Documentary and Imaginative Literature 1880-1920

HISTORY AND LITERATURE

1880-1920

Documentary and Imaginative Literature 1880-1920

J. A. V. CHAPPLE

Senior Lecturer in English,
University of Manchester

Barnes and Noble, Inc.
Publishers, Booksellers
Since 1873

First published 1970

© Blandford Press Ltd
Published in the United States
by Barnes & Noble, Inc.

SBN 389 04015 0

Printed in Great Britain

To Kathleen

ACKNOWLEDGMENTS

Acknowledgments for permission to quote from copyright material are due as follows:

Rudyard Kipling—Mrs. George Bambridge, Methuen & Co. Ltd and Macmillan & Co. Ltd; Doubleday & Co. Inc. *W. B. Yeats*—M. B. Yeats & Macmillan & Co. Ltd; Macmillan Co., New York. *Sir Henry Newbolt*—Peter Newbolt, Esq. *H. G. Wells*—The executors of the estate of H. G. Wells; Wm. Heinemann Ltd. for *The War of The Worlds*. *Siegfried Sassoon*—The literary executor. *Thomas Hardy*—the trustees of the Hardy estate and Macmillan & Co. Ltd, publishers of the *Collected Poems*; Macmillan Co., New York; The Macmillan Co. of Canada Ltd. *Ezra Pound*—Faber & Faber Ltd; New Directions Publishing Corp. *T. S. Eliot*—Faber & Faber Ltd; Harcourt, Brace & World, Inc. *A. E. Housman*—the Society of Authors as the literary representatives of the estate and Jonathan Cape Ltd, publishers of the *Collected Poems*; Holt, Rinehart & Winston, Inc. *Joseph Conrad*—J. M. Dent & Sons Ltd, acting on behalf of the trustees of the estate.

ERRATA

Page 159, line 25; for 'They' read 'He'.
Page 160, line 2; for 'hid' read 'hide'.

Contents

ACKNOWLEDGEMENTS

Acknowledgement is due to the following for their kind permission to reproduce photographs:

The Art Institute of Chicago, No. 24
Bloomsbury Group and The New English Library, Nos, 16, 17, 18, 19
British Museum, Nos. 1, 4 (reproduced from Jesse Collings: *Land Reform, etc.*, Longmans 1908), 5 (reproduced from Richard Jefferies: *The Story of My Heart*, Longmans 1891), 13 (reproduced from H. Belloc: *Emmanuel Burden*, Methuen 1915), 15 (reproduced from M. Beerbohm: *A Book of Caricatures*, Methuen 1907)
Ferrers Galley, London, No. 22
Mrs. M. Kennedy and Manchester University Press, No. 9
Provost and Fellows of King's College, Cambridge, No. 20
Los Angeles County Museum of Art, No. 25
William Morris Gallery, Walthamstow, No. 6
National Gallery of Ireland, No. 10
National Gallery of Scotland, No. 8
Penguin Books Ltd., No. 12
Private Collection, New York No. 23
Radio Times Hulton Picture Library, Nos. 11, 14
Maurice Rickards, No. 21
Weidenfeld and Nicolson, No. 2
No. 3 is reproduced from *The Saturday Book*, edited by L. Russell, Hutchinson 1945
No. 7 is reproduced by permission of *Punch*

List of Illustrations

Preface

THIS is neither a history nor a literary history of the period 1880–1920. It is a book intended to bring out the many and fascinating ways in which history can be connected with literature. Though the works of the period's major authors have been given most attention, a number of minor works and other pieces not usually found in histories of literature have been looked at. The chapters, too, are organised about themes of a broadly historical nature. On the other hand, while it might seem that many good authors have little historical interest and belong almost entirely to the histories of literature—Jane Austen and Emily Brontë are often mentioned in this connexion—one finds in practice that even the notorious *fin de siècle* writers are well worth consideration and might even be said to have a special relevance in a book like this.

History and literature can be studied together both horizontally and vertically. It is not at all difficult to place works of literature alongside more or less contemporary events and then, using the criteria of both disciplines as they seem appropriate, try to establish the significance of such juxtapositions; but as often as not, I think, it is just as valuable to look for ancestors and descendants, following the course of cultural relationships changing in time as astronomers follow the complex movements of binary stars through space. In these cases the boundaries of the period 1880–1920 could have been a nuisance: in the series as a whole, however, they have not been rigidly interpreted. It has also seemed most helpful to spend several pages on a single work, quite often, rather than struggle to coin an epigram in every other sentence about hundreds of examples. Paragraphs that begin, 'Equally of interest in the field of prison reform in the first decade are the following fifteen works . . .' are very discouraging and it is not realistic to expect that even a keen interest will survive such bald lists.

Finally, a study of this nature depends on the work of many scholars and critics, to whom reference has been made in the text and notes, but I owe a particular debt to past and present colleagues of the University of Manchester. They have provided me with both maps and compasses. I must also thank my wife and Mrs Shelagh Aston for invaluable help in preparing this book for the press.

August 1969

1 : Introduction

J. R. HALE, in his book *The Evolution of British Historiography* (1967), drew attention to Elizabethan contempt for writers of history whose only model of construction can have been a heap, an accumulation of item after item without plan or system worth speaking of. One of my own vivid memories is of excitedly opening a bulky parcel containing the manuscript remains of an antiquarian, to find a mass of unsorted and unsortable papers of all shapes and sizes, colours and states of decay, some crumbling at the edges, others as fresh almost as the day when they left the papermaker. The compiler—this seems a very apt name—had evidently spent his life in copying pedigrees, leases, tombstones, letters, printed books and anything else that came to hand. In the phrase used by Thomas Hearne, somebody had been 'making collections', for a history of the shire, the knights of the North . . . who knows? The collecting had been unsystematic; no principle of order had been devised or discovered, so no ordering principle could be the shaping factor of any finished work. When we speak in these broad and general terms, it is clear that there is a fundamental sense in which historians and creative artists face similar problems in dealing with the confused mass of detail that needs moulding into a work of history or a work of literature. There are in practice enormous differences, some of which are explored in this book, but with the possible exception of some kinds of modern literature the need to order is common to both. Other common factors are neatly indicated in Conrad's remarkable appreciation of Henry James (1905), when he wrote that the novelist is 'a historian, the preserver, the keeper, the expounder, of human experience'. If novelists can stand for creative writers in general, Conrad's insight becomes a basic premise for the study of history and literature. It is not surprising to discover that critics of literature often have very definite historical interests: Conrad himself, for instance, has inspired books with such titles as *Conrad's Polish Background* and *Conrad's Eastern World*, by Zdzislaw Najder and Norman Sherry respectively. The materials and workings of the creative mind are perennially fascinating and the preliminary approaches at least are plainly historical in nature.

If literary critics have involved themselves in the discipline of history, there have been, conversely, a number of historians whose methods were highly literary. Names like Macaulay, Carlyle and Froude come to mind at once. As long ago as 1923 Herbert Butterfield turned his attention to the subject, but more recently, in a section entitled 'History as a Branch of Literature' of his book *History and Human Relations* (1951), he has pursued his enquiries into the value of this kind of historiography, drawing the useful distinction between historians who depict and narrate and those who analyse and dissect. The former tend to see history as a work of 'resurrection', the latter as an analytical study of processes. In very simple terms, one might ask what happened or why and how it happened. Literary-minded historians might well adopt a sentence from Froude's biography of Carlyle as their motto: 'We must have the real thing before we can have a science of a thing.' Professor Butterfield suggests that such historians have often sought more widely for the truth and could even perform certain historical tasks more efficiently, since, as he says, 'perhaps only a high degree of literary art can solve the problem of portraying a movement that takes place in different dimensions—delineating the past in its broad expanse for example, but showing that it is moving all the time.' For this relatively sophisticated form of communication considerable literary craftsmanship is needed. Besides this, a historian with talents of a literary kind is likely to possess the sort of sympathetic intelligence that can really look deep into the minds of people in the past; he would be, as Keats wrote in a letter of 27 October 1818 about the chameleon nature of the poet, 'continually informing and filling some other Body'. And he might also possess the kind of assured taste and judgment that could recognise the greatest attainments of past ages and estimate the quality of their finest culture. To imagination would be joined a sense of values.

Imagination and a sense of values, it is not too partial to suggest, are terms that invite us to look more closely at literature again. Literature is very often history being recorded more or less as it happens; it reflects contemporary people and events. But we know that this is too simple a statement, because the way in which literature acts as the mirror of its time can itself be affected by movements of history. Authors, like historians, respond to the spirit of their age and consequently mould their evidence in ways that embody their less tangible attitudes and values. We have only to think for a moment of literature written in the heat of intellectual, religious or political engagement. A certain degree of refraction must be allowed for. Even then there is a possible source of disappointment. Professor Butterfield drew up a profit and loss account when he wrote of his literary historians that while partisanship drives them to much fuller investigation and re-creation of the past than usual, it also leads to a defect in historical analysis, which vitiates history at precisely those points where inferences for conduct are drawn. It does exactly the same for literature; one remembers James Joyce's remark to David Fleischman in this context: 'I believe the three writers of the nineteenth century who had the greatest natural talents were D'Annunzio, Kipling, and Tolstoy—it's strange that all three had semi-fanatic ideas about religion or about patriotism.' Yet Joyce's use of 'semi-' is a reminder that even partisan writers are not all goat, and any serious work of literature has a special value as a document of its time, which deserves at very least all the care historians are accustomed to give when weighing historical evidence.

Serious works of literature can also possess more purely aesthetic characteristics; they live by their own principles and have their individually distinctive forms. Here we may suggest that it is literary critics who are accustomed to studying these aspects and who, at their best, make precise, subtle assessments of the shape and linguistic texture of particular works of art. Without claiming that form and content are inseparable, it is a dangerous thing to believe that all writings can be chopped up without more ado. William Morris's *News from Nowhere* (1890), for example, which is considered at some length in chapter 4 below, must be read as a tightly integrated work; otherwise, it seems to me, it just falls apart into a number of ideas and prophecies of dubious value. Its narrative form is significant. In practice, of course, works of literature have to be broken down to make them amenable to discussion, and with some kinds of writer this hardly matters; but special care is needed when analysing works for which the concept of 'organic form' we inherit from Coleridge has any relevance. A true work of literature, he believed, was not just put together: it grew according to some inner and living principle. (His analysis of *The Tempest* in the 1811–12 lectures on Shakespeare is well worth looking at in this connexion.) We might also be prepared to believe that in works of this vital, non-mechanical nature will be found unique insights into the truth of the age which saw its birth. Their authors were not just 'making collections'. In the *Kenyon Review* for 1958, in an article entitled 'Historicism Once More', R. H. Pearce put matters this way: 'In a poem there is outline, texture, form; and there is something happening. The important point is that there is something *still* happening, and the organicity and wholeness which formalist criteria will help us remark are such because, as the poem first happened, it still happens. As it still happens, it brings, inseparably, the life of its culture with it. If we accept the form, we accept the life. If we accept the life, we accept the culture. That is historical understanding and historical knowledge.'

    ·   ·   ·   ·   ·   ·

It will be useful to extend these rather theoretical points by looking at some particular writings—thereby avoiding, incidentally, the constant discomfort of feeling that there is always an exception to prove the rule. In 1912 there occurred the greatest disaster at sea of the period. The White Star liner *Titanic* sank on her maiden voyage through collision with an iceberg in the mid-Atlantic. This was the complete loss of what was then the world's largest ship; 1,635 persons died, although another 732 were saved by the other vessels brought by that new invention, wireless. The information is from a standard history. It tells us the main facts and also brings out the significance in maritime history of the new invention. Something else, however, is given by Hardy's poem on the disaster, 'The Convergence of the Twain':

> In a solitude of the sea
> Deep from human vanity,
> And Pride of Life that planned her, stilly couches she.

> Steel chambers, late the pyres
> Of her salamandrine fires,
> Cold currents thrid, and turn to rhythmic tidal lyres.

> Over the mirrors meant
> To glass the opulent
> The sea-worm crawls—grotesque, slimed, dumb, indifferent.

Here is a strange defunctive music! In these three short stanzas taken from the poem, Hardy has turned a sardonic gaze upon the defeat of human aspiration, brought out the weirdly mythical sea-change undergone by the products of modern technology and shown the blind inhumanity of the natural world. The phrase 'glass the opulent' might bear the implication that the social life of Hardy's culture was superficial, though the main tensions are undoubtedly between the exhilaration Hardy believed his contemporaries had in the thought of their own powers and his personal, more saturnine belief that the real power controlling our destiny is unintelligently hostile:

> Jewels in joy designed
> To ravish the sensuous mind
> Lie lightless, all their sparkles bleared and black and blind.

> Dim, moon-eyed fishes near
> Gaze at the gilded gear
> And query: 'What does this vaingloriousness down here?'

> Well: while was fashioning
> This creature of cleaving wing,
> The Immanent Will that stirs and urges everything

> Prepared a sinister mate
> For her—so gaily great—
> A Shape of Ice, for the time far and dissociate!

> And as the smart ship grew
> In stature, grace, and hue.
> In shadowy silent distance grew the Iceberg too . . .

The historian of ideas might well wish to discuss Hardy's view of destiny and refer, say, to Arthur Schopenhauer's view that no individual has value for a nature that only cares about the preservation of the species. (His book of 1818, *The World as Will and Idea*, had been translated from the German by R. B. Haldane and J. Kemp in 1883–6.) Students of literature will probably recall something like chapter 2 of Conrad's *Lord Jim* (1900), where he writes that now and then 'there appears on the face of facts a sinister violence of intention—that indefinable something which forces it upon the mind and the heart of a man, that this complication of accidents or these elemental furies are coming at him with a purpose of malice, with a strength beyond control, with an unbridled cruelty that means to tear out of him his hope and his fear, the pain of his fatigue and his longing for rest: which mean to smash, to destroy, to annihilate all he had seen, known, loved . . .' I break off at this point, because it must be obvious that whatever philosophical similarities there may be, there is all the difference in the world between Conrad's over-heated prose and Hardy's condensed, individual, poetic vision. Works of literature record the life of a culture, but they also show its rich diversity. Their differences in form cannot be passed over in the pursuit of thematic interests.

· · · · · ·

I sometimes think that at the heart of the relationship between history and literature is the difference between the fate of whole nations, societies, groups—all the larger units of mankind which so often engage the attention of historians—and the life of the private individual and his own immediate circle, so often the subject of literary works. The poem we have just looked at proves that this is no more than a generalization, for Hardy showed concern with

the character of the civilisation in which he lived, but it is worth
considering another poem of Hardy's in this light:

> Only a man harrowing clods
>   In a slow silent walk
> With an old horse that stumbles and nods
>   Half asleep as they stalk.
>
> Only thin smoke without flame
>   From the heaps of couch-grass;
> Yet this will go onward the same
>   Though Dynasties pass.
>
> Yonder a maid and her wight
>   Come whispering by;
> War's annals will cloud into night
>   Ere their story die.

This little poem, 'In Time of "The Breaking of Nations" ', establishes opposites: the routine of ordinary life continuing against the
background of dynasties which have reached their moments of
crisis; the simple actions of human lovers against the portentous
happenings of war and battle. Its expression might be criticised.
'Stalk' is perhaps a word imposed by the need to rhyme; the third
stanza could be called trite, though the archaism 'wight' is probably
meant to associate these lovers with many others before them and
the last lines perhaps gain strength from the memory of the closing
couplets of certain Shakespearian sonnets. But where could one
find a finer symbol than the heaps of couch-grass burning? There
is not even a flame to add drama, just thin smoke which continues
whilst the pomp and circumstance of grand affairs pass away. The
lesser things abide.

I feel that by now the social historians are beginning to burst
forth from a variety of containers like angry djinns—and not only
the social historians—but I must stick to my guns. In the reading
done for this book Hardy's little poem came to stand for the two
opposing *tendencies* of history and literature. Historians dig and
investigate and bring together facts of all kinds, including the
human ones—especially the human ones, one might admit. But so

often this is done in the service of larger ideas, controlled general-isations from the masses of material. And while literary men care equally for facts and undoubtedly express thoughts of far-ranging scope, even the more visionary writers usually keep a firm hold on the specific and personal. They work through such means: the slow, silent walk of a man harrowing clods with an old horse is fast enough. This is, it is true, a special case, and one knows that Wordsworth is behind the conviction that basic truths are most clearly seen in low and rustic life. He may well have been right, however, in his more general search for 'the essential passions of the heart'; works set on far less rustic earth are at bottom products of the same quest. The belief that literature is valuable for its basic humanity is a bias that it has been impossible to avoid.

Fortunately, in reading over the following chapters it became equally clear that complexity and elaborate artistry had received a good deal of attention, coming close at times to being admired for their own sake. Readers might wish to bear in mind the delightful Chinaman whose driving instructor reported that the only English words he had heard him utter in a number of lessons were 'yes', 'no' and 'Oh-my-God!' He passed his driving test, and obviously had enough in him to pass tests of a far more serious kind. Complexity and high artistry in the use of language are by no means indispensable in life or in literature. Yet such aestheticism is perhaps, a useful counterbalance to the weight that 'basic humanity' has been given in this book. And to reinforce as powerfully as possible the comments made earlier about the distinctiveness of literary forms, here is a passage on the same theme of continuity during grandiose disasters as the Hardy breaking-of-nations poem:

> Since the bouts of Hebear and Hairyman the cornflowers have been staying at Ballymun, the duskrose has choosed out Goatstown's hedges, twolips have pressed togatherthem by sweet Rush, townland of twinedlights, the whitethorn and the redthorn have fairygeyed the mayvalleys of Knockmaroon, and, though for rings round them, during a chiliad of perihely-gangs, the Formoreans have brittled the tooath of the Danes and the Oxman has been pestered by the Firebugs and the

Joynts have thrown up jerrybuilding to the Kevanses and
Little on the Green is childsfather to the City (Year! Year!
and laughtears!), these paxsealing buttonholes have quadrilled
across the centuries and whiff now whafft to us, fresh and
made-of-all-smiles as, on the eve of Killallwho.

James Joyce's *Finnegans Wake* (1939) is the source of this splendid
passage, which we know on the best authority (Richard Ellmann's
biography) is a version of a French piece by Edgar Quinet—about
the flowers that manage to survive the crashing and collision of
civilisations and then reappear as fresh and as laughing as they had
ever been on the days of battles. Set Joyce's intricate interweavings
of syllables beside Hardy's simple stanzas and it becomes very
clear that amongst all the documents that can speak to us out of
dead mouths, works of creative literature have a special and
unique status. At the same time, they were undoubtedly created
in a particular period of history and can be only partially
considered out of it. Our period stretches from one century to
another. We may begin our preliminary survey with the reminder
that the title of the literary journal devoted to this period is *English
Literature in Transition*.

II

The age surveyed in this book may not be one that is long in
years but it is certainly one that resists easy summary. Viewed
externally, it seems to have the prime characteristic of medieval
tragedy; its history might well be termed 'A Tragical Discourse of
many who have fallen from high Estate to extreme Misery' if we
take in one grand sweep the events between Queen Victoria's
Golden Jubilee of 1887 and the Great War. The celebration of the
two Jubilees (there was a second, Diamond Jubilee, in 1897) were
for most ordinary people the proper recognition of Britain's
imperial glory. Bonfires, reviews of the fleet, parish tea-parties,
colonial conferences, the entertainment of the representatives of
foreign powers were all signs of Britain's progress, expansion and
joy. But many of the works of literature we are to look at in the

following chapters show the other side of the coin: the years of decline and economic depression, the social unrest, the increasing momentum of class struggle and the Irish question, which developed to a point when rebellion was being hatched in Ulster by Carson and Bonar Law while both there and elsewhere nationalists rushed to join the National Volunteers. Precarious foreign relations were another feature of the period, together with an actual war in South Africa, in which yet again British incompetence and mismanagement were shown up and during which the old Queen, a symbol of stability, died. The early years of the twentieth century saw more industrial strife, the turning of a section of the suffragette movement towards violence and the bitterness of political struggle which ended in the breaking of the power of the House of Lords by the Liberal party, with the assistance of Irish nationalists and the new Labour members. Finally, it is almost unnecessary to say, came 'the war to end war', in which the loss of men even now, in the light of all that has happened since the Treaty of Versailles, is unbearable to contemplate for long.

Many writers have commented upon the more inward aspects of this breakdown, and stressed the rapidly changing climate of thought and belief. The lights were going out long before the actual outbreak of war in 1914. G. K. Chesterton, in a little book that came out in the newly founded Home University Library in 1913 and is still going strong, *The Victorian Age in Literature*, wrote of a 'coincident collapse of both religious and political idealism' roughly about 1880. This

> produced a curious cold air of emptiness and real subconscious agnosticism such as is extremely unusual in the history of mankind. It is what H. G. Wells, with his usual verbal delicacy and accuracy, spoke of as that ironical silence that follows a great controversy. It is what people less intelligent than Wells meant by calling themselves *fin de siècle*; though, of course, rationally speaking, there is no more reason for being sad towards the end of a hundred years than towards the end of five hundred fortnights. There was no arithmetical autumn, but there was a spiritual one. And it came from the fact suggested in the

paragraphs above: the sense that man's two great inspirations had failed him together. . . . The years that followed on that double disillusionment were like one long afternoon in a rich house on a rainy day. It was not merely that everybody believed that nothing would happen; it was also that everybody believed that anything happening was even duller than nothing happening. It was in this stale atmosphere that a few flickers of the old Swinburnian flame survived; and were called Art. The great men of the older artistic movement did not live in this time; rather they lived through it. But this time did produce an interregnum of art that had a truth of its own; though that truth was near to being only a consistent lie. (Section 4.)

Despite the frantic phrase-making (which must always be condemned firmly by cooler, incapable spirits), this passage contains several acute comments and much that is probable about the state of feeling. Chesterton was born in 1874, we might remember, and he wrote his *Victorian Age* only a dozen years after Queen Victoria's death in 1901. His account receives confirmation from the exceptional interest aroused by the publishing of Mrs Humphry Ward's somewhat old-fashioned novel *Robert Elsmere* in 1888, the story of a clergyman who had lost his faith and resigned his living. (There is a clergyman of a similar type in Elizabeth Gaskell's *North and South*, 1855, and her own father had resigned his preaching appointment as a Unitarian minister for reasons of conscience in the 1790s.) An article by Gladstone in *The Nineteenth Century* on Mrs Ward's novel roused yet more attention. *Robert Elsmere* undoubtedly has historical interest. But an even greater collapse of religious belief is recorded in Bertrand Russell's elaborate rhetoric in 'A Free Man's Worship', first printed in *The Independent Review* of December 1903:

That Man is the product of causes which had no prevision of the end they were achieving; that his origin, his growth, his hopes and fears, his loves and his beliefs, are but the outcome of accidental collocations of atoms; that no fire, no heroism, no intensity of thought and feeling, can preserve an individual life beyond the grave; that all the labours of the ages, all the devotion, all the inspiration, all the noonday brightness of human genius, are destined to extinction in the vast death of the solar system, and that the whole temple of man's achievement must inevitably be buried beneath the debris of a universe in ruins—all these things, if not quite beyond dispute, are yet so nearly certain that no philosophy which rejects them can hope to stand. Only within the scaffolding of these truths, only on the firm foundation of unyielding despair, can the soul's habitation henceforth be safely built.

Russell's summary of the secular alternative to religious belief is uncompromising, but his stance on such paradoxical ground— 'the firm foundation of unyielding despair'—is not at all what we find in the writings of the most influential of Victorian critics, Matthew Arnold. In *God and the Bible* of 1875 we find Arnold anticipating that the religion of the future would be a 'Catholicism purged, opening itself to the light and air, having the consciousness of its own poetry, freed from its sacerdotal despotism and freed from its pseudo-scientific apparatus of supernatural dogma.' In the first year of our period he wrote a general introduction to T. H. Ward's *The English Poets*. Here he asserted that religious beliefs and traditions were declining, particularly the more dogmatic ones, and went on to suggest that we should therefore

conceive of poetry worthily, and more highly than it has been the custom to conceive of it. We should conceive of it as capable of higher uses, and called to higher destinies, than those which in general men have assigned to it hitherto.

Then follows one of the most famous of all his pronouncements:

More and more mankind will discover that we have to turn to poetry to interpret life for us, to console us, to sustain us. Without poetry, our science will appear incomplete; and most of what now passes with us for religion and philosophy will be replaced by poetry.

The statement of the last sentence, if looked at closely, is not as bold as it might seem. Exercising, perhaps, what he once satirically labelled 'the God-given right of every Englishman to do as he likes', he defined religion and philosophy to suit himself. We have seen his idea of a religion of the future. Later in his introduction he wrote of contemporary religion, 'parading evidences such as those on which the popular mind relies now; our philosophy, pluming itself on its reasonings about causation and finite and infinite being; what are they but the shadows and dreams and false shows of knowledge?' At another time, crossing swords with Professor T. H. Huxley for his scorn of medieval education, Arnold allows his contention that science had forced new conceptions of the universe 'fatal to the notions held by our forefathers'—a large allowance—but goes on:

> The Middle Age could do without humane letters, as it could do without the study of nature, because its supposed knowledge [delivered by Scripture and by the Church] was made to engage its emotions so powerfully. Grant that the supposed knowledge disappears, its power of being made to engage the emotions will of course disappear along with it,—but the emotions themselves, and their claim to be engaged and satisfied, will remain. Now if we find by experience that humane letters have an undeniable power of engaging the emotions, the importance of humane letters in a man's training becomes not less, but greater, in proportion to the success of modern science in extirpating what it calls 'medieval thinking'.
>
> (Literature and Science, in *Discourses in America*, 1885)

It all seems to swing upon very reduced definitions of both science and humane letters, but apart from this, there does seem to be a particular importance for us in his substitution of 'humane letters' for 'what now passes with us for religion and philosophy'. Arnold was striving to adapt the culture of his time in a changing climate of thought and belief—in an age, it seemed to him, of inevitable transition and transformation.[1] Literature to his mind was the last possible refuge of values when traditional beliefs were yielding to assault. Does it appear strange today that he should imagine writers might take this burden on their shoulders? It is worth looking at the status of authors in Victorian society.

·　　·　　·　　·　　·　　·

The position of a great Victorian man of letters who lived on into our period, Alfred Tennyson, is almost unbelievable today. As poet laureate he produced the expected effusions on, say, the 'Opening of the Indian and Colonial Exhibition by the Queen' in 1886 or on the Golden Jubilee in the following year:

> Fifty years of ever-broadening Commerce!
> Fifty years of ever-brightening Science!
> Fifty years of ever-widening Empire!

But in a far more real way than this he was the spokesman for many of his contemporaries. He told James Knowles that *In Memoriam*, the series of poems he had begun in 1833 on the death of his friend Arthur Hallam and added to year after year until it was finally published in 1850, was 'rather the cry of the whole human race than mine.' (Quoted in C. Ricks's fine edition, *The Poems of Tennyson*, 1969, which has provided me here with several other valuable notes.) Tennyson's popularity in his time, though it fluctuated to some extent, underlines the justice of this claim as far as his fellow-countrymen were concerned. It is therefore valuable to look at a poem he published in 1886, 'Locksley Hall Sixty Years After', which is in effect a long and sweepingly comprehensive attack on the state of the age as Tennyson saw it. The title of this poem refers back to his earlier 'Locksley Hall', published in 1842, an involved poem which yet manages to end with a positive cry:

> Not in vain the distance beacons. Forward, forward let
>   us range,
> Let the great world spin for ever down the ringing grooves
>   of change.
>
> Through the shadow of the globe we sweep into the
>   younger day:
> Better fifty years of Europe than a cycle of Cathay. . . .

Though the first poem contains social protest, it is balanced by aspiration and the hope in progress implied in those 'ringing grooves of change'. (Tennyson thought the first train from Liverpool to Manchester back in 1830 ran in grooves at the time he

actually wrote this line.) The second poem is much more vituperative, to such an extent that he makes his speaker say:

> Heated am I? you—you wonder—well, it scarce becomes
>   mine age—
> Patience! let the dying actor mouth his last upon the stage.
>
> Cries of unprogressive dotage ere the dotard fall asleep?
> Noises of a current narrowing, not the music of a deep?

And even these lines, we learn, were added late in the composition
of the poem; throughout its drafting Tennyson attempted to
damp down his invective, in fact. But his estimate of his age in the
1880s is still incredibly bitter and pessimistic:

> When was age so crammed with menace? madness? written,
>   spoken lies?
>
> Envy wears the mask of Love, and, laughing sober fact to
>   scorn,
> Cries to Weakest as to Strongest, 'Ye are equals, equal-born.'
>
> Equal-born? O yes, if yonder hill be level with the flat.
> Charm us, Orator, till the Lion look no larger than the Cat,
>
> Till the Cat through that mirage of overheated language loom
> Larger than the Lion,—Demos end in working its own doom.
>
> Russia bursts our Eastern barrier, shall we fight her? shall
>   we yield?
> Pause! before you sound the trumpet, hear the voices from the
>   field.
>
> Those three hundred millions under one Imperial sceptre now,
> Shall we hold them? shall we loose them? take the suffrage
>   of the plow.
>
> Nay, but these would feel and follow Truth if only you and
>   you,
> Rivals of realm-ruining party, when you speak were wholly
>   true.

The particular points will be considered later in this book; for the present purpose I wish to emphasise how the ageing Tennyson, a major and a representative poet in a sense unknown today, was buried in the depths of depression when he looked at his own time. As in the first 'Locksley Hall' poem, a more positive note is struck, but in the interrogative form:

> All diseases quenched by Science, no man halt, or deaf or
>   blind;
> Stronger ever born of weaker, lustier body, larger mind?
>
> Earth at last a warless world, a single race, a single
>   tongue—
> I have seen her far away—for is not Earth as yet so
>   young?

Before very long, the poem sinks right back into pessimism as the hopes associated with scientific progress and social advance seem to bear Dead Sea fruit—again, matters that will be taken up in subsequent chapters:

> Is it well that while we range with Science, glorying in
>   the Time,
> City children soak and blacken soul and sense in city
>   slime?
>
> There among the glooming alleys Progress halts on palsied
>   feet,
> Crime and hunger cast our maidens by the thousand on
>   the street. . . .

It is, I think, difficult for us today to take an onslaught like this seriously and we are tempted to believe that the extreme criticisms and the exaggerated emotions that are inextricably associated with them belong to the speaker of the dramatic monologue, meant to be, as we have seen, in his 'unprogressive dotage.' But one contemporary, as prominent in the sphere of politics as Tennyson was in that of literature, had no doubt that the poem called for a direct, personal reply. William Gladstone, then just a few months out of office as Prime Minister, wrote for the January 1887 number of *The Nineteenth Century* an elaborately grave and majestically serious answer. He winds into his article, first noting how the 'passionate or emotional part of nature comes into rivalry with the reflective organ' and then admitting that Tennyson 'is shrouded behind the veil his art has woven'. But, writes Gladstone with massive simplicity, not every reader can bear in mind the distinction between Tennyson and his character. After a reference to the generally sanguine nature, of the earlier 'Locksley Hall', he pens the nearest thing to a reproof in the entire article: 'Perhaps the tone may even, at times, be thought to have grown a little hoarse'! After this brief descent into the savage arena he reaches the heart of his reply, a large review of the political and social progress of England during the past fifty years. Tennyson had roused Gladstone to take stock. He admits there are still social problems, but contends that wages are fairer, dwelling houses are better, legislative and private charity flourishes, an empire of 'exacting though imposing magnitude' has been built up, slavery has been abolished, unfair laws of combination and of contract have been repealed, the suffrage has been extended and so on. England has led the world to cheap communications (witness Mr Cook's travel idea, a 'humanizing contrivance of the age'), pugilism is now 'rare, unobtrusive and modest' and swearing, duelling and cruel sports less frequent. There is more, but enough has been given to show the consideration that men of letters were accorded by statesmen. It is hard to think of subsequent examples which can really compare with this exchange on the summit of Mount Olympus. The Wells-Churchill debate in the *Daily Express* of 1920 has some very slight claim, perhaps.

The grand accumulations of 'facts' are probably typical of this kind of debate, which rarely amounts to true argument, but they seem particularly appropriate in a time when Charles Booth began to collect masses of social statistics. His well known estimate that 30.7 per cent of the population of London lived in poverty according to his definition was derived from an enquiry conducted in the following year, 1888 (the year, too, of the strike of the East End match-making girls). Looking at 'Locksley Hall Sixty Years

After' and Gladstone's reply, it seems that in them we have two examples not only of great Victorian seriousness but also of that extraordinary centrifugal force which sends men spinning in opposite directions. To some extent it is no more than a matter of temperament—optimists versus pessimists, tender versus tough-minded and so on—but the literature of the 1880–1920 period leaves one with the very strong impression that writers especially were inclined to deplore the course history was taking in their time. An author like Trollope is exceptional,[2] and it is hard not to agree with John A. Lester, who writes in his *Journey Through Despair 1880–1914: Transformations in British Literary Culture* (Princeton, N.J., 1968):

> My contention is that the years from 1880 to 1914 severely jarred and shifted the bearings of man's imaginative life and left him at times bewildered as to how to recover his lost meaning and purpose. Such times are necessarily painful, and they carry overtones of tragedy. In literature it was a time of confusion and a nervous, often frenzied, search for new terms on which the imagination could live.

We have already seen in Arnold that he believed 'humane letters' should play a major role in providing new meaning and purpose in life. Many writers found 'new terms on which the imagination could live', but often in ways that left them isolated from the main movements of thought and feeling in their own society; that in a sense cut them off from the main currents of history, if we take history as broadly defined in the first part of this introduction. Leaving out of consideration the *fin de siècle* writers as a rather special case, the deliberate refusal to compromise with public demands by certain major writers in the new century, their 'obscurity' according to popular standards of communication, has meant that they have never had the wide popularity of authors like Galsworthy, Wells, Bennett and Shaw. It would be impossible to ignore the work of popular writers, some of whom can be shown to have influenced the course of events in a very direct manner indeed, but it would be equally short-sighted to neglect the difficult 'moderns' like Pound, Eliot and Joyce, who with a little more

trouble can be shown to have had a distinctive interest in history
and its bearing upon the times they lived in.

·   ·   ·   ·   ·   ·

There is no grand and simple theme in this book. History and
literature are intertwined with each other like Laocoön and the
serpents, and we should be grateful for it. Social historians,
aestheticians, sociologists, economic historians and many others
will all find food for thought in the relationships between them
and will be led to their own kinds of assessments. For the general
reader, they offer opportunity to cultivate flexibility of mind and
discover the continuity of a culture in one of its most sensitive
aspects. I have attempted in what follows to give some direct
contact with the variety of possible interrelationships and to make
the appropriate value judgments, within the obvious limitations
imposed upon my thinking by my own specialist training in English.
But all this is the business of criticism, an interest and a discipline—
and quite secondary. 'What fine chisel/Could ever yet cut breath?'
asks Leontes raptly gazing on the statue of Hermione in the last
scene of *The Winter's Tale*. The past will revive in its works of art;
it is to them we look for its warm life. As we read through the
literature of the period 1880–1920, we can live once more in the
days when Britain was finally ceasing to be an agricultural nation
and when what came to be called mass civilisation was beginning
to exert its full pressures upon the human spirit. We can experience
again the social and political conflicts of that age, know their
reflections in foreign affairs as a great Empire reached its apogee.
The widening gulf between artists and society can be studied in
relatively minor but significant writers and, intimately connected
with their strange history, the tense attempt of one of the finest
authors of the period to reconcile the ever-conflicting claims of
art and life as public events involved him in even more acute
difficulties. These problems, and their most terrible manifestation
in a world war, have been re-created for us in literature registering,
it has been rightly said, a change in sensibility of a kind that can
never be reversed. Finally, as the last topic of this book, the end of
Victorianism—or some semi-mythical variants of it—will be shown

in a number of writers. What it meant to be 'modern' all those years ago will be documented in works some of which retain their modernity half a century later for the average reader; but, strangest of all, history itself will in a sense be overturned by the long-delayed publication in 1918 of a volume of 'modern' poems—written by a great *Victorian* author, Gerard Manley Hopkins. This would seem to be unmatchable, were it not for a purely internal literary event recorded in F. E. Hardy's *The Later Years of Thomas Hardy 1892–1928* (1930): 'I have a faculty (possibly not uncommon) for burying an emotion in my heart or brain for forty years, and exhuming it at the end of that time as fresh as when interred. For instance, the poem entitled "The Breaking of Nations" contains a feeling that moved me in 1870, during the Franco-Prussian war, when I chanced to be looking at such an agricultural incident in Cornwall. But I did not write the verses till during the war with Germany of 1914 and onwards. Query: where was that sentiment hiding itself during more than forty years?' Where indeed? In such ways history is annihilated.

NOTES

[1] David Daiches has laid great stress upon the excellence of the comparable effort by the lesser known William Hale White, author of *The Autobiography of Mark Rutherford* (1881) and *Mark Rutherford's Deliverance* (1885): 'White goes much beyond Arnold in redefining the nature and purpose of religion, for he was continually coming down to cases and asking in specific detail exactly what need it was that religion served' (*Some Late Victorian Attitudes*, 1969, Lecture 3).

[2] 'But then we do not put very much faith in Mr Carlyle—nor in Mr Ruskin and his other followers. The loudness and extravagance of their lamentations, the wailing and gnashing of teeth which comes from them, over a world which is supposed to have gone altogether shoddy-wards, are so contrary to the convictions of men who cannot but see how comfort has been increased, how health has been improved, and education extended—that the general effect of their teaching is the opposite of what they have intended' (*Autobiography*, 1883, II, pages 209–10).

2 : Crisis in the Country

WHEN in 1846 J. H. Dixon brought out his *Ancient Poems, Ballads, and Songs of the Peasantry of England* for the Percy Society, he triumphantly asserted the rout of 'that Utilitarian spirit which, seeking to turn everything it touches into gold, would invade the realm of Fancy and Romance, banish the bright day-dreams of our youth, and leave us nothing but a cold Saducean philosophy in its stead'. With his references to cold philosophy and the destructiveness of the Utilitarian spirit he was undoubtedly writing in the century that saw the publication of Keats's *Lamia* (1820) and Dickens's *Hard Times* (1854), but an interest in 'peasant-rhymes' is of much longer ancestry. Without going back as far as Sir Philip Sidney's commendation of 'Chevy Chase', we can see this interest fighting to survive in a cultivated age when many, at least amongst the educated, would 'think it ridiculous enough to enter seriously into a Dissertation upon Ballads', to quote from the preface to the second volume of *A Collection of Old Ballads* (1723). Its anonymous editor, however, is very clear about the virtue of the ballads he has collected: nobody is likely to find in them or in 'Chevy Chase'

> one Piece of false, or as a modern Author calls it, *Gothick* Wit; no vile Conceit, no Low Pun, or double Entendre; but the whole is of a Piece, apparell'd in Majestick Simplicity, and the true Political Genius appears in every Line.

The eighteenth-century stress upon the virtue, simplicity and truth of popular poetry is repeated just as strongly in Queen Victoria's reign, when Robert Bell undertook the revising and enlarging of the original Percy Society volume of *Ancient Poems, Ballads, and Songs:*

C

The value of this volume consists in the genuineness of its contents, and the healthiness of its tone. While fashionable life was masquerading in imaginary Arcadias, and deluging theatres and concert rooms with shams, the English peasant remained true to the realities of his own experience, and produced and sang songs which faithfully reflected the actual life around him. . . . It is in this particular aspect that the poetry of the country possesses a permanent and moral interest.

Rustic life is a true one; so is the literature that faithfully reflects it: this is the bold claim made for rural literature in general, even when it is produced by authors who can hardly be regarded as genuine peasants. Indeed, we have not yet measured the full extent of the claim, for with 'Majestick Simplicity', we saw, went 'true Poetical Genius', or, to use the words of Dixon in the next century, 'the inspired breathings of a Burns, a Bloomfield, and a Clare'.

Not only reality, in fact, but a higher reality can be found in rural life, discovered by that faculty in man which is closest to the divine. The histories of criticism will trace 'inspiration theory' back to Skelton's *Replycacion* and beyond, but it is easier to take Dixon's hint and glance briefly at a peasant poet, John Clare. Clare, as his recent editors are at pains to make clear, writes with sharp, direct accuracy in both prose and verse about life in his native Helpstone during the early decades of the nineteenth century, not even allowing 'that awkward squad of pointings called commas colons semicolons etc . . . drilled hourly daily and weekly by every boarding school Miss who pretends to gossip in correspondence' to come between him and the first-hand experience he was rendering! (Introduction, *Selected Poems and Prose of John Clare*, chosen and edited by Eric Robinson and Geoffrey Summerfield, 1967.) At the same time, they go on to say, Clare's native place was also his Paradise, his Garden of Eden; it had 'a deeper identity':

> Theres more then music in this early wind
> Awaking like a bird refreshed from sleep
> And joy what Adam might in eden find
> When he with angels did communion keep . . .
> The very grass in joys devotion moves

Cowslaps in adoration and delight
This way and that bow to the breath they love
Of the young winds that with the dew pearls play
Till smoaking chimneys sicken the young light
And feelings fairey visions fade away

Clare is, admittedly, a very special case, in that loss of mental stability meant 'his mind was unable to keep separate at all times the world of reality and the world of his soul's longing'; but he thereby shows in a peculiarly concentrated way the dual allegiance of much rural literature. We look to it for writing that is both record and vision—which in our period turns out to be largely a record of decline and a vision of Paradise Lost. In the rest of this chapter four books will be given particular attention in order to bring out the distinction between documentary and imaginative literature, and to throw some light upon the way in which writers of fiction approach the reality of their day and age. In later chapters we will see how the smoke from Clare's cottage chimneys sickening the young light of the morning turns into the fumes of industry, belching forth by day and by night, and cities become abodes of the damned.

·   ·   ·   ·   ·   ·

Agriculture ceased to be the country's major industry in the early years of the twentieth century. By 1911, we are told by J. D. Chambers and G. E. Mingay in their recent book, *The Agricultural Revolution 1750–1880* (1966), only 7.6 per cent of the working population was engaged in farming. Its decline had been painful: the Great Depression of British Agriculture is the phrase used to describe the events of the years between 1873 and 1896 in particular, the most evident symptom of depression being the disastrous fall in wheat prices. The development of wheat-growing abroad in such countries as the United States and Canada, where the huge acreage meant that machines could be fully utilised to sow, reap, bind and thresh, combined with the constantly falling costs of transport by rail and by steamship, brought unparalleled competition to British farmers. Many of them could not stand up to it.

Nevertheless, historians like T. W. Fletcher, probing more deeply into the general view of those times, have discovered and stressed the fact that it was arable farmers who suffered most. Livestock farmers actually gained by lower costs of cereal and fodder prices, 'because corn is to them an input not an output' (*Economic History Review*, 1960–61). We are told also that there was an expanding market for meat and dairy products. During the thirty or so years of the Great Depression of British Agriculture the population increased by a figure of ten millions, and in addition people were beginning to demand such products rather than the bread they had once had to be content with. Imports of meat and dairy products from countries like Denmark and Holland did increase but they had nothing like the adverse effects on the home market of the corn imports. The depression, though real enough in some quarters, was not general.

T. W. Fletcher's article, it is clear from this brief summary, is notable for the way in which he strives to get behind the general statistics of agricultural decline and what he calls 'an abstraction like "the national farm" '. Towards the end of his article he goes yet further, speculating about the possible human motives for the failure of a number of arable farmers to see the writing on the wall and convert to livestock farming. He suggests, for example, rigidity of mind, a kind of stubbornness and conservatism that led them to resist change even when it was essential for economic survival. In ways like this a historian shows an undoubted concern with the human realities of the situation, but it is startling to find how Fletcher's discussion springs to life when he illustrates 'rigidity of mind' by quoting the actual words of an observer in the Essex of 1896: 'newcomers are going in for milk, cheese, butter, fruit, and sheep but with the average Essex farmer it is corn, corn, corn'. The final words, coming as they do after the innocuous list of dairy products, suddenly hammer home the real sense of exasperation felt by 'a Lancashire farmer'. In writing of this kind we in our day can appreciate what it was to live, and feel, in such times. A historical phenomenon like the great depression of agriculture can be viewed in a detached manner, in an intellectually refined and balanced way, but its consequences in personal life are told with most immediacy by contemporary observers or participants. Their narratives will be partial and often untypical; they will still be communicated to us on a level at which the majority of readers can respond most easily.

A book which has since come to be regarded as a classic in social history illustrates this claim in its own most distinctive way. In 1880 Richard Jefferies collected a number of articles he had written for a London newspaper, *The Standard*, and gave them the title of *Hodge and His Masters*. It is a classic for the extraordinary descriptive power with which Jefferies conveys what he has known and experienced, a power which is manifest on the very first page of the book. There is no sense of a man fumbling or tentatively searching for his theme; indeed, he is confident enough to start with a most unpromising subject:

> The doorway of the Jason Inn at Woolbury had nothing particular to distinguish it from the other doorways of the same extremely narrow street. There was no porch, nor could there possibly be one, for an ordinary porch would reach half across the roadway. There were no steps to go up, there was no entrance hall, no space specially provided for crowds of visitors; simply nothing but an ordinary street-door opening directly on the street, and very little, if any, broader or higher than those of the private houses adjacent.

The negatives accumulate, until the reader begins to feel that the author is foolishly cutting the ground from under his feet; but Jefferies knows the one important fact about the doorway, and is keeping it for the end of his paragraph:

> The dead, dull wall was worn smooth in places by the involuntary rubbings it had received from the shoulders of foot-passengers thrust rudely against it as the market-people came pouring in or out, or both together.

The doorway is significant because of constant contact with human beings, the press and bustle of those who passed through it on business or pleasure. The Jason Inn is not a quaint place to be admired; it is a place to be used. A visitor has to force his way in off the crowded street, past the loungers just inside the doorway and along the sanded passage to see the bar,

> which is full of farmers as thick as they can stand, or sit. The rattle of glasses, the chink of spoons, the hum of voices, the stamping of feet, the calls and orders, and sounds of laughter, mingle in confusion. Cigar-smoke and the steam from the glasses fill the room—all too small—with a thick, white mist, through which rubicund faces dimly shine like the red sun through a fog.

It is evident that Jefferies calculated his literary effects exactly, even to the reasonably efficient quality of the last simile, 'like the red sun through a fog'. Imaginative enough, but hardly so startling that a literal-minded reader would be put off. Nor is his descriptive power confined to evocation of sights, sounds and movements. Besides being able to describe physical environments with brilliant precision, Jefferies can bring out the characters and achievements of, say, a solicitor, a scientific farmer or a 'gigantic agricultural speculator', placing them all firmly in fully realised and convincing settings. He can reveal the influence of mechanical inventions or international trade movements upon the countryside, and demonstrate a real grasp of the interactions between men, environment, institutions and external factors. Rural England, from the miniature cyclone whirling up a column of hay above the trees to the career of the ambitious young squire who went cleverly, cautiously, to work to get himself a nomination to a parliamentary seat, is caught in a web of words. It is also caught at what Jefferies saw as a time of historical crisis in the countryside, for Jefferies was, of course, writing of his part of the country, North Wiltshire and South Gloucestershire, in the first phase of the agricultural depression.

The sense of crisis is fully brought out, especially in such chapters as 'A Wheat Country'. The farmer's dependence upon a number of factors, the weather and seasons, the foreign producer, and the markets influenced by the conditions of trade at large, is stressed. To farmers under pressure from these factors, Jefferies maintains, the last straw is extravagant labour demands for high wages. His

analysis of the situation is pushed further in the chapter entitled
'Landlord's Difficulties. The Labourer as a Power. Modern
Clergy'. He writes of the general ferment in the countryside, the
prevalence of strikes and indignation meetings and—significant
phrase—the 'preaching of doctrines which savour much of Com-
munism'. Whatever justification labourers had for their unrest,
he saw them essentially as losing respect for authority and the
general order of society. He was also acute enough to see that while
agricultural labourers were then usually voteless and on the whole
lacked organisation, supporting newspapers and powerful patrons,
they were yet a power in the land. They were able to bring pressure
to bear that might one day destroy what Jefferies believed to be a
peculiarly attractive way of life. He ends by making two important
points. First, although he condemns the typical labourer's 'moral
apathy and contempt of property—i.e. of social order', he shows
a clear-sighted recognition that the clock cannot be put back:

> Free of mental restraint, his own will must work its way for
> good or evil. It is true that the rise or fall of wages may check
> or hasten the development of that future. In either case it is
> not, however, probable that he will return to the old grooves;
> indeed, the grooves themselves are gone, and the logic of events
> must force him to move onwards. That motion, in its turn,
> must affect the rest of the community.

Second, Jefferies emphasises the unity of thought being supplied
by education, not only at school but after it when young men form
their own moral, political and social opinions, and continues:

> In short, the future literature of the labourer becomes a serious
> question. He will think what he reads; and what he reads at
> the present moment is of anything but an elevating character.
> He will think, too, what he hears; and he hears much of an
> enticing but subversive political creed, and little of any other.
> There are busy tongues earnestly teaching him to despise
> property and social order, to suggest the overthrow of existing
> institutions; there is scarcely anyone to instruct him in the
> true lesson of history. Who calls together an audience of
> agricultural labourers to explain to and interest them in the

story of their own country? There are many who are only too anxious to use the agricultural labourer as the means to effect ends which he scarcely understands. But there are few, indeed, who are anxious to instruct him in science or literature for his own sake.

There is much in this paragraph which we in the twentieth century recognise only too easily: the existence of strong public opinion which can yet be formed and controlled by manipulating the means of communication and, even more significant, the use of history, or rather of particular interpretations of history, as the content of propaganda. Jefferies is himself providing just this type of literature, giving his readers a particular view of historical process and attempting to influence its future course by guiding it into patterns acceptable to conservative thinkers. We should not fail to notice what can so easily happen when literature becomes too involved with propaganda.

The word Hodge, a diminutive of Roger, has been used since Chaucer to indicate a rustic and can become a term of contempt for bucolic simplicity. Even if contempt is not intended, *Hodge and His Masters* shows how the *incidental* use of this word in a sentence here and there can drain a human being of the life that is in him, making the country labourer of little more account than a property stool on a stage:

> Hodge eating his luncheon under the hedge in October, as he slowly munched his crust, watched the squire strolling about the fields with his gun under his arm, and wondered why he did not try the turnips.

The last chapter of the book, which is an extended and successful account of an old labourer who died in the workhouse, shows the depth of imaginative sympathy and knowledge that Jefferies at his best could bring to the life of a countryman, one who had been carried off to the workhouse because there was then a great movement against outdoor relief:

> The dormitories were clean, but the ward was not his old bedroom up the worm-eaten steps, with the slanting ceiling, where as he woke in the morning he could hear the sparrows

chirping, the chaffinch calling and the lark singing aloft. There was a garden attached to the workhouse, where he could do a little if he liked, but it was not his garden. He missed his plum-trees and apples, and the tall pear, and the lowly elder hedge. He looked round, raising his head with difficulty, and he could not see the sign-post, nor the familiar red-bricked farmhouse. He knew all the rain that had fallen must have come through the thatch of the old cottage in at least one place, and he would have liked to have gone and re-thatched it with trembling hand.

It is not too hard to see why Raymond Williams, in the introduction to a recent edition, should claim that in this chapter about the old man Jefferies was 'working essentially as a novelist'. We can see how the description is caught up with the feelings of the old man about the new place and how the prose takes on in consequence the rhythm of a lament. This is not the expression of Jefferies the objective observer of a rural specimen: it is the language of a man who has found his way into the responses of another human being. We are worlds away from the distant tone of 'In short, the future literature of the labourer becomes a serious question'.

In this final chapter, called 'Hodge's Last Masters. Conclusion', a serious question has found a solid substance and embodiment, which reveals that in Jefferies was the power not only of a novelist but of a poetic novelist:

> The end came very slowly; he ceased to exist by imperceptible degrees, like an oak-tree. He remained for days in a semi-unconscious state, neither moving nor speaking. It happened at last. In the grey of the winter dawn, as the stars paled and the whitened grass was stiff with hoar frost, and the rime coated every branch of the tall elms, as the milker came from the pen and the young ploughboy whistled down the road to his work, the spirit of the aged man departed.

Not that he forgets his moral, social or political purpose, but the relevant questions he immediately goes on to pose soon modulate into the 'reality' he has created:

What amount of production did that old man's life of labour represent? What value must be put upon the service of the son that fought in India; of the son that worked in Australia; of the daughter in New Zealand, whose children will help to build up a new nation? These things surely have their value. Hodge died, and the very gravedigger grumbled as he delved through the earth hard-bound in the iron frost, for it jarred his hand and might break his spade. The low mound will soon be level, and the place of his burial shall not be known.

In this passage Jefferies in a sense makes us gravediggers for our customary insensibility to the claims of men like the old labourer, thus attempting to break down our frost-bound sympathies; which makes it all the more surprising when we catch in Jefferies a note of the economic callousness of the *laissez-faire* tradition so strong in the earlier part of the nineteenth century. Dealing in the chapter called 'Grass Countries' with the efforts of labour organisations to encourage corn land because it supports more labourers, he can only conclude that the situation 'must settle itself, and be governed entirely by the same conditions that affect other trades—i.e. profit and loss'. Much of the history of political thought of the nineteenth century is the record of the struggle against that deterministic 'entirely' and its implications, the narrowness of the view that human beings should be left to the unregulated operation of the market. Too much weight cannot be given to a single word, which may not have been written fully intending all its implications, but it is tempting to consider such a general cast of thought as leading to Jefferies' failures in imaginative insight. At the time he was writing agricultural unionism had lost the impulse given to it in the seventies by Joseph Arch and was all but dead. It had been killed by many factors, such as the fall in grain prices, the lock-outs and use of blackleg labour from Ireland, and also the arguments mounted against unionism generally by those who claimed that working men were dupes of agitators where they were not plain idle. Jefferies comes into this category of anti-union critics and it is disappointing to discover him producing, in the chapter called 'A Winter's Morning', one of the most durable of stereotypes, lazy navvies:

I watched the process. Using the right hand as a fulcrum and keeping it stationary, each navvy slowly lifted his pick with the left half-way up, about on a level with his waist-coat, when the point of the pick was barely two feet above the ground. He then let it fall—simply by its own weight—producing a tiny indentation such as might be caused by the kick of one's heel. It required about three such strokes, if they could be called strokes, to detach one single small stone. After that exhausting labour the man stood at ease for a few minutes, so that there were often three or four at once staring about them, while several others lounged against the wooden railing placed to keep vehicles back.

The facile sarcasm ('exhausting labour') and imprecision ('several others') of the last sentence casts doubt on the promising Sterne-like detail of the earlier sentences. As a whole it does not ring true, any more than similar caricatures of bloated capitalists in works of the opposite persuasion, or if it comes to that, ideal working men like Stephen Blackpool in Dickens's *Hard Times*. There is no feeling, as there is in the chapter about the old labourer dying in the workhouse, that Jefferies is communicating the truth of his experience rather than what suits his uninspired and abstract purposes. The distinction between the two descriptions—if it is indeed valid and not just an indirect expression of impatience on my part with the triteness of the thought about the navvies—is of some importance. It draws attention to the fundamental difference between writing which though committed to its own beliefs about life is in certain respects indisputable, and writing which is open to denial or modification. Jefferies is unrivalled in his ability to communicate the truth of his experience, but he can undoubtedly lose force and quality when ideology is uppermost in his mind.[1]

·   ·   ·   ·   ·   ·

It is not hard to allow for at least the possibility of various kinds of bias in writings of a documentary nature. When we read on the first page of Flora Thompson's fascinatingly detailed account of her life, which began in a little Oxfordshire hamlet in the 80s of the last century, that 'the ripened cornfields rippled up to the door-steps of the cottages and the hamlet became an island in a sea of dark gold' (*Lark Rise to Candleford*, World's Classics, 1954), the imagery alerts us to the fact that this is no artless writer providing a naive record to be taken just at its face value. Again, W. H. Hudson goes to the extent of ending his *Nature in Downland* (1900) with an open confession that emotional memories of West Sussex scenery could affect his rational convictions about the county, and a recent writer, John Burnett, quotes a passage from Hudson's *Hampshire Days* (1902) as an illustration that even Hudson's country informants were probably allowing their judgement to be clouded by 'romantic nostalgia for the past' (*Plenty and Want: A Social History of Diet in England From 1815 to the Present Day*, 1966). In fact, a double corrective has to be applied in this last case, though still one of a relatively straightforward nature—*two* pinches of salt, so to speak.

But when we turn our minds to wholly creative literature, we see that it is not always easy to strike a balance between the fictional data and the historical facts to which they are so often related. Our period, we might remember, was also a great era of collecting and reviving folk-music, and it is just as difficult to say how far works by composers like Holst or Vaughan Williams transcend the folk-music with which they are often intimately connected as it is to disentangle Thomas Hardy's novels from the rural history of his day. Critics, with their responsibility to expound and elucidate, can only envy the splendid simplicity of one of Elgar's pronouncements on this topic: 'I am folk-music'!

Many of Hardy's novels and poems are set in a region he called, after the ancient southern English kingdom, Wessex. He himself tells us in the preface to *Far From the Madding Crowd* that

> the press and the public were kind enough to welcome the fanciful plan and willingly joined me in the anachronism of im-agining a Wessex population living under Queen Victoria;—a modern Wessex of railways, the penny post, mowing and reap-ing machines, union workhouses, lucifer matches, labourers who could read and write, and National school children.

But Wessex was far from being purely fictional, as Hardy makes very clear in the most useful General Preface (1912)[2] he provided for the definitive Wessex Edition of his writings. After saying that the people in most of his novels were meant to be 'typically and essentially those of any and every place', that they shared a common humanity, he continues:

But whatever the success of this intention, and the value of these novels as delineations of humanity, they have at least a humble supplementary quality of which I may be justified in reminding the reader, though it is one that was quite unintentional and unforeseen. At the dates represented in the various narrations things were like that in Wessex: the inhabitants lived in certain ways, engaged in certain occupations, kept alive certain customs, just as they are shown doing in these pages. And in particularizing such I have often been reminded of Boswell's remarks on the trouble to which he was put and the pilgrimages he was obliged to make to authenticate some detail, though the labour was one which would bring him no praise. Unlike his achievement, however, on which an error would as he says have brought discredit, if these country customs and vocations, obsolete and obsolescent, had been detailed wrongly, nobody would have discovered such errors to the end of Time. Yet I have instituted inquiries to correct tricks of memory, and striven against temptations to exaggerate, in order to preserve for my own satisfaction a fairly true record of a vanishing life.

Wessex may be an imaginary region, and in many respects as much of a creation as William Faulkner's Yoknapatawpha county, but it is based upon actual fact. Hardy brought together real details, even if, it is worth noting, he differed from many of his Victorian readers when he called the results of his efforts no more than a 'humble supplementary quality'. (Kenneth Graham notices the 'fairly common inability to distinguish between fiction and history, or biography' in his *English Criticism of the Novel 1865–1900* and tartly remarks that 'informativeness of any kind [was] enough to ensure many pseudo-novels serious critical attention.') Hardy admittedly changed and re-shuffled his real details—the place-names of the boundaries of his region, Bath, Plymouth, Southampton and the like, are an exception—but this is the inevitable result of making fiction out of history or biography. His Preface makes it clear that he strove hard to recapture the very quality of life in the rural, south-western counties of England during the reign of Queen Victoria, life in those communities where, he once wrote, 'happiness will find her last refuge on earth, since it is among them that a perfect insight into the conditions of existence will be longest postponed'.

He had himself been born and brought up in a little country place, Higher Bockhampton near Dorchester, and his knowledge of country characters and customs, habits and traditions, was minute and extensive, something that can be seen most clearly in the article from which the last quotation was taken ('The Dorsetshire Labourer', published in *Longman's Magazine* for July 1883). Here, in this article, is the kind of detailed and intimate knowledge that finds its way into the Wessex novels and poems. Many of the novels relate to an earlier date. *The Mayor of Casterbridge*, for instance, is set in the years before the repeal of the corn laws in 1846. *Tess of the D'Urbervilles* (1891), however, is set in the 1880s and includes material drawn directly from the earlier article. One has only to compare the descriptions of a family removal on Lady Day in both texts:

> The goods are built up on the waggon to a well-nigh unvary-ing pattern, which is probably as peculiar to the country labourer as the hexagon to the bee. The dresser, with its finger-marks and domestic evidences thick upon it, stands importantly in front, over the backs of the shaft horses, in its erect and natural position, like some Ark of the Covenant, which must not be handled slightingly or overturned.

This quotation is from the article, but with minor verbal changes and the addition of the information that this was the migration of the Durbeyfield family it might have come from chapter 52 of *Tess*. Hardy was bringing home to us how precarious was the situation of the migratory farm labourer in the 80s. No longer did such men usually stay for their whole life upon one farm as had once been the custom. Hardy writes in his article of certain positive gains: the minds of the workfolk were stimulated by change and their general outlook became wider. Nevertheless—and here we see him striking the balance appropriate in an expository article—they undoubtedly lost touch with their native place, and lost, too, 'that sense of long local participancy which is one of the pleasures of age'.

We begin to realise the degree of divergence between the novel and the article when we see how much more powerful *Tess of the D'Urbervilles* is in its recreation of historical circumstance. It provides such a dense accumulation of particulars that it is hard to know which passage to choose as an illustration. We might refer to the description of the heroine as a field woman by Flintcomb Ash:

> Thus Tess walks on; a figure which is part of the landscape; a fieldwoman pure and simple, in winter guise; a grey serge cape, a red woollen cravat, a stuff skirt covered by a whitey-brown rough wrapper, and buff-leather gloves. Every thread of that old attire has become faded and thin under the stroke of raindrops, the burn of sunbeams, and the stress of winds. There is no sign of young passion in her now—

One can sense the insistence with which Hardy is crushing Tess's individuality from her; she was sinking to a low point of bare existence:

> The swede field in which she and her companion were set hacking was a stretch of a hundred odd acres, in one patch, on the highest ground of the farm, rising above stony lanchets or lynchets—the outcrop of silaceous veins in the chalk formation, composed of myriads of loose white flints in bulbous, cusped and phallic shapes. The upper half of each turnip had been eaten off by the livestock, and it was the business of the two women to grub up the lower or earthy half of the root with a hooked fork called a hacker, that it might be eaten also. Every leaf of the vegetable having already been consumed, the whole field was in colour a desolate drab; it was a complexion without features, as if a face, from chin to brow, should be only an expanse of skin. The sky wore, in another colour, the same

likeness; a white vacuity of countenance with the lineaments gone. So these two upper and nether visages confronted each other all day long, the white face looking down upon the brown face, and the brown face looking up at the white face, without anything standing between them but the two girls crawling over the surface of the former like flies.   (Chapter 43.)

A nadir of existence has been reached. Tess is lost in a landscape which is itself featureless, engaged in a task which is itself a kind of ultimate reduction—only the earthy halves of what had once been whole roots with fresh green springing from the top are left to be grubbed up. She and her companion in the field are reduced to the status of insects crawling on a surface without character or meaning.

As a piece of description this is more imaginative than what can be found in most works of a documentary nature, though the best passages in Jefferies show that it is not unattainable nor necessarily different in kind. It is possible to quote from *Tess of the D'Urbervilles* many a similar passage, all of which succeed through Hardy's intense concentration on the whole quality and texture of the life he imagines as well as on the basic, accumulated facts. And yet such descriptions are strictly subordinate in the novel as a whole: *Tess* almost incidentally reveals the harshness of a fieldwoman's lot or the failure of an independent haggler like Tess's father or the fatalism of country people in a world of incomprehensible happenings. Such things are matters of historical record and highly important in their own right, but in the world of the novel they are part of a much wider vision that sees the course of human history primarily in the shape of an individual's story, the *invented* history of a fictional character. The unity and fullness of Hardy's total creation conveys to an exceptional degree the feeling of inevitability about the successive events of Tess's life. The blankness of her existence upon the stony soil of Flintcomb Ash could not contrast more with the earlier phase of her life in the lush valley of the Great Dairies, when Angel Clare had been irresistibly drawn to her as summer heat intensified:

Amid the oozing fatness and warm ferments of the Froom Vale, at a season when the rush of juices could almost be heard below the hiss of fertilization, it was impossible that the most fanciful love should not grow passionate. The ready bosoms existing there were impregnated by their surroundings.

(Chapter 24.)

Yet this paradisial fertility is as completely appropriate in its phase as the flinty negation that succeeds it when Tess is deserted by Angel Clare. Different as the two settings are from each other, they function in the same way. They are inseparably bound up with the stages of Tess's career, providing a kind of external impulse and sanction. Moreover, it is not only external nature that is involved in giving us a sense of total coherence. The major pattern of Tess's life is like that of her own family's when they are driven from their assured place in village society. The death of her father lost them the cottage which, like so many at that period of history, was tied to the lifetime of a certain person. The family consequently lost 'that sense of long local participancy' with their native place and by a bitter irony were forced to set up the family bed over the tombs of their ancestors, the only piece of land remaining to them. Again, as Hardy stresses at the beginning of chapter 51, their removal is far from unique: Tess's uprooting, and that of her family, is the pattern of the loss of stability of a whole rural society. *Tess* is Hardy's vision of the remorseless destructive flow of history, the 'vanishing life' he spoke of in his Preface to the Wessex Edition.

But always in the foreground of the novel is a fictional character, Tess, unable to save herself from destruction, and whose tragedy springs, we must note, from her individuality. Despite what has been said so far, she is in some ways at odds with her rural society. Hardy early underlines the difference between the primitive, superstitious mother and Tess, 'with her trained National teachings and Standard knowledge under an infinitely Revised Code.' When Tess and her mother were together, Hardy writes in an epigrammatic phrase, 'the Jacobean and the Victorian ages were juxtaposed'. He likewise goes out of his way to distinguish Angel Clare, unable in conscience to take Orders while his Church refused 'to liberate her mind from an untenable redemptive theolatry', and his father,

D

a vicar of the ardent Evangelical school, conservative and unyielding in his beliefs. Both Tess and Angel Clare, at their different social levels, stand apart from their world and are alienated from their parents. He achieves even more emphasis (and aesthetic symmetry) by showing that they were also distinguished from their coevals, carefully giving Angel Clare two temporising brothers able to take Orders without any difficulty and providing Tess with fellow milkmaids who constantly remark on her uniqueness. Most memorable of all, however, are the thoughts Hardy gives to Angel Clare:

> He was surprised to find this young woman—who though but a milkmaid had just that touch of rarity about her which might make her the envied of her housemates—shaping such sad imaginings. She was expressing in her own native phrases—assisted a little by her Sixth Standard training—feelings which might almost have been called those of the age—the ache of modernism. The perception arrested him less when he reflected that what are called advanced ideas are really in great part but the latest fashion in definition—a more accurate expression by words in *logy* and *ism*, of sensations which men and women have vaguely grasped for centuries. (Chapter 19.)

That striking phrase, 'the ache of modernism', shows that Hardy sees in Tess the spirit of his own age, with its lack of inner resources in the face of a hostile universe and its inevitable 'sad imaginings' about the course of human life. In accordance with his beliefs these profound thoughts are voiced in Tess's simple words to Clare:

> 'The trees have inquisitive eyes, haven't they?—that is, seem as if they had. And the river says,—"Why do ye trouble me with your looks?" And you seem to see numbers of tomorrows just all in a line, the first of them the biggest and clearest, the others getting smaller and smaller as they stand farther away; but they all seem very fierce and cruel and as if they said, "I'm coming! Beware of me! Beware of me!..." (Chapter 19.)

The same troubled, painful spirit is expressed in 'Faith Giving Way', a drawing by Jan Toorop of 1894, and there can be no doubt that Hardy is reaching out to larger concerns than those invariably found in rural society.

In these passages just quoted from chapter 19 are a number of Shakespearian echoes. They are so subdued that one would hardly imagine them to be deliberate; nevertheless, the milkmaid with a touch of rarity especially brings the heroine of *The Winter's Tale* into illuminating comparison with Tess. Perdita, like the other heroines of Shakespeare's Last Plays, is a type of perfection, virginal, springlike, a goddess on earth in the eyes of her lover Florizel— she seems the very reverse of Tess, who even looks upon herself after she has been seduced as 'a figure of Guilt intruding into the haunts of Innocence'. But according to Hardy this is precisely what she is not. She was wrong about herself; and Angel Clare was wrong about her when he ceased to see her as a perfect being after she had confessed her past to him and he consequently rejected her love. To Hardy she was, as he firmly insists in the sub-title of the novel, 'A Pure Woman'; only by the mistaken social conventions of the Victorians or in the sight of Christians not living up to their highest standards could she be regarded as impure. In other words, Hardy's fiction, like Jefferies' journalism, was directed at public beliefs and attitudes of his time.

In the main, however, *Tess of the D'Urbervilles* is a work of art, not a manifesto. There are, it is true, places where Hardy intrudes with barely relevant commentary in a way that rends the dense created texture of his work. One example is the bitterness with which he attacks Wordsworth's lines in the Immortality Ode, 'Not in utter nakedness/But trailing clouds of glory do we come': he writes that

> to Tess, as to not a few millions of others, there was ghastly satire in the poet's lines ... To her and to her like, birth itself was an ordeal of degrading personal compulsion, whose gratuitousness nothing in the result seemed to justify, and at best could only palliate. (Chapter 51.)

When, we might ask with Dorothy Van Ghent,[3] had he shown Tess as the kind of girl who would be likely to react so critically to philosophic poetry? Who are the 'few millions'? It is probably impossible to justify these intrusions if we object to the way in which they break the continuity of our belief in the story as we read it. At the same time, they make us sharply aware of the author himself, usually at moments of intense response to the life of his own creation. In an odd manner these interruptions serve as a guarantee of the likeness of the fiction to real life at certain points, since we feel that Hardy the author would not have let his personal emotions show so openly had not the course of his narrative suddenly touched him on a raw nerve as a man with experience of life outside his book. But on the whole his powerful shaping of historical particulars must mean that whatever the local likenesses of the invented story to real life may be, he has generally rejected any balanced, fully objective view for the sake of his imaginative creation and its own internal logic.

Many years later he wrote that he would like to place before his novels the simple phrase, 'Understand that however true this book may be in essence, in fact it is utterly untrue'. The statement is extreme, for the sake of emphasis, but it is a basic view of the relationship between imaginative literature and history—one stated as long ago as the third century B.C. in Aristotle's *Poetics*: 'Poetry is more philosophical than history'. Or, as Wordsworth wrote in the 1800 Preface to *Lyrical Ballads*:

> Aristotle, I have been told, has said that Poetry is the most philosophic of all writing: it is so: its object is truth, not individual and local, but general and operative; not standing upon external testimony, but carried alive into the heart by passion; truth which is its own testimony, which gives competence and confidence to the tribunal to which it appeals, and receives them from the same tribunal.

Aristotle and Wordsworth speak of poetry, but the same holds for all fiction: it goes well beyond the record of the bare facts and deploys them very much for its own purposes, creating its own unity and leading to its own necessary conclusion. For Hardy these purposes involved very much more than a plain reflection of life in the rural south-west, as we have seen with *Tess*.

In general we cannot fail to remark that his novels now draw increasing praise from literary critics when contemporary writers of similar fiction are all but ignored. Eden Phillpotts may stand here as a regional writer who produced novel after novel about Dartmoor and its people in the early years of this century, beginning with *Children of the Mist* in 1899. Novels like *The Whirlwind* (1907) and *Widecombe Fair* (1913) are good reading. The fact remains that they are actually read by few today in comparison with the multitudes who call for the successive reprints of Hardy's works. Nor is Hardy's popularity with literary critics anything to do with fine writing in the ordinary sense. Many a sentence must have been composed on the subject of his inconsistent and unsophisticated style. (One of the wittiest was T. S. Eliot's in *After Strange Gods*: 'at times his style touches sublimity without ever having passed through the stage of being good'.) We might maintain that Hardy's substantial realisation of Wessex is important, especially the way in which he reflects the great rural decline in his lifetime, but he himself (in 'The Profitable Reading of Fiction', *Forum*, New York, March 1888) faced up to the tempting idea that faithful reproduction of life was enough and decided that it simply was not:

> To distinguish truths which are temporary from truths which are eternal, the accidental from the essential, accuracies as to custom and ceremony from accuracies as to the perennial procedure of humanity, is of vital importance in our attempts to read for something more than amusement. There are certain novels, both among the works of living and the works of deceased writers, which give convincing proof of much exceptional fidelity, and yet they do not rank as great productions; for what they are faithful in is life garniture and not life. . . . But what of it, after our first sense of its photographic curiousness is past? In aiming at the trivial and the ephemeral they have almost surely missed better things.

Hardy's actual achievement confronts us with universal themes, and I do not think it is ludicrous to suggest that his words above can be prescriptively applied to the writing of history—provided we bear in mind that invention on a large scale is denied to the historian. 'Poetry is usually more fictional than history', so to speak. But that does not prevent historians in their study of the past from defining what is contingent and what has continuing relevance. It is at the centre of their effort. Hardy, I think, therefore deserves the attention he has been given in the present context and by critics generally. As a man he straddled the old and the new, the Victorian and the modern world. As an artist he gives us aesthetic pleasure of an unusual kind and, I would say, writing of an essentially historical nature, in that much of his work provides a distinctive evaluation of his own times and their place in the course of human affairs.

His success as a writer brings problems when we look at later rural literature. Many lesser works were written in his shadow, culminating in the famous *Precious Bane* (1924) by Mary Webb; how far such works relate to real life and how far they are Hardyesque repetitions in another context causes difficulties of interpretation. Looking very briefly at Galsworthy's play, *A Bit o' Love* (1915), we can see how very typical of its author are themes of unhappiness in marriage and society's inhuman conventions, but when Act II opens with a village-inn setting, a bucolically heavy joke and a little maid sent for six clay pipes, we are distracted by memories of Warren's Malthouse in *Far From the Madding Crowd* (1874) and Hardy's comparable introduction of a piece of local colour in the shape of the God-forgive-me. We can gain a new perspective by going outside the narrowly English tradition of rural literature.

·   ·   ·   ·   ·   ·

The name of Sir James Barrie immediately brings to mind writing both fanciful and beautiful, especially that whimsically poetic play of 1904, *Peter Pan*. Yet Barrie began life as a journalist; he first came to fame by publishing collections of sketches and tales about Scottish country folk and was part of a literary movement of the time known derisively as the Kailyard School, 'writers of fiction describing, with unsparing use of the vernacular, common life in Scotland' according to the *Concise Oxford Dictionary*. These were authors like Ian Maclaren (John Watson) or 'George Douglas', whose *The House with the Green Shutters* (1901) is far from contemptible in its successful avoidance of the prevailing fault of the

School, a tendency to sentimentalise Scottish life. An early volume of Barrie's, *Auld Licht Idylls* (1888), attempts to achieve a degree of realism in its evocation of life in the little town of Thrums amongst the strictest of its four religious sects, the Auld Lichts. The book opens with a description of a deep winter scene and goes on to underscore in many ways the quality of life in that part of Scotland, whether by the passing mention of the cold skeletons of deserted houses on the hill or by the more elaborate description of a bothy, the lodging place of agricultural labourers:

> 'Hands' are not huddled together today nowadays in squalid barns more like cattle than like men and women, but bothies in the neighbourhood of Thrums are not yet things of the past. . . . Here is a picture of a bothy of today that I visited recently. Over the door there is a water-spout that has given way, and as I entered I got a rush of rain down my neck. The passage was so small that one could easily have stepped from the doorway on to the ladder standing against the wall, which was there in lieu of a staircase. 'Upstairs' was a mere garret, where a man could not stand erect even in the centre. It was entered by a square hole in the ceiling, at present closed by a trap-door in no way dissimilar to the trap-doors on a theatre stage. I climbed into this garret, which is at present used as a store-room for agricultural odds and ends. At harvest-time, however, it is inhabited—full to overflowing. A few decades ago as many as fifty labourers engaged for the harvest had to be housed in the farm out-houses on beds of straw. . . .   (Chapter 2.)

To a large extent Barrie succeeds. We find as we read that Thrums comes to life in our imagination, not so much as a physical place, despite the early part of the book, but rather as a community of people with its own highly idiosyncratic character. In that respect it is a kind of Scottish Cranford. But Barrie intended more than simple objective realism.

The Auld Licht sect, in his eyes, was an object of satire—for its severity when the Sabbath day was broken, however slightly, the length of prayers over sinners, the old wives who would grumble if the minister did not look in 'to despair of their salvation', the minister who heckled and warned, exhorted and admonished, 'tried to tear the devil out of the pulpit rails' and who could even reduce a stone-deaf parishioner to tears of repentance. There is the story of the white-haired old lady who would march ostentatiously out of the kirk when the psalm began because she disapproved of the way it was no longer read and sung reverently line-by-line. It seems utterly ridiculous, but Barrie turns the anecdote at the end to take away any real bite from the satire. His narrator, the local school-master, finishes in this way:

> Once some men, capable of anything, held the door from the outside, and the congregation heard Tibbie rampaging in the passage. Bursting into the kirk she called the office-bearers to her assistance, whereupon the minister in miniature raised his voice and demanded the why and wherefore of the ungodly disturbance. Great was the hubbub, but the door was fast, and a compromise had to be arrived at. The old lady consented for once to stand in the passage, but not without pressing her hands to her ears. You may smile at Tibbie, but ah! I know what she was at a sick bedside. I have seen her when the hard look had gone from her eyes, and it would ill become me to smile too.   (Chapter 3.)

This, it seems to me, is too blatantly done for us to be charitable and say that Barrie was trying to be a fair historian of the Auld Lichts by giving both sides.

He is a disarming writer, certainly; satire mingled with quaintness and touching sentiment is not easy to resist. *Auld Licht Idylls*, too, is the kind of book that can make its readers laugh aloud, as when we come across the tale of Tammas Haggart who married a gipsy lassie and always maintained that the marriage turned out better than he had expected, 'though he had his trials like other married men':

> Among them was Chirsty's way of climbing on to the dresser to get at the higher part of the plate-rack. One evening I called in to have a smoke with the stone-breaker, and while we were talking Chirsty climbed the dresser. The next moment she was on the floor on her back, wailing, but Tammas smoked on

imperturbedly. 'Do you not see what has happened, man?' I cried. 'Ou,' said Tammas, 'she's aye fa'in off the dresser.'

(Chapter 12.)

At the end of the book Barrie demonstrates exceptional technical skill by bringing together the two main value-systems involved in *Auld Licht Idylls*, the narrow *mores* of a primitive sect and those of the wider morality to be discovered in literature: the one the principal subject-matter of the book and the other informing the whole approach and treatment of that subject-matter. Thrums, his narrator tells us, got many of its books and pamphlets from the 'flying stationers', men who usually bore their stock on their backs:

It was from Sandersby that Tammas Haggart bought his copy of Shakespeare, whom Mr Dishart [the minister] could never abide. Tammas kept what he had done from his wife, but Chirsty saw a deterioration setting in and told the minister of her suspicions. Mr Dishart was newly placed at the time and very vigorous, and the way he shook the truth out of Tammas was grand. The minister pulled Tammas the one way and Gavin [chairman of the literary club] pulled him the other, but Mr Dishart was not the man to be beaten, and he landed Tammas in the Auld Licht kirk before the year was out. Chirsty buried Shakespeare in the yard.

The splendid last sentence thuds home dead centre. It could hardly be more final, nor could it strike more unerringly at the spiritual certitude that would unhesitatingly reject the larger scheme of values represented by Shakespeare's works. 'Old Light seeking light doth light of light beguile', in fact.

.   .   .   .   .   .

Barrie is a canny writer; though when the charm has faded and the delight died down one begins to ponder about the amount of selection and modification that went to produce his effects. Had he not shaped his material the result would not be art, merely compilation. Churlishness, too, is probably the besetting sin of literary critics, especially when they suspect that they have been cajoled into a good humour. Yet for all that, I feel Barrie went too far in manipulating reality. Local authenticity may abound in *Auld Licht Idylls*: one is not convinced of the truth of the whole. For such a quality I would rather turn to a similar collection of tales about Irish life, George Moore's *The Untilled Field* (1903), which is hardly as entertaining as *Auld Licht Idylls* but which possesses the kind of large verisimilitude we look for when we are considering works of literature as valuable historical records of their time and place.

George Moore had his hobby-horses. The word 'America' appears throughout, bringing to mind the positively catastrophic decline of rural Ireland during the nineteenth century, its population halved—the cliché 'decimated' is quite inadequate in this context—by famine and continued emigration. Where in Hardy's *Tess of the D'Urbervilles* the family lost touch with its native village, hundreds of thousands of the Irish were separated from their native land itself. As far as Moore was concerned, the desertion of Ireland was not only a matter of economics but also related to the power wielded in society then by the clergy. The story called 'The Wild Goose' is a very direct expression of one man's refusal 'to accept all the base moral coinage in circulation' and his decision to leave his wife, child and work in Ireland for a freer life abroad. The theme, specifically a social-historical one, recurs throughout the book. Even so, Moore seems to write with less prejudice and externality than Barrie. His care for truth glows strongly when he concentrates on rendering the mental life of an individual responding to his circumstances, as in 'Home Sickness', the tale of an Irish American returning to his native village to convalesce after an illness. He becomes engaged to a local girl and all goes well, since his American savings and his dowry will give the young couple extraordinarily hopeful prospects in an impoverished land. At this stage comes a letter from an American friend who used to serve drinks with him in a Bowery bar, asking when he was coming back:

> He tried to forget the letter, and he looked at the worn fields, divided by walls of loose stones, and a great longing came upon him.
> The smell of the Bowery slum had come across the Atlantic,

and had found him out in this western headland; and one night he awoke from a dream in which he was hurling some drunken customer through the open doors into the darkness. He had seen his friend in his white duck jacket throwing drink from glass into glass amid the din of voices and strange accents; he had heard the clang of money as it was swept into the till, and his sense sickened for the bar-room.

And so he goes back to America, wondering how it was that 'the smell of the bar seemed more natural than the smell of fields, and the roar of crowds more welcome than the silence of the lake's edge.' We might think that this is a pleasant paradox. Pope had used it for comic effect in an Epistle to Teresa Blount—'On her leaving the Town after the Coronation' for 'wholesome country air', only to find to her disgust that

> She went to plain-work and to purling brooks,
> Old fashion'd halls, dull aunts and croaking rooks:
> She went from op'ra, park, assembly, play,
> To morning-walks and pray'rs three hours a-day . . .

We might also claim that it rounds off the tale nicely—the happy land of Arcady tried and found wanting. But Moore has felt his way into human life and its untidiness far more deeply than could be expressed in a neatly symmetrical form. In a few additional sentences he tells succinctly how his character eventually retired from a successful business career in America, his wife died and his children went off; and then, in the loneliness that came upon him,

> it seemed to him that a memory was the only real thing he possessed, and the desire to see Margaret again grew intense. But she was an old woman, she had married, maybe she was dead. Well, he would like to be buried in the village where he was born.
>
> There is an unchanging, silent life within every man that none knows but himself, and his unchanging, silent life was his memory of Margaret Dirken. The bar-room was forgotten and all that concerned it, and the things he saw most clearly were the green hillside, and the bog lake and the rushes about it,

and the greater lake in the distance, and behind it the blue line
of wandering hills.

There *is* a twist at the end of the story, but not one imported like
Barrie's in order to produce a more acceptable mixture of satire
and sentiment. It seems to me that Moore deeply felt that human
beings change in time and would not palter with the truth he knew,[4]
even if it meant the story spilling over the edge of the neat shape it
had taken by the time he wrote the words quoted above about the
silence of the lake's edge. His sense of form was controlled by his
reactions to life, not predetermined by abstract considerations.

It is not easy to do sufficient justice to these stories and the
sensitive informality of their making. Moore gives only what is
needed, cutting out inessentials to a surprising extent. 'Home
Sickness' begins in a most laconic way. In the first sentence a man
is telling his doctor that he must be back at work in the Bowery
by eight the next morning; about a dozen lines later that man is
landing in Cork. The technique is very un-English, that is if one
thinks of the exuberantly Dickensian as being the central tradition
of prose fiction. When James Joyce brought out his volume of
stories called *Dubliners* in 1914, they were welcomed at once by
Ezra Pound for virtues he considered rare at that time—clarity of
outline even in subjective matters, swift and vivid presentation of
people, the avoidance of 'neat little diagrams' and the rigorous
selection of the presented detail. This last quality especially, Pound
thought, marked Joyce as belonging to the 1910s rather than to the
writers of the previous decade. Pound may well be right in general
terms, but Moore's *The Untilled Field* of 1903 deserves similar
praise. A fine modern critic has termed Moore's collection 'an
obvious ancestor' of *Dubliners*, noting the parallel cadences of their
prose and other likenesses in feeling and treatment. (See Graham
Hough, *Image and Experience: Studies in a Literary Revolution*,
1960, chapter 6.)

Professor Hough has also underlined Moore's wish 'to paint the
portrait of my country' and the likeness of this to Joyce's words
when he described to his publisher the purpose of *Dubliners*: 'to
write a chapter of the moral history of my country'. We have

already seen that Moore could present human beings without balking at their changeableness. We might go on to indicate that the most effective way he found of really associating those human beings with their own land was to use the Irish countryside to provide a delicately clear notation of their moral qualities. In the following description of a natural scene the underlying serenity belongs just as much to the nature of its observer, a gentle priest (a type, incidentally, we might have thought Moore would not understand or care for):

> He walked on and on. When they had walked six miles he sat down and took a piece of bread out of his pocket. As he ate it his eyes wandered over the undulating bog, brown and rose, marked here and there by a black streak where the peasants had been cutting turf. The sky changed very little, it was still a pale, dove colour; now and then a little blue showed through the grey, and sometimes the light lessened; but a few minutes after the sunlight fluttered out of the sky again and dozed among the heather.   ('A Letter to Rome')

There are many other possible examples, some of the most distinguished being in the story called 'The Wedding Gown', which displays an almost incredible coalescence of scene and changing situation, both outer and inner. We do not, to take just one brief instance from the tale, need to be told directly of the death of an old, senile woman at the very moment she is bathed in memories of her wedding day:

> The moonlight lay still upon her knees, but little by little the moon moved up the sky, leaving her in the shadow.

More extended analysis belongs to pure literary criticism; for the present we must leave this author in subtle control of one of the constants of rural literature, the natural scene—described not only for its own sake but for what it can convey of human lives in time.

George Moore had the literary skill needed to paint the portrait of Ireland and the Irish at the turn of the nineteenth century. We see in his stories a strong respect for reality combined with a great regard for aesthetic effect; a dual allegiance also displayed in the actual paintings of his Victorian namesake, Albert Moore, which suggests that in them we witness the rise of an artistic movement that would result in work valuable both as a record and as a source of delight. It is significant that the use of photographs was a well-established studio practice followed by artists like Albert Moore and Alma-Tadema, according to Graham Reynolds in his *Victorian Painting* (1966), yet they could achieve exquisite decorative effects in the finished painting. Naturalism and a tendency towards art for art's sake are not necessarily opposites; they can exist in a creative balance together, inspiring works in which extreme care about formal perfection matches the desire to give 'the thing as it is', reality. The word 'reality' slips easily into the argument, though it is not always easy to explain its precise meaning.[5] For me it is best focussed here by a comment of Professor Hough's on two historical novels by Moore, *The Brook Kerith* and *Héloise and Abelard*:

> Moore has no historical axe to grind; he shows people behaving as they do behave; alike, in his view, in the first century as in the twelfth, or the nineteenth.

We are back, I think, at Hardy's essay on 'The Profitable Reading of Fiction', but now we can modify his use of words like 'distinguish' —the eternal from the temporary, the accidental from the essential, and so on. Hardy's philosophy no doubt dictated his particular phraseology. I would rather claim that such artists can reveal the eternal embedded in the temporary—that each discovers to us a continuing human truth in the actuality they so beautifully present.

NOTES

[1] Raymond Williams, in his introduction to *Hodge and His Masters*, 2 vols, 1966, notes that in later years Jefferies' position changed. He recommends several other works, including 'the remarkable "Primrose Gold in Our Village"—an account of modern Conservatism—and "Thoughts on the Labour Question"—with its near-marxist section on "The Divine Right of Capital" (in *Field and Farm*, collected 1957).'

[2] A number of minor pieces like this preface have been brought together very usefully indeed in one volume, edited by Harold Orel, *Thomas Hardy's Personal Writings: Prefaces, Literary Opinions, Reminiscences* (1967).

[3] See D. Van Ghent, *The English Novel: Form and Function* (New York, 1953).

[4] Compare what Conrad's wife wrote about him in her memoir: 'I have a firm conviction that for a long time before his death he felt the call of his native land—though he was as good an 'Englishman' as any born and bred, as loyal to her interests and as devoted to the English people' (*Joseph Conrad As I Knew Him*, 1926, page 16).

[5] A short work on the subject has recently been published in the Critical Idiom Series: *Realism*, by Damian Grant.

3 : The Rural Myth

Up till now we have mostly investigated rural life and its literature in the closing years of the nineteenth century. For a book which both covers this period and takes us through the years that follow we may refer to M. K. Ashby's biography of her father, *Joseph Ashby of Tysoe 1859-1919: A Study of English Village Life* (1961). Built up from memories and oral traditions like W. H. Hudson's *A Shepherd's Life* (1910), but also stiffened by consultation of personal writings, parish registers, overseers' accounts, council minutes, etc., Miss Ashby's book traces the career of an exceptional man. Joseph Ashby began life as the illegitimate child of a poor village girl and ended as an employer, county councillor and Justice of the Peace. He was a Methodist and a Liberal, and his life demonstrates in the limited setting of Warwickshire how men of character and intelligence felt that they were denied the scope they desired to control their own religious and political affairs. The trouble Jefferies had fearfully anticipated came to Tysoe as it did to other places, large and small, for in Britain as a whole the first decades of the twentieth century brought major changes in the structure of society. 'Controversy raged in the street', writes M. K. Ashby of the Nonconformist opposition to the Education Act of 1902, resisted in Tysoe on the grounds that it used the rates to maintain Church of England elementary schools. Her most vivid illustration of strife is the exasperated cry of the school-master, whenever the children kept out of the lessons in religion returned making some sort of disturbance: 'Tell your fathers it is for pennies, not for conscience that you are kept away!' He knew that they had often been doing useful jobs at home in the interval.

The General Election of 1906, with its overall majority for the Liberal party, also brought a group of Labour members:

> In his 'Villager' column of the *Warwick Advertiser* Joseph welcomed this group without qualms. He had not yet made the acquaintance of the young doctrinaires of Ruskin College or his comments might have been a little different. He assumed that the new group were men like village Radicals—a trade union version of local preachers, and as to most of them he was right.

The new Government managed to get through a number of Acts of Parliament—the Justices of the Peace Act (1906), the Agricultural Holdings Bill (1908), the Licensing Bill (1908), the Old Age Pensions Bill (1908) are singled out by M. K. Ashby—but by 1909 the tension between a Liberal House of Commons and a Conservative House of Lords reached crisis point over Lloyd George's budget. Two General Elections later and after the threat of a number of new peerages, the Parliament Bill to effectively limit the powers of the Lords became law in 1911.[1] All these events, though national in scope and importance, were reflected in rural Warwickshire and its neighbourhood. Joseph Ashby, as might have been expected of a man who had toured the countryside some years before on behalf of the Land Restoration League in a red van with slogans like JUSTICE TO LABOUR and ABOLITION OF LANDLORDISM emblazoned on its sides, was out electioneering for the Liberals; his fellow-magistrate, Lord Willoughby de Broke, was one of the foremost defenders of the House of Lords:

> A group of die-hard peers were all for the utmost resistance to a reduction of the powers of their House. Lord Willoughby became more and more fluent, more and more bold, the most prominent of all the Last Ditchers from the 'backwoods'. In the end, however, a majority of peers voted against their rash brethren. The struggle over, the great foxhunter was back on his estate, writing his charming essays on foxhunting and his autobiography. The dead hand of the past had been loosened from English villages. (Chapter 18.)

For a brief space, M. K. Ashby writes, peace and tolerance came to villages like Tysoe, only to be lost irrevocably in 1914. Army sergeants appeared to seize the horses; agricultural labourers were called up and women once more worked the land; refugee children arrived, and so did an unusual source of labour, conscientious objectors; submarine warfare made the labourers left at home so important that they 'positively gained social consideration, not to say prestige'. Not only labourers gained in status, for a social revolution of immense magnitude was increasing in momentum. In 1910 especially a flood of land sales had broken up the great country estates and, most important, the whole way of life associated with them. The result, we are told by F. M. L. Thompson in his *English Landed Society in the Nineteenth Century* (1963), was that tenant farmers tended to buy their own holdings and thus become owners themselves. A new race of yeomen was forming, while the sellers of great estates lost their former prestige and position. The old 'landed interest' (or 'landlord interest', as its enemies called it) practically ceased to exist. The year 1919 in particular broke all records in land sales: probably well over a million acres were sold in the course of the year. 'England is changing hands' was the popular phrase at the time and indeed, F. M. L. Thompson states that such a permanent transfer of land had not been known since the dissolution of the monasteries in the sixteenth century.

It is no wonder that Siegfried Sassoon, when he came to write his *Memoirs of A Foxhunting Man* (1928), should have had to make a deliberate effort to look back to those pre-war days in order to recapture what had been for him a leisured, idyllic way of life, ordered and hierarchical:

Ten minutes late, in the hot evening sunshine, my train bustled contentedly along between orchards and hop gardens, jolted past the signal-box, puffed importantly under the bridge, and slowed up at Baldock Wood. The station was exactly the same as usual and I was very pleased to see it again. I was back from Ballboro' for the summer holidays. As I was going forward to the guard's van to identify my truck and my wooden play-box, the station-master (who, in those days, wore a top-hat and a baggy black frock-coat) saluted me respectfully. Aunt Evelyn always sent him a turkey at Christmas.

(Part 2, 1.)

This passage is somewhat written up, a degree more than the last passage quoted (the *Memoirs*, unlike *Joseph Ashby*, is part-fictional), but it is still instructive to compare the family-retainer attitude of the Station-master with the action of Joseph Ashby when his children were told by a new Vicar that the girls should curtsy and the boys touch their caps to their betters: he stormed off at once to see the Vicar and tell him that he 'would not have his children taught ridiculous manners'. The new independence of such strong-minded individuals was finding its appropriate context in the nature of the general changes in society during the period of Radical agitation and reform. Rural life today is in consequence very different, except perhaps in some of the more isolated and out-of-the-way spots. Yet in reading Sassoon's evocation of a vanished rural past, or an anthology piece like W. S. Blunt's 'The Old Squire', I do not think we in our own age remain utterly unaffected by their characteristics; something certainly survives as a kind of potent myth to which we can still respond two generations and two wars later.

.   .   .   .   .   .

The myth was in fact largely created in reaction to the great changes outlined above. At its simplest it is a sentimental refusal to admit change in the countryside at all:

> Let hound and horn in wintry woods and dells
> Make jocund music though the boughs be bare,
> And whistling yokel guide his teaming share
> Hard by the homes where gentle lordship dwells.
> Therefore sit high enthroned on every hill,
> Authority! and loved in every vale;
> Nor, old Tradition, falter in the tale
> Of lowly valour led by lofty will;

And, though the throats of envy rage and rail,
Be fair proud England, proud fair England still.
>   (A. Austin, 'Why England is Conservative', III.)

C. K. Stead, who quotes these lines in his excellent book, *The New Poetic* (1964), thinks they are typical of poetry at the end of the first decade of this century. They are mere idealisation of a supposed unchanging England, and he regards their trite generality as dishonest 'in the face of the realities of poverty and injustice'. It is interesting to see how poetry of this kind, which so positively propounds political philosophy rather than implying it, seems to invite a literary critic to apply his historical knowledge, to relate the verse statements to 'the realities' of the time. Judgment—remembering the evidence in B. S. Rowntree and M. Kendall, *How the Labourer Lives* (1913)—rightly goes against Austin's poem.[2] It would be fairer to find a more sophisticated version of the myth of rural England; one more in touch with the realities of the time, more evolved from actual observation and more aware of the qualities of the 'lowly' objects of leadership. Hardy had insisted in his article on the Dorsetshire labourer that there was more to the impenetrable 'Hodge' than met the eye and his comparatively brief suggestion later received great amplification in a series of works by George Sturt, who used to write under the pen-name of George Bourne. As if these were not enough, much of Sturt's *Journal*, 1890–1927, has recently been published in two volumes with an introduction by E. D. Mackerness (1967). Altogether they provide a better source of information about the myth in the period with which we are concerned.

Sturt had inherited a wheelwright's shop in Farnham, Surrey. This position gave him a vantage point which undoubtedly prevented complete involvement with his work-people but which did allow him to be close enough to know them more intimately than many a squire or—always irritating to Sturt—retired and prosperous newcomers. He called them, rudely, Resident Trippers. He saw the countryside under siege by people who were able to buy up without a second thought cottages in which men and their families had lived for many years, dispossessing them at a week's notice:

A Mr. Croker Stuart (who bought his house across the valley about 18 months ago, and has enlarged it, etc. etc.) secured three of the Smith Wright cottages neighbouring his own place. It was told me, at the time, that his object was to dispossess the present tenants in favour of a more respectable variety: and I could believe it—for he has the blackguard look and walk and cigar-smoke of a retired publican or book-maker trying to do the 'gentleman at his little place in the country'—one of the most selfish and worthless-looking specimens of mankind, in fact, that I have seen. . . .

A week's notice! 'Tis almost like the calamities of war. This man Edwards has been in this cottage for years—longer than I have lived here: he has brought up a big family there. Even now two or three of his children attend the Council School. But, in one little week, he has to root himself up—he, and his wife and children, and never mind about their comfort, or their education, or anything. Nothing matters; he must go.

(4 July 1909.)

Here is the factual detail that is valuable to the social historian, but more important is the application of the myth. From our longer perspective we may share, naturally, Sturt's sympathy with the dispossessed, but we may also notice the likeness of Mr Croker Stuart as described by him to some stock figure of a villain in Victorian melodrama. The cigar-smoke is a nice touch! We may also have a shrewd suspicion that today many descendants of Resident Trippers are standing shoulder to shoulder with indigenous countryfolk to fight Sturt's rearguard action, striving to repel the assault from the cities.

Even so, our reservations should not be pushed too far, since Sturt has much more to say than we have allowed him. Turning on to the *Journal* entry for 19 July, we meet a confirmation of Richard Jefferies' plaint about the aged poor which then expands into a much more explicit and at the same time widely ranging historical idea:

Old Wooderson was here this morning, bringing a few eggs; but he was in a pitiful plight, with asthma. 'I didn't 'ardly know how to git up the lane', he said, with a wan smile. It seems that he is under the Doctor's hands—his club-doctor—but he had been trying to see another (viz. Tanner) having heard people speak well of him. 'But I can't *pay* a doctor', he said; 'so I got a Parish order for to see him. He didn't seem to take much notice. He said I'd best go into the Infirmary, and he'd let me have an order. But I don't *care* 'bout *that*. I thought I'd sooner die at home' ...

As he stood painfully panting, I fetched a chair from the kitchen, and for a minute or two he sat down to rest, visibly relieved, there by the back door. And so we fell into a talk, that was like a little bit of old peasant England getting itself vocal for a minute, so full it was of a fine rustic sentiment, so suggestive of a more established, sane, dignified and happy life than is known now in the village, where all the old traditions are practically dead. This old man had even, I felt for a moment or two, almost an orderly outlook—not a cultivated philosophy of course, yet a scheme of ideas by which details might be judged.

Sturt goes on to give the substance of their talk, the craft of thatching, with all its simple yet subtle practices discovered by generations of thatchers and passed on to their successors. Similarly, Sturt's most fascinating book, *The Wheelwright's Shop* (1923), describes the work of his own craftsmen, who, for example, were willing to satisfy an individual carter they knew by adding another half-inch of curve to his wagon-bottom. From his great mass of detailed observations of this nature Sturt had come to his belief in what has been called 'the organic community', in which life could be lived by folk-values which were the complete opposite of aggressive, selfishly individualistic attitudes. These, fundamentally, are the two poles of his total pattern of thought about rural life.

His *Change in the Village* (1912; with introduction by Geoffrey Grigson, 1955) is a notable account of the myth he was so urgently yet carefully communicating. The chapter entitled 'The Peasant System' in particular provides a coherent statement of his beliefs about the 'home-made civilization of the rural English', which he thought was in the process of being destroyed. In the past, people were not only able to get their living, they were able to live well in all senses. Self-subsistent by and large, they were expert at looking after themselves with all the necessary skills and crafts; unhurried, taking pleasure in jobs like wine-making, pig-tending or bee-keeping, they could spare the time to decorate and make beautiful their iron-work or field-gates; they knew in their bones the qualities and potentialities of their physical environment, to such a degree that the peasant

> did not merely 'reside' in it; he was part of it, and it was part of him. He fitted into it as one of its native denizens, like the hedgehogs and the thrushes. All that happened to it mattered to him. He learnt to look with reverence upon its main features, and would not willingly interfere with their disposition. But I lose the best point in talking of the individual peasant: these things should rather be said of the tribe—the little group of folk—of which he was a member.

Best of all, according to Sturt, the countryman insensibly gained 'a sort of *savoir vivre*', an unwritten code by which he could live. He was strong, frugal and handy. Where such a society 'really flourished it ultimately led to gracefulness of living and love of what is comely and kindly'. At the end of *Change in the Village* he gives his reasons for expecting a renaissance after the 'disillusionments of this present time of transition'.

Sturt has been criticised for not taking account of the reverse side of the penny, the bad conditions in the past. In other words, his organic society as a matter of historical fact is an illusion, his beliefs about it rosier than the reality. Against this attack he can be defended: one has only to read a few pages into *Change in the Village* to discover Sturt openly admitting that rural life had not always been perfect:

> Then, besides the distresses brought upon the people by their own folly, there were others thrust upon them by their economic condition. Of poverty, with its attendant sicknesses and neglects, there has never been any end to the tales, while the

desolations due to accidents in the day's work, on the railway, or with horses, or upon scaffoldings of buildings, or in collapsing gravel-quarries, have become almost a commonplace. In short, there is no room for sentimentality about the village life. Could its annals be written they would make no idyll; they would be too much stained by tragedy and vice and misery.

He could hardly have been more explicit. In general, however, he saw change as sheer loss in human terms. Like John Clare, or J. L. and B. Hammond in *The Village Labourer* (1912), he thought that the enclosure of common land had seriously affected poor country people. For the old peasant thrift, he would say, had been substituted a modern commercial thrift; competitive wage-earning took the place of mutual and kindly help; the successful discarded their provincial habits and speech, bringing humiliation upon those who had once been their fellows, the insistence that they should know their place and so on. Summary does scant justice to the way in which Bourne supports his case by examples drawn from his experience, though it is necessary to mention the work of recent historians who are more sceptical about the unfortunate results of enclosure than Sturt or the Hammonds. (See Chambers and Mingay, *The Agricultural Revolution*, chapter 4.)

Warnings of this kind, however, hardly affect what is truly central and vital in Sturt's myth. It is vulnerable in detail, inevitably. It is not wholly original: Goldsmith's *The Deserted Village* of 1770 comes immediately to mind as a precursor. But it has been an acknowledged influence, as we may see from the length and number of quotations from Sturt's works in *Culture and Environment* (1933), a book itself designed for educational use by F. R. Leavis and Denys Thompson.[3] Another instance might be a letter of 1939 from Siegried Sassoon to Sydney Cockerell, in which he writes that a *signature* of Hardy's is like 'order in chaos, isn't it? (& craftsmanship in a world of machines!)' (*The Best of Friends: Further Letters to Sydney Carlyle Cockerell*, ed. V. Meynell, 1956.) Sturt's writings are also the developed version of a myth all-pervasive in the thought-patterns of the age with which we are

concerned, when Sassoon grew up, and which appears with a variety
of shadings or stressings in the most diverse writers:

> Nations may have brilliant epochs—more or less long-
> continued—of commercial prosperity, with vast accumulations
> of money wealth, but their strength, virility, permanence, and
> resisting power must ever depend on a numerous rural
> population. The combatant in classic story who, when hurled
> to the ground by his antagonist, gained renewed life and vigour
> by each contact with Mother Earth, is an apt illustration of the
> strength and recuperative power of a nation whose people are
> rooted in the soil.

This somewhat florid passage is taken from the introduction to
Jesse Collings, *Land Reform Occupying Ownership Peasant Proprietary and Rural Education* (2nd edition, 1908), a work by a
Member of Parliament, the President of the Rural Labourers'
League, full of detailed history, statistics, references to authorities,
the text of a parliamentary bill and other weighty matters. But the
quotation above, precisely because of the way in which it stands
out from its more prosaic context, does more than hint at the
motivating force of the myth inspiring Collings and his political
aim of restoring occupying owners to the beleaguered countryside.
Another sign, a visual one, is the plate that follows his rather
wordy and serious title-page. (This plate is reproduced amongst
the illustrations, fig. 4).

An occasional emotional paragraph, however, or an odd photograph or two in a political tract is not to be compared with D. H.
Lawrence's *inferno* vision in chapter 12 of *The Rainbow* (1915):

> Wiggiston was only seven years old. It had been a hamlet of
> eleven houses on the edge of healthy, half-agricultural
> country. Then the great seam of coal had been opened. In a
> year Wiggiston appeared, a great mass of pinkish rows of thin,
> unreal dwellings of five rooms each. The streets were like
> visions of pure ugliness; a grey-black macadamized road,
> asphalt causeways, held in between a flat succession of wall,
> window, and door, a new-brick channel that began nowhere,

and ended nowhere. Everything was amorphous, yet everything repeated itself endlessly. . . .

The place had the strange desolation of a ruin. Colliers hanging about in gangs and groups, or passing along the asphalt pavements heavily to work, seemed not like living people, but like spectres. The rigidity of the blank streets, the homogeneous amorphous sterility of the whole suggested death rather than life. There was no meeting place, no centre, no artery, no organic formation. There it lay, like the new foundations of a red-brick confusion rapidly spreading, like a skin-disease.

This quotation is taken from the body of the novel; by the time we come to the very last pages Lawrence's style has risen to a high intensity of imagery and rhythmic utterance:

She saw the stiffened bodies of the colliers, which seemed already enclosed in a coffin, she saw their unchanging eyes, the eyes of those who are buried alive: she saw the hard cutting edges of the new houses, which seemed to spread over the hillside in their insentient triumph, the triumph of horrible, amorphous angles and straight lines, the expression of corruption triumphant and unopposed, corruption so pure that it is hard and brittle: she saw the dun atmosphere over the blackened hills opposite, the dark blotches of houses, slate roofed and amorphous, the old church-tower standing up in hideous obsoleteness above raw new houses on the crest of the hill, the amorphous, brittle, hard-edged new houses advancing from Beldover to meet the corrupt new houses from Lethley, the houses of Lethley advancing to mix with the houses of Hainor, a dry, brittle, terrible corruption spreading over the face of the land, and she was sick with a nausea so deep that she perished as she sat. And then, in the blowing clouds, she saw a band of faint iridescence colouring in faint colours a portion of the hill. And forgetting, startled, she looked for the hovering colour and saw a rainbow forming itself. In one place it gleamed fiercely, and, her heart anguished with hope, she sought the shadow of iris where the bow should be. Steadily the colour gathered, mysteriously, from nowhere, it took presence upon itself, there was a faint, vast rainbow. The arc bended and strengthened itself till it arched indominable, making great architecture of light and colour and the space of heaven, its pedestals luminous in the corruption of new houses on the low hill, its arch the top of heaven.

And the rainbow stood on the earth. She knew that the sordid people who crept hard-scaled and separate on the face of the world's corruption were living still, that the rainbow was arched in their blood and would quiver to life in their spirit, that they would cast off their horny covering of disintegration, that new, clean, naked bodies would issue to a new germina-tion, to a new growth, rising to the light and the wind and the clean rain of heaven. She saw in the rainbow the earth's new architecture, the old, brittle corruption of houses and factories swept away, the world built up in a living fabric of Truth, fitting to the over-arching heaven.

This is the end of the novel: a passage of obsessive and oppressive power, in a style utterly transcending the more workaday prose of authors like Sturt. E. M. Forster wrote that Lawrence was 'the only living novelist in whom the song predominates, who has the rapt bardic quality' (*Aspects of the Novel*, 1927). His language finds its literary affinities in poetry like the final apostrophes of John Masefield's *The Everlasting Mercy* (1911), or in the impas-sioned dramatic prose of the last scene of his *Tragedy of Nan*, first performed in 1908. Actors would have to chant such speeches. Masefield's preface to this play, dated 4 April 1911, is worth a glance:

Tragedy at its best is a vision of the heart of life. The heart of life can only be laid bare in the agony and exultation of dread-ful acts. The vision of agony, or spiritual contest, pushed beyond the limits of the dying personality, is exalting and cleansing. It is only by such vision that a multitude can be brought to the passionate knowledge of things exulting and eternal. . . .

It is possible to find in Lawrence's novels passages on, say, Morel as a good workman (*Sons and Lovers*, 1913, chapter 4) that are as straightforwardly true-to-life as Sturt's descriptions of his workmen in *The Wheelwright's Shop*, but Lawrence in our period was beginning to break with ordinary traditions of writing—in great as well as in small ways. His famous letter of 5 June 1914 to the puzzled Edward Garnett warns him not to look for 'the old stable ego of the character', nor to expect

> the development of the novel to follow the lines of certain characters: the characters fall into the form of some other rhythmic form, as when one draws a fiddle-bow across a fine tray delicately sanded, the sand takes lines unknown.

In fact, he was turning away from the simple pattern of a story told largely for its own sake and instead producing the myth he felt made most sense of the history of his own time in England just before and during the Great War. This myth, with its triple movement of degeneration, crisis and rebirth, tends to control the course of his novels in an extraordinary way. There is, for instance, no obvious narrative reason why Ursula should encounter the terror of the horses in the last chapter of *The Rainbow*: it leads to no new twist or turn of the actual story—insofar as there *is* one. In one sense her collapse under their dark and savage power is random and cannot be accounted for in ordinary terms. Yet it was clearly a deliberate artistic stroke by Lawrence to bring his character to this extremity, to her nadir (like Tess):

> As she sat there, spent, time and the flux of change passed away from her, she lay as if unconscious upon the bed of the stream, like a stone, unconscious, unchanging, unchangeable, whilst everything rolled by in transience, leaving her there, a stone at rest on the bed of the stream, inalterable and passive, sunk to the bottom of all change.

In this deep, and in the depth of the delirium that followed, Ursula won through to a spiritual rebirth, crossing 'the void, the darkness which washed the New World and the Old'. Unlike Hardy, who kept the individual, Tess, so firmly in the forefront of his novel,

Lawrence makes Ursula at the visionary end of the book point directly to a new life for others, even if only for a select number of them. The novel as a whole begins in a simple farming community and ends in the urbanised, industrial world—in Lawrence's myth a process of degeneration which had come to the moment of crisis before renewal. In another letter of 7 February 1916 Lawrence tells Lady Cynthia Asquith that he did not know what the message of *The Rainbow* was, 'except that the older world is done for, toppling on top of us. . . . There must be a new world.'[4]

The general conclusions to be drawn are, I think, fascinating. The facts of rural history in our period are those of a decline in importance and a submission to new commercial or industrial interests. Labourers were becoming 'hands' while landowners were becoming capitalists. These changes have been registered by historians, of course, but also by creative writers like Hardy. Many writers, as soon as they attempted to assess the human implications of rural history, concluded that a whole way of life was failing and with it much that had given people a valuable, sustaining 'sense of long local participancy' in their native place and with each other. In a writer like George Sturt this loss in human terms is amplified and emphasised, and also he brings into frequent, damaging comparison with rural virtues the new values, those of the 'mass society'. (Hence, sometimes, that asperity which sits so oddly on lovers of 'what is comely and kindly' and the general temptation to slip into the pessimistic belief that all change is change for the worse.) At this point we think of Lawrence's *The Rainbow* and *Women in Love*, which involves an even deeper pessimism and loss of faith. In many ways his future writing can be seen as a search for the deep source of lost vitality. He also allowed the pattern he apprehended in recent English history, his individual version of the myth common to his contemporaries, to dictate the looser, less logical, more intuitive shape of his novels. He rejected—quite explicitly in his letters—the usual conventions in character-portrayal and the ordinary narrative sequences of previous novels.

What this meant in practice can be seen most sharply by a comparison with an older novelist like Elizabeth Gaskell. Her novel *North and South* (1854–55) also uses the industrial and the rural as conflicting elements in a myth about the England of her day; at her stage of the Industrial Revolution she could see with great clarity how the dynamic but heartless existence in the 'shock cities' of the North was taking the place of the slower way of life still found in a more patriarchal and agricultural South. As we might expect, her characters are solidly drawn, her story-line strong and brought to a neat, an over-neat, conclusion. Most revealing of all, however, is the cool rationality in the mid-Victorian novelist that proposed an accommodation between industrial North and rural South, the retention of the best values of both societies. This is a moderation of a kind alien to Lawrence and to many others by the turn of the century, as we will see in the next chapter. That Ursula Brangwen should, like Margaret Hale (Mrs Gaskell's heroine), be plunged by her creator into an illness as much spiritual as physical, one in which she achieves a true sense of herself, is a similarity of little account beside the radically different outcome in each case: Margaret Hale comes to an acceptance of aspects of life she had originally repudiated, but Ursula Brangwen rejects the present wholly in favour of the new life to come. Mrs Gaskell, though strongly dissatisfied with the conditions she saw about her in Manchester, was certainly not so pessimistic as to believe that 'the older world is done for, toppling on top of us'. Modern as she may have been in her treatment of an individual woman discovering her full potentialities for action in the world, that action itself was hardly revolutionary. The existing world could be saved, she thought, given intelligence and good will on the part of all the individuals concerned. Nor did Mrs Gaskell feel that she had to be revolutionary in the way she wrote. She was able to accept the form of the novel as she found it, though ensuring that the story she invented and the characters she created had thematic relevance; Lawrence, on the other hand, rejected society as it had developed up to his day and with it the existing form of the novel. Noticing the many open references to actual historical events in *North and South* and the relative dearth of them in *The Rainbow* we might well think of claiming that Elizabeth Gaskell was the more 'historical' writer, yet in Lawrence a way of seeing the course of history became the essential form of his novel, the pattern he dis-

covered was the mould of his fiction. This is a much deeper connexion between history and literature than any obvious injection of
historical circumstances could ever be.[5]

. . . . . .

The Rainbow, of course, contains rural elements used in a much
more conventional and unsurprising manner. While Lawrence
tended to eliminate precise references to people and events from
his novels, his work is still the embodiment of his own experience,
often in the most essential sense. Chapter 13 of *The Rainbow* can
be read with a recently printed letter of 28 February 1909. Both
deal with the experience of school-teaching, but where the documentary record, the letter, touches lightly on the subject: 'School is
really very pleasant here [Croydon]. I have tamed my wild beasts—
I have conquered my turbulent subjects, and can teach in ease and
comfort. But I still long for the country and for my own folks . . .',
the fictional account makes life infinitely more soul-destroying,
for the teacher, Ursula, and for the taught:

> So that, pale, shut, at last distant and impersonal, she saw
> no longer the child, how his eyes danced, or how he had a
> queer little soul that could not be bothered with shaping hand-
> writing so long as he dashed down what he thought. She saw no
> children, only the task that was to be done.

This is a very brief quotation, but it is very apparent how in the
novel (written some years later) Lawrence was claiming that
teaching of this kind was a defeat of the true self and also something unnatural and mechanical. For this the proper countertheme is the countryside:

> She came to school in the morning seeing the hawthorn
> flowers wet, the little, rosy grains swimming in a bowl of dew.
> The larks quivered their song up into the new sunshine, and the
> country was so glad. It was a violation to plunge into the dust
> and greyness of the town.
> So that she stood before her class unwilling to give herself
> up to the activity of teaching, to turn her energy, that longed
> for the country and for joy of early summer, into the dominat-

ing of fifty children and the transferring to them some morsels of arithmetic.

And in the same letter that was so casual about the business of teaching there is a much closer parallel in feeling when the country-side is the theme:

> The snowdrops one buys in bunches, with their poor little noses packed tight together, turned upwards to the winter sky, like white beans stuck in a green cup—these are not snowdrops gathered in the mill garden on the banks of the Wreake—these are not snowdrops from under the hazel brake in the steep dell in the woods of Strelley. Louisa, oh Louisa, my heart aches for the country, and those splendid hours we have had. The town too is good; it has books, and people; it is not so desolating; one cannot there be lonely enough to feel the wistful misery of the country; above all, the town is valuable for the discipline it gives one's nature; but, in the end, for congenial sympathy, for poetry, for work, for original feeling and expression, for perfect companionship with one's friends—give me the country.

The words about the town noticeably strive for a kind of intellectual balance that is quite absent from the fiction (where it would only serve to muffle the main effects and blur the force of the presentation). As far as the country is concerned, however, the rhythms in this part of the letter are even more yearning in their swoops than those in Jefferies' description of the old labourer in the workhouse (pages 40–1, above). The hard brutality of the image for *town* snowdrops, 'like white beans stuck in a green cup', can be brought out by comparison with some finely delicate lines from a poem by Walter De La Mare, 'The Snowdrop':

> Beneath these ice-pure sepals lay
> A triplet of green-pencilled snow,
> Which in the chill-aired gloom of day
> Stirred softly to and fro.

In his writing on this theme Lawrence is striking through to a fundamental human response, for there are very many who would give whole-hearted assent to a sentence later in the letter, which is more than can be said for a number of Lawrence's propositions:

> Richmond Park is glorious; it is history, it is romance, it is allegory, it is myth.

It could have come straight out of Mrs Gaskell's letters. Once more we are in touch with the country as an emotional force; ultimately, perhaps, an irrational force, productive of myths, but undeniable as a fact of life, then and now.

Snowdrops are the subject of a conversation in Lawrence's first novel, *The White Peacock* (1911), where they are a mysterious link with the distant past:

> 'They remind me of mistletoe, which is never ours, though we wear it,' said Emily to me.
>
> 'What do you think they say—what do you make you think, Cyril?' Lettie repeated.
>
> 'I don't know. Emily says they belong to some old wild lost religion. They were the symbol of tears, perhaps, to some strange-hearted Druid folk before us.'
>
> 'More than tears,' said Lettie. 'More than tears, they are so still. Something out of an old religion, that we have lost. They make me feel afraid.'
>
> 'What should you have to fear?' asked Leslie.
>
> 'If I knew I shouldn't fear,' she answered. 'Look at all the snowdrops'—they hung in dim, strange flecks among the dusky leaves—'look at them—closed up, retreating, powerless. They belong to some knowledge we have lost, that I have lost and that I need. I feel afraid they seem like something in fate. Do you think, Cyril, we can lose things off the earth—like mastodons, and those old monstrosities—but things that matter—wisdom?'
>
> (Part 2, Chapter 1.)

The expression is rather facile and Late-Romantic, but the passage points to something very common at that time. Europe seems to have been full of seekers after esoteric wisdom, knowledge from the past almost lost but preserved by little circles of initiates, the

Order of the Golden Dawn and the like. To some extent these groups were the product of the decline of formal religious observance during the nineteenth century and the uncongenial rationalisation of society demanded by new inventions, both technological and commercial. A later version in Lawrence, which again takes the rural as its mode and which brings out his pattern of thinking about the whole nature of life in his time, its values and the only proper responses to them, is to be found in the short story called 'England, my England' (in *Complete Short Stories*, vol. 2, Phoenix edition, 1955). This is a story about a young man and his bride, whose rich father enables them to live deep in the heart of rural England, in a 'timbered cottage' which

> with its sloping, cloak-like roof was old and forgotten. It belonged to the old England of hamlets and yeomen. Lost alone on the edge of the common, at the end of a wide, grassy, briar-entangled lane shaded with oak, it had never known the world of today.

We are back in a mythological world again, with, as we have come to expect, roots stretching far back into the past; in this case to a very remote and even pre-human past:

> One day Winifred heard the strangest scream from the flower-bed under the low window of the living-room: ah, the strangest scream, like the very dark soul of the dark past crying aloud. She ran out, and saw a long brown snake on the flower-bed, and in its flat mouth the one hind leg of a frog was striving to escape, and screaming its strange, tiny, bellowing scream. She looked at the snake, and from its sullen flat head it looked at her, obstinately. She gave a cry, and it released the frog and slid angrily away.
>
> That was Crockham. The spear of modern invention had not passed through it, and it lay there secret, primitive, savage as when the Saxons first came. And Egbert and she were caught there, caught out of the world.

'The spear of modern invention' is almost as striking a phrase as Hardy's 'ache of modernism', and expresses the spiritual death associated with progressive Western society. But this existence is

F

always, Lawrence makes clear, dependent upon the father working at business in the world of London, sustaining the 'living romance' of his children. And eventually, full historical actuality, in the shape of the Great War, breaks in upon them. Egbert's deepest instincts were against the war: he 'had no conception of Imperial England'—a creation of much more recent history than Saxon; he 'recoiled inevitably from having his feelings dictated to him by the mass feeling' and was fundamentally unwilling to submit himself to military discipline, 'the power of the mob-spirit of a democratic army'. He does at length submit, but is then a prisoner 'in his gritty, thick, sandpaper khaki and puttees and the hideous cap'. Like Ursula, he has been reduced to a mechanism, and again we see the rural countertheme in use, for only when Egbert returned to Crockham did he regain his humanity:

> This summer still it would flame with blue anchusas and big red poppies, the mulleins would sway their soft, downy erections in the air: he loved mulleins: and the honeysuckle would stream out scent like memory, when the owl was whooing. Then he sat by the fire with the friends and with Winifred's sisters, and they sang the folk-songs. He put on thin civilian clothes and his charm and his beauty and the supple dominancy of his body glowed out again.

There is in this story a good deal of direct statement of values, but what proof or demonstration there is resides in the creative substance of passages like the one just quoted. Phrases of the order of 'the supple dominancy of his body glowed out again' are their own justification, especially considering that instinctive knowledge of self is the theme. Unlike Hardy, Lawrence did not subscribe to a neo-Platonic and abstract reality behind appearances; as he wrote in *Studies in Classic American Literature* (1924),

> Art speech is the only truth. An artist is usually a damned liar, but his art, if it be art, will tell you the truth of his day. And that is all that matters. Away with eternal truth. Truth lives from day to day, and the marvellous Plato of yesterday is chiefly bosh today.

· · · · · ·

It can hardly be thought that Lawrence was alone in thus seeing the ruination of England, though no one has ever been so tragically intense as he was in some of his letters or in chapter 12 of *Kangaroo* (1923). The England he saw dying was a rural vision, lit by 'the dawn of all dawns':

> The wet lawn drizzled with brown, sodden leaves; the feathery heap of the ilex tree; the garden-seat all wet and reminiscent.
>
> Between the ilex tree and the bare, purplish elms, a gleaming segment of all England, the dark plough-land and wan grass, and the blue, hazy heap of the distance, under the accomplished morning.
>
> (To Lady Ottoline Morrell, 1 December 1915.)

A more conventional summary of contemporary opinion is contained in the chapter called 'The Countryside' in C. F. G. Masterman's *The Condition of England* (1909). In it we find him quoting from books with titles like *The Ruin of Rural England* and *Where Men Decay* (which glances back at Goldsmith's *Deserted Village*, where 'Wealth accumulates and Men decay'). George Bourne's *Memoirs of a Surrey Labourer* is summarised at length and even the Liberal successes of recent years are felt to be illusory:

> Already the manifestations of resistance and of aspiration, associated with the democratic victories of the last election, are sinking back into the older acquiescence: as the rulers of the countryside exhibit, by a combination of kindliness and austerity, how undesirable is such an overthrow of the accepted ways. Villas and country houses establish themselves in the heart of this departing race: in it, but not of it, as alien from its ancient ways as if dropped from the clouds into another world. Wandering machines, travelling with an incredible rate of speed, scramble and smash and shriek all along the rural ways. You can see them on a Sunday afternoon, piled twenty or thirty deep outside the new popular inns, while their occupants regale themselves within.

After-events have made his impassioned rhetoric seem understated in places—twenty or thirty cars piled deep would be a sign of commercial failure today for the sort of inn that caters to whole fleets of coaches. On the other hand, the more moderate *Joseph Ashby of Tysoe* suggests that temperamental outbursts of this kind are not really comparable to cries of personal despair or their fictional counterparts.

In a later chapter, 'Literature and Progress', Masterman looks for the manifestations of a 'spirit of joy as well as of reason', for an inspiration which is truly humanist and which triumphantly affirms 'the greatness of Present Things'. Surprisingly, his main example is Richard Jefferies' nature mysticism, carefully distinguished from that of Wordsworth, whose pantheistic Nature and piously tranquil Poor, Masterman claimed, could never satisfy the spirit of the early twentieth century. He characterises Jefferies as a Life Worshipper, a despiser of asceticism, a man who accepted the evidence of his senses with delicacy and avidity, who condemned the mere getting of wealth and power, and who was bored with the claims of science. 'His strength was in himself. It was from that hidden, mysterious source of vitality that the colours appeared which he sought in field and flower, that rain of fairy gold which flung itself over the common things till every bush was burning with fire'. Nevertheless, in his next chapter Masterman makes the important reservation that contemporary writings are highly unlikely to influence more than a few, certainly not the 'contented, boisterous spirit of Middle Class England', let alone the 'huge and inarticulate multitudes of the city people'. A work like Jefferies' *The Story of My Heart* (1883) would suit an even more limited readership—the 'Autobiography of a Soul, or of Thought'; full of words like 'soul-emotion', 'soul-life', 'soul-work', 'soul-entity'; and always attempting to reach outside and beyond the limitations of humanity, insisting upon man directing his own future to the achievement of immortality. Much of his mystical exaltation starts in nature:

I looked at the hills, at the dewy grass, and then up through the elm branches to the sky. In a moment all that was behind me, the house, the people, the sounds, seemed to disappear, and to leave me alone. Involuntarily I drew a long breath, then

I breathed slowly. My thought, or inner consciousness, went up through the illumined sky, and I was lost in a moment of exaltation. This only lasted a very short time, perhaps only part of a second, and while it lasted there was no formulated wish. I was absorbed; I drank the beauty of the morning; I was exalted. When it ceased I did wish for some increase or enlargement of my existence to correspond with the largeness of feeling I had momentarily enjoyed. Sometimes the wind came through the tops of the elms, and the slender boughs bent, and gazing up through them, and beyond the fleecy clouds, I felt lifted up. The light coming across the grass and leaving itself on the dewdrops, the sound of the wind, and the sense of mounting to the lofty heaven, filled me with a deep sigh, a wish to draw something out of the beauty of it, some part of that which caused my admiration, the subtle inner essence. . . . I desired the beauty—the inner subtle meaning—to be in me, that I might have it, and with it an existence of a higher kind.

(Chapter 5.)

But Jefferies does not stay with nature and, amongst objections to the logic of science and to the kind of arguments that proceed from premises to conclusions, soon loses himself in statements of near blank opacity: 'The only idea I can give is the idea that there is another idea', for instance.

Perhaps the expansiveness of prose is too tempting. It does seem, if we look at lines with similar content from Edward Thomas's poem, 'The Glory', that the discipline of poetic form brings advantage:

> The glory of the beauty of the morning,—
> The cuckoo crying over the untouched dew;
> The blackbird that has found it, and the dove
> That tempts me on to something sweeter than love;
> White clouds ranged even and fair as new-mown hay;
> The heat, the stir, the sublime vacancy
> Of sky and meadow and forest and my own heart:—
> The glory invites me, yet it leaves me scorning

> All I can ever do, all I can be,
> Beside the lovely of motion, shape and hue,
> The happiness I fancy fit to dwell
> In beauty's presence.

The claim can be debated, however. This poem, it is only fair to say, is psychological rather than mystical and becomes even more so as it goes on, turning into a series of self-questionings. It is therefore bound to seem more compactly real than Jefferies' higher flights. Nevertheless, if ever Thomas sees a garden of Eden in a rural scene, he quickly returns from myth to common life: 'This beauty made me dream there was a time/Long past and irrecoverable' gives up its lark song for the song of sedge-warblers, 'that lacks all words, all melody,/All sweetness almost', but which is the true voice of the present moment. He is, too, the poet who praises the dusty nettles in the corner of a farmyard, an old nursery melody on a penny whistle or swedes revealed when the roof of clay is lifted from their pile. There has never really been a terrible crush of poets singing of swedes.

Not that Thomas writes of lesser and underestimated things as part of a programme—these poems spring from an honesty of intent that proves itself in the grave patience of lines like the following from 'Haymaking':

> In the field sloping down,
> Park-like, to where the willows showed the brook,
> Haymakers rested. The tosser lay forsook
> Out in the sun; and the long waggon stood
> Without its team: it seemed it never would
> Move from the shadow of that single yew.
> The team, as still, until their task was due,
> Beside the labourers enjoyed the shade
> That three squat oaks mid-field together made
> Upon a circle of grass and weed uncut,
> And on the hollow, once a chalk-pit, but
> Now brimmed with nut and elder-flower so clean.
> The men leaned on their rakes, about to begin,
> But still. And all were silent. All was old,

This morning time, with a great age untold,
Older than Clare and Cobbett, Morland and Crome,
Than, at the field's far edge, the farmer's home
A white house crouched at the foot of a great tree.

This is rural England seen, quietly and without fuss, in the perspective of history, the record of Cobbett's *Rural Rides* and Clare's poetry, of Crome and Morland's paintings of the country scene. The tradition is even more strongly evoked in the long poem called 'Lob', which begins as a search for an old man seen at hawthorn-time in Wiltshire but soon turns into the discovery that 'Everybody has met one such man as he':

The man you saw,—Lob-lie-by-the-fire, Jack Cade,
Jack Smith, Jack Moon, poor Jack of every trade,
Young Jack, or old Jack, or Jack What-d'ye-call,
Jack-in-the-hedge, or Robin-run-by-the-wall,
Robin Hood, Ragged Robin, lazy Bob,
One of the lords of No Man's Land, good Lob,—
Although he was seen dying at Waterloo,
Hastings, Agincourt, and Sedgemoor too,—
Lives yet. He never will admit he is dead
Till millers cease to grind men's bones for bread,
Nor till our weathercock crows once again
And I remove my house out of the lane
On to the road.

It *is* a vision of a kind, but a very limited one; strictly controlled by the interlaced and progressing shapes of the language, irregular, but cunningly wrought in a style that itself takes us right back to Shakespeare or his contemporary, Dr John Bull the musician. The artistic impulse that shaped Petruchio's energetic excursus on the name Kate (*Taming of the Shrew*, II. i. 184) or Bull's marvellous setting of a Flemish carol ('Een kindekin is ons geboren', I) does not seem to me to be essentially different. Yet Thomas's historical vision of England is also anchored in its own time by sensitive reproduction of turns of speech (and thought) he himself must have heard:

> All he said was: 'Nobody can't stop 'ee. It's
> A footpath, right enough. You see those bits
> Of mounds—that's where they opened up the barrows
> Sixty years since, while I was scaring sparrows.
> They thought as there was something to find there,
> But couldn't find it, by digging, anywhere.'

This rings very true to me. 'Lob' draws upon folk stories and country traditions; it rests upon rustic names and places; it can still assimilate the most up-to-date of inventions:

> There was both Alton Barnes and Alton Priors.
> All had their churches, graveyards, farms and byres,
> Lurking to one side up the paths and lanes,
> Seldom well seen except by aeroplanes;
> And when bells rang, or pigs squealed, or cocks crowed,
> Then only heard. Ages ago the road
> Approached. The people stood and looked and turned.
> Nor asked it to come nearer ...

Thomas seems to treat the aeroplane in the same way as people treated the road: it flew into his rustic verse—so be it!

·   ·   ·   ·   ·   ·

Edward Thomas did not compose a great deal of poetry. He did not begin writing it until he was in his thirties and was killed a few years later in the Great War. But the success of his pastoral poetry is, I think, unequalled, and in its unemphatic strength finds the perfect course between the Scylla of vague mysticism and the Charybdis of solid information. He was not alone in writing poetry of this nature: the tradition from Hardy would include good poetry from D. H. Lawrence, Edmund Blunden, W. H. Davies and Robert Graves. This tradition, however, suffered a disastrous decline as R. H. Ross points out in his *The Georgian Revolt: Rise and Fall of a Poetic Ideal 1910–22* (1967). Ross quotes a poem by Harold Monro, published in the third volume of *Georgian Poetry* (1917), which plainly shows why some poets of rural England eventually attracted the derisive name of 'weekend poets'. Monro's poem is, in fact, called 'Weekend':

The train! The twelve o'clock for paradise.
   Hurry, or it will try to creep away.
Out in the country every one is wise:
   We can only be wise on Saturday.
There you are waiting, little friendly house:
   Those are your chimney-stacks with you between,
Surrounded by old trees and strolling cows,
   Staring through all your windows at the green.
Your homely floor is creaking for our tread;
   The smiling tea-pot with contented spout
Thinks of the boiling water, and the bread
    Longs for the butter. All their hands are out
     To greet us, and the gentle blankets seem
     Purring and crooning: 'Lie in us, and dream.'

I suppose that the comic association of 'strolling' with 'cows' is some sort of reward for reading this coyly sentimental piece. Thomas knew that mere idyll or naive myth is helpless in the face of the common experience of humanity; our eye, he wrote in 'The Path' sees

   . . . but the road, the wood that overhangs
   And underyawns it, and the path that looks
   As if it led on to some legendary
   Or fancied place where men have wished to go
   And stay; till, sudden, it ends where the wood ends.

   This is not, it must be emphasised, the simpler external realism of John Masefield's *The Everlasting Mercy* (1911), a poem which, Ross claims, set the pre-war renaissance of poetic realism in motion and which, oddly enough, I have used above to provide a parallel for the impassioned note in Lawrence's prose. Actually, Masefield takes a very long run before delivering an eloquent ball; what struck the first readers of *The Everlasting Mercy* were its bald colloquialisms and the fairly earthy realism of the main narrative. It is a long poem in doggerel metre, the ostensible topic the life of a wild poacher called Kane ('I drunk, I fought, I poached, I whored'). Readers in those gentler days were apparently taken aback by passages like this:

Now when he saw me set my snare,
He tells me 'Get to hell from there.
This field is mine,' he says, 'by right;
If you poach here, there'll be a fight.
Out now,' he says, 'and leave your wire;
It's mine.'
   'It ain't.'
      'You put.'
         'You liar.'
   'You closhy put.'
   'You bloody liar.'
   'This is my field.'
   'This is my wire.'
   'I'm ruler here.'
   'You ain't.'
   'I am.'
   'I'll fight you for it.'
   'Right, by damn.'

Ross quotes Robert Lynd's comment that these must be 'the most innocent swear-words in literature'. Professor Pinto has seen in this dutiful attention to the underdog a counterpart in poetry of the 'emotional radicalism of Lloyd George and the sentimental socialism of the young Ramsay Macdonald' (*Crisis in English Poetry 1880–1940*, 5th edition, 1967), for Masefield shows up the social hypocrisy of his time through his rebellious poacher, though ultimately bringing him to a state of grace. But while Lawrence often went too far in incorporating rural life in a highly individual myth of his own, however extraordinary its expression, and Richard Jefferies can be said to have deviated into mystical abstraction, however intense its presentation, this poetry of Masefield's gives too many hostages to the actualities of life. Besides, the conversation quoted above may be realistic in itself, but the way in which it is manipulated as an element in the whole is crucial: Kane's speech is an index of the spontaneous vitality of rebelliousness but also of its inadequacy—this poacher, for all his surface realism, is a straw man in a larger argument.

We come back to Edward Thomas, whose range, incidentally, is greater than I have indicated. In this necessarily limited context of commitment to England and its rural life he seems the clearest, sanest and most genuine of all. For his generation the Great War proved to be a profound psychic upheaval and Thomas was not alone in clinging to an idea of rural England to set against horrors. This is not to claim that all his poetry called forth by war was admirable. 'This is No Case of Petty Right or Wrong' is far too oratorical; 'Tears' after an especially fine opening falls off rather. Yet other poems are very impressive. One feels, for instance, that he is perfectly right to see in 'fifty faggots/That once were underwood of hazel and ash' and now, cut down, are crept through and nested in by small birds, a symbol of something that will last out the war:

> Before they are done
> The war will have ended, many other things
> Have ended, maybe, that I can no more
> Foresee or more control than robin or wren.

And such humility before the facts, together with a careful avoidance of the grand gesture Thomas must have been capable of making, ensure that for me at least a poem like 'In Memoriam (Easter 1915)' is not over-sentimental. It neither distorts nor exploits its image of rural England:

> The flowers left thick at nightfall in the wood
> This Eastertide call into mind the men,
> Now far from home, who, with their sweethearts, should
> Have gathered them and will do never again.

History is here given most poignant literary expression.

NOTES

[1] There is a very lively account of this in George Dangerfield's *The Strange Death of Liberal Englaand* (1935), Part 1.

[2] But see Leonard Woolf's autobiographical volume *Sowing* (1960), pages 36–7, for a defence (by a lifelong Socialist) of the *quality* of life in more prosperous households of the time.

[3] These quotations were, of course, selected for the purposes of the argument in

Culture and Environment. It is therefore essential to take the writers' advice and look at Sturt's works for their own sake. His views can be easily misrepresented.

⁴ In a carefully analytical article, 'The Genesis of *The Rainbow* and *Women in Love*' (*D. H. Lawrence Review*, 1968), Keith Sagar has suggested that this quotation is much nearer the 'message' of *Women in Love*, and he later quotes very aptly from a letter in which Lawrence wrote, 'This actually does contain the results in one's soul of the war: it is purely destructive, not like *The Rainbow*, destructive-consummating.'

⁵ When working out this brief comparison between *The Rainbow* and *North and South*, I was greatly helped by a lecture given by Professor Frank Kermode on *The Rainbow, Women in Love* and *Middlemarch*. See especially his 'Lawrence and the Apocalyptic Types' (in *Word in the Desert*, ed. C. B. Cox and A. E. Dyson, 1968), which suggests further reasons for the differences between these novels of crisis and also brings out their fundamental likenesses in the light of a particular mode of historical explanation.

⁶ See J. T. Boulton, *Lawrence in Love: Letters to Louie Burrows*, Nottingham, 1968.

4 : Progress and Poverty

READING the better rural literature of the period is often disheartening. Undoubtedly individual authors carefully qualified their conclusions, as we have seen in the case of George Sturt, but the general view seems to be that the process of historical change was unwelcome. A great author like Thomas Hardy found in the countryside an appropriate setting for his fictions of decline and failure, thus swinging the powerful influence of an influential novelist and poet behind the common lament that a whole authentic way of life was being lost. It can be argued that Hardy became progressively less certain that rural life was an entirely good way of life, but this only deepens the gloom. Other writers turned to view with loathing the spread of industry:

> The smoke of their foul dens
> Broodeth on Thy fair Earth as a black pestilence,
> Hiding the kind day's eye. No flower, no grass
>   there groweth,
> Only their engines' dung which the fierce furnace
>   throweth.
> Their presence poisoneth all and maketh all unclean.
> Thy streams they have made sewers for their dyes
>   analine.
> No fish therein may swim, no frog, no worm, may
>   crawl,
> No snail for grime may build her house within their
>   wall.

These lines are taken from one of Satan's speeches in *Satan Absolved: A Victorian Mystery* (1899), by Wilfred Scawen Blunt.

(See *Poetical Works*, 1914, vol. 2.) They are not put forward here as good poetry; in a way their very awkwardness seems to illustrate the inability of many to do more than throw themselves into simplified attitudes of protest at industrialisation and its cost, in human as well as in natural terms. The title of a highly influential book, *Progress and Poverty* (San Francisco, 1879: London, 1881), reached the heart of the matter for those who could see a little further. Its author, Henry George, voiced their near-despair at a dreadful paradox; material progress, far from bringing joy and a better life for all, was generating new horrors. To quote from the rolling oratory of its introduction, the

> march of invention has clothed mankind with powers of which a century ago the boldest imagination could not have dreamed. But in factories where labour-saving machinery has reached its most wonderful development, little children are at work; wherever the new forces are anything like fully utilized, large classes are maintained by charity or live on the verge of recourse to it; amid the greatest accumulations of wealth, men die of starvation, and puny infants suckle dry breasts; while everywhere the greed of gain, the worship of wealth, shows the force of the fear of want. The promised land flies before us like the mirage. The fruits of the tree of knowledge turn as we grasp them to apples of Sodom that crumble at the touch.

The detailed survey of the conditions of city living in the earlier part of the period can be found in sources like the seventeen-volume *Life and Labour of the People in London* (1902–3), which prints the data gathered in an extensive enquiry set on foot by Charles Booth in 1886. His attempt, he tells us, was

> to produce an instantaneous picture, fixing the facts on my negative as they appear at a given moment and the imagination of my readers must add the movement, the constant changes, the whirl and turmoil of life. (Vol. I, page 26.)

There are similar books on York (B. S. Rowntree, *Poverty: A Study of Town Life*, 1901) and on Northampton and Warrington (A. L. Bowley and A. R. B. Hurst, *Livelihood and Poverty*, 1915), but the quotation above indicates a very definite limitation of their interest for the non-specialist reader. Their picture is a static one. This is by no means to say that they cannot give us vivid glimpses of life in the poorest parts of a city:

> They go to their shop as an ordinary housewife to her canisters: twice a day they buy tea, or three times if they make it so often; in 35 days they made 72 purchases of tea, amounting in all to 5s. 2¾d., and all most carefully noted down. The 'pinch of tea' cost ¾d. . . . (Vol. I, page 142.)

But fascinating as such information may be, it is still anonymous, and very often general or statistical as well, so that we naturally want to follow up Booth's recommendation of George Gissing as a novelist exceptional for the truth to life of his writing (Vol. 1, page 157).

.   .   .   .   .   .

As it happens, Gissing himself turned his mind to the question of the relationship between literature and life in his *Charles Dickens: A Critical Study* (1898; revised 1903) and proved acutely aware that Dickens's art hardly met the standards of relatively objective reporting current in the later years of the century. In chapter 4, however, Gissing repudiated what he called 'schools of rigid "naturalism" ' and asked for sincerity of purpose above all. In chapter 11 he returned to the subject, making the very positive statement that a true artist 'gives us pictures which represent his own favourite way of looking at life', so that 'a master's general conception of the human tragedy or comedy must be accepted as that without which his work could not take form'. Mere imitation of life was not enough. On these premises it is worth looking first at one notable way of expressing a 'general conception of the human tragedy or comedy', i.e. the use of analogy—a technique, incidentally, which is not necessarily confined to formal works of literature.

When the young Beatrice Webb was making investigations in the East End for an article on Dock Labour (published first in 1887), she met a Mr Kerrigan, School Board Inspector for the

Stepney Division. He spoke to her on one occasion about the casual labourers he knew:

> They do not migrate out of the district, but are constantly changing their lodgings: 'they are like the circle of the suicides in Dante's Inferno; they go round and round within a certain area.' (Page 299).

These words, taken from Beatrice Webb's autobiographical *My Apprenticeship* (1926), show that contemporary history and past literature came together very easily in Mr Kerrigan's mind: he found an analogue of his everyday experience in a medieval poem. (The Dante revival at the beginning of the nineteenth century was proving oddly useful to Victorians interested in social problems.) Mr Kerrigan was not unique, for references to Hell of one kind or another, we find, are frequent in the literature of the period when industrial civilisation is the topic. Gissing's novel *The Nether World* (1889) is an unusually elaborate example. Its title is both significant and exact, because his 'general conception' of slum existence was 'Hell on earth'. This was the all-embracing analogy he used to help guide our reactions to the swarming particulars of his novel and mould them into a single main response—in the dispiriting words of one of the characters, Mad Jack:

> 'This life you are now leading is that of the damned; this place to which you are confined is Hell! There is no escape for you. From poor you shall become poorer; the older you grow the lower shall you sink in want and misery; at the end there is waiting for you, one and all, a death in abandonment and despair. This is Hell—Hell—Hell!'

Just as W. Harrison Ainsworth in *Old St Paul's* (1841) called his mad prophet 'the genius of the pestilence', so we can see the wandering Mad Jack as the genius of Stygian London; his weird ravings powerfully enforce the correspondence between the slums and the infernal regions. In the long extent of the novel, however, he only appears at intervals and in the course of reading it is the multitude of naturalistically treated details and events that make the most continuous impact on us. Page follows page describing

cellar and sordid room, wife-beating and the rage for strong drink.
Our physical senses are revolted by the accounts of squalid meals
and our moral sensibility is outraged by the depiction of base
treachery, ingratitude, drudgery, futility and horror. In some ways,
even, this protracted portrayal of urban misery might be thought
of as a secular substitute for the kind of traditional sermon on the
tortures of the damned so stunningly re-created by James Joyce
in his *A Portrait of the Artist As A Young Man* (1916). In Gissing's
The Nether World the speeches of Mad Jack survive as a fossil
deposit of the earlier mode.

Gissing's pressure is relentless. The few gleams of light, such as
the description of a richly rural Essex in chapter 19, are probably
inserted to show up the prevailing gloom, though it is not always
absolutely certain. One of the most terrible chapters. 'On the Eve
of Triumph', reveals how the tenuous friendship between two poor
actresses in a provincial theatre collapses the moment a chance to
take the lead is offered to one at the expense of the other. The
episode ends with disfigurement by acid-throwing and the discovery of 'the body of a woman, train-crushed, horrible to view'.
Yet this chapter sets out with apparently inappropriate touches
of humour. Not to overstate the case, one could argue that the
grimly humorous criticism directed at

> a certain town of Lancashire, one of those remarkable centres
> of industry which pollute heaven and earth, and on that
> account are spoken of with somewhat more of pride than
> stirred the Athenian when he named his Acropolis,

possesses an acceptable sarcastic bite. Can this be said of another
sentence taken from the same early paragraph?

> As leading lady he had the distinguished Miss Erminia
> Walcott; her part was a trying one, for she had to be half-
> strangled by ruffians and flung—most decorously—over the
> parapet of London Bridge.

Is it really possible to give that rather funny aside, 'most decor-
ously', a sufficiently sardonic turn? Should we here infer that life
for poor actors and actresses is, like the melodrama they play, a

savage, primitive affair beneath the gloss of respectability it is often given? We seem to be straining interpretative muscles for what may well be a careless addition of no significance.

Gissing is not an easy writer to come to terms with in more fundamental ways. Authenticity is, as all critics note, patently there in his novels. We know that he drew some of his characters from real people, like Westlake (based on William Morris) in *Demos: A Story of English Socialism* (1886); that he spent hours in Lambeth making notes for his *Thyrza* (1887), 'a book which will contain the very spirit of London working-class life'; and that *The Nether World* especially is closely based on observation of real life. [Jacob Korg, to whose *George Gissing: A Critical Biography* (Seattle, 1963) I am indebted for these facts, refers very pertinently to the contemporary cartoon of Emile Zola 'plunging under the hooves of a pair of cab horses, notebook in hand, in search of first-hand experience'.] Such exemplary care in the imitation of real life ought to result in work of obvious value to the social historian; and to an extent it did. But still we come to the end of *The Nether World* convinced that for all the credibility of its drab documentation the whole is saturated in the emotions and beliefs of the novelist; which gives the work a satisfying unity of theme and expression but creates the complication that for historians interested in the actual conditions of life in the 1880s, a novel like *The Nether World* reflects the individual spirit of Gissing as much as it does the external realities of contemporary London. This is not to claim that it portrays the inner landscape of its creator's mind to anything like the same degree as James Thomson's despairing *The City of Dreadful Night* (1874), but undoubtedly pessimism dictates the course and nature of the main narrative and directs our attention to the most dismal thematic analogues. For Gissing the state of the poor was hopeless, attempts at reform bound to fail. He deliberately rejected conventional remedies like thrift and charity, and stated blankly that

> there is no chance of a new and better world until the old be utterly destroyed.
>
> (Chapter 12.)

Intransigence of this kind places Gissing, at least as far as *The Nether World* is concerned, with Lawrence (compare page 76 above) rather than with the more sanguine social-problem novelists of the 40s and 50s (Disraeli, Charles Kingsley, Elizabeth Gaskell, etc.) and raises the question of how far his depressed inner world is representative of a radical change in temper during his own time—how far, in fact, his bleak views were historically conditioned.

.   .   .   .   .   .

We might look first at a book called *In Darkest England and The Way Out* (1890), written by General William Booth, founder of the Salvation Army, with the assistance of the famous journalist W. T. Stead. Its opening chapter is an involved explanation of the title. The explorer Henry Stanley had just published *In Darkest Africa* (1890), which had struck the public imagination with its sensational description of the immense forest of equatorial Africa, dank, decaying and joyless, its pigmy inhabitants at the mercy of brutal ivory raiders, their lives a morass of despair. Booth and Stead were not slow to exploit the possibilities:

> As in Africa, it is all trees, trees, trees with no other world conceivable; so is it here—it is all vice and poverty and crime. To many the world is all slum, with the Workhouse as an intermediate purgatory before the grave. And just as Mr. Stanley's Zanzibaris lost faith, and could only be induced to plod on in brooding sullenness of dull despair, so the most of our social reformers, no matter how cheerily they may have started off, with forty pioneers swinging blithely their axes as they force their way into the wood, soon become depressed and despairing. Who can battle against the ten thousand million trees? Who can hope to make headway against the innumerable adverse conditions which doom the dweller in Darkest England to eternal and immutable misery?

Their pessimism might seem to prove that Gissing really is a man of his time, especially in the contention that even the reformers were losing heart.

In Darkest England is again like *The Nether World* in its resort
to analogy to colour our reactions. Quite apart from the major
parallel between Africa and England, within a page of the above
quotation the dreadful reign of King Stephen ('It seemed to them
as if God and his Saints were dead', wrote the old chronicler),
Bunyan's Slough of Despond and Dante's Hell have all been
pressed into service. We are irresistibly drawn to think of the
Salvation Army itself—its name, its discipline, its military titles
and structure of command; or, to take from an Appendix a few
minor items, lesser ramifications of the major image of an army
of salvation—its 'Prison Gate Brigades', 'Training Garrisons' and
'Large Vans for Evangelising the Villages (known as Cavalry
Forts)'! When the Army marched down the street people saw a
metaphor in action. In *action*, of course, and not as a form of
entertainment. The whole was and is organised as an army for very
practical reasons indeed and, to return to *In Darkest England*, so
was the resort to analogy a coolly propagandistic decision. 'An
analogy', we read, 'is good as a suggestion; it becomes wearisome
when it is pressed too far.' Except for chapter 1 it is not pressed
very far at all; much the greater part of the book is taken up with
an analysis of social evils and numerous suggestions for coping
with them, down to the proper price for Boiled Jam Pudding ($\frac{1}{2}$d.).
They used analogies as they used graphic art in the symbolic
coloured chart folded behind the front cover of *In Darkest England*,
for strictly limited and practical purposes. Gissing sought to bring
Hell and London together; Booth and Stead *ultimately* kept Africa
and England quite distinct. The larger strategy of their book
matches their tactics of style. Unlike Gissing again, Salvationists
had many practical answers to specific social problems and however hard they may have beaten rhetorical drums in their prose,
or real ones in the streets for that matter, their basic aims were as
positive and as down-to-earth as the actual rescue work the Army
did in the slums.

We may well judge that their optimistic outlook shows that
Gissing is not an entirely representative figure of the time, but it
is also true to say that *In Darkest England* looked backward in
some respects, or, to put it another way, was thoroughly traditional:

I am under no delusion as to the possibility of inaugurating a millenium by my Scheme; but the triumphs of science deal so much with the utilisation of waste material, that I do not despair of something effectual being accomplished in the utilisation of this waste human product. The refuse which was a drug and a curse to our manufacturers, when treated under the hands of the chemist, has been the means of supplying us with dyes rivalling in loveliness and variety the hues of the rainbow. If the alchemy of science can extract beautiful colours from coal tar, cannot Divine alchemy enable us to evolve gladness and brightness out of the agonised hearts and dark, dreary, loveless lives of these doomed myriads.

(Part II, Chapter 1, Section 1.)

Along with the standard Victorian belief that the minds of men capable of subduing brute nature by science and technology must be able to solve social problems—a belief which, already shaken badly, underlies the passage quoted above from George's *Progress and Poverty* (1879)—went a specifically religious drive to give direct help to the victims of society. This is reminiscent of the mid-century 'Christian Socialism' of F. D. Maurice and J. M. Ludlow. But Socialism towards the end of the nineteenth century was, apart from bodies like the Anglican Guild of St Matthew, very much more of a secular phenomenon, in the tradition of Owen and Paine. It was also much more abstract in some quarters; to such an extent that *In Darkest England* devoted some space to criticising its newer manifestations under the significant heading of 'Socialist Utopianism' (Part 1, Chapter 9) while at the same time maintaining sympathy with the Socialist spirit and aims. Within limits one can see their point. Would all the theorising they read from Socialist pens actually help the man who was even then knocking at the door of a Salvation Army shelter begging for aid? When, precisely, would the millennium start? There is truth in the suggestion that for men with the cast of mind of Booth and Stead Socialism was a matter of literature and little else. To them, fine words were buttering no obvious parsnips.

.   .   .   .   .   .

The famous volume called *Fabian Essays* might be one example. It came out in 1889, published by the numerically small but intelligent Fabian Society and edited by George Bernard Shaw. (There is a recent edition, 1962, with introduction by Asa Briggs.) It sold well enough—a thousand within a month of publication— and has sold ever since, though to look through the table of contents is hardly to find the marks of a popular success. The volume contains Shaw on the economic basis of socialism, followed by Sidney Webb on the historical basis, William Clarke on the industrial basis and Sydney Olivier on the moral basis; which can be no more tempting to most people than the four other essays by Graham Wallas, Annie Besant, Hubert Bland and Shaw on topics like property and industry. But we have not far to look to find why these essays live. Sidney Webb, for instance, writing on the progressive enfranchisement of one class after another during the century, found a striking ending for one section of his essay:

> The full significance of this triumph is as yet unsuspected by the ordinary politician. The Industrial Revolution has left the labourer a landless stranger in his own country. The political evolution is rapidly making him its ruler. Samson is feeling for the pillars.

This kind of writing is neither bald nor dull, two frequent faults of specialists who take pen in hand. The last sentence in particular is splendidly expressive of the shackled power of labouring men and, from Webb's angle of vision, the justice and inevitability of their forthcoming victory. To put these words beside the passages quoted from Jefferies (on pages 39–40 above) is also a worthwhile exercise, since to have similar analyses of an aspect of contemporary life made in opposite tones, one apprehensive and the other sympathetic, is to realise afresh how much general beliefs about man and society can temper historical statements and our consequent reactions to them.

We expect brilliant and animated writing from Bernard Shaw and we are not disappointed. Even his most amusing flights in this volume display substantial sense:

Numbers of young men, pupils of Mill, Spencer, Comte and
Darwin, roused by Mr Henry George's *Progress and Poverty*,
left aside evolution and freethought; took to insurrectionary
economics; studied Karl Marx; and were so convinced that
Socialism had only to be put clearly before the working-
classes to concentrate the power of their immense numbers in
one irresistible organization, that the Revolution was fixed for
1889—the anniversary of the French Revolution—at latest. I
remember being asked satirically and publicly at that time how
long I thought it would take to get Socialism into working
order if I had my way. I replied, with a spirited modesty, that
a fortnight would be ample for the purpose.

(Fabian Essays, 1962, pages 220–221.)

Shaw's fun deflates his own youthful chiliasm, but the early desire
for 'catastrophic' change and its replacement by a Fabian policy
of 'gradualism' in the pursuit of the millennium is one aspect of a
distinctive phase in the history of Socialism in Great Britain. Asa
Briggs stresses in his introduction to *Fabian Essays* (1962) that
gradualism was grounded deep in the nature of British life, the
continuousness of change in our society since the seventeenth
century rather than resort to sudden or violent convulsions. In
this he is supported by Shaw's contemporaries. Robert Blatchford
wrote in *Merrie England* (1894), a simple but exceedingly popular
piece of Socialist propaganda, that Socialism would 'grow up
naturally out of our surroundings, and will develop naturally and
by degrees' (chapter 14). H. M. Hyndman, leader of the Social
Democratic Federation, who in the early 1880s used to have long
talks with Karl Marx at his London home, the two of them pacing
up and down on opposite sides of a table for hours on end,
reports:

I frequently spoke with him about the Chartist movement,
whose leaders he had known well and by whom, as their
writings show, he was greatly esteemed. He was entirely sympathetic with my idea of reviving the Chartist organisation,
but doubted its possibility; and when speaking of the likelihood
of bringing about a great economic and social transformation

in Great Britain politically and peacefully he said: 'England is
the one country in which a peaceful revolution is possible;
but', he added after a pause, 'history does not tell us so.' 'You
English,' he said on another occasion, 'like the Romans in
many things are most like them in your ignorance of your
own history.'

This passage was taken from Hyndman's autobiography, *The
Record of an Adventurous Life* (1911).

If the revolution in Britain was not to be nasty, brutish
and short, then there was a place for the longer processes of
persuasion and argument. The Fabians aimed at changing society
by convincing its leaders of opinion; they undertook the task of
remaking the general political and social outlook till it was in
accord with their idea of the facts. Hubert Bland, whose very
readable essay shows that Shaw did not have a monopoly of
vivacity amongst Fabians, demonstrates one of their historical
'facts', the conviction that Socialism was coming in on the flood
tide. It is fascinating to see how his conscious exploitation of this
particular belief makes for generally effective propaganda:

> For it is largely instinctive and wholly self-preservative, this
> change in the position of the working people towards the State
> —this change by which, from fearing it is an actual enemy,
> they have come to look to it as a potential saviour. I know
> that this assertion will be violently denied by many of my
> Socialist brethren. The fly on the wheel, not unnaturally, feels
> wounded at being told that he is, after all, not the motive
> power; and the igniferous orators of the Socialist party are
> welcome, so far as I am concerned, to all the comfort they can
> get from imagining that they, and not any great, blind, evolu-
> tionary forces are the dynamic of the social revolution. Besides,
> the metaphor of the fly really does not run on all fours (I
> forget, for the moment, how many legs a fly has); for the
> Socialist does at least know in what direction the car is going,
> even though he is not the driving force. Yet it seems to me
> that the part being, and to be, played by the Socialist, is

notable enough in all conscience; for it is he who is turning instinct into self-conscious reason; voicing a dumb demand; and giving intelligent direction to a thought-wave of terrific potency. (*Fabian Essays*, 1962, pages 244–5.)

Asked to comment on the style of this passage, we might start with the parenthesis about a fly's legs—the insertion of a pure joke, for its own sake, into a sequence of argument. It is not surprising to learn that all the essays were originally given as lectures, for most people keep a stricter control of relevance when they write than when they talk; but it is also true that harmless jokes slipped into lectures relieve tedium and bring speaker and audience into a mutual sympathy. You are, he implies, intelligent enough not to be distracted by a bit of harmless fun; you have, too, the sort of lively minds that could never be content with plain stodge. Transferred to print, this is one style of the journalist who intends to be just as well received by his readers as a popular speaker. Actually, Shaw mentions in an entertaining letter he wrote about the Fabian Society on 27 May 1887 that 'the eye-glassed and indomitable Bland' was the editor of *Today*, a Socialist magazine. Hubert Bland seems to have been an influential writer and the passage above is typical of the combined vigour and ease of his prose style. It might also be evidence, judging by the hyperbole of some of its phraseology, that his beliefs about history were generating the higher emotional temperature of a myth, something able to subsist even if its links with reality were not at all as strong as he appeared to think. The power of a myth admittedly depends less on its truth than on the assent it can win, but phrases like 'great, blind, evolutionary forces' and 'terrific potency' are for the converted rather than the uncommitted in the more intelligent circles addressed by Fabian essayists.

For students of history in its relations with literature the case of the Fabian Society is especially fascinating. It more or less ignored in its *Essays* the growing Trade Union movement, though Sidney Webb and Beatrice Potter produced a *History of Trade Unionism* and *Industrial Democracy* a few years afterwards. Despite the presence in their ranks of what Shaw in a revealing phrase from the letter of 27 May called 'a genuine working man in the lathe and plaster line' (which makes him sound like a kind of mascot, an object of pride but quite unique), Fabians were predominantly middle-class intellectuals. They believed in providing Socialist ideas and projects for all; even political opponents, according to Sidney Webb in the Preface he wrote for a 1920 reprint of the *Essays*. He also tells us in this Preface that the seven essayists had by 1920 been responsible for over a hundred volumes, not to mention 'an uncounted host of minor publications.' It is therefore difficult to estimate the real importance of these 'communicative learners', so far from the factory, the docks or the farm, in the rise of Socialism. Asa Briggs in his introduction pays tribute to the ideas they provided for the British labour movement and their 'invitation to a permanent review of what was happening'. E. J. Hobsbawm is sceptical, making sharp comments to the effect that their exceptional literary fluency gave them the unfair advantage of being able to establish their own sunny place in history, somewhat to the detriment of other pioneering worthies. (See 'The Fabians Reconsidered', in *Labouring Men: Studies in the History of Labour*, 1964). This is an awkward criticism for any Fabian apologist to deal with and deserves more extended discussion than is possible here. It is certainly an oddly relevant sidelight on the protean relationship between history and literature.

.　　.　　.　　.　　.　　.

If Booth and Stead thought groups like the Fabians too impractical, the Fabians themselves had a similar line to draw. In the Appendix Bernard Shaw wrote for E. R. Pease's *The History of the Fabian Society* (1916) he claims that most of his colleagues were 'inveterate Philistines' and on the whole kept aloof from anything so frivolous as Art and Literature. Shaw obtained for *Fabian Essays* a striking cover designed by Walter Crane and a decorative back by May Morris, but he was unable to make Fabians do justice to her father's *News From Nowhere* (1890). To us this neglect of William Morris is impossible, for his work in art as well as literature is not only significant in the history of western culture but it also provides some of the more intricate insights into the connexion between history and literature—not to mention simple pleasure.

No-one can miss in Morris the dislike, even hatred, of contemporary civilisation and its staggeringly ugly works, grotesque, shoddy products of an accelerated manufacturing system. After a period of escapism his response was to turn, in the early 1880s, to Socialism:

> The hope of the past times was gone, the struggles of mankind for many ages had produced nothing but this sordid, aimless, ugly confusion; the immediate future seemed to me likely to intensify all the present evils by sweeping away the last survivals of the days before the dull squalor of civilization had settled down on the world. . . . So there I was in for a fine pessimistic end of life, if it had not somehow dawned on me that amidst all this filth of civilization the seeds of a great change, what we others call Social-Revolution, were beginning to germinate. . . . But the consciousness of revolution stirring amidst our hateful modern society prevented me, luckier than many others of artistic perceptions, from crystallizing into a mere railer against 'progress' on the one hand, and on the other from wasting time and energy in any of the numerous schemes by which the quasi-artistic of the middle classes hope to make art grow when it no longer has any root, and thus I become a practical Socialist.
>
> How I became a Socialist. *Justice* (16 June 1894).

The view of history and the analysis of the age is broadly like Lawrence's—even some of the imagery, perhaps inevitably, is similar—but the consequence, a life devoted to writing, lecturing and other kinds of activism in the Socialist cause, could hardly have been more different. Many specimens of Morris's Socialist writings can be turned up in the pages of *The Commonweal*, a paper he edited for the Socialist League from 1885, in the very first number of which he printed one of his own poems called 'March of the Workers'. This is a good example of a poem which may be of historical interest, but which is of very slight literary value; however stirring and affecting it may have been in its day, it is now little more than old-fashioned propaganda:

> On we march then, we the workers, and the rumour
>   that ye hear
> Is the blended sound of battle and deliv'rance
>   drawing near;
> For the hope of every creature is the banner that
>   we bear,
> And the world is marching on.
>
>> Hark the rolling of the thunder!
>> Lo the sun! and lo thereunder,
>> Riseth wrath, and hope, and wonder,
>>   And the host comes marching on.

Nascent Socialist fervour is obsolete now and this poem cannot revive it for us; for all the rousing vigour of the statement, its use of language is tired.

Morris's revolutionary commitment found more lasting form in his prose *News From Nowhere* (1890), a romance of the future set in the twenty-second century after the presumed breakdown of the existing capitalist system. In this it resembles Edward Bellamy's *Looking Backward*, published a short time before in 1888, the story of which is set in Boston of the year 2000. (This American Utopia is a useful reminder that the problems of industrial society were by no means confined to Great Britain and that our historical perspectives should not be limited.) In *News From Nowhere* Morris reverses the flow of history in his time, sweeping away factories and anything else associated with the degraded inside of industrial life. His vision of a better world is highly optimistic, though not, one must admit, truly forward-looking. Bellamy's new city shows clearly that Morris's dream of a future London is a reversion to an idealised Middle Ages. There is nothing of what John Evelyn endearingly called '*Cut-work and Crinkle-Crankle*' about Bellamy's monumental vision:

At my feet lay a great city. Miles of broad streets, shaded by trees and lined with fine buildings, for the most part not in continuous blocks but set in larger or smaller enclosures, stretched in every direction. Every quarter contained large open squares filled with trees, among which statues glistened and fountains flashed in the late afternoon sun. Public buildings of a colossal size and an architectural grandeur unparalleled in my day raised their stately piles on either side.

(Chapter 3.)

Morris is much more decorative at the same stage of his story. He is the one who is looking backward, in fact:

I was going to say, 'But is this the Thames?' but held my peace in my wonder, and turned my bewildered eyes eastward to look at the bridge again, and thence to the shores of the London river; and surely there was enough to astonish me. For though there was a bridge across the stream and houses on its banks, how all was changed from last night! The soap-works with their smoke-vomiting chimneys were gone; the engineer's works gone; the lead-works gone; and no sound of rivetting and hammering came down the west wind from Thorneycroft's. Then the bridge! I had perhaps dreamed of such a bridge, but never seen such a one out of an illuminated manuscript; for not even the Ponte Vecchio at Florence came anywhere near it. It was of stone arches, splendidly solid, and as graceful as they were strong; high enough also to let ordinary river traffic through easily. Over the parapet showed quaint and fanciful little buildings, which I supposed to be booths or shops, beset with painted and gilded vanes and spirelets. The stone was a little weathered, but showed no marks of the grimy sootiness which I was used to on every London building more than a year old. In short, to me a wonder of a bridge. (Chapter 2.)

A passage of this kind is probably only really successful when its attitudes, rather simple ones, are shared by its readers. Bellamy tended to predict the future by projection of existing tendencies. Morris, on the other hand, cut away what he disliked about his own age and so evaded the real problem: he removed some at least of its essential terms. Similarly, N. Pevsner has found it necessary to emphasise that important as Morris was for his claims that art should be in touch with everyday life and that mundane things like chairs and wallpaper are worthy of an artist's imagination, he could not take the further, necessary step of wholeheartedly welcoming machinery and its design potential. (*Pioneers of Modern Design From William Morris to Walter Gropius*, 1960, chapter 1.) Though it is true that Morris did not reject the machine outright, there is no passage in *News From Nowhere* comparable in content to the following panegyric from chapter 7 of H. G. Wells's *A Modern Utopia* (1905):

> Art has scarcely begun in the world.
>
> There have been a few forerunners and that is all. Leonardo, Michael Angelo; how they would have exulted in the liberties of steel! There are no more pathetic documents in the archives of art than Leonardo's memoranda. In these, one sees him again and again reaching out as it were, with empty desirous hands, towards the unborn possibilities of the engineer. And Dürer, too, was a Modern, with the same turn towards creative invention. In our times these men would have wanted to make viaducts to bridge wild and inaccessible places, to cut and straddle great railways athwart the mountain masses of the world. You can see, time after time in Dürer's work, as you can see in the imaginary architectural landscape of the Pompeian walls, the dream of structures, lighter and bolder than stone or brick can yield.

Wells here follows in the tradition of writers like Zola and Whitman, cited by Professor Pevsner as the first preachers of the Modern Movement, men who were 'carried away by the overwhelming marvels of modern civilization and modern industry'.

Not that Morris should therefore be dismissed, because *News From Nowhere* is remarkable for other and perhaps in the long run more important qualities. First, it comes as something of a surprise to learn that his account of the beginnings of the breakdown of the capitalist system is directly based on the agitation in 1887 which culminated in 'Bloody Sunday' (13 November), when crowds of demonstrators on their way to protest in Trafalgar Square were broken up by the police. ('We *skedaddled*', Bernard Shaw wrote in a letter at the time.) Second, this and similar drafts on the real (for it is not unique) do no more than offset the ideal when viewed in complete context. We can best show how by a brief literary analysis of the book's structure, especially of its beautifully managed ending. After the narrator has been taken on a tour of the new London and has had many conversations with its future inhabitants, in which the contrasts with nineteenth-century life are drawn as emphatically as possible to the latter's disadvantage, there is a trip up the river Thames to a haymaking. We are made to look forward to this haymaking as to the crowning experience of all that is good about the new life; or more particularly, as the end draws near, to a haymakers' feast in a church, a symbol of the unity and perfect harmony of the new society that has sprung from the dead stock of the past. Then, at the moment the narrator stands ready to join in, the blow falls:

> I stood on the threshold with the expectant smile on my face of a man who is going to take part in a festivity which he is really prepared to enjoy. Dick, standing by me, was looking round the company with an air of proprietorship in them, I thought. Opposite me sat Clara and Ellen, with Dick's place open between them: they were smiling, but their beautiful faces were each turned towards the neighbours on either side, who were talking to them, and they did not seem to see me. I turned to Dick, expecting him to lead me forward, and he turned his face to me; but strange to say, though it was as smiling and cheerful as ever, it made no response to my glance—nay, he seemed to take no heed at all of my presence, and I noticed that none of the company looked at me. A pang shot through me, as of some disaster long expected and suddenly realised.
>
> (Chapter 32, 'The Feast's Beginning—The End'.)

Once done, it seems inevitable that Morris should have made the narrator, who had originally materialised in a mysterious manner in the future, suddenly become insubstantial at this exact moment. The last sentence of the passage, too, is the drawing together of several minor but disquieting thoughts and experiences in the preceding narrative: glimmerings of fear, oppressive memories of past sorrows and the days when 'it was thought poetic and imaginative to look upon life as a thing to be borne, rather than to be enjoyed'. (James Thomson's *The City of Dreadful Night*, with its sequence of despairing, terrible visions, will again serve for illustration.) The names in the passage remind us of the close relationships that have been established in the narrator's new life in the future, so that the sense of personal loss is quite as intense as that, for instance, experienced by Gulliver when his beloved Houhynhymn master tells him he has to leave the land of the horses. And the whole setting is the last of many calm, clear descriptions of nature and a life lived close to nature which fill the latter part of *News From Nowhere*. An earlier example might be taken from chapter 23:

> . . . so I got up, and found that, early as it was, someone had been stirring, since all was trim and in its place in the little parlour, and the table laid for the morning meal. Nobody was afoot in the house as then, however, so I went out a-doors, and after a turn or two round the superabundant garden, I wandered down over the meadow to the river-side, where lay our boat, looking quite familiar and friendly to me. I walked up stream a little, watching the light mist curling up from the river till the sun gained power to draw it all away; saw the bleak speckling the water under the willow boughs, whence the tiny flies they fed on were falling in myriads; heard the great chub splashing here and there at some belated moth or other, and felt almost back again in my boyhood.

The language here obviously lacks the compressed precision of, say, a *Journal* entry by Gerard Manley Hopkins ('wavelets edged with fine eyebrow crispings'), but nevertheless all these descriptions lend their accumulated force to other aspects of the narrative.

The blow that eventually falls upon the unfortunate narrator has been carefully prepared for and is correspondingly devastating. The feeling of immense disappointment communicated to us at the end of the book brings home the vital force of Morris's idea of

what life *could* be like, how perfect an existence would be possible
if only the system he detested in his own time were to be overthrown.
News from Nowhere, whatever its defects as a prophecy of the
future—sad to say, the date of the dawning of the new age is given
as 1952—is unusually successful in conveying the quality of an
ideal life for human beings. Literature, one could say in this case,
embodied potential history in order to inspire the men and women
who might have made it actual ... and unlike 'March of the
Workers' retains its power to move us even when the course of
history has falsified many of its central political aspirations.

.   .   .   .   .   .

Once again, however, it is H. G. Wells we must pick out as more
attuned to preliminary movements of sensibility in his time.
Writing only fifteen or so years later he was unable to approach the
reader as directly as Morris had. The organisation Wells felt
impelled to give his *A Modern Utopia* seems highly significant in
itself, for he tells us in prefatory notes that we must think of
his book as a hybrid between a lecture and a work of fiction,
imagining as we read 'a moving picture of Utopian conditions'
rather erratically presented on a screen behind a lecturer. And
why did Wells invent such a complicated and untransparent form
for his work? Because, he writes in a brief note at the end, he
could not reconcile two kinds of vision, two distinct ways of
looking at life:

> For I see about me a great multitude of little souls and
> groups of souls as darkened, as derivative as my own; with the
> passage of years I understand more and more clearly the
> quality of the motives that urge me and urge them to do what-
> ever we do. ... Yet that is not all I see, and I am not altogether
> bounded by my littleness. Ever and again, contrasting with
> this immediate vision, come glimpses of a comprehensive
> scheme, in which these personalities float, the scheme of a
> sympathetic wider being, the great State, mankind, in which
> we all move and go, like blood corpuscles, like nerve cells, it
> may be at times like brain cells, in the body of a man. But the

H

two visions are not seen consistently together, at least by me, and I do not surely know that they exist consistently together.

Both Morris and Wells felt deeply that 'the desire is boundless, and the act a slave to limit' (*Troilus and Cressida*, III. ii. 80), but whereas Morris, as we have seen, did not allow the specks of sad reality to seriously obscure the clear surface of his imagined ideal existence and in the end brought his narrative back to an image of real life with firm decision, Wells found himself quite unable to be so positive. The form he evolved for *A Modern Utopia* embodied the incompatibility of human pettiness and human aspiration continuously. His pictures of perfect society flickered spasmodically behind the two personalities he had created to stand for defective humanity; his *A Modern Utopia* 'began upon a philosophy of fragmentation and [ended], confusedly, amidst a gross tumult of immediate realities, in dust and doubt, with, at the best, one individual's aspiration.' Both Morris and Wells feared their utopias were built upon sand, but Wells had the extra fear that it was quicksand.

Another author, then, had concluded that the very shaping of his work must correspond with his response to his own age, both in the superficial aspect of finding a model in the very new art-form of moving pictures and in the more fundamental aspect of believing that lack of spiritual certainty could be reflected in a disjointed work of literature[1]. Older utopias showed by their relatively straightforward structures that their authors had been possessed by an equally uncomplicated vision of the perfect life, but modern man, Wells claimed, knew that 'One grasps at the Universe and attains— Bathos.' Some years before T. S. Eliot's 'The Love Song of J. Alfred Prufrock' Wells knew that he had time 'for a hundred visions and revisions'; and the kaleidoscopic shapes he created as a result anticipate in a minor way the course to be taken by modernist poetry a few years later.

· · · · · ·

Eliot is a major twentieth-century poet. His greatest works, which began with *The Waste Land* (1922), will be studied in the next volume of this series, but his early poems certainly fall into the tradition of urban, social literature we are at present investigating. One poet in this tradition, John Davidson, has stated the main thesis for us. For him, the poet has become a kind of historian of his age and, moreover, that age in its most sordid and common-place aspects:

Poetry is not always an army on parade: sometimes it is an army coming back from the wars, epaulettes and pipe-clay all gone, shoeless, ragged, wounded, starved, but with victory on its brows; for Poetry has been democratized. Nothing could prevent that. The songs are of the highways and the byways. The city slums and the deserted villages are haunted by sorrow-ful figures, men of power and endurance, feeding their melancholy not with heroic fable, the beauty of the moon, and the studious cloisters, but with the actual sight of the misery in which so many millions live. To this mood the vaunted sweetness and light of the ineffective apostle of culture [Matthew Arnold] are, like a faded rose in a charnel house, a flash of moonshine on the Dead Sea. It is not now to the light that 'the passionate heart of the poet' will turn. The poet is in the street, the hospital. He intends the world to know it is out of joint.

He goes on to claim that the newspaper was a potent force in moulding the character of poetry:

It was in the newspapers that Thomas Hood found the 'Song of the Shirt'—in its place the most important English poem of the nineteenth century; the 'woman in unwomanly rags plying her needle and thread' is the type of the world's misery. . . . Poetry passed by on the other side. It could not endure the woman in unwomanly rags. . . . But the woman in unwomanly rags, and all the insanity and iniquity of which she is the type, will now be sung. . . . The offal of the world is being said in statistics, in prose fiction; it is besides going to be sung.

(*A Rosary*, 1903.)[2]

We have already seen something of the statistics and prose. In poetry W. E. Henley was early on the scene with his *Hospital*

Sketches (1875) and *London Voluntaries* (1892) and other poets like
Arthur Symons and Lawrence Binyon also found their subject-
matter in the city. Davidson's own most famous poem, 'Thirty Bob
a Week', appeared first in *The Yellow Book* (July 1894) and is an
attempt to reproduce the spoken language of a London clerk, with
all the characteristics of his normal expression:

> For like a mole I journey in the dark,
>   A-travelling along the underground
> From my Pillar'd Halls and broad Suburban Park,
>   To come the daily dull official round;
> And home again at night with my pipe all alight,
>   A-scheming how to count ten bob a pound.
>
> And it's often very cold and very wet,
>   And my missus stitches towels for a hunks;
> And the Pillar'd Halls is half of it to let—
>   Three rooms about the size of travelling trunks.
> And we cough, my wife and I, to dislocate a sigh,
>   When the noisy little kids are in their bunks.
>
> But you never hear her do a growl or whine,
>   For she's made of flint and roses, very odd;
> And I've got to cut my meaning rather fine,
>   Or I'd blubber, for I'm made of greens and sod:
> So p'r'aps we are in Hell for all that I can tell,
>   And lost and damn'd and serv'd up hot to God.

This poem of sixteen stanzas has received very high praise from
T. S. Eliot, who read it at an impressionable age (his late teens)
and found that it made 'a terrific impact' on him. To some degree
this was a technical matter: Davidson, he considered, had freed
himself from the poetic diction of his time by use of colloquial,
everyday language, but Eliot goes on to say, in a Preface to
M. Lindsay's selection,

> I am sure that I found inspiration in the content of the poem,
> and in the complete fitness of content and idiom: for I also had
> a good many dingy urban images to reveal. Davidson had a
> great theme, and also found an idiom which elicited the great-

ness of the theme, which endowed this thirty-bob-a-week clerk with a dignity that would not have appeared if a more conventional poetic diction had been employed. The personage that Davidson created in this poem has haunted me all my life, and the poem is to me a great poem for ever.

There are echoes here of another famous Preface, Wordsworth's, prefixed to *Lyrical Ballads* (1800). The need to free poetry from poetic diction, regarded as a barrier to truth, is present in both. The nub of the matter, though, is reached in Eliot's remarks about dignity. It is again Wordsworthian—as modified by a new historical context, for the history of literature is not insulated from general history. We could say that a personage like Wordsworth's leech-gatherer, the old man who used to wander over the moors and seemed an integral part of rural nature, changed into a city wage-slave—just as life during the nineteenth century became ever more urbanised. The parallel between clerk and countryman holds in several ways: both were lowly figures, in extremely adverse circumstances; both bore up with resolution and independence, and both were possessed of an inalienable personal dignity. There is, of course, a major difference: to Wordsworth the leech-gatherer seemed shown by a 'leading from above', but to Davidson, as the reference to Hell in his poem indicates, the clerk could no longer be regarded in a religious light:

> My weakness and my strength without a doubt
> Are mine alone for ever from the first:
> It's just the very same with a difference in the name
> As 'Thy will be done.' You say it if you durst!

The urban and secular nature of this poem does not disguise its essential Wordsworthian romanticism, which if teased out shows the basic belief that poetry should present the truth of man *in his time*, with the inevitable corollary that the language used could never merely repeat what had been used and in a sense worn out in the past. There must be a perpetual struggle with words and meanings; each new venture must be a raid on the inarticulate. These are two of Eliot's later formulations of his basic approach to literary expression.

Reproduction of colloquial idioms and language is not the only technique Davidson employed. In order to capture the sense of contemporary city life going on about the death-bed of the mother in the semi-autobiographical 'A Woman and Her Son' (1897), he made a selection of significant details. At first it reads like some eighteenth-century poetical catalogue of types:

> The working-men with heavy iron tread,
> The thin-shod clerks, the shopmen neat and plump
> Home from the city came.

That last syntactic inversion reinforces our dating, but then Davidson seems to become far more interested in rendering experience as it seeps into consciousness, though his lines still retain a certain formality of style:

> On muddy beer
> The melancholy mean suburban street
> Grew maudlin for an hour; pianos waked
> In dissonance from dreams of rusty peace,
> And unpitched voices quavered tedious songs
> Of sentiment infirm or nerveless mirth.

The mother's anxious voice plucks at the attention of her nurse:

> 'Has he come yet?'
>   'Be still or you will die!'

> And when the hour of gaiety had passed,
> And the poor travellers were gone to bed,
> The moon among the chimneys wandered long,
> Escaped at last, and sadly overlooked
> The waste raw land where doleful suburbs thrive.

Without laying too much stress on the anticipation of T. S. Eliot's famous title in the last line of this extract, it is evident that some of his early poetry is very similar indeed. There was, it is true, an intermediate source: Eliot tells us that the influence of poets like Davidson, or Arthur Symons and Ernest Dowson from the same period, the nineties, melted into the inspiration he gained a little later from the French symbolist poets like Laforgue. (See *John*

Davidson, ed. Lindsay, page 9.) Nevertheless, a comparison of a passage from Eliot's 'Preludes II' (in *Prufrock and Other Observations*, 1917) with the Davidson quoted above reveals likenesses in subject-matter and the technique used to capture sense-impressions of urban reality:

> The morning comes to consciousness
> Of faint stale smells of beer
> From the sawdust-trampled street
> With all its muddy feet that press
> To early coffee-stands.

Or a passage from Eliot's 'Morning at the Window' (in the same collection) is comparable to Davidson's poem in its strangely complex mood:

> They are rattling breakfast plates in basement kitchens,
> And along the trampled edges of the street
> I am aware of the damp souls of housemaids
> Sprouting despondently at area gates.

Words like 'thrive' and 'sprouting', certainly as far as their associations of vitality and life are concerned, do not march logically with words like 'doleful' and 'despondently': both Davidson and Eliot are either using the same kind of critical irony or simply responding to the same contradictory quality of their urban impressions. Are they being moralists or annalists? It is not always easy to tell, especially with Eliot, though we can be reasonably sure about some lines later in Davidson's poem:

> Far off a clank and clash of shunting trains
> Broke out and ceased, as if the fettered world
> Started and shook its irons in the night.

> .   .   .   .   .   .

There was clearly an important widening of subject-matter in the nineties as poets followed the prose writers (and painters, too, if we think of James Whistler's impressionist Nocturnes, or Atkinson Grimshaw's suburban street scenes) in reflecting urban life. As town life became the normal condition of twentieth-century man the old Pastoral opposition of town and country was growing less and less relevant; it was, we have seen in Gissing, still part of mental life and consequently used by writers, but it was becoming distinctly old-fashioned. Modern authors began to identify modern life with urban life, and this in turn could often only be compared with hell or nightmare. In an essay on Baudelaire, whose poetry Eliot was reading in about 1907 or 1908, there are some illuminating remarks on the *intensity* of his urban imagery; Eliot has also said:

> I think that from Baudelaire I learned first, a precedent for the poetical possibilities, never developed by any poet writing in my own language, of the more sordid aspects of the modern metropolis, of the possibility of fusion between the sordidly realistic and the phantasmagoric, the possibility of the juxta-position of the matter-of-fact and the fantastic.

Eliot himself was to use Baudelaire very directly in Part I of *The Waste Land*, when he wrote of the 'Unreal city' where the spectre in broad daylight reaches out to grasp the passer-by, and he gave in his notes to this whole passage two major references, Dante's *Inferno*, canto III, and the Baudelaire poem beginning:

> Fourmillante cité, cité pleine de rêves,
> Où le spectre en plein jour raccroche le passant!

Reality and spectral horror fuse in this poetry, just as they do in a posthumously published poem by John Davidson called 'The Crystal Palace'.

No longer was the Crystal Palace the 'blazing arch of lucid glass' which leapt like a fountain to meet the sun, as celebrated by Thackeray at its opening in the proud May of 1851, but rather, Davidson concluded in insistently modish scientific imagery, like some

> Immense crustacean's gannoid skeleton,
> Unearthed, and cleansed, and polished! Were it so
> Our paleontological respect
> Would shield it from derision; but when a shed,
> Intended for a palace, looks as like
> The fossil of a gigantic myriapod . . .

In this striking poem, written when his early views had changed considerably and posthumously published in 1911, Davidson poured scorn upon the crowd making its glum gala-day in this 'Victorian temple of commercialism', hordes of people all frantically pleasure-bent but at bottom consumed by ennui. It is the complete opposite to the simple human pleasure experienced by H. G. Wells' Kipps and Ann in their day at the Crystal Palace (*Kipps*, 1905, Book 2, chapter 9). True, even Kipps and Ann eventually become uneasy and leave, but Davidson is from the beginning totally committed to devastating criticism. In verse of shifting tones and movement he switches from scene to scene in the vast edifice:

> ... That?
> King Francis—by Clesinger—on a horse.
> Absurd: most mounted statues are.—And this?
> Verrochio's Coleone. Not absurd:
> Grotesque and strong, the battle-harlot rides
> A stallion; fore and aft, his saddle, peaked
> Like a mitre, grips him like a vice.
> In heavy armour mailed; his lifted helm
> Reveals his dreadful look; his brows are drawn;
> Four wrinkles deeply trench his muscular face;
> His left arm half-extended, and the reins
> Held carelessly, although the gesture's tense;
> His right hand wields a sword invisible;
> Remorseless pressure of his lips protrudes
> His mouth; he would decapitate the world.
>
> The light is artificial now; the place
> Phantasmal like a beach in hell where souls
> Are ground together by an unseen sea.
> A dense throng in the central transept, wedged
> So tightly they can neither clap nor stamp,
> Shouting applause at something, goad themselves
> In sheer despair to think it rather fine:
> 'We came here to enjoy ourselves. Bravo,
> Then! Are we not?' Courageous folk beneath
> The brows of Michaelangelo's Moses dance
> A cakewalk in the dim Renascence Court.

The fine set-piece description of a striking work of art, defying time in its sculptured moment of remorseless power, is placed immediately before a desperate and insufficient modern reality, so lacking in true sense of purpose that it is a spiritual desert. In Davidson's poem art has more real substance than life, and in the last three lines quoted above he brings them together in bizarre conjunction, as Eliot did in the line, 'O O O O that Shakespeherian Rag!' We could parody Eliot's *Sweeney Agonistes* and proclaim that for a cakewalk, 'Any old Court is just my sort', even if it means regarding a copy of Michaelangelo's statue of Moses as no more than dance-hall *décor*. Davidson 'intends the world to know it is out of joint': he is a critical and disgusted Hamlet in a rotten state of Denmark. The poetic tour of the Crystal Palace, 'a building lacking life,/A house that must not mellow nor decay'—quite non-organic—is designed to bring out the total meaninglessness of people's frantic quest for pleasure and enjoyment. They are, variously, 'an unhappy locust swarm', 'a stranded shoal of folk', 'deluded myriads', or just plain 'Mob'.

Davidson is partial, no doubt. Another intriguing poem in the posthumous volume, 'The Testament of Sir Simon Simplex Concerning Automobilism', is written on the preposterous assumption that

> Railways are democratic, vulgar, laic;
> And who can doubt Democracy's archaic? . . .
> But convalescence with the car begins
> And petrol expiates our railway sins.

Nevertheless, whatever our opinion of Davidson's views, there is no doubt he held them strongly and gave them the kind of memorable and intense presentation we expect from poetry beyond any other literary form. Literature generally is one of the main ways in which society becomes conscious of itself as it was and is; it makes the diagnoses which are the first histories of an age. Later writers, with that hindsight which is always the best improver of histories, will modify and clarify the preliminary diagnoses, but they can never give the full sense of what it was actually like to be alive in what is being analysed. This may be an impossible ideal but of those who interpret an age for later generations the poets with their more flexible, creative use of language speak most powerfully to us. If we examine the history of the novel, we find it is a form that has increasingly allowed veins of poetry to run through its more solid narrative substance. Lecture, analysis, discourse, argument—all add their valuable quota to its primary embodiment of experience, but a novel is most completely alive when the blood is coursing through those veins.

. . . . . .

Society, once conscious of itself and of its patterns of being, begins to judge itself. We have already seen that one of the most tempting ways of reaching judgement is to work by analogy or, in effect, measure against other societies and modes of existence in both space and time. In time can mean, as far as late nineteenth-century urban literature is concerned, being set against past traditions of hell or against speculative, perfect societies of the future; in space might be against primitive cultures still surviving outside Europe, since the North-country shepherd and his like had already been affected—some would say corrupted—by civilisation. One of the most remarkable literary works of our period, Conrad's *Heart of Darkness* (1899), is worth mentioning in this rather technical connexion, though it will be given much more detailed attention in a later chapter. The story starts on the river Thames, 'a waterway leading to the uttermost ends of the earth', just as darkness was falling. Its main narrator, Marlow, suddenly reminds his audience that even the splendid Thames was once a dark and savage place to men from the civilised Mediterranean lands, and then he returns to the nineteenth-century present by beginning his account of a journey he had once taken into the darkness of the Congo—as much a moral darkness of so-called civilised men as of primitive peoples:

The word 'ivory' rang in the air, was whispered, was sighed. You would think they were praying to it. A taint of imbecile rapacity blew through it all, like a whiff from some corpse. By Jove! I've never seen anything so unreal in my life. And outside, the silent wilderness surrounding this cleared speck on

the earth struck me as something great and invincible, like evil
or truth, waiting patiently for the passing away of this fantastic
invasion.

European traders are a 'fantastic invasion', while Africa is profoundly ambiguous in value, 'like evil or truth'. For Marlow it
posed a 'choice of nightmares . . . in the tenebrous land invaded by
these mean and greedy phantoms.' In such deliberately arranged
clashes between cultures separated in space or time literature
provides a parallel to historiography of the Toynbeian variety,
setting whole societies against each other, though imaginative
literature can to a far greater extent allow itself the licence to
choose unreal or visionary options. These, in their turn, can be
given such verbal substance that even real life and people are made
to appear inferior in comparison, as with *News From Nowhere*, or
quite insubstantial, as with the passages quoted above from Eliot,
Davidson and Conrad. The real and solid becomes spiritually null
and is repudiated; which shows what a major impulse the search for
values must be in such works. Human beings do not like to be left
without a pattern and a meaning.

NOTES

[1] Compare Charles Kingsley's defence of the 'fragmentary and unconnected form'
of his novel *Yeast* (1848). In an epilogue he refers to stereotyped traditional systems
breaking up like ice in a thaw and 'a thousand facts and notions' which cannot
be classified pouring in like a flood. Such a subject demands an appropriately
expressive form, he claims. See also A. J. LaValley, *Carlyle and the Idea of the
Modern*, New Haven 1968.

[2] Quoted from *John Davidson: A Selection of His Poems*, ed. M. Lindsay (1961).

5 : The Search for Values

Values, standards by which we sometimes lead our own lives and more often judge the lives of others, are found in most works of literature; but there are many cases of which we must say that any *search* for values occurred at a stage well in advance of actual composition. Only a limited number of books seem to have been written on the assumption that values ought to be discovered rather than just communicated. All writers, perhaps, start by analysing life, looking into themselves and out at the society around them, trying to make sense of the complexities and peculiarities of existence. Then they diverge. One group, the larger, soon finds a clear enough pattern in character and event and therefore proceeds at once to direct criticisms and definite proposals; the other undertakes a much more tentative analysis and then might even go so far as to present a version of the search itself in the hope that the values it ultimately reveals will not have been distorted by premature codification and removal from a living context. To some extent the division is a matter of literary history. A writer like Pope was much more liable to start from prepared positions than Keats, whose first version of *Hyperion*, for instance, survives as a shell that could not contain his fast-growing spirit. From the time of the Romantics to W. B. Yeats, who wrote in the last weeks of his life—he died in 1939—that 'Man can embody truth but he cannot know it', it became increasingly unlikely that perceptive readers would accept a set of formulas, however prettily they were dressed up.

Oscar Wilde, in Act I of *An Ideal Husband* (1895), touched amusingly on the general philosophical problem when he made his Mrs Cheveley propose that women at least could not be logically and simply explained:

Sir Robert Chiltern You prefer to be natural?

Mrs Cheveley Sometimes. But it is such a very difficult pose to keep up.

Sir Robert Chiltern What would all those modern psychological novelists, of whom we hear so much, say to such a theory as that?

Mrs Cheveley Ah! the strength of women comes from the fact that psychology cannot explain us. Men can be analysed, women . . . merely adored.

Sir Robert Chiltern You think science cannot grapple with the problem of women?

Mrs Cheveley Science can never grapple with the irrational. That is why it has no future before it, in this world.

Wilde is being witty about what was a great movement of thought away from narrowly rational and oversimplified accounts of human experience and behaviour. Science was in fact beginning to grapple with the irrational, even if it was using reason to do so. The idea of the unconscious mind arrived at by Freud, and especially the attention he gave to what he called the Id, a seething cauldron of instinctual energy where the laws of logic (not to mention morality) do not hold, is a major instance. The philosopher William James, in his *Pragmatism: A New Name for Some Old Ways of Thinking: Popular Lectures on Philosophy* (1907, Lecture 2), write that modern scientists were turning away from certitudes and regarding their theories as 'instruments not answers to enigmas':

When the first mathematical, logical, and natural uniformities, the first *laws*, were discovered, men were so carried away by the clearness, beauty and simplification that resulted, that they believed themselves to have deciphered authentically the eternal thoughts of the Almighty. His mind also thundered and reverberated in syllogisms. He also thought in conic sections, squares and roots and ratios, and geometrized like Euclid. . . . But as the sciences have developed farther, the notion has gained ground that most, perhaps all, of our laws are only approximations. The laws themselves, moreover, have grown so numerous that there is no counting them; and so many rival formulations are proposed in all the branches of science that investigators have become accustomed to the notion that no theory is absolutely a transcript of reality, but that any one of them may from some point of view be useful. . . . Thus human arbitrariness has driven divine necessity from scientific logic.

One of Einstein's scientific papers, we might note here, has for its title: 'On a heuristic point of view concerning the generation and transformation of light' (1905). 'Heuristic' means 'serving to discover', and therefore not to be regarded as final. In the light of such general movements of thought many of the dramatists of the period can be seen as bringing over-definite mental processes to bear upon material too indeterminate for rigid solutions. What they put forward as artistic 'transcripts of reality' are in many cases quite unacceptable.

    ·   ·   ·   ·   ·   ·

In 1891, for example, H. A. Jones published a play first staged in 1884, *Saints and Sinners*, with a preface. He begins by saying that the passing of the American copyright act would encourage dramatists to print their plays since they no longer had to fear the loss of American stage profits, which in turn would encourage dramas of a more literary type. He himself had done well in the past out of stage melodrama. He was therefore in a position to please himself—now that 'the intellectual ferment of the age' had reached the theatre—by writing this play of a higher type, a play based on life rather than on theatrical conventions. Considering what follows, this preamble was about as unfortunate as the letter to himself he quotes from in the preface. The letter was from Matthew Arnold, who wrote that by plays like *Saints and Sinners* 'faith in the middle-class fetish' would be weakened and that 'its representative middle-class man (Hoggard) was well drawn.' Hoggard is pure caricature: a hypocritical chapel deacon. How anyone could for a moment imagine that dialogue like the following was either representative of real life or well drawn is almost beyond belief:

> *Prabble* I find the members of the congregation are going to the Stores, and I've asked Mr. Fletcher [the Minister] more than once to preach against them. I'm a grocer, and I've got eleven children, and how can I pay my rates and taxes and bring up my family if the Stores are allowed to undersell me, eh? I ask you that as a member of the great tax-paying middle classes.
>
> *Hoggard* Very true, Prabble. The middle classes are the great backbone of this country. It's such men as you and I, Prabble, that are the source of England's greatness. We have made England what she is today.   (Act III.)

Even if one admits that drama demands bolder, plainer strokes than almost any other form of art, only prejudice could find such a situation and dialogue at all credible.

It is not surprising to find that Jones has added to this material a conventional plot of seduction and betrayal, placing his contemporary economic villains beside familiar upper-class rogues like Captain Eustace Fanshawe:

> When a man has been as badly used by womankind as I have been, damn it all! he owes it to his own sense of justice to be revenged on womankind as often as he can. (*Chuckling*) I don't think I shall get to be much *worse* than I am! (Act II.)

The chuckle is rather winning—but only if he stays in an out-and-out melodrama. Jones's attempts to write a play that was more than mere entertainment is an artistic failure, yet it is at the same time a symptom of the determination of dramatists of the time to achieve social relevance. It was in this period that Ibsen's work began to exercise its powerful influence, particularly his 'realistic' social plays. And these plays sprang from disillusionment with the course of history in his time, according to one of Ibsen's admirers in England, Edmund Gosse. In an 1889 article, reprinted in his *Northern Studies* (1890), Gosse repeats for us a good many of the contentions outlined in the last chapter:

> During the Franco-German war [of 1870], it would seem that his sentiment with regard to life and history underwent a

1 Walter Crane: book cover

2 G. Doré: *A Street in London*

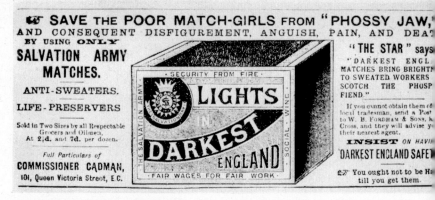

3 Salvation Army advertisement

A NOBLE PEASANT WOMAN
TO WHOSE CHERISHED MEMORY THIS BOOK IS INSCRIBED BY THE
YOUNGEST AND LAST SURVIVOR OF HER MANY CHILDREN

4 From Jesse Collings: *Land Reform, etc.*

5 W. Strong: *Richard Jefferies*

William Morris: design for the 'Avon' chintz

7   From *Punch*, 20 November 1879

"IMPERIUM ET LIBERTAS."

"Nor deal in watchwords overmuch."—Tennyson.

Albert Moore: *Beads*

9 Robert Gregory: *Coole Lake*

10 J. B. Yeats: *W. B. Yeats,*

1   William Ewart Gladstone

12   Jan Toorop:
Faith Giving Way

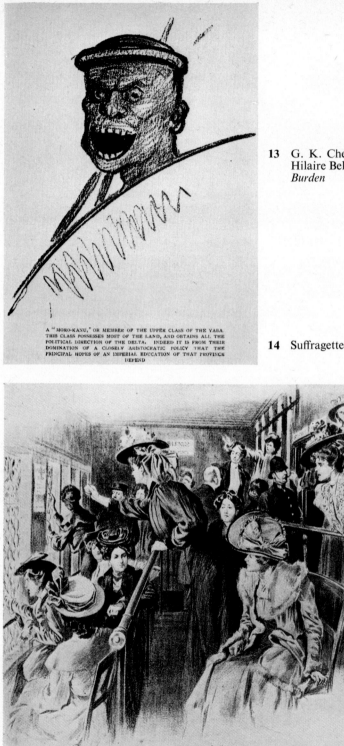

A "MORO-KANU," OR MEMBER OF THE UPPER CLASS OF THE VABA. THIS CLASS POSSESSES MOST OF THE LAND, AND OBTAINS ALL THE POLITICAL DIRECTION OF THE DELTA. INDEED IT IS FROM THEIR DOMINATION OF A CLOSELY ARISTOCRATIC POLICY THAT THE PRINCIPAL HOPES OF AN IMPERIAL EDUCATION OF THAT PROVINCK DEPEND

13 G. K. Chesterton: cartoon Hilaire Belloc's *Emmanuel Burden*

14 Suffragettes in Parliament

15 Max Beerbohm: *Mr. Henry James revisiting America.* Extract from his Un-
spoken Thoughts: ". . . So that in fine, let, without further beating about the bush,
me make to myself amazed acknowledgement that, but for the certificate of birth
which I have – so quite indubitably – on me, I might, in regarding (and, as it
somewhat were, overseeing) *à l'oeil de voyageur* these dear good people, find hard
to swallow, or come to take by subconscious injection, the great idea that I am – oh
ever so indigenously! – one of them . . ."

VOLPONE

16 A. Beardsley: Frontispiece to *Volpone*

A. Beardsley: *Et in Arcadia Ego*, from *The Savoy*

18 A. Beardsley: *Of a Neophyte,* from *The Pall Mall Magazine*

19 A. Beardsley: *Design for the Opening Meeting*, invitation card of the Princes Ladies' Golf Club, Mitcham

HOOD BATTALION,
2nd NAVAL BRIGADE,
BLANDFORD,
DORSET.

(5)
The Soldier.

If I should die, think only this of me:
  That there's some corner of a foreign field
That is for ever England. There shall be
  In that rich earth a richer dust concealed;
A dust whom England bore, shaped, made aware,
  Gave, once, her flowers to love, her ways to roam,
A body of England's, breathing English air,
  Washed by the rivers, blest by suns of home.

And think, this heart, all evil shed away,
  A pulse in the eternal mind, no less
    Gives somewhere back the thoughts by England
                                              given;
Her sights and sounds; dreams happy as her day;
  And laughter, learnt of friends; and gentleness,
    In hearts at peace, under an English heaven.

20 Rupert Brooke: *The Soldier*   *Kings College, Cambridge*

21 First World War poster

MACHINE GUN CORPS
PRISONERS OF WAR FUND

2 Atkinson Grimshaw: *A Moonlight Scene*

23 Pablo Picasso: *Girl with a Mandolin*

4　Juan Gris: *Hommage à Picasso*　　　　　　*Art Institute of Chicago*

25 Kurt Schwitters: *Construction for Noble Ladies*

complete revolution. He woke up to see, or to think he saw, that we were living in the last scene of the last act of a long drama; that all which politics, morals, literature were giving us was but the last and driest crumbs swept up from under the table of eighteenth-century revolution . . . The hope of the immediate future had sunk behind the Seine, and Ibsen turned from watching the horizon to diagnose the symptoms of that mortal moral disease of which, as it appeared to him, Europe was fast advancing towards social death. The hypocrisy of society and the brutality of personal egotism—these were the principal outward signs of that inward but universal malady beneath which he saw the world sinking. It was with no thought of reforming society, with no zeal of the missionary or the philanthropist, that he started on his new series of studies. He would spend the few years left to him before the political agony of Europe in noting down, with an accuracy hitherto unparalleled, the symptoms of her disorder.

Pessimism, the sense that civilisation was on its last legs, the attempt at accuracy of record, severe social criticism—though this is certainly not a total account of Ibsen's drama it echoes much of what has already been said of English novelists and shows very distinctly what Ibsen meant to an English populariser of plays like *The Pillars of Society*, *Ghosts* or *The Wild Duck*.

If Jones could be so inadequate, perhaps Bernard Shaw's plays will supply the need. Author of a book called *The Quintessence of Ibsenism* (1891) and a man who could say that he would always be a 'revolutionary writer, because our laws make law impossible; our liberties destroy all freedom; our property is organized robbery; our morality is an impudent hypocrisy; our wisdom is administered by inexperienced or malexperienced dupes, our power wielded by cowards and weaklings, and our honor false in all its points' ('First Aid to Critics', *Major Barbara*, 1907), Shaw appears to write out of a feeling that society needed radical change—although it is true that the quoted passage comes from a section entitled 'Sane Conclusions', which was designed to qualify his previous indictment of society for driving men with a conscience into anarchist

I

outrages. Some of his plays Shaw actually used to call 'bluebook'. In the Appendix to his first published drama, *Widowers' Houses* (1893), an exposure of slum landlords, he wrote that the official blue-bound reports of social problems were in his play's ancestry rather than the dramatic tradition. (He makes an exception of the line running through dramas like Charles Reade's *It's Never Too Late to Mend*, 1864.) He even stated that *Widowers' Houses* was intended to make people vote on the Progressive side at the next County Council Election in London, but later removed from the play some of the specific propaganda it contained. Nevertheless, when it was published together with *Mrs Warren's Profession* (1894) and *The Philanderer* (1895), the general title he gave the volume was *Plays Unpleasant*. Whatever reservations one has to make about the exact strength of Shaw's revolutionary impulses, in his early plays he undoubtedly took society as his subject, wrote them as propaganda, and set out to shock audiences in order to help bring about change.

Martin Meisel's study, *Shaw and the Nineteenth-Century Theater* (Princeton, 1963), takes us a stage farther when he compares Shaw with a contemporary dramatist, Arthur Wing Pinero. Pinero's *The Second Mrs Tanqueray* (1893) is the tragedy of a 'woman with a past' and therefore in subject-matter is connected with Shaw's *Mrs Warren's Profession* (not performed publicly until 1925 because of censorship). But Mrs Warren, Meisel claims, is the anti-type to all stage courtesans: she is not beautiful and careless but prospering, vulgar and shrewd; she did not regret her lost innocence nor desire above all things else to regain respectability; rather she saw her childhood as the time when she feared being sent to work in the white-lead factory where her sister had died of lead poisoning, and she was perfectly content to continue with her wealthy and expanding business of prostitution. Like Undershaft, the munitions manufacturer in *Major Barbara* (1907), she makes no bones about her way of life, considering the condemnation she receives from society to be a measure of society's hypocrisy. Meisel's final point is that Shaw wished to show in Mrs Warren and her profession 'the cold logic of her economic choice' in society as then constituted. There is no 'feverish sexual glamour, because Mrs Warren represents prostitution as a social and economic phenomenon, rather than prostitution as forbidden fruit, personal temptation and fall.'

While we must admit that Shaw dealt with society in a much more direct way than Pinero, he does not thereby escape the accusation of having schematised real life. Topicality is undoubtedly a main feature of many of his plays. To the examples already given we might add his brilliant updating of Leporello from Mozart's *Don Giovanni*, the chauffeur Henry Straker in *Man and Superman* (1903)—a 'new man' to match the 'new woman' of the play, mechanically minded, practical, prouder of his education at Board School and Polytechnic than if he had ornamented Eton and Oxford, taking more trouble 'to drop his aitches than ever his father did to pick them up'—Shaw was, I think, on to a genuinely new phenomenon of his time and one that has flourished ever since. But in general the artistic development he gave his material produces sparkles to beguile the mind while at the same time they blind us to the consumption of substance. His wit, in fact, can be self-defeating. Consider this meeting from *Man and Superman*, Act III:

> *Mendoza (posing loftily)* I am a brigand: I live by robbing the rich.
> *Tanner (promptly)* I am a gentleman: I live by robbing the poor. Shake hands.

Or this dialogue in *Major Barbara*, Act II, on the subject of the Salvation Army:

> *Undershaft* All religious organizations exist by selling themselves to the rich.
> *Cusins* Not the Army. That is the Church of the poor.
> *Undershaft* All the more reason for buying it.
> *Cusins* I don't think you quite know what the Army does for the poor.
> *Undershaft* Oh yes I do. It draws their teeth: that is enough for me—as a man of business—
> *Cusins* Nonsense! It makes them sober—
> *Undershaft* I prefer sober workmen. The profits are larger.
> *Cusins* —honest—
> *Undershaft* Honest workmen are the most economical.

Cusins —attached to their homes—
Undershaft So much the better: they will put up with anything
  sooner than change their shop.
Cusins —happy—
Undershaft An invaluable safeguard against revolution.
Cusins —unselfish—
Undershaft Indifferent to their own interests, which suits me
  exactly.
Cusins —with their thoughts on heavenly things—
Undershaft (*rising*) And not on Trade Unionism nor Socialism.
  Excellent.

In performance this dialogue rushes along like a stream in spate
and is just as irresistible; there is no surrounding terrain to be dis-
tracting. Sober workmen bring profits for capitalists, very possibly.
Do they also save themselves from blinding headaches the morning
after? This kind of question is ruled out by Shavian pace and
rodomontade in the theatre, though a glance at some of Shaw's
unplayable stage-directions proves that he wrote his plays for
reading as well. And even in performance, perhaps, his habit of
pushing matters to logical extremes can bring diminishing returns.
The clearer his intellectual argument becomes, the less likely we
are to accept it. 'I am not one of those men who keep their morals
and their business in watertight compartments', says Undershaft,
and the moral bullet strikes. 'All the spare money my trade rivals
spend on hospitals, cathedrals and other receptacles for conscience
money, I devote to experiments and researches in improved
methods of destroying life and property', he continues. 'All the
spare money'? We realise that the bullet has passed harmlessly
through and out the other side. Undershaft is beginning to sound
like the naively villainous Ithamore in Marlowe's *Jew of Malta*.
The conventions of drama Shaw exploits so successfully for serious
moral purposes begin to take their revenge.

·   ·   ·   ·   ·   ·

Somerset Maugham's first novel, *Liza of Lambeth* (1897), is not
a major piece of work, nor is it entirely consistent in its accomplish-

ment, but it at least suggests that the novelists of the time were producing more acceptable 'transcripts of reality' than the dramatists. A double influence affected this novel: Maugham's reading of the great French naturalist writers—he mentions Guy de Maupassant in a preface written for a later edition—and first-hand experience as obstetric clerk at St Thomas's Hospital in London—on call day and night for a period of three weeks, during which he attended sixty-three confinements in ill-lit, stuffy rooms up the dark and stinking alleys of Lambeth. Looking back on it all nearly half a century later, after many books of a very different kind, Maugham still thought that the best advice to give to a young writer was to tell him to write only about the things he knew (Preface to *Works*, volume 1, 1951). Apart from an occasional smartness of phrase (children without mud are as 'disconsolate as poets') and some lapses, especially in the conversation between Liza's mother and a nurse at the end of the book, into the kind of writing that draws the label 'rich gallery of English character', Maugham is a careful historian of lower-class life in those days. Dancing to a barrel organ; a Bank Holiday trip to Chingford in a brake crammed with huge baskets of food and cases of beer under the seats, the driver's legs and the vehicle itself; the sheer difficulty (for the poor) of assignations with a married man in winter time; a visit to the performance of a melodrama—Maugham adequately fulfils his purpose of showing middle-class readers how the other half lives, mostly with a kind of cool sympathy. There is none of the intensity given to the same kind of material in *The Nether World*. It is Gissing without the demonology.

The odd thing about *Liza of Lambeth* is that it is focussed on the life of the main character and yet one remembers it as a study of an environment and a society. These imposed a pattern of behaviour upon the heroine; her character and her career stand out but only as more strikingly representative of her class. She is no Tess of the D'Urbervilles. Cockney girls dancing to the barrel organ in the street are gravely dignified; when Liza appears, 'if the others were as stately as queens, she was as stately as an empress.' Her joys and her sorrows are more exuberant versions of those belonging to her fellows. Even her death is not unique:

'I've been very unfortunate of lite,' remarked Mrs. Hodges, as she licked her lips, 'this mikes the second death I've 'ad in the last ten days—women, I mean, of course I don't count bibies.'

Maugham's later contention that he was forced to stick to facts because of 'the miserable poverty' of his imagination is over-modest: there is a wealth of implication as well as a bare record in that not counting babies' deaths. The casual remark suddenly reveals a strange standard of values and we look for a reason in the conditions of life at the time, with the result that Maugham's account of individual lives in Lambeth turns into the study of the lower level of urban society. It is, of course, very limited in scope and not at all subtle, but Shaw's plays are made to seem very abstract in comparison though he too sought to reflect society in representative types.

.   .   .   .   .   .

Moving on into the twentieth century we meet another social-problem dramatist in John Galsworthy. Though he is better known as a novelist, his plays fill a thick volume (1929). Not all of these plays are committed. *Old English* (1924) is in intention a character-piece, a vehicle for the leading actor. It presents the ancient, amoral Chairman of the Island Navigation Company of Liverpool, an 'early Victorian' well able to look after his own interests in the teeth of his creditors. One might learn something of how the affairs of a company were conducted by certain old-fashioned business types, but it is really a play devoted to a 'grand old fightin' gintle-man! The great old sinner he was!' *The Silver Box* (1906) is more germane, designed to demonstrate that even in courts of justice it is safer to be rich than poor. The scapegrace son of a Liberal M.P. gets into a position where he gives evidence against an unemployed drunkard, but the drunkard's attempts to accuse the son of a theft which had in fact instigated his own retaliatory theft are suppressed by the court. Social concern is very strong, but it is a poor play.

Strife (1909) is much better. It is about a factory on strike and the struggle between the union and the board of directors. Between the leaders of the two sides there is no agreement, since both are extremists. The Chairman holds tenaciously to the harsher standards of the past in labour relations:

> It has been said that times have changed; if they have, I have not changed with them. Neither will I. It has been said that masters and men are equal! Cant! There can only be one master in a house! Where two men meet the better man will rule. . . . There is only one way of treating 'men'—with *the iron hand*. This half-and-half business, the half-and-half manners of this generation has brought all this upon us. (Act III.)

He actually goes on to say that if he were in the men's place he would share their views, and in this respect there is a connection made between the two sides. Roberts, the leader of the men, is just as strong, just as unbending, just as contemptuous of his own side for weakness and inclination to temporise. When he is told that the men have no heart for the strike because they feel for the suffering of their wives, his answer is immediate: 'Ah! So they say! They can remember the women when their own bellies speak! The women never stops them from the drink; but from a little suffering to themselves in a sacred cause, the women stop them fast enough.' The play is embedded in an awareness of the course of events and changing times, the altering relationship between capital and labour and the inevitable defeat of intransigents.

Strife is a carefully constructed piece. It has great symmetry of structure, neat cross-cutting between boardroom and poor cottage and the major irony that both Chairman and strike leader, hamstrung by their older attitudes, are in the end betrayed by their own sides for of all things the terms originally drawn up and refused. *Strife* is as strongly organised and as committed as a Shaw play, but it retains more of the feeling of actuality than Shaw's socioeconomic projections. Shaw does, however, provide a more continuously stimulating texture, in that Galsworthy's language here deserves no more than the damning adjective 'adequate'. *The Foundations* (1917) is on this account more attractive. There is a great deal of topical interest in its references to sweated labour in the clothing industry, the possibility of a bomb attack by an anarchist, the behaviour of reporters ['*Press* (*writing furiously*)

"Lady William stood like a statue at bay" '], the relationship between servants and children, or between officers and men, and so on. There is also humour, though as we can see from the following thematic speech about the aristocracy it could hardly be called mordant—prophetic in some ways, of course:

> *Lemmy* Wot I sy is: Dahn wiv the country, dahn wiv everyfing. Begin agyne from the foundytions. [*Nodding his head back at the room*]. But we've got to keep one or two o' these 'ere under glawss, to show our future generytions. An' this one is 'armless. His pipes is sahnd, 'is 'eart is good; 'is 'ead is *not* strong. 'Is 'ouse will myke a charmin' palace o' varieties where our children can come an' see 'ow they did it in the good old dyes. Yer never see sich waxworks as 'is butler and 'is four conscientious khaki footmen.   (Act III.)

Justice: A Tragedy (1910) is another play that is inconclusive beside drama like that of Bernard Shaw; this, however, was a play written in the cause of prison reform. Its staging of the horrors of solitary confinement, then all too common, and the ultimate suicide of a ticket-of-leave prisoner as he was being re-arrested had an extraordinary effect upon the emotions of the audience. It also affected the Home Secretary of the time, Winston Churchill, who wrote to Galsworthy about its influence. Inconclusive it might have been, but it helped persuade others to conclusions of direct practical relevance.

Decent, humanitarian and concerned, but not revolutionary, Galsworthy is really very typical of a certain kind of writer. His plays and early novels may be critical of the religion of property, but it has often been noted that the satire in *The Man of Property* (1906) is sharper than in the later volumes of *The Forsyte Saga*, *In Chancery* (1920) and *To Let* (1921). The change in the characterisation of Soames Forsyte is the index of Galsworthy's more tolerant temper. Dudley Barker also notes the diminution of satire in the other novels he wrote about different sections of society: *The Country House* (1907), in which 'the crass self-importance of the squirearchy' is attacked; *Fraternity* (1909), which shows the futility of London intellectuals in their idealistic attempts at brotherhood with slum-dwellers; and *The Patrician*

(1911), which depicts the aristocrats of the time. Ultimately, he was to admit to Edward Garnett that these works were 'simply the criticism of one half of myself by the other . . . a bit of spiritual examination'. (See D. Barker, *The Man of Principle: A View of John Galsworthy*, New York, 1963, chapter 14.)

．　　．　　．　　．　　．　　．

I do not think that the work of any of the authors so far considered in this chapter could be called deeply satisfying. They tend towards ideological abstraction, or schematisation, or naivety, or sentimentality. They all offer values, and some can get a bulldog grip on the ordinary reader, who is fascinated by the strong fidelity o f their reflection of life as he knows it or can easily believe it to have been at the time. But they are all, even Shaw, the most verbally outrageous of the three, comfortable. We are not disturbed by a vision of life that illuminates more than we ourselves could have imagined possible, nor are we surprised by their technique to any great degree. And here the position of Henry James in English literature is crucial. It is one of the odder facts of literary history that in the period with which we are concerned many of the greatest figures were not English: Conrad was a Pole; Joyce and Yeats were Irish; Eliot, Pound and James were American.[1] It must seem even more strange to mention the name of Henry James in a chapter where most of the works deal with the social problems springing from industrial and urban conditions. His usual subject-matter, international and cultured, does not recall that of Shaw and Galsworthy, any more than his developed prose style brings to mind the modes of propaganda or polemic. The style in particular can be an instrument of incredible flexibility, turning in upon itself, hesitating, circling, plunging abruptly onto a colloquialism that is often startlingly appropriate amongst the cultured tortuosities of its context. Long residence in Europe and prolonged dedication to his art made James into the most cosmopolitan and sophisticated of writers, a point fully brought out in Max Beerbohm's cartoon of him visiting his native land—a cartoon which also includes, delightfully, a parody. (It is reproduced in this book.) In very important respects James was a foreigner in any country; although he settled in England he remained a stranger. One of the Secretaries at the American Embassy in London recorded that he resented a lady making a remark which implied that he was, like herself, a member of the middle class: James, he noted, had no wish to be 'adjudged a place in English society in accordance with English standards' (Leon Edel, *Henry James: the Conquest of London 1870–1883*, 1962, page 324).

James, then, had a most subtle and independent mind, which mainly occupied itself with the delicate probing and assessment of the characters, manners, morals and traditions of several nations, though amongst them all the English are our main concern. And of them he early wrote to a friend, using a turn of phrase we have already come across in connection with George Moore and James Joyce: 'It seems to me many times the strongest and richest race in the world—my dream is to arrive at the ability to be, in some degree, its moral portrait-painter' (Edel, *James*, page 281).[2] The task required dedication. In the preface he wrote for one of his best novels, *The Portrait of a Lady* (1881), he made a number of revealing statements about its genesis and development, which again cause us to think about the differences between a truly creative artist and one who is no more than an observer and judge of life. James recalls in this preface some of the workshop revelations he had heard in Paris from a fellow-author, Ivan Turgenieff, who maintained that first of all he had a 'vision of some person or persons'; afterwards he had to 'find for them the right relations, those that would most bring them out; to imagine, to invent and select and piece together the situations most useful and favourable to the sense of the creatures themselves, the complications they would be most likely to produce and to feel.' James was aware of just this characteristic in himself, a propensity to see the character before the setting or the fable in which the character would act. Yet this creative trick of James's imagination is not, he claims, divorced from his stated desire to be a *moral* portrait-painter, because he found in the fullness of his perceptions a moral quality:

There is, I think, no more nutritive or suggestive truth in this connexion than that of the perfect dependence of the 'moral' sense of a work of art on the amount of felt life concerned in producing it. The question comes back thus, obviously, to the kind and the degree of the artist's prime sensibility, which is the soil out of which his subject springs. The quality and capacity of that soil, its ability to 'grow' with due freshness and straightness any vision of life, represents, strongly or weakly, the projected morality. That element is but another name for the more or less close connexion of the subject with some mark made on the intelligence, with some sincere experience.

The Portrait of a Lady is the creation of a sensibility that by its richness, precision and delicacy enlists us to follow the fate of a young American girl, Isabel Archer. She was generous, aspiring and free, and quite unfettered by Old World presumptions and requirements—as James had insisted he himself was. He saw her as capable of choosing her own destiny and employing the freest of criteria to do so:

> 'But I always want to know the things one shouldn't do.'
> 'So as to do them?' asked her aunt.
> 'So as to choose', said Isabel.   (Chapter 7.)

By her standards, in fact, 'the strongest and richest race in the world' did not come up to scratch: she rejects the proposal of marriage made to her by Lord Warburton, who offered her in many ways a very splendid way of life. But there were deficiencies—his home, for instance:

> Within, it had been a good deal modernised—some of its best points had lost their purity; but as they saw it from the gardens, a stout, grey pile, of the softest, deepest, most weather-fretted hue, rising from a broad, still moat, it affected the young visitor as a castle in a legend. The day was cool and rather lustreless; the first note of autumn had been struck, and the watery sunshine rested on the walls in blurred and desultory gleams, washing them, as it were, in places tenderly chosen, where the ache of antiquity was keenest.   (Chapter 9.)

Ancient, calm, legendary—we recognise the traditional myth of an older England and acknowledge its force, but we are also meant to respond to the loss of purity and the first note of autumn. Early in the novel, in the very first chapter, the background of social and political change is brought up in conversation. Lord Warburton has not been unaffected; he is a radical. Another character, Ralph Touchett, explains this when he says that Warburton

> occupies a position that appeals to my imagination. Great responsibilities, great opportunities, great consideration, great wealth, great power, a natural share in the public affairs of a great country. But he's all in a muddle about himself, his position, his power and indeed about everything in the world. He's the victim of a critical age; he has ceased to believe in himself and he doesn't know what to believe in.   (Chapter 8.)

Touchett's father is even more astringent upon the subject of nobility like Warburton:

> You see they're very luxurious, and these progressive ideas are about their biggest luxury. They make them feel moral and yet don't damage their position.

It was the 'position' which made Isabel Archer reject Warburton's offer of marriage. In his assured status he appeared set and established in a system that would blunt her personal standards and hamper her freedom: 'A certain instinct, not imperious, but persuasive, told her to resist—murmured to her that virtually she had a system and an orbit of her own' (chapter 12). To refuse Lord Warburton was *not* the mistake for which she was to suffer.

Subdued intimations of a rawer, more strenuous existence, on which these subtleties of civilised living and fine gradations of moral choice were no more than the lightest of surface foam, are occasionally voiced in *The Portrait*. *The Princess Casamassima* (1886) intensifies them. Its main character, Hyacinth Robinson, is actually swept into a revolutionary movement. He is shown as committing himself in a far more positive way than Lord Warburton to the forces that were in real life going to change society radically in the next few decades. We wonder what could have been the first germ of this novel, so unusual in the James canon, and discover from its preface that it was the impact of urban living, the myriad impressions made upon James during the first year of his residence in London. He used to walk about the streets of the city and imagine the lives it could have formed. He thought of a character who had been excluded from the rich, powerful and free life he himself had been fortunate enough to be born to. The novel develops this theme of a young man, Hyacinth Robinson, whose first contacts had been with the Gissing world of labour, ignorance and sordid struggle, who felt the torment of living in this world but who also grew to divine very thoroughly what precious things he was cut off from. His subsequent history comes from this sensitive awareness; he turns, despite his charged sense of the beauty of the life he cannot lead, to revolutionary courses and becomes involved in actual plots. But then, James tells us in the preface, 'what was essential with this was that he should have a social—not less than a socialist— connection, find a door somehow open to him into the appeased and civilised state, into that warmer glow of things he is precisely to help to undermine.' Hence the relationship with Princess Casamassima. But here we must pause and take stock. First, the general historical pressure that caused James of all people to feel the 'nearness (to all our apparently ordered life) of some sinister anarchic underworld, heaving in its pain, its power and its hate; a presentation not of sharp particulars, but of loose appearances, vague motions and sounds and symptoms, just perceptible pres- ences and general looming possibilities', is remarkable in itself. (An even more unexpected literary reflection of anarchism, perhaps, is an immature play of 1880 by Oscar Wilde, *Vera, or the Nihilists*. This is, however, set in Russia.) But second, the way in which James's artistic imagination develops the original *donnée* brings home how much it is an individual's heightened consciousness that is important and an individual's choice that matters. And if accused of vagueness he had a defence that it was true to his own most genuine (and representative) experience:

Shouldn't I find it in the happy contention that the value I wished most to render and the effect I wished most to produce were precisely those of our not knowing, of society's not knowing, but only guessing and suspecting and trying to ignore

what 'goes on' irreconcilably, subversively, beneath the vast
smug surface? I couldn't deal with that positive quantity for
itself—my subject had another too exacting side; but I might
perhaps show the social ear as on occasion applied to the
ground, or catch some gust of the hot breath that I had at
many an hour seemed to see escape and hover.

It is, then, a novel that deliberately avoids confronting anarchism,
but which does display the ominous stability of Victorian middle-
class ease and comfort and its position on a great base of raw
poverty and unrest.

Apart from this it is difficult to know how far in this novel
James was an observer of life and how much he was a reader of
literature, Dickens in particular. One can believe he himself had
seen small children, unwashed and unchidden, spending 'most of
their time either pushing each other into the gutter or in running to
the public house at the corner for a pennyworth of gin'; one can
credit that, in chapter 5, the description of Hyacinth's excursion in
the streets of London at night-time in the autumn repeats and
gathers up James's own excursions, when 'big clumsy torches
flared and smoked over hand-carts and costermongers' barrows
drawn up in the gutter.' But the following brief passage almost
seems a paradigm of the way in which the robust spirit of Charles
Dickens could take hold of Henry James and inspire an unsubtle
and therefore anomalous energy of narrative:

> 'Now *ain't* he shrinking and sensitive?' demanded Miss
> Pynsent, who had pounced upon him and, holding him an
> instant at arm's length, appealed eagerly to her visitor. 'Ain't
> he delicate and high-bred, and wouldn't he be thrown into a
> state?' Delicate as he might be, the little dressmaker shook him
> smartly for his naughtiness in being out of the way when he
> was wanted, and brought him to the big square-faced, deep-
> voiced lady who took up, as it were, all that side of the room.

Actually, the humour and the child's-eye view of the young
Hyacinth here seem derived from Dickens; the delicacy that made
the grown-up Hyacinth first espouse and then reject the revolu-

tionary cause belongs to James. This novel is remarkable in that it so interestingly reflects the social concerns of the time, but it cannot for one moment be pretended that James either places them in the centre of the picture or gives them moral precedence. Like his hero, he 'saw the immeasurable misery of the people, and yet he saw all that had been, as it were, rescued and redeemed from it: the treasures, the felicities, the splendours, the successes of the world' (chapter 35). James's main subject as a writer was civilisation—the duty to be 'finely aware and richly responsible'—and the tragedy of his own life was that he never found its full, free manifestation anywhere, not even in England.

.   .   .   .   .   .

'In story after story', writes F. R. Leavis in *The Great Tradition* (1948), 'James, with the exasperation of an intellectual writer, expresses his disdainful sense of the utter unintellectuality of the country-house class. He always knew that he hadn't really found the ideal civilization he looked for . . .' In a later chapter Leavis brings up the case of Lord Lambeth, a character in the story called *An International Episode* (1879), who in himself was 'a symbol that there would be no poets or philosophers' wherever he appeared! Vapidity, then, is one of James's accusations against the English upper class. Cupidity is another. In the story called *The Spoils of Poynton* (1897) he portrays the Brigstock family, upper-class vulgarians; they were people who smothered their home with 'trumpery ornament and scrapbook art, with strange excrescences and bunchy draperies, with gimcracks that might have been keepsakes for maid-servants and nondescript conveniences that might have been prizes for the blind'. Taste is here used as a moral index, but not in a simple way. The house of the Brigstocks is indeed the opposite of Poynton, which was a gem created by Mrs Gereth and her husband in twenty-six years of planning and seeking the right contents for an exquisite Jacobean house. Nevertheless, when those contents are taken away from Poynton by a widowed Mrs Gereth into another, smaller house to 'save' them from the Brigstock daughter her son was going to marry, they become spoils. Beautiful in themselves, wonderfully arranged in their new home, they 'seemed to suffer like chopped limbs'. The image is graphic. For all her aesthetic taste Mrs Gereth was a barbarian in matters of conduct and had, as James writes, a 'strange, almost maniacal disposition to thrust in everywhere the question of "things", to read all behaviour in the light of some fancied relation to them'. The tide of Edwardian materialism and vulgarity was soon to come in and would be bewailed by James in his private life and letters even more explicitly.

In the preface to *The Spoils of Poynton* James writes memorably: 'Life being all inclusion and confusion, and art being all discrimination and selection, the latter, in search of the hard latent *value* with which alone it is concerned, sniffs round the mass as instinctively and unerringly as a dog suspicious of some buried bone.' Mrs Gereth, too, compared with the Brigstocks, was all discrimination and selection, but she was not in the least concerned with matters of value—only things. There is some kind of analogy, perhaps, between the art of living and the art of writing, and increasingly James found frustration in the England of his day. In life he withdrew more and more from Society. In art, John Holloway has stressed, 'the plutocracy of his time is studied from the point of view of the writer: over and over again James reveals his conviction, sometimes with bitterness, that the social world of his time at bottom had little to offer the artist save a velvet-gloved exploitation and the kind of hollow applause which destroyed his real life and real work' ('The Literary Scene', in *The Modern Age*, ed. Boris Ford, 1961). This critique of society was made by a man of high intelligence and aspiration, able to judge by reference to international standards; but inevitably over a limited area. It has even been suggested that he did not really meet the most truly civilised members of the society in which he moved. The historical evidence registered on a fine and sensitive plate, but the luminous moral intelligence that shaped it for us was working on a partial record. This does not prevent us from appreciating the inner values of his writing. As we noted with William Morris, the ideals survive. And even for those who miss or do not care to come to terms with the major artistry that shaped entire works, bright chips of wisdom lie scattered throughout: 'a man to whom one could say anything in the world provided one didn't think it of more importance to be sympathised with than to be understood' (chapter 14), for instance, is a description to make us pause and think when reading *The Princess Casamassima*, while 'I never really have believed in the existence of friendship in big societies—in great towns and great crowds' (chapter 2) is an exclamation from a character in *The Awkward Age* (1899) that loses none of its truth as the twentieth century grinds on.

.   .   .   .   .   .

James's high concern for the novel as a work of art was definitely not shared by his contemporary, H. G. Wells. Their conflict, a classic one, has been documented by L. Edel and G. N. Ray in *Henry James and H. G. Wells* (Urbana, 1958). Remembering James's 'art is all exclusion and selection', we can realise the difference expressed in the following passage from H. G. Wells's *Boon* (1915): 'But if the novel is to follow life it must be various and discursive. Life is diversity and entertainment, not completeness and satisfaction. All actions are half-hearted, shot delightfully with wandering thoughts—about something else. All true stories are a felt of irrelevances. But James sets out to make his novels with the presupposition that they can be made continuously relevant.' Along with this criticism Wells maintains that James omitted opinions and strong feelings and prejudices in favour of fully thought-out individualities, whereas he himself was quite prepared to make use of rather sketchy scenes and individuals in order that the novel should become 'a help to conduct'. It should help ordinary people adjust to their environment and to each other in real life.

There were other, more wounding criticisms of James in *Boon*:

It is leviathan retrieving pebbles. It is a magnificent but painful hippopotamus resolved at any cost, even at the cost of its dignity, upon picking up a pea which has got into a corner of its den. Most things, it insists, are beyond it, but it can, at any rate, modestly, and with an artistic singleness of mind, pick up that pea . . .

To this attack James replied with massive self-possession. The novel was not, and never could be, a kind of bag into which one

K

just stuffed life. Literature, he wrote, 'is admirable exactly by its range and variety, its plasticity and liberality, its fairly living on the sincere and shifting experience of the individual practitioner'; literature exists for 'extension of life'; it is 'art that *makes* life, makes interest, makes importance, for our consideration and application of these things, and I know of no substitute whatever for the force and beauty of its process.' The conflict between the two men is irreconcileable, at least when pushed to these extremes. Sometimes Wells on James sounds like Chesterton on W. H. Gilbert: 'The typical satire of this period remained what Gilbert himself loved to preserve it, an airy, artistic, detached and almost dehumanised thing; not unallied to the contemporary cult of art for art's sake.' (This is taken from Chesterton's contribution to *The Eighteen-Eighties*, edited by W. De la Mare, Cambridge, 1930.) Literature is just a means to a larger end; literature contains its end and therefore demands the most devoted service of its means—the division between Wells and James is very patent. It is also of special relevance for us, for on the one hand we find writing of exceptional topicality and obvious connection with the facts of real life in its time, and on the other we meet writing that establishes values as it communicates the total sense of life of its creator, an exceptional being in his time.

Wells, it is true, was deeply stirred by ideas and values. Given that his novels were always likely to be flawed—not unified, economical works of art—there is much in them which is valid criticism of life and idealist in intent. There is nothing of a search for values; they are, so to speak, injected, but they are none the less there. James referred to 'the particular rich receptacle of intelligences and impressions emptied out with an energy of its own, that your genius constitutes.' We might go further and say that Wells provides an analysis of whole areas of society with a kind of fervent authenticity and raw passion that we miss in James, however poorly the many intelligences and impressions have been fused into a whole. He wrote a number of novels out of his own experience, giving us both social and intellectual history as it impinged upon a man with the talents to view and assess the course of his own life. In *Love and Mr. Lewisham* (1900), we are mostly in the realm of pure experience: the progression of a young and ambitious assistant master at a Sussex Proprietary School (wages £40 a year), who wins a place at the Normal School of Science (now Imperial College) in Kensington and a guinea a week to live on from the State—'there being an inadequate supply of qualified Science teachers in England.' Socialism, an improvident marriage, the sordid round of lodgings and later, scholastic agencies, the activities of a fake medium and forger are all described in some detail, but there is little theme other than the inevitable abandonment of grandiose intellectual plans for the future. Later novels take a much wider view.

Kipps (1905) is the story of a draper's apprentice who inherited a fortune. It is a rather obviously structured piece of writing. His fortune encourages him to try to escape from his class, only to discover that he has left happiness, true affection and genuine living behind him; the contrast in the behaviour demanded of him by his two fiancées, one a lady and the other a maidservant, brings this out in a variety of ways. Wells himself is quite prepared to intrude with a lecture, or to deliver one through the mouth of a character:

All the way up and all the way down the scale there's the same discontent. No one is quite sure where they stand, and everyone's fretting. The herd's uneasy and feverish. All the old tradition goes or has gone, and there's none to make a new tradition. Where are your nobles now? Where are your gentlemen? They vanished directly the peasant found out he wasn't happy and ceased to be a peasant. There's big men and little men mixed up together, and that's all. None of us know where we are. Your cads in a bank holiday train, and your cads on a two-thousand-pound motor, except for a difference in scale there's not a pin to choose between them.

(Book 2, chapter 7. iv.)

It is remarkable how this passage summarises so much of what we have been looking at in authors from Hardy to James, but if we look at the whole series of speeches from which it comes we will then see how Wells has given them a more analytical or sociological turn of his own: 'Man is a social animal with a mind nowadays that goes round the globe, and a community cannot be happy in one part and unhappy in another. . . . The fact is, Society is one body, and it is either well or ill.' This is the stage before McLuhan's 'electronic village', I suppose.

An even more elaborate and broader analysis of society is found in *Tono-Bungay* (1909). It begins by presenting a presumed Victorian order and stability, taking a great country house, Bladesover, as a symbol. It is the aristocratic centre of its own system and is seen by those who live in it as corresponding to all the other social centres which go to make up England. But scepticism and other destructive forces had already begun their insidious work. There comes the substitution of plutocracy ('It is nonsense to pretend that finance makes any better aristocrats than rent') and, more important by far, the impact of all that is represented by the astounding Uncle Ponderevo:

> 'Lord! there's no end of things—no end of *little* things. Dill-water—all the suff'ring babes yowling for it. Eucalyptus again —cascara—witch hazel—menthol—all the toothache things. Then there's antiseptics, and curare, cocaine . . .'
> 'Rather a nuisance to the doctors,' I reflected.
> 'They got to look out for themselves. By Jove, yes. They'll do you if they can, and you do them. Like brigands. That makes it romantic. That's the Romance of Commerce, George. You're in the mountains there! Think of having all the quinine in the world, and some millionaire's pampud wife gone ill with malaria, eh? That's a squeeze, George, eh? Eh? Millionaire on his motor-car outside, offering you any price you liked. That 'ud wake up Wimblehurst . . . Lord! You haven't an Idea down here. Not an idea. Zzzz.' (Book 1, chapter 3. i.)

Blindly irresponsible, dubiously ethical, socially reprehensible; creative, energetic, enterprising: Ponderevo with his patent medicines and his business amalgamations stands for Wells's idea of the new men of commerce in his time. 'By all modern standards the business was, as my uncle would say, "absolutely bona fide".

We sold our stuff and got the money, and spent the money honestly in lies and clamour to sell more stuff.' So speaks Ponderevo's nephew George in the novel, but though Wells was writing fiction it has a very strong connection with such historical phenomena as the late-Victorian tendency to form trusts and combines, thus establishing monopolies in various products, or the sea-change in the character of journalism pioneered by Alfred Harmsworth, later Lord Northcliffe. (He began his halfpenny *Daily Mail* in 1896, which soon reached a sale of half a million and became very attractive to advertisers in consequence.) The last chapter of *Tono-Bungay* expounds Wells's contemptuous vision of his time: a 'spectacle of forces running to waste, of people who use and do not replace, the story of a country hectic with a wasting, aimless fever of trade and money making and pleasure-seeking'; the 'incurable tradition of commercialised Bladesovery, of meretricious gentry and nobility sold for riches'—all reflected in 'a story of activity and urgency and sterility'.

The trouble is that Wells's own words about the content of *Tono-Bungay* are just as true of its form. As literature it is loose and repetitive, and it compares very badly with the simpler novel he published in the following year, *The History of Mr Polly* (1910). This gains by concentrating on the life of a single individual. Its attitudes are warmer and more sympathetic; there is more of an attempt to feel into the life of one of the less fortunate members of society, a small shopkeeper and disappointed husband, who eventually manages to escape from all that had been constricting his genuine originality. The censorious generalisations and lectures are much rarer; in fact a severe critic might diagnose sentimentality and wish-fulfilment. But it is not easy to imagine such ingratitude. After encountering this great stream of comic energy, scene after scene of high farce, characters sketched with bold and lavish absurdity, and such exuberantly mimetic speech ('D'bloved we gath'd gether sighto' Gard 'n face this con'gation join gather Man Woom Ho Mat-mony whichis on'bl state stooted by Gard in times mans in'cency . . .'), to carp seems as ill-advised as it was to entangle the ferociously active Uncle Jim in a best tablecloth. The book will escape as easily as Uncle Jim did. It is surely more 'strategious' to sit back and enjoy one of the most straightforwardly entertaining works written in the period.

Another book of this type is Arnold Bennett's *The Card* (1911). Its main character, Edward Henry Machin, known as Denry, is as amusing as Mr Polly but for quite opposite reasons. He has never been at the mercy of life since his schooldays and always manages to fall on his feet whatever the odds against him. He bests all opponents and controls his environment by a combination of an eye to the main chance, the kind of original actions that take people's fancy and plain luck. The episodes follow each other as an unbroken success story: the poor son of a widowed washerwoman in the Potteries town of Bursley (Burslem) ends as its mayor. In *The Card*, however, the Midlands environment is only sketched in. In other works it is drawn with immense solidity and richness, showing to what an extent *The Card* is a kind of holiday from Bennett's main concerns. The choice of his own native region as setting for the early novels means that he can be immensely knowing about it, not in a deeply probing manner but in innumerable central, commonplace and average ways. By sheer application to every detail of existence and a total sense of how the middle class lived in the towns of Staffordshire, Bennett fully recreates a portion of the English industrial past for readers today. In *Anna of the Five Towns* (1902) we are steeped in the constricted life of the daughter of a miser, surly and uncompromising, the very antithesis of a card. (Denry was capable of acts of wild generosity.) There is a real insight into Anna's predicament, an heiress when she came of age ('Total face value . . . forty-eight thousand and fifty pounds, producing a net annual income of three thousand two hundred and ninety pounds or thereabouts'), but not allowed to control her own affairs, even to the spending of a few pounds. Her situation is underlined by giving her contacts with another family who use money rather than hoard it, especially the spoilt daughter, and by making Anna, through her father's demands, drive a debtor to suicide. One might object that none of this is very subtle and complain that Bennett is always telling us about the values involved, but what he has to tell of the narrowness of provincial society is often worth reading and certainly of great documentary value.[3]

The Old Wives' Tale (1908) and *Clayhanger* (1910) are two more remarkable novels set mainly in the Potteries. *Clayhanger* especially provides a good example of the connection between literature and history, in that he prepared himself for the creation of old Darius Clayhanger by reading in histories of Staffordshire during the 1840's. In this way Bennett was able to proclaim his idea of the absolutely formative effect a terrible childhood could have upon a grown man: successful as Darius was with his printing works, he saw his whole career as a miracle of escape from the rope's end and destitution. Dudley Barker points out that Bennett was writing this section of his book in Brighton during the tumult of the January 1910 General Election and, while he was bringing out the horrors of child labour in the past, was haunted by the feeling that the comforts and luxuries of Tory Brighton were 'founded on a vast injustice to the artisan-class.' It is not only the description of Darius's childhood that has been influenced by contemporary political history. The Radicalism of Edwin Clayhanger, Darius's son, and such lesser matters as Mrs Hamp's foolish conviction that Parnell's fall and death (in 1891) are the result of 'the inherent viciousness' of Gladstone's Home Rule for Ireland campaign (Book IV, chapter 1), reflect the same pressures. All this, however, is subsidiary to Bennett's protracted presentation of a father-son conflict, the attempt of Edwin to resist his father's powerful drive to dominate his entire life. The social and political events Bennett refers to are aids to sharpen the intensely domestic drama, which is the classic tension found in works like Samuel Butler's *The Way of All Flesh* (1903) and Edmund Gosse's *Father and Son* (1907). Gosse's opening words stress that his book is 'the record of a struggle between two temperaments, two consciences and almost two epochs' and it is in this respect that *Clayhanger* succeeds most interestingly. Darius's death and the news of a Tory election success in Bursley against a Labour candidate come in the same chapter, entitled 'The Chain Broken'. Edwin's reaction is significant:

It was in his resentment, in the hard setting of his teeth as he confirmed himself in the rightness of his own opinions, that he first began to realise an individual freedom. 'I don't care if we're beaten forty times,' his thoughts ran. 'I'll be a more out-and-out Radical than ever! I don't care, and I don't care! And he felt sturdily that he was free.

The individual becomes his own measure of value. The twentieth century is round the corner.

.   .   .   .   .   .

Verloc, a character in Conrad's novel *The Secret Agent* (1907), carries this to an extreme; his egotism is positively sublime. From the early pages of the book where we learn that he was accustomed to breakfast in bed and remain 'wallowing there with an air of quiet enjoyment till noon every day', and that although he was a police informer, double agent and dealer in pornography, the instincts of conventional respectability in him were 'only overcome by his dislike of all kinds of recognised labour', we are caught up by the sustained critical irony of Conrad's treatment. We discover that Verloc's wife had married him in the hope of obtaining a home for her half-witted brother, that the greatest desire of her life was to bring her husband and brother together almost as father and son; that instead Verloc, by using the boy to carry a bomb for an anarchist outrage, brings about his death. Verloc then fails to realise that his wife could have deep feelings for anybody but himself and the danger he had been in: 'Upon this matter, his ethical notions being in agreement with his vanity, he was completely incorrigible.' More than this, he does not know that his wife is in possession of the true facts of the case, which brings us to the final dramatic scene between Verloc and his wife, 'one of the most astonishing triumphs of genius in fiction' in the opinion of F. R. Leavis. When 'the note of wooing' finally causes his wife to plunge a carving knife into his corpulent body, the scene achieves its blackly comic climax.

It must be already evident that Conrad has written the first of a line of books dealing with the underworld of spying and intrigue, thrills and murder. His work, however, also emphasises the connection of this world with the one above it; in society there is almost a symbiotic connection between the two levels, a strange and disturbing relationship between criminals and respectable people. Conrad is very explicit about this when describing Chief Inspector Heat:

> Thieving was not a sheer absurdity. It was a form of human industry, perverse indeed, but still an industry exercised in an industrious world; it was work undertaken for the same reason as the work in potteries, in coal mines, in fields, in tool-grinding shops. It was labour, whose practical difference from the other forms of labour consisted in the nature of its risk, which did not lie in ankylosis, or lead-poisoning, or fire-damp, or gritty dust, but in what may be briefly defined in its own special phraseology as 'Seven years hard'. Chief Inspector Heat was, of course, not insensible to the gravity of moral differences. But neither were the thieves he had been looking after. They submitted to the severe sanctions of a morality familiar to Chief Inspector Heat with a certain resignation. They were his fellow-citizens gone wrong because of imperfect education, Chief Inspector Heat believed; but allowing for that difference, he could understand the mind of a burglar, because, as a matter of fact, the mind and the instincts of a burglar are of the same kind as the mind and the instincts of a police officer.
>
> (Chapter 5.)

Chief Inspector Heat, whose actions are shown to spring largely from expediency (he is quite prepared to *get up* evidence), and the deplorable Verloc are not alone as targets of Conrad's sardonic irony. *The Secret Agent* is a complex attack upon the clear-cut, comforting assumptions of people at all levels in society, especially those who are convinced of their own moral superiority—humanitarians, politicians and the like. In the above passage, however, we notice how the working of Conrad's imagination led him to associate prison sentences with occupational hazards in industrial society. Elsewhere in the novel he states that Verloc had the appearance of 'a well-to-do mechanic in business for himself' and something more:

> the air of moral nihilism common to keepers of gambling hells and disorderly houses; to private detectives and inquiry agents;

to drink sellers and, I should say, to the sellers of invigorating
electric belts and to the inventors of patent medicines. But of
that last I am not sure, not having carried my investigations so
far into the depths.   (Chapter 2.)

The Socialist H. G. Wells was to perform that last task for the
radical conservative. Yet in this novel, which deals with such
crudely melodramatic material, Conrad has carried his investigations far into mass society and revealed a torpor of morality in
almost every segment of it.

Little wonder, then, that in the world of *The Secret Agent*
London's familiar presence should become alien and seem to
exhibit an unnatural power over its inhabitants:

And Mr Verloc, steady like a rock—a soft kind of rock—
marched now along a street which could with every propriety
be described as private. In its breadth, emptiness and extent it
had the majesty of inorganic nature, of matter that never dies.
The only reminder of mortality was a doctor's brougham
arrested in august solitude close to the curbstone. The polished
knockers of the doors gleamed as far as the eye could reach,
the clean windows shone with a dark opaque lustre. And all
was still. But a milk cart rattled noisily across the distant
perspective; a butcher boy, driving with the noble recklessness
of a charioteer at Olympic Games, dashed round the corner
sitting high above a pair of red wheels. A guilty-looking cat
issuing from under the stones ran for a while in front of Mr
Verloc, then dived into another basement; and a thick police
constable, looking a stranger to every emotion, as if he, too,
were part of inorganic nature, surging apparently out of a
lamp-post, took not the slightest notice of Mr Verloc. With a
turn to the left Mr Verloc pursued his way along a narrow
street by the side of a yellow wall which, for some inscrutable
reason, had No.1 Chesham Square written on it in black
letters. Chesham Square was at least sixty yards away, and
Mr Verloc, cosmopolitan enough not to be deceived by
London's topographical mysteries, held on steadily, without a
sign of surprise or indignation.   (Chapter 2.)

The rationality of the last sentence preserves the naturalistic surface of the description, but to see Mr Verloc as 'a soft kind of rock' is wierdly evocative—a grotesque parody of Wordsworth's first vision of the Leech Gatherer. Critics who adopt an archetypal approach to literature might well remark on the general similarity of Conrad's inorganic image to that of the Gorgon myth and, later in the novel, might comment on the labyrinthine mysteries of the streets of London. They are like a 'slimy aquarium', 'an immensity of greasy slime and damp plaster interspersed with lamps, and enveloped, oppressed, penetrated, choked and suffocated by the blackness of a wet London night'; they are where a

> van and horses, merged into one mass, seemed something alive —a square-backed black monster blocking half the street, with sudden iron-shod stampings, fierce jingles and heavy, blowing sighs. The harshly festive, ill-omened glare of a large and prosperous public-house faced the other end of Brett Street across a wide road. This barrier of blazing lights, opposing the shadows gathered about the humble abode of Mr Verloc's domestic happiness, seemed to drive the obscurity of the street back upon itself, make it more sullen, brooding, and sinister.
>
> (Chapter 7.)

Plain sarcasm is again evident in the phrase 'humble abode of Mr Verloc's domestic happiness', but at the same time the poetic intensity that invests the ordinary appearances of urban life with inhuman and macabre qualities is constantly reinforcing the more realistic presentation of moral issues. The book's metal, so to speak, is heated to a baleful glow. This constant resonance and suggestiveness of Conrad's symbolic writing is beyond the capability of writers like Bennett and Galsworthy, just as the range, subtlety and complexity of his analysis of social evils surpasses their achievement.

In most ways, however, we could not claim that *The Secret Agent*, great as it is, embodies a *search* for values. It is, of course, infinitely removed from the simple-minded scheme of a work like *Saints and Sinners* and the very depth of the analysis means that it breaks into the moral complacency and obtuseness of many a reader. The most sympathetic character in the novel, the Assistant Commissioner, is not immune from criticism—and he is to some extent a self-portrait of Conrad. Its uncompromising attacking irony does not spare either the individual or the collection of strangely related types who made up contemporary society for Joseph Conrad. In an essay he published in 1905, 'Autocracy and War' (in *Notes on Life and Letters*), he demonstrates that this same penetration and power could also be applied on an international level:

> The idea of ceasing to grow in territory, in strength, in wealth, in influence—in anything but wisdom and self-knowledge is odious to them [States] as the omen of the end. Action, in which is to be found the illusion of a mastered destiny, can alone satisfy our uneasy vanity and lay to rest the haunting fear of the future—a sentiment concealed, indeed, but proving its existence by the force it has, when invoked, to stir the passions of a nation.

It is to this aspect of our subject that we must now turn our attention.

NOTES

[1] Eliot and James became British citizens and lived in England.

[2] In 1864 Edmond and Jules de Goncourt wrote of the Novel beginning to be the History of contemporary morals, through its analysis and psychological research (Preface, *Germinie Lacerteux*).

[3] Lawrence, however, complained with some justice that it was not truly tragic: 'I hate Bennett's resignation. Tragedy ought really to be a great kick at misery. But *Anna of the Five Towns* seems like an acceptance . . .' (*The Collected Letters of D. H. Lawrence*, ed. H. T. Moore, 1962, page 150).

6 : The Imperial Theme

An idea can be a powerful historical fact. The last years of the nineteenth century saw an immense expansion of British power overseas; often against the real desires of the statesmen concerned, territory after territory was occupied till at length the point was reached when mere contemplation of its vast unity could inspire a kind of ecstasy. Alan Sandison, whose book *The Wheel of Empire: a Study of the Imperial Idea in Some Late Nineteenth and Early Twentieth-Century Fiction* (1967) is clearly relevant to the concerns of this chapter, quotes a highly enthusiastic passage from a rectorial address made by Lord Rosebery at Glasgow University in 1910:

> How marvellous it all is! Built not by saints and angels but the work of men's hands; cemented with men's honest blood and with a world of tears, welded by the best brains of centuries past; not without the taint and reproach incidental to all human work, but constructed on the whole with pure and splendid purpose. Human and yet not wholly human, for the most heedless and the most cynical must see the finger of the Divine. Growing as the trees grow, while others slept; fed by the faults of others; reaching with the ripple of a resistless tide over tracts and islands and continents, until our little Britain woke up to find herself the foster-mother of nations and the source of united empires. Do we not hail in this less the energy and fortune of a race than the supreme direction of the Almighty?

There is much to notice in this passage: the religious sense of Divine destiny, the racial pride, the humble sense of human imperfection (though 'the faults of others' seem more serious in their outcome) and the belief in the strength of the 'resistless tide' (which yet only ripples gently in practice!) The whole passage, written by a man who had been Liberal Foreign Secretary for two years before taking over the Premiership from Gladstone, is a testimony to the complex strength of an idea that had become for many a major component of their moral life, a precious heritage to be guarded, defended and passed on to the best of the country's youth. One of the most succinct illustrations of this I have noticed is the publisher's advertisement of Sir Henry Newbolt's *Clifton Chapel and Other School Poems* (1908):

> The whole collection deals with English School life, mainly in its Imperial aspect; it is published by special request for the use of Clifton College, and will, it is hoped, commend itself to members of other Public Schools.

Two stanzas of the title-poem, an exhortation addressed to a school-boy in the chapel of the school, may be aptly set beside Lord Rosebery's speech to demonstrate the pattern of ideals set before the future rulers of the British Empire:

> To set the cause above renown,
> To love the game beyond the prize,
> To honour, while you strike him down,
> The foe that comes with fearless eyes;
> To count the life of battle good,
> And dear the land that gave you birth,
> And dearer yet the brotherhood
> That binds the brave of all the earth—
>
> My son, the oath is yours: the end
> Is His, Who built the world of strife,
> Who gave His children Pain for friend,
> And Death for surest hope of life.
> Today and here the fight's begun,
> Of the great fellowship you're free;
> Henceforth the School and you are one,
> And what You are, the race shall be.

There is a large directness about these lines; the rhythm, too, is appropriately open and flowing in the first stanza, then brought to a definite, firmly resolute movement in the next one. The last line, 'And what You are, the race shall be', is an epigram of the kind that remains in the mind, effective both in itself and as a culmination of the previous lines. Once again, any criticism has to go beyond more narrowly technical considerations: in terms of simple expression this is a successful poem and probably inspired the audience it was written for. But, despite its rhetorical amplitude, is it not resting upon narrow foundations? Important as Clifton and similar schools were in their day, 'the race' and its nature is determined by many more factors than they could control. Newbolt was writing for 'a fellowship', one which cannot really be thought to include the much larger group of which it was only a part.

Not that all his poems are open to this criticism. 'Drake's Drum', from the collection entitled *Admirals All, and Other Verses* (1897), has long been an anthology piece and, in its musical setting, a great standby for male soloists. Narrative, open drama ('Capten, art tha sleepin' there below?'), sentiment and the evocation of a people's historical continuity are a potent recipe for popularity, giving this particular poem more claim to stand as a witness of the culture in which it was born. Its continuing popularity until very recent years is a sign how such literature helps preserve certain characteristics of society and transmit them to future generations. Another anthology piece by Newbolt from the same volume, 'He Fell Among Thieves', achieves a quaintly attractive juxtaposition of a scene from the far-flung empire with a picture of the cosy English countryside:

> He did not hear the monotonous roar that fills
>   The ravine where the Yassin river sullenly flows;
> He did not see the starlight on the Laspur hills,
>   Or the far Afghan snows.
>
> He saw the April noon on his books aglow,
>   The wistaria trailing in at the window wide;
> He heard his father's voice from the terrace below
>   Calling him down to ride.

> He saw the gray little church across the park,
>   The mounds that hid the loved and honour'd dead;
> The Norman arch, the chancel softly dark,
>   The brasses black and red.

Stanzas like these seem a degree more acceptable than Alfred Austin's lines about rural England quoted in an earlier chapter (see page 66). They are sentimental and generalised, it is true, but they are attached to an individual and therefore have a certain dramatic propriety; though as with Tennyson this is a line of defence that cannot be very strongly urged. It fails when we come to the end of the poem, with its cinematic treatment of the hero's death-scene:

> Light on the Laspur hill was broadening fast,
>   The blood-red snow-peaks chill'd to a dazzling white;
> He turn'd, and saw the golden circle at last,
>   Cut by the Eastern height.

> 'O glorious Life, who dwellest in earth and sun,
>   I have lived, I praise and adore thee.'
>   A sword swept.
> Over the pass the voices one by one
>   Faded, and the hill slept.

A seventeenth-century poem like George Herbert's 'Redemption', with its 'ragged noise and mirth / Of thieves and murderers' comes closer to the probable realities of such a situation.

.   .   .   .   .   .

In practice some propagandists of the imperial idea were so extravagant that it is even possible to find criticism of them by Rudyard Kipling, who of all authors must be the one most associated with the cause of empire and regarded as its most power-fully effective literary missionary. In a short story of 1912, 'The Vortex', which is to be found in the collection entitled *A Diversity of Creatures* (1917), Kipling deliberately sets out to show the dis-comfiture of an enthusiast for imperialism. Lingnam, the character in question, is depicted as a citizen from an unnamed Dominion who has already nearly cured his own land of imperialism by excruciating eloquence on the subject, and has now come to England to lend the most verbose of voices to Imperial Councils. On a motor trip through the English countryside, Kipling writes,

> He admitted that a man obsessed with a Central Idea—and after all, the only thing that mattered was the Idea—might become a bore, but the World's Work, he pointed out, had been done by bores. So he laid his bones down to that work till we abandoned ourselves to the passage of time and the Mercy of Allah, Who Alone closes the Mouths of His Prophets. . . .
>
> The thick thunderous June airs brought us gusts of melody from a giddy-go-round steam-organ in full blast near the pond on the village green. Drums, too, thumped and banners waved and regalia flashed at the far end of the broad village street. Mr Lingnam asked why.
>
> 'Nothing Imperial, I'm afraid. It looks like a Foresters' Fête —one of our big Mutual Benefit Societies,' I explained.
>
> 'The Idea only needs to be co-ordinated to Imperial scale—' he began.
>
> 'But it means that the pub will be crowded,' I went on.

Lingnam's windy abstractions are neatly deflated at the end of this passage by reference to much more basic matters, and it is worth noting how throughout the story his large ideas are always propounded against the background of many and concrete English facts, including quantities of infuriated English bees in the end. Of course, it is not Imperialism itself that Lingnam, with rather cruel fun, is finally cured of—only its oratorial superstructure. He is brought from prolixity and sweeping condemnation of what he calls 'the vortex of Militarism' Europe is engulfed by to an uncompromising belief in imperial 'Co-ordinated, Offensive Operations . . . without any respect to the merits of any *casus belli*, instantaneously, automatically, and remorselessly at the first faint buzz of war.' This is undoubtedly exaggerated—partly for the sake of the joke involved and for the contrast with Lingnam's former verbosity. We can still see very clearly the spiritual ancestry of Brigadier Ritchie-Hook, one of the most amusing characters in Evelyn

L

Waugh's *Sword of Honour*. We might regret, however, the complete absence in Kipling of Waugh's longer and more complex view of a predeliction for simple 'biffing'.

Another short story in Kipling's *A Diversity of Creatures*, 'In the Presence', is supposed to be told by a Sikh Havildar-Major. It openly exploits the symbolic grandeurs of the lying-in-state of Edward VII:

> When all was in order, the new King said, 'Give entrance to all people,' and the doors were opened, and O my uncle! O my teacher! all the world entered, walking through that Temple to take farewell of the Dead. There was neither distinction, nor price, nor ranking in the host, except an order that they should walk by fours. . . . the coffin itself was as a shoal in the Ravi river, splitting the stream into two branches, one on either side of the Dead; and the watchers of the Dead, who were soldiers, stood about It, moving no more than the still flame of the candles. Their heads were bowed; their hands were clasped; their eyes were cast upon the ground—thus. They were not men, but images . . .

Precisely, we could interject at this point. They stood for something much larger than themselves. Quite obviously, as the story goes on, it becomes clear that the four Indian watchers in the Presence— only four, when Grenadiers had thousands available for relief duties—stand for the highest ideals of soldierly duty and honour maintained by these men from a major part of the overseas Empire towards the King-Emperor who had been the focus of its unity. The story will, however, yield further meaning, especially when we notice how Kipling intensifies the difficulties surmounted by his four Indian watchers: they are old men; there are almost insur-mountable problems about providing their food; the height of the stocks under their chins means that they almost choke themselves in attempting to look as deeply sorrow-stricken as other soldiers there wearing bearskins; one has to stand duty for four hours on end while the others deliver flowers at Windsor. While all this evidently works towards stressing the inspirational force of the

imperial idea, it also brings with it the sense that no longer is the
imperial stance sublimely self-confident and outward-looking;
rather, we must feel, it is embattled; resisting and firm; nevertheless, under stress:

> He threw out one hand palm upward to show that the
> tale was ended.
> 'We came well and cleanly out of it,' said the
> Subadar-Major.
> 'Correct! Correct! Correct!' said the Regimental
> Chaplain. . . .

And here, when we might expect from the Chaplain some remark
like, 'It was all quite splendid', he is made to continue with words
that in their implications raise the multitude of contemporary
spectres threatening the sublime ideal:

> 'In an evil age it is good to hear such things, and
> there is certainly no doubt that this is a very evil age.'

It is an unexpected literary pleasure to turn from these late,
somewhat defensive and cripplingly public versions of the imperial
idea to the documentary records made by men who had in fact
been involved in the acquisition of an overseas empire in the
previous century. What has been called 'the essential amateurishness' of British foreign policy-making in the earlier part of our
period ensured that real political decisions were recorded in
private correspondence and notes, which were usually taken away
by the Minister concerned when he left office. Uninhibited by fear
of publication in a Blue book, devoted to closely practical concerns
rather than to the mere creation of a public image, these politicians
can write in a way that is eminently readable as well as historically
significant. A number of such writings have been printed as the
second volume of C. J. Lowe's *The Reluctant Imperialists: British
Foreign Policy 1878–1902* (1967).

The documents produced by the Foreign Secretary, Lord
Salisbury, in particular, are often admirable for the economical
clarity of his prose style:

As to our policy—the defence of it lies in a nutshell. When you have got a neighbour and faithful ally who is bent on meddling in a country in which you are deeply interested—you have three courses open to you. You may renounce—or monopolize —or share. Renouncing would have been to place the French across our road to India. Monopolizing would have been very near the risk of war. So we resolved to share.

(To Northcote, 16 September 1881.)

Forcible directness is often diversified by lively, telling images, which demonstrate that not only was Salisbury a man who could think clearly, he must also have had the enviable ability to communicate the results of his thinking to others:

We are steering in very narrow channels and we are in constant danger of running aground on one side or the other. . . . [Bismarck's] policy in a humbler walk of life would be called *chantage* [blackmailing]. He is perpetually telling us of the offers France is making of reconciliation on the basis of an attack upon England in Egypt, and of the sacrifices which Germany makes by refusing these proposals; sacrifices for which, he adds, England must make some return, and then he demands this and that. I heartily wish we had never gone into Egypt. Had we not done so, we could snap our fingers at all the world. But the national, or acquisitional feeling has been roused; it has tasted the fleshpots and it will not let them go . . .

(To Drummond-Wolff, 23 February 1887.)

Nor is Salisbury's lucidity won at the expense of subtlety and humour, as we may see from a memorandum for the Cabinet about the complications of African imperial affairs:

To the north of Lake Tanganyika the English claim rests wholly upon the Treaties which Mr. Stanley, and possibly Mr. Jackson, have made with the King of Uganda and other natives. The weak point of such Treaties, as a ground of title, is that generally they are confronted by a parallel set of Treaties made with another European Power by the same native

Potentates, or by native Potentates claiming the same country; and Mr. Stanley's and Mr. Jackson's Treaties do not seem to be exempt from this inconvenient flaw.

(Extract, 2 June 1890.)

It seems only a moderate claim that writings of this kind provide an exceptionally painless way of acquiring historical information—a pleasant side-effect of the recent tendency to publish documents along with conventional historical writing.

.   .   .   .   .   .

It is not really possible, however, to remain behind the scenes admiring Salisbury's elegance and humour. He himself was forced to recognise the existence of public opinion, although he disliked it and only allowed it to exert a negative force in foreign affairs, according to Lowe. He was no Gladstone. But there was one occasion at least when popular feeling ran very high indeed, which gives us an example of literature utterly immersed in the tide of public affairs: Sir William Watson's *The Purple East: A Series of Sonnets on England's Desertion of Armenia* (1896). The difficulties of defending a particular part of the Empire, the land frontiers of India, had produced the strategy of diversionary action elsewhere if ever they were attacked. Consequently arose Britain's great interest in the Ottoman Empire, for Russia could not be attacked in the Black Sea without the goodwill of the Sultan of Turkey. In 1894 a series of Turkish massacres of the Armenians had outraged public opinion in Britain but had not caused the British government to take any steps. Agitation in Britain, Lord Salisbury wrote to Currie on 17 December 1895, 'approaches frenzy in its intensity'—this was after a fresh wave of massacres had occurred in September of that year—but again it led to no positive initiative. A number of Watson's sonnets on the subject had been published in the *Westminster Gazette* and had roused the poet laureate, Alfred Austin, to reply with three sonnets entitled 'A Vindication of England'. These in their turn inspired extremes of sarcasm and indignation in Watson: supine drivers of the steeds of empire are basely passive, 'Treachery's apologist' (the poet laureate, that is) remonstrates with him—'while a people bleeds/To death'.

As we read through the slim pamphlet in its purple cover our sensibilities become blunted and numb, Watson's attack is so extravagant, however just his cause may have been. 'Ghastly graves', 'the deadliest fangs of ravening seas', 'the Dragon ramps with fiery gorge', 'rot by the wayside'—phrases of this type lead on to perfectly wholesale onslaughts, very like some in 'Locksley Hall Sixty Years After':

> Still in your midst there dwells a remnant, who
> Love not an unclean Art, a State no less
> Unclean, a gibing and reviling Press,
> A febrile Muse, and Fiction febrile too . . .

And so it continues: 'slime' . . . 'rank miasma' . . . 'sloth' . . . 'torpor' . . . 'Till ye can feel nought keenly, see nought plain'. There's an ironical line, one feels. Watson, in fact, was a liberal imperialist, as we can soon see by looking at a number of poems in his works: 'Gordon', 'Our Eastern Treasure', 'England and Her Colonies', 'On Being Styled Pro-Boer' or 'The True Imperialism', this last being a poem that remarks on the difference between overseas achievements and the 'starved and stunted human souls' at home, exhorting us to 'build within the mind of Man/The Empire that abides.' Larger considerations of imperial defence did not matter beside what he saw as more fundamental issues, but the consequent diatribes in *The Purple East* are ridiculously extreme. In effect Watson reduced the *genre* that includes Milton's exalted sonnet on the massacre of the Vaudois, 'Avenge O Lord thy slaughter'd Saints . . .', to the level of the Gothic horror novel. He deserved Max Beerbohm's caricature in *The Poet's Corner* (1904).

Much of the literature of imperialism is insensitive. It is often written on the assumption that the poet's duty is to express the values of his own people as slavishly as possible, 'chant to them, for example, their own morality, their own religion, their own patriotism', wrote Newbolt. (Quoted in Stead, *The New Poetic*.) That this is too limited an intention is shown by the poetry of

W. E. Henley, who had been the Tory editor of the *Scots Observer* ('An Imperial Review') when it printed Kipling's 'Barrack Room Ballads' in 1890. The Boer War drew from Henley a volume of patriotic verse with an appropriate title, *For England's Sake: Verses and Songs in Time of War* (1900); it includes his most famous poem of all, 'England, My England', though this had been written some years before in 1892. Here is a poem that openly recognises what Lord Rosebery was to call the 'taint and reproach incidental to all human work', even in imperial affairs, but then goes on to make the 'taint and reproach' not incidental but integral by glorying in them:

> They call you proud and hard,
>   England, my England:
> You with worlds to watch and ward,
>   England, my own!
> You whose mail'd hand keeps the keys
> Of such teeming destinies,
> You could know nor dread nor ease
>   Were the song on your bugles blown!
>   England,
> Round the Pit on your bugles blown!

The poems in this volume that were actually written during wartime are much worse, whipping up emotion with wildly flailing rhythms,

> From Gib to Vancouver, from Thames to Yukon,
> The live air is loud with you—*Storm along, John!*

A brief sample of this poem is enough.

Such literary phenomena of the time are properly associated with the pitch of hysteria reached by London crowds at the news of the successful defence of Mafeking, which actually gave the language a new word. It is illuminating to see *The Times*'s explanation for 'mafficking' in the issue of 22 May 1900 (quoted in B. Gardner's *Mafeking: A Victorian Legend*, 1966):

> It is instinctively felt that in Mafeking we have the common-man of the Empire, the fundamental stuff of which it is built,

with his back to the wall, fighting an apparently hopeless battle without ever losing hope ... We have here the demonstration of the fundamental grit of the breed, the unanalysable qualities that have made the Empire, in spite of foolish politicians and blundering generals and the secular ineptitude of officials ... With the aid of his brave subordinates Baden-Powell has saved the isolated British station, which the folly, the neglect, and the ignorance of others had endangered.

Likewise, Henley's verse becomes intolerably jingoistic when he comes to write about the successes of Lord Roberts, the commander-in-chief who replaced Sir Redvers Buller in South Africa and whose strategy brought about a reversal of the series of humiliations inflicted by the Boers in the field:

> By the dismal fords, the thankless hills, the desolate,
> half-dead flats
> He has shepherded them like silly sheep, and cornered
> them like rats.
> He has driven and headed them strength by strength,
> as a hunter deals with his deer,
> And has filled the place of the heart in their breast with
> a living devil of fear.

The note of brutal exaltation and the lack of compassion for a beaten foe are very much what Dr Basil Cottle remarked in a poem by Laurence Minot about King Edward's victory over Spaniards at Winchelsea as long ago as 1350. (See an earlier volume in this series, *The Triumph of English 1350–1400*, 1969, chapter 2.) Such poems must spring from basic human reactions in time of war, responses common to human beings in all ages; but in Henley's case it is also impossible to forget that he was a cripple. Well before the South African War he had been writing poetry like 'The Song of the Sword', published in 1892:

> Clear singing, clean slicing;
> Sweet spoken, soft finishing;
> Making death beautiful.

There is a strange, perhaps compensatory, preoccupation with death and violence in this lengthy poem, dedicated, incidentally, to Kipling. But then, violence was not just a freakish strain in Henley's individual psychology, it was a particular feature of this age. Historians would undoubtedly recall that just a year later pitched battles were fought in Wales during a miners' lockout and that for the second time in the period with which we are concerned deaths occurred in civil commotions, when rioting strikers were fired upon by troops in Yorkshire. Two men were killed. There was apparent incendiarism in the docks at Hull, too, and a fight on the floor of the House of Commons, further if slighter indications of the precarious temper of the country about this time. Outside Britain this same year saw the ending of the power of the Matabeles in South Africa—put down by a certain Doctor Jameson, with machine-guns.

In the last decade of the century perfectly natural patriotic feelings became associated as never before with great racial arrogance and intolerance of others, often combined with a near-worship of force and might. How all this appeared to a contemporary observer may be seen in a dense essay by the aged philosopher Herbert Spencer, 'Re-barbarization', in his *Facts and Comments* (1902). With the air of a man yet again bringing reason to bear upon the irrationalities of his contemporaries, he points to the Church services held for troops going to South Africa, with hymns 'used in a manner which substitutes for the spiritual enemy the human enemy'; the rise of cadet-corps in various public schools; the mobs physically attacking those known to be against the Boer War; the popularity of football with thousands of spectators—and here one has a real moment of *déja vu*—'whose natures are such that police are often required for the protection of umpires'. Spencer continues by noting the revival of pugilism and various kinds of athleticism, including cricket, and then goes on to state that literature, journalism and art have encouraged re-barbarization. The millions of tales of bloodshed and fighting circulated amongst the young (he refers to an article on them in the *Academy* of 5 June 1897 here) are noted; the war-books that 'followed in the wake of Prof. Creasy's *Fifteen Decisive Battles of the World* and its thirty-odd editions' are coupled with the immense popularity of Kipling, 'in whose writings one-tenth of nominal Christianity is joined with nine-tenths of real paganism', and the proliferation of memoirs by generals, admirals, even privateers and pirates, not to mention the violent sanguinary fiction and portraits in the magazines and illustrated newspapers. There is not much doubt by this point that Spencer doth protest too much: pugilism leading to actual deaths is one thing but it is very hard to believe in the atavistic savagery of competitive cricket! The mental pictures one has of both crude woodcuts of massacres and exceedingly glossy colour photographs of atrocities are also sufficient reminder that popular art and literature has always been devoted to supplying a constant demand. Given the fact, however, that as so often happens in polemic, lack of measure answers lack of measure, the real interest of Spencer's article is that it draws attention to the way in which imperial adventures abroad could lead to a perceptible degeneration of the national life at home.

This decline is mirrored in literature at various levels, and even if we ignore cruder forms of journalism entirely, though from a sociological point of view they are no less significant, we are still forced to recognise, sadly, some of the reasons for the waste of Henley's great talent. It is a shame that he should ever have become so knotted with prejudice. It is a pity that he arrived at the hectoring of *For England's Sake* after writing his remarkable *Hospital Sketches* about a lengthy stay under Joseph Lister in Edinburgh Infirmary. These poetic sketches were first published by Leslie Stephen in the *Cornhill Magazine* for 1875; they show how very easily Henley could achieve the sharpness of detail and credibility of personal impression that are lacking in the public poetry he later wrote. Lines like,

> The stature and strength of the horses,
> The rustle and echo of footfalls,
> The flat roar and rattle of wheels!
> A swift tram floats huge on us . . .

seem to bear no relation to the later verse and in their distance from it are the measure of what Henley lost. He had not found the

secret of combining private and social concerns in poetry that did
no violence to either.

.   .   .   .   .   .

According to Ensor in his standard work, *England 1870–1914*,
the South African War pricked the bubble of imperial annexation,
but myths are slow to respond to the pressure of facts and occasions
of symbolic importance in the imperial context continued to
inspire expansive literary expression. Watson's 'Ode on the
Coronation of Edward VII' (1903) begins with majestic amplitude:

> Sire, we have looked on many and mighty things
> In these eight hundred summers of renown
> Since the gold Dragon of the Wessex Kings
> On Hastings' field went down:
> And slowly in the ambience of this crown
> Have many crowns been gathered, till, today,
> How many peoples crown thee, who shall say?
> Time and the ocean and some fostering star,
> In high cabal have made us what we are,
> Who stretch one hand to Huron's bearded pines,
> And one on Kashmir's snowy shoulder lay,
> And round the streaming of whose raiment shines
> The iris of the Australasian spray.
> For waters have connived at our designs,
> And winds have plotted with us and behold,
> Kingdom in kingdom, sway in oversway,
> Dominion fold in fold . . .

This is a deliberate and successful attempt at slow-paced grandeur
of utterance, but Professor Pinto's application of the phrase
'expensive vagueness' seems very apt (*Crisis in English Poetry*,
page 104). Who can be sure what 'things' are meant in Watson's
first line? 'How many peoples crown thee, who shall say?' is
another vague line, and one that is not even clear when first read.
In this lack of clarity it resembles a line from an earlier poem on
the death of Tennyson: 'I see the hands a nation's lyre that strung.'
Watson obviously wished to gain the effect of nobility of utterance

through the use of archaic syntax, but it is no compensation for the loss of lucidity. Significantly enough, we are forbidden to see Tennyson as a simple poet:

> Ev'n as the linnet sings, so I, he said:
> Ah, rather as the imperial nightingale . . .

For a contemporary comment on the general tendency we might turn to E. M. Forster's *Howards End* (1910). In this novel, a character called Ernst Schlegel, a German who has settled in England, is asked by a nephew if he thought the Germans were stupid. He replies,

> Your Pan-Germanism is no more imaginative than is our Imperialism over here. It is the vice of a vulgar mind to be thrilled by bigness, to think that a thousand square miles are a thousand times more wonderful than one square mile, and that a million square miles are almost the same as heaven. That is not imagination. No, it kills it. When the poets over here try to celebrate bigness they are dead at once, and naturally.

At this stage of our survey it is useful to refer to the revaluation of certain writers that has been a feature of recent years. To read on into Watson's Coronation poem is to find that he was doing more than celebrate size. He goes on, in fact, to write of those 'That greatly loving freedom loved to free' and ends with visualising the giving up of Empire at the appropriate time. Uncomplicated criticism of the kind voiced by Forster's Ernst Schlegel is not always relevant. Similarly, one of the main purposes of Sandison's *Wheel of Empire* is the radical modification of the traditional belief that Rider Haggard, Rudyard Kipling and John Buchan were simple-minded imperialists.

Although it is true that Rider Haggard actually ran up the flag in Pretoria when the Transvaal was annexed and at times wrote as a believer in Britain's imperial destiny, none of this made him naively paternalistic or superior towards native races. Sandison maintains that in stories like *Nada the Lily* (1892), *Marie* (1911–12) and *Child of Storm* (1913) full value is allowed to Zulu culture:

it is not foolishly disparaged and, while very different from ours, is regarded as being civilised in its own way. In Haggard's most famous novel, *King Solomon's Mines* (1885), there is a sensitive 'identification of native and European spiritual life', so that Rachel Dove assumes the role of Inkosazana y Zoola in a very genuine sense. In the background of this breadth of tolerance, Sandison believes, is Darwin's *On the Origin of Species*, published in 1859 when Haggard was three years of age. A possible implication of evolution by 'natural selection from *accidental* variations' is a denial of Divine Purpose in the universe, and this leads to Haggard's cultural relativity. His awareness of the enormous evolutionary time-scale, in which man changes as well as everything else, made him disinclined to believe that particular value-systems were final or possessed universal validity. He had a sense of the whole of humanity, which includes both Europeans and non-Europeans, struggling to survive and, in addition, trying to find order and meaning in the incomprehensible processes of the universe. Mere imperialism is dwarfed, especially in the crude Darwinian variant that interpreted 'survival of the fittest' as implying the inevitable preservation of superior Europeans.

We may look briefly at *She* (1886–7) to see this working out. Once in Africa, the young and handsome Englishman Leo, for example, was an object of admiration to the women of the strange tribe that had captured him. One of the most beautiful of them leaned forward and kissed him full on the lips; immediately Haggard puts into his mouth a reference to the customs of the early Christians and in the next paragraph adds the explicit comment: 'in direct opposition to the habits of almost every savage race in the world, women among the Amahaggar are not only upon terms of equality with the men, but are not held to them by any binding ties.' But matters are not left with early Christians or savage races, for Haggard continues to bring them nearer home:

I am bound, however, to say that the change of husbands was not nearly so frequent as might have been expected. Nor did quarrels arise out of it, at least among the men, who, when their wives deserted them in favour of a rival, accepted the matter much as we accept the income tax or our marriage laws, as something not to be disputed, and as tending to the good of the community, however disagreeable they may prove to the individual in particular instances.

The attitude of the social anthropologist talking of the relative nature of custom is very much to the fore; the contention is that different countries have different habits, thus 'making morality an affair of latitudes, and what is right and proper in one place is wrong and improper in another.' We can associate with this Haggard's 'scientific' descriptions of flora and fauna: the party of Englishmen shoot a wild goose, for instance, with 'a spur about three-quarters of an inch long growing from the skull between its eyes ... a "sport" or a distinct species. In the latter case this incident may interest naturalists.' There is a fascinating parallel also with Bishop J. W. Colenso of Natal, who found that prolonged residence amongst the Zulus had made him realise the sense, in their society, of the practice of polygamy. He wrote a pamphlet defending it and then, troubled by other questions raised by the Zulus, went on in the 1860s and 1870s to attack the literal credibility of the Old Testament. An Evangelical upbringing, A. O. J. Cockshut tells us in his *Anglican Attitudes: A Study of Victorian Religious Controversies* (1959), made him see *Genesis* and its succeeding books 'as *pure history*, with no symbolical elements whatsoever', even when he was questioning it. He was also a mathematician, so much so that his friend F. D. Maurice said, 'His idea of history is that it is a branch of arithmetic'! Deposed from his bishopric and excommunicated; restored by the Privy Council and confirmed in the temporal rights of his see: A. O. J. Cockshut brings out clearly the effect that Zulus had on Colenso and through him on the whole Anglican Church, its order and its authority.

Of course, Haggard is first of all a writer of adventure stories. Any reader who gets past the opening pages of *She* will proceed with bated breath: an enormous wave will bear Leo back from the jaws of Death, a magnificent waterbuck will go off with a mighty

bound as swift as an arrow, a lion and a crocodile will fight together
—no, duel to the death—mysterious men whose spears gleam
cruelly will carry us off in palanquins to the mouth of a great cave
where eventually, 'mad with rage and that awful lust for slaughter
which will creep into the most civilised of us when blows are flying,
and life and death tremble on the turn', we will fight for our lives.
The pronouns of the last sentence run quite easily into the first
person plural, such is the sense of involvement for the reader who
is not alert to cliché and stock phrase. We might, too, notice how
the thrilling romance and exoticism is occasionally set against the
sullen ground of life back in Cambridge amongst 'eminently
respectable fossil friends'. When Newbolt's 'They Fell Among
Thieves' harked back to England it was to imply that its values
were superior and inspired the bravely noble death of the hero.
The imagination of both writers was stimulated to explore distant
scenes and exotic behaviour, but they often travelled by very
different moral compasses and directed their sympathies in quite
opposite directions. The literature of imperialism has more than
one aspect, as these minor writers show. It also includes the work
of one major writer, Rudyard Kipling.

·　·　·　·　·　·

It should be admitted at the outset that there are many critics
who would not agree with this plain statement. That he was a man
of remarkable talent, a great craftsman with surprising range and
variety in his work, a virtuoso of literature whose originality is
infinitely greater than Haggard's—all this would hardly be denied.
In addition, he is one of the very few writers who could say with
Dryden that he was able to run his thoughts into verse or give
them 'the other harmony of prose': he was highly competent in
both. In both, too, he was an amazing exponent of history as
'resurrection', as we will see. Nor does it seem possible to claim
that Kipling was incapable of 'moulding outer things in sympathy
with inner values', as Santayana puts it in *Reason in Art*, since
there is no doubt that his writing is more than superficial entertainment. But Santayana goes on to say that art, having moulded its
significant forms, 'establishes a ground whence values may con-

tinually spring up.' This, with its claim for moral progress and growth, is denied by Edmund Wilson in his 1941 essay, 'The Kipling that Nobody Read', for Kipling, he wrote,

> has committed one of the most serious sins against his calling which are possible for an imaginative writer. He has resisted his own sense of life and discarded his own moral intelligence in favour of the point of view of a dominant political party. To Lord Roberts and Joseph Chamberlain he has sacrificed the living world of his own earlier artistic creations and the heterogeneous human beings for whom they were offered as symbols. Here the constraint of making the correct pro-imperialist point is squeezing out all the kind of interest which is proper to a work of fiction. . . . He lacked faith in the artist's vocation.
>
> (From *Kipling's Mind and Art*, essays edited by Andrew Rutherford, 1964.)

In the face of such lack of faith, all Kipling's expertise and historical interest, about which Edmund Wilson writes brilliantly, are seen as wasted. The new technique that closely and efficiently reflected the triumph of the machine and the accurate accounts of neurosis at a time when 'the human engine was going wrong' are no compensation for the central failure to maintain artistic integrity—especially in the longer novels of his middle period, which unlike the short stories gave him the opportunity to display the fullness of his creative power.

I do not myself think that *Kim* (1901) bears out Edmund Wilson's judgement. It is, as he begins by saying, a book that is enchanting, complex and dense. The following passage illustrates several of its finest qualities:

> 'A blessing on thee.' The lama inclined his solemn head. 'I have known many men in my so long life, and disciples not a few. But to none among men, if so be that thou art woman-born, has my heart gone out as it has to thee—thoughtful, wise and courteous; but something of a small imp.'

'And I have never seen such a priest as thou.' Kim considered the benevolent yellow face wrinkle by wrinkle. 'It is less than three days since we took the road together, and it is as though it were a hundred years.'

'Perhaps in a former life it was permitted that I should have rendered thee some service. Maybe'—he smiled—' I freed thee from a trap; or, having caught thee on a hook in the days when I was not enlightened, cast thee back into the river.'

'Maybe,' said Kim quietly. He had heard this sort of speculation again and again, from the mouths of many whom the English would not consider imaginative. 'Now, as regards that woman in the bullock-cart, *I* think she needs a second son for her daughter.'

'That is no part of the Way,' sighed the lama. 'But at least she is from the Hills. Ah, the Hills, and the snow of the Hills!'

He rose and stalked to the cart, Kim would have given his ears to come too, but the lama did not invite him; and the few words he caught were in an unknown tongue, for they spoke some common speech of the mountains. The woman seemed to ask questions which the lama turned over in his mind before answering. Now and again he heard the sing-song cadence of a Chinese quotation. It was a strange picture that Kim watched between drooped eyelids. The lama, very straight and erect, the deep folds of his yellow clothing slashed with black in the light of the *parao* fires precisely as a knotted tree-trunk is slashed with the shadows of a low sun, addressed a tinselled and lacquered *ruth* which burned like a many-coloured jewel in the same uncertain light. The patterns on the gold-worked curtains ran up and down, melting and re-forming as the folds shook and quivered to the night wind; and when the talk grew more earnest the jewelled forefinger snapped out little sparks of light between the embroideries. Behind the cart was a wall of uncertain darkness speckled with little flames and alive with half-caught forms and faces and shadows. The voices of early evening had settled down to one soothing hum whose deepest note was the steady chumping of the bullocks above their chopped straw, and whose highest was the tinkle

M

of a Bengali dancing-girl's *sitar*. Most men had eaten and
pulled deep at their gurgling, grunting hookahs, which in full
blast sound like bull-frogs.   (Chapter 4.)

The passage is long but well worth close attention; like all first-
class prose its language is not muffled or approximate and it
cannot be diminished by rigorous analysis. The last paragraph is
a masterpiece of description, cunningly presented to us as the
sights Kim saw between drooped eyelids and the sounds he heard as
he lay stretched on the ground by the fire. He was free to submit
his whole being to the registering of the outside world. He looks
upon a scene that is rich, various and beautiful, the animation of
light and colour playing against a darker background, which is
matched by the continuous and prolonged sound of Chinese
quotations, bullocks chumping and noisy hookahs. That the
water-pipes in full blast sounded like bull-frogs is a touch of
grotesquerie which helps save the description from lush monotony,
just as the sudden focussing on the jewelled forefinger which *snapped*
out little sparks of light as the talk grew more earnest brings
a welcome touch of astringency to the lambency of the curtains in
the night wind. Nor is the sudden bite unrelated to the character
of the occupant of the *ruth* or family bullock-cart with its broidered
canopy: that ancient grandmother's imperious manners, strong
will and sharp, realistic intelligence are only barely contained in
the tinselled and laquered vehicle with its gold-worked, shivering
curtains. Stubborn conservatism makes her travel in the old-
fashioned way rather than by rail in a screened compartment, but
it is not at all surprising that she should keep bursting out of her
filigree chains. Back go the curtains at every opportunity and she
lives the life of India vicariously. 'And truly the Grand Trunk Road
is a wonderful spectacle', wrote Kipling, and truly the spectacle
is wonderfully conveyed. The Road they are all travelling on is
'a river of life as nowhere else exists in the world'; on it trot long-
haired, strong-scented Sansis, given ample room by other castes;
a newly released prisoner walks along stiffly, the memory of his
leg-irons still on him; a wild-eyed Sikh devotee, women with babes
on their hips, older boys dragging rude brass models of loco-

motives, a gang of *changars*, 'the women who have taken all the embankments of all the Northern railways under their charge—a flat-footed, big-bosomed, strong-limbed, blue-petticoated clan of earth carriers, hurrying north on news of a job . . .' People and sensations crowd and jostle in upon us as we read.

But look back at the passage we are analysing and notice the clean contrast of the lama's appearance, 'the deep folds of his yellow clothing slashed with black', so severe against the garish, kaleidoscopic sights by which he is surrounded. His outward look more truly represents his inner being. His robe, we notice, is like 'a knotted tree-trunk slashed with the shadows of the low sun' . . . a rather more speculative idea rises in the mind and again forces us to consider the relationship of the details in this passage to their wider context. This lama is old and wrinkled, *his* sun is low; he is, besides, in the last stages of his release from the Wheel of Things, almost entirely divorced from the bustle and confusion of this world, nearly freed from illusion. This means that the snatch of dialogue about the Hills and the snow of the Hills is not accidental, expressive of no more than the lama's nostalgia for his native place. The Hills are his native place in a spiritual sense as well; they are alien to men from the softer plains. The Hills are where the 'dry air [is] taken sobbingly at the head of cruel passes' and where, in a later chapter, Kim and the lama

> meditated often on the Wheel of Life—the more so since, as the lama said, they were freed from its visible temptations. Except the grey eagle and an occasional far-seen bear grubbing and rooting on the hillside; a vision of a furious painted leopard met at dawn in a still valley devouring a goat; and now and again a bright-coloured bird, they were alone with the winds and the grass singing under the wind.
>
> (Chapter 13.)

The Hills with their plain severity and emblematic nature are utterly different from the Grand Trunk Road; they are a world in which from a distance a man walking under an umbrella looks to other travellers like a wind-blown hare-bell nodding down the valleys and round the mountain sides. We must not allow the

unexpected descriptive grace of that harebell to disguise the way
in which the image also asserts the reduction of a human being's
importance. The mountains, Kipling tells us, rise enormously
above men; on them lies the eternal snow, 'changeless since the
world's beginning, but changing to every mood of sun and cloud.'
Now we can see the connection with another part of the passage
we are considering, the dialogue which refers to a former incarna-
tion when the lama might perhaps have rendered Kim some
service (and which, incidentally, involves an echo of Rider
Haggard's sympathetic appreciation of the spirituality of other
races). The lama, like everybody and everything else, is on the
Wheel of Life, but few are as near as he is to the ending of successive incarnations. The hillman's garments are in their simple
colours symbolic of his progression from multiplicity to unity,
the moment when the soul passes beyond the illusions of Time
and Space and Things.

Finally, since this passage is like a leaf that reveals its tree, there
is the opening conversation between Kim and the lama. In these
two speeches is summed much of the vital warmth of the relationship between them. Kim is always an 'imp of this world' as well
as being thoughtful, wise and courteous to his lama. At the end of
the book when the lama is telling him of the conclusion of his
search and the immersion he has taken in the holy River of the
Arrow to cleanse the last traces of evil from his soul, Kim wonders
if the lama got very wet and what the earthy old grandmother had
to say on the subject. But the lack of worldly wisdom does not
make the lama an object of pity to Kim: 'It is less than three days
since we took the road together, and it is as though it were a
hundred years.' The lama is ancient, and innocent in the ways of
this world in which Kim becomes so expert; he could easily be an
object of contempt, as he is in the next chapter to the Reverend
Arthur Bennett ('Bennett looked at him with the triple-ringed
uninterest of the creed that lumps nine-tenths of the world under
the title of "heathen".') Kim and the lama show in their love for
each other what most imperialist Europeans have missed altogether. They are very different beings—one active and the other
contemplative—but distinction, always maintained, does not

bring contemptuous intolerance. Relationships extend from them. Early in the story the lama and Kim meet a cobra, which Kim wishes to kill but which the lama sees as being bound on the Wheel like themselves:

> 'Let him live out his life.' The coiled thing hissed and half opened its hood. 'May thy release come soon, brother!' the lama continued placidly. 'Hast *thou* knowledge, by chance, of my River?'

This is a key-note of the book. No one could be more unlike the lama than Mahbub Ali, one of Kim's mentors in the very worldly business of intrigue, spying, excitement and rule by superior cunning and strength. This burly Afghan horse-coper begins by giving a rougher imitation of the Reverend Bennett where the lama is concerned: 'God's curse on all unbelievers!' He ends, however, by being able to 'see holiness beyond the legs of a horse.' He will not accept the lama's Way, of course; he remains himself, just like the fourth great Indian character, Hurree Babu. In many ways a figure of fun, Hurree still 'selves, goes himself', to borrow a way of putting it from Gerard Manley Hopkins. Hurree may be 'a beast of wonder' and a fearful man, but he displayed great courage by going alone with robbed and angry foreigners . . . 'And he *is* a fearful man', stresses Kim. He has to be accepted as such.

Kim is actually of Irish birth, though an orphan who has been brought up as an Indian. Edmund Wilson sees in the novel as a whole two opposite forces meeting but never genuinely engaging. In Kim, the child of sahibs whose most real experiences and most inspiring visions have come from the service of an old lama, a powerful conflict might have been developed; in even larger perspective, Kipling might have made him realise eventually that by Secret Service work 'he is delivering into bondage to the British invaders those whom he has always considered his own people.' This is surely an external scheme. To begin with, India being in bondage to British invaders is not an issue in *Kim*. It is tenable that Kipling should have written a novel to flesh out a scheme of this kind: that he did not try to do so seems indisputable. Second, the recovery of Kim after his physical and spiritual collapse at the end of the book is thereby given a wrong interpretation and stress. Kim goes out into the world again and is overwhelmed; he felt,

> though he could not put it into words, that his soul was out of gear with its surroundings—a cog-wheel unconnected with any machinery, just like the idle cog-wheel of a cheap Beheea sugar-crusher laid by in a corner. The breezes fanned over him, the parrots shrieked at him, the noises of the populated house behind—squabbles, orders and reproofs—hit on dead ears.
> 'I am Kim. I am Kim. And what is Kim?' His soul repeated it again and again.

'But he now gets this unattached soul to find a function in the working of the crusher—note the mechanical metaphor', writes Mr. Wilson; 'dissociating himself from the hierarchy represented by the Abbot-Lama, he commits himself to a role in the hierarchy of a practical organisation' (the British Secret Service). The *mechanical* metaphor isn't important. In the story called 'The Bridge Builders' a low-pressure cylinder is 'not half a bad thing to pray to' and in any case, Kim's healing is completed by Mother Earth: 'The many-rooted tree above him, and even the dead manhandled wood beside, knew what he sought, as he himself did not know.' More important, in this context it is misleading to say that Kim committed himself to the hierarchy of the Service helping to keep India in thrall. What Kipling wrote was this:

> Things that rode meaningless on the eyeball an instant before slid into proper proportion. Roads were meant to be walked upon, houses to be lived in, cattle to be driven, fields to be tilled, and men and women to be talked to. They were all real and true—solidly planted upon the feet—perfectly comprehensible—clay of his clay, neither more nor less. He shook himself like a dog with a flea in his ear, and rambled out of the gate.

It is conceivable that in a sequel Kim might have gone back to the Secret Service, but here it is ordinary daily life that he rejoins.

·   ·   ·   ·   ·   ·

One cannot pretend that *Kim* has no larger perspective and is no more than the story of a few individuals. There is an essay by Noel Annan called 'Kipling's Place in the History of Ideas' reprinted in Rutherford's collection; in this he states that

> The centre of Kipling's world is society itself, and he related man to society in a way different from that of any other late Victorian writer. His understanding of society resembles that of a sociologist—and, what is more odd, it owed nothing to the theories of society then current in England. He is indeed the sole analogue in England to those continental sociologists —Durkheim, Weber and Pareto—who revolutionised the study of society at the beginning of this century. The same problems which forced them to invent new methods of analysing human behaviour led him to conclusions similar to theirs.

He goes on to say that this new breed of sociologists thought society could be studied in a truly empirical way, rather than through philosophy or ethics. They saw society existing in a nexus of groups and it was these groups, with the patterns of behaviour they established for individuals, which could promote order or instability in society. Kipling, too, was fascinated with the problem of social order. India, where he had been born and began his career, was a bewilderingly diverse network of groups and, as Annan emphasises, had almost succeeded in annihilating the caste to which Kipling belonged, Anglo-India, back in the days of the Mutiny. The England of Kipling's day was much more stable. (We have to think back to the position of John Dryden to find a literary analogy.) Kipling's answer to the question of what actually held Indian society of his day together was the 'forces of social control'—religion, law, custom, convention and morality, 'which imposed upon individuals certain rules which they broke at their peril.' Ultimately, Kipling would claim, civilisation rests upon the Law, something common and universal that transcends the variations of particular cultures, which is accepted as good by all groups—Annan lists such virtues as the keeping of promises, loyalty to friends, bravery, generosity, respect for parents, and so on. Thus, for Annan the real fault in Kipling's writings is that everything is explained in terms of social processes, relationships and forces; Kipling tries to prove his social theory in art and ends with a schematic presentation of life that ignores and flattens out the total human situation.

There is no doubt that in a story like 'The Head of the District' (see *Life's Handicap: Being Stories of Mine Own People*, 1891) we are very soon aware in broad outline of what is going to happen; all that we lack are the details of how the initial situation will work out—and very distasteful those details turn out to be. When a great literary craftsman decides to present violence we undoubtedly feel 'the soft *wheep*, *wheep* of unscabbarded knives' and experience the slow roll across the floor of 'the crop-haired head of a spectacled Bengali gentleman, open-eyed, open-mouthed—the head of Terror incarnate.' Early in the story the first lines of the diagram are drawn for us: we know what is bound to happen when a cultured and clever Bengali is appointed, against all the advice of men on the spot, to take over a northern district where the fighting men of a frontier clan have only just been won over to 'the paths of moderate righteousness' (a true meiosis) by British genius for government. Disorder is the expected result.

For some Kipling stories the word diagram is too open—maze might be a more appropriate description of their structure—but in far too many of them a pre-existing pattern of some kind is rigidly imposed. Rutherford has noted the 'tract-like nature' of the tales in *Stalky & Co.* (1899) and the 'remorselessly recurring pattern of "stalkiness" bringing its own reward' ('Officers and Gentlemen', in *Kipling's Mind and Art*). His general comment that Kipling tended 'to convert actuality to myth' revives for us a concern of earlier chapters and it is therefore interesting to read his assessment of one book in which Kipling triumphantly surmounted the consequent artistic problems. In *Puck of Pook's Hill* (1906), Rutherford contends, the mythical blends much more easily and less schematically with the realistic. Instead of dealing directly with the North-West frontier or the Prussian menace of his day, Kipling has gone back in history to the Great Wall of Northern Britain during Roman days. (T. S. Eliot wrote in his preface to his selection of Kipling's verse that the simplest summary of the change in Kipling during his middle years as a writer was 'the development of the imperial into the historical imagination'.) Distanced, then, from contemporary pressures he was able to give an individual hero like Parnesius 'a finer fuller humanity' and to assert the civilised values he stood for with 'new tact, new subtlety and an imaginative power that has no trace of propagandist zeal'.

Kipling at his best could remain in the present without writing schematically. The early story called 'Without Benefit of Clergy' (in *Life's Handicap*) is often praised for its human qualities. It is the tale of an Englishman in Lucknow who lived with a young Indian woman. Their perfect happiness is crowned with the birth of a small son, but before very long the child dies of fever and the mother of cholera. The very house they lived in falls into ruin and is to be demolished; the tragedy is complete. Annan regards the demolition of the house as symbolising 'the impossibility of fusing British and Indian culture through love', since love between individuals of the two races was in the social climate of the time quite out of the question. I would rather say that the social attitude exists as a very solid background. Certainly Ameera is always talking of the white women to whom her lover Holden will return one day. The attitude is emphasised to an unbearable extent when Holden cannot even mention his son's death as fond English fathers boast of their offspring's performances. But it is 'Nature' that brings about the ruin of the three lives and the ruin of the house. Society, in the form of marital shibboleths or the Municipality that always wanted to make a road across the house from the burning-ghaut to the city wall, is on a par with cholera, the greedy mother of Ameera, the rain that tears down the mud-pillars of the gateway of the house, the mildew and, in fact, everything else that is insentient or death-dealing. 'When the birds have gone what need to keep the nest?', says the landlord at the end of the tale. The loss is that of the birds who lived in the nest in their brief life. Society is by no means slighted but, as with Hardy's work, this story reaches to something at once larger and smaller than society: human beings suffer from life itself or, to extend the case to *Kim*, human individuals find themselves fully in life itself.

I believe, in fact, that Kipling's best work will stand with that of other great authors of the time and for very similar reasons. It is tempting to claim that an author who is interested in problems of social order is more relevant today than ever, but this would be to ignore his most vital qualities and those which give his work continuing rather than temporary relevance.[1]

·   ·   ·   ·   ·   ·

Kipling's most famous piece of imperialist writing is 'Recessional'. In its heyday the imperial theme was invested with many of the trappings of a living myth, a ritual and a liturgy. Queen Victoria's Diamond Jubilee in 1897 was celebrated with great national ceremony, bonfires, a Grand Review of the Fleet and so on, imperialism being an important aspect of the celebrations. But rejoicing is not the mood of Kipling's contribution to the liturgy. The whole poem is quoted below and it can be seen how, when one reaches the end of the first stanza, a major qualification is made, which is repeated with gathering emphasis in the next three stanzas. The poem ends with a plea for mercy on account of 'frantic boast and foolish word'. Spoken in the Jubilee celebrations? One might well ask.

> God of our fathers, known of old,
>   Lord of our far-flung battle-line,
> Beneath whose awful Hand we hold
>   Dominion over palm and pine—
> Lord God of Hosts, be with us yet,
> Lest we forget—lest we forget!
>
> The tumult and the shouting dies;
>   The Captains and the Kings depart:
> Still stands Thine ancient sacrifice,
>   An humble and a contrite heart.
> Lord God of Hosts, be with us yet,
> Lest we forget—lest we forget!
>
> Far-called, our navies melt away;
>   On dune and headland sinks the fire:
> Lo, all our pomp of yesterday

Is one with Nineveh and Tyre!
Judge of the Nations, spare us yet,
Lest we forget—lest we forget!

If, drunk with sight of power, we loose
   Wild tongues that have not Thee in awe,
Such boastings as the Gentiles use,
   Or lesser breeds without the Law—
Lord God of Hosts, be with us yet,
Lest we forget—lest we forget!

For heathen heart that puts her trust
   In reeking tube and iron shard,
All valiant dust that builds on dust,
   And guarding, calls not Thee to guard,
For frantic boast and foolish word—
Thy mercy on Thy people, Lord!

Stanza 4 is notorious, but it is not at all certain which race or races
are meant by 'Gentiles' and 'lesser breeds without the Law'. One
remembers Fielding's telling remark in *Tom Jones* to the effect that
Mob can be found in all classes. In any case it is clear that Kipling's
main desire was that the British people should not fail; his concern,
like Herbert Spencer's, was with the centre of Empire.

   Some of Kipling's South African War poetry is thickly involved
with the course of political events. His long poem 'The Islanders'
is a bitter attack upon England for its supine lack of care and only
improves upon William Watson's verses by reason of never-failing
powers of pungent expression:

And ye vaunted your fathomless power, and ye
   flaunted your iron pride,
Ere—ye fawned on the Younger Nations for the men
   who could shoot and ride!
Then ye returned to your trinkets; then ye
   contented your souls
With the flannelled fools at the wicket or the
   muddied oafs at the goals. . . .

Arid, aloof, incurious, unthinking, unthanking, gelt,

> Will ye loose your schools to flout them till their
> brow-beat columns melt?
> Will ye pray them or preach them, or print them,
> or ballot them back from your shore?

'The Dykes' is a much better and more distanced version of the same theme, but we cannot ignore the fact that some of the poems of this time are journalism of genius. 'Stellenbosch', for instance, expresses the point of view of the soldier who does all the dirty work under incompetent commanders:

> And it all goes into the laundry,
> But it never comes out in the wash,
> 'Ow we're sugared about by the old men
> ('Eavy-sterned amateur old men!)
> That 'amper an' 'inder an' scold men . . .

Indeed, Kipling's extraordinary powers of catching the exact tone of the moment have, paradoxically, given poems of this dramatic kind qualities that will always be valid. A poem like 'Chant-Pagan (English Irregular, discharged)' belongs to more than its immediate occasion, as the following verses from it will show. They catch a mood and a style of expressing it that are bound to recur:

> Me that 'ave been what I've been—
> Me that 'ave gone where I've gone—
> Me that 'ave seen what I've seen—
>   'Ow can I ever take on
> With awful old England again,
> An' 'ouses both sides of the street,
> And 'edges two sides of the lane,
> And the parson an' gentry between,
> An' touchin' my 'at when we meet—
>   Me that 'ave been what I've been?
>
> Me that 'ave watched 'arf a world
> 'Eave up all shiny with dew,
> Kopje on kop to the sun,
> An' as soon as the mist let 'em through
> Our 'elios winkin' like fun—

Three sides of a ninety-mile square,
Over valleys as big as a shire—
'*Are ye there? Are ye there? Are ye there?*'
An' then the blind drum of our fire . . .
An' I'm rollin' 'is lawns for the Squire,
Me!

The speaker of this poem eventually leaves England for South Africa, but Kipling's literary explorations of Empire essentially ended in the land where 'the virtue stays' and 'the clinging magic runs'.

Settled in Sussex, he wrote poetry of a kind we have already met in earlier chapters, for it is English rural life seen in its historical depth that is the source of his values. It seems incredible that the man who could write a poem like 'Mandalay', so heavily nostalgic for 'somewheres East of Suez', the temple-bells and the flying fishes, could ever contract himself to England, and often to small portions of England. But these poems have their extension in history, as 'The Land' shows: this is centred on a piece of river-land in the Weald, once owned by Julius Fabricius, then by Ogier the Dane, then by William of Warenne and latterly by a modern owner—who knows perfectly well that whoever pays the taxes 'old Mus' Hobden' actually owns the land where his family has been settled from British times. Two brief quotations will demonstrate the exceptional technical ease and competence of this poem:

Well could Ogier work his war-boat—well could
Ogier wield his brand—
Much he knew of foaming waters—not so much of
farming land.
So he called to him a Hobden of the old unaltered
blood,
Saying: 'What about that River-piece; she doesn't
look no good?'

The alliterative simplicities of heroic days vanish before later legal niceties, but Hobden survives, of course:

Georgii Quinti Anno Sexto, I, who own the
River-field,

Am fortified with title-deeds, attested, signed and
    sealed,
Guaranteeing me, my assigns, my executors and
    heirs
All sorts of powers and profits which—are neither
    mine nor theirs.

I have right of chase and warren, as my dignity
    requires,
I can fish—but Hobden tickles. I can shoot—
    but Hobden wires.

This concentration upon 'the *core* of empire . . . something older, more natural and more permanent', T. S. Eliot wrote, is given its finest expression in the poem called 'The Way Through the Woods':

They shut the road through the woods
Seventy years ago.
Weather and rain have undone it again,
And now you would never know
There was once a road through the woods
Before they planted the trees.
It is underneath the coppice and heath
And the thin anemones.
Only the keeper sees
That, where the ring-dove broods,
And the badgers roll at ease,
There was once a road through the woods.

Yet, if you enter the woods
Of a summer evening late,
When the night-air cools on the trout-ringed pools
Where the otter whistles his mate,
(They fear not men in the woods,
Because they see so few.)
You will hear the beat of a horse's feet,
And the swish of a skirt in the dew,
Steadily cantering through
The misty solitudes,

As though they perfectly knew
The old lost road through the woods. . . .
But there is no road through the woods.

This beautiful poem comes from the collection of stories and poems
called *Rewards and Fairies*, published in 1910. Without any context
it seems patiently descriptive and plainly musical in the manner of
some Edward Thomas poems, with a touch of De La Mare's
mystery in the second stanza. But it has, I feel, an extended meaning
though its symbolism is very subdued indeed—the symbols can, so
to speak, live a life of their own in the poem and have not been
flung down like counters. Propagandist seems the last word one
could apply. Even so, Kipling did come to feel that imperialism
had lost its way, that Britain's civilising influence had been prevented and that the great idea of Empire was one with Nineveh
and Tyre. It is odd to see something like civilisation in the reduced
form of a 'road through the woods', but odder still to find something as pleasant as badgers rolling at ease where that road had
once been. There is, if it is legitimate to be so blunt in interpretation of symbols, a kind of retirement from the fray. In the next
great writer we must look at, Joseph Conrad, a larger scepticism
on the subject of imperialism and Western Europe's civilising
mission in general is given hectic expression in one of his most
important works. In it, the primitive dark gods are allowed to run
riot and prodigies of rhetoric have to be exerted in the attempt to
keep them under artistic control. It might even be fitting to apply
to Conrad the lines Kipling wrote about Britain's spiritual position
in 1902:

Ninefold deep to the top of the dykes the
    galloping breakers stride
And their overcarried spray is a sea—a sea on the
    landward side.

The very last defences are almost down.

NOTES

[1] There are useful introductory books on Kipling by Bonamy Dobrée and by
J. I. M. Stewart.

7 : Critics of Imperialism

JOSEPH CONRAD, the astonishing Pole who became successively a British master mariner and then a major novelist, had in the course of his strange career been the commander of a boat sailing on the Congo river in Central Africa. This was in 1890, and since the beginning of the decade the activities of the King of Belgium's agents there had come under growing international suspicion; reports filtering out claimed that the commercial exploitation of the Congo State's resources involved appalling mistreatment of the native inhabitants. Ruth Slade's *King Leopold's Congo: Aspects of the Development of Race Relations in the Congo Independent State*, 1962, chapter 8) gives details of the situation and describes the report made in 1904 by a man who later became famous in Irish history, Consul Roger Casement. This report was entirely adverse, as was, in fact, the report prepared by King Leopold's own commission, which he had been forced by international pressure to set up in 1904. Leopold bitterly resented and resisted interference, thus inspiring equally bitter opposition: see, for example, just two lines from 'Leopold of Belgium' in Sir William Watson's *New Poems* (1909):

> Merely he loosed the hounds that rend and slay
> That he might have his fill of loathsome gold.

The last chapter, I think, has shown how extremes provoke extremes; the language of both supporters and opponents is flawed in just the same way. Fire drives out fire, flaring up very strongly ... for a brief space. Even across the Atlantic weirdly exotic reverberations of Congolese affairs sounded in the verses of Vachel Lindsay, in whose poem called 'The Congo' cannibals, Leopold in Hell, wild crap-shooters, cake-walk princes, witch-men and negro revivalists mingle in syncopated excitement. It is a strange poem, giving as odd a slant upon persons and events as his 'General William Booth Enters Into Heaven', but verses of this kind undoubtedly show up the limitations, the narrow range, of Watson's lines. One begins to appreciate something of Samuel Johnson's preference for the grandeur of generality.

Before all this, however, Conrad had published in *Blackwood's Magazine* for 1902 a fictional version of his own Congo experiences, the short novel *Heart of Darkness* (written slightly earlier, in 1899). This work is now regarded as a classic. It is without doubt a remarkable piece of writing, starting in personal history (we may compare the simple documentary record in Conrad's own Congo diary, published after his death in *Last Essays*, 1926) but then intensely recreated and transformed in his imagination. It is, as well, a work that runs to extremes, so that it is necessary to ask why in this case cooler critics do not put it in the same low class as much of the imperialist or anti-imperialist literature written about the turn of the century. The short answer, I think, is that Conrad's language in this work almost never congealed into cliché; or, to go behind the language, an emotional drive of great power did not become unresponsive to nuance. *Heart of Darkness* leaves an indelible mark on the sensibility of the reader, but not because it is a coarsely obvious scrawl in 'desp'rate charcoal'.

One of the engineering achievements of the age was the driving of a railway into the interior of the Congo, a manifestation of Victorian progress bringing more horrors in its wake than the poverty so deplored by Henry George. It is therefore fitting that one of the most sombrely impressive passages in *Heart of Darkness* is the description of the chain-gang of African labour building the railway, allowed to crawl away and die when they were no longer capable of work:

> At last I got under the trees. My purpose was to stroll into the shade for a moment; but no sooner within than it seemed to me that I had stepped into the gloomy circle of some Inferno. The rapids were near, and an uninterrupted, uniform, head-

N

long, rushing noise filled the mournful stillness of the grove, where not a breath stirred, not a leaf moved, with a mysterious sound—as though the tearing pace of the launched earth had suddenly become audible.

Black shapes crouched, lay, sat between the trees, leaning against the trunks, clinging to the earth, half coming out, half effaced within the dim light, in all the attitudes of pain, abandonment and despair. Another mine on the cliff went off, followed by a slight shudder of the soil under my feet. The work was going on. The work! And this was the place where some of the helpers had withdrawn to die.

They were dying slowly—it was very clear. They were not enemies, they were not criminals, they were nothing earthly now—nothing but black shadows of disease and starvation, lying confusedly in the greenish gloom. . . . Then, glancing down, I saw a face near my hand. The black bones reclined at full length with one shoulder against the tree, and slowly the eyelids rose and the sunken eyes looked up at me, enormous and vacant, a kind of blind, white flicker in the depths of the orbs, which died out slowly.

We hardly need the by now familiar reference to Dante's *Inferno* to darken the dire and dreadful atmosphere of this grove of death; it is conveyed by the unexpected evocation of the earth's rush through empty, inhuman space, by the insistent repetitions of parts of speech, by the reduction of a living man's flesh and blood to 'black bones' and by the final, labouring syntax of the last few lines as they depict the extinction of a human life.

As a commentator on one form of imperialism in practice, we must add, Conrad sees well beyond the ruin of its unfortunate victims; he also sees how its positive triumphs are wasted. E. J. Hobsbawm, in his *Industry and Empire: an Economic History of Britain Since 1750* (1969), maintains that Britain made a fatal mistake in not modernising her economy to escape from the Great Depression (1873–96); instead she merely exploited her traditional situation by exporting to 'the backward and satellite economies (as in cotton)' and by making 'what she could from the last of the great technical innovations she had pioneered, the iron steam-ship (as in ship-building and coal exports)'. One might almost read the following passage from *Heart of Darkness* as a symbolic illustration of a similar thesis, a sign of the basic futility of colonial advance into Africa:

> I came across a boiler wallowing in the grass, then found a path leading up the hill. It turned aside for the boulders, and also for an undersized railway-truck lying there on its back with its wheels in the air. One was off. The thing looked as dead as the carcass of some animal. I came upon more pieces of decaying machinery, a stack of rusty nails.

Mary Kingsley spoke for many in her time when she maintained that to her the railway engine was the manifestation of the superiority of her race (*West African Studies*, 1899). It is odd to think that one day our descendants will have to struggle to recapture the complex of feelings with which we ourselves hear of earth-orbits and moon-shots, but without such an effort of the historical imagination we will lose the full symbolic effectiveness of that railway truck on its back like a dead animal. More obviously and permanently effective, perhaps, is the French gunboat described earlier in the story, 'firing into a continent', uselessly, with no perceptible results, while its crew died of fever at the rate of three a day. A futile action is always just that.

In *Heart of Darkness*, Conrad's narrator, Marlow, is relating his own experience, telling the little audience in a yawl on the Thames of what had been at once 'the farthest point of navigation and the culminating point of [his] experience'. Also, as noticed in an earlier chapter (see page 123), the nineteenth-century colonisation of Africa by Europeans is set in a much larger historical context when, by an imaginative leap, Marlow is made to recall that even London had at one time been one of the dark places of the earth—to colonisers from Rome, men driven two thousand years ago by the same incongruous mixture of greed and idealism:

> The conquest of the earth, which mostly means the taking it away from those who have a different complexion or slightly flatter noses than ourselves, is not a pretty thing when you

> look into it too much. What redeems it is the idea only. An
> idea at the back of it; not a sentimental pretence but an idea;
> and an unselfish belief in the idea—something you can set up,
> and bow down before, and offer a sacrifice to. . . .

Ignoring the complication that Conrad may differ from his
narrator, is this a concession to the undoubted ideals that inspired
men like Rhodes and Henley, Rosebery and Kipling? It is to some
extent; but I do not really think that the story itself does anything
but throw an ironical light upon idealism. (In his autobiographical
A Personal Record, 1916, Conrad rather perfunctorily puts idealism
forward as the motive behind the ludicrous behaviour of a local
General's daughter in Kent, who used to war against 'the decay
of manners in the village children' and execute 'frontal attacks on
the village mothers for the conquest of curtseys'. The metaphors
here are clearly satirical.) In any case, *Heart of Darkness* goes much
deeper than the economic or idealistic aspects of imperialism. On
the literal level, which Conrad's astounding capacity to make us
see in all its peculiar and solid presence ensures that we will never
pass over lightly, Marlow is sailing up the Congo in search of a
man called Kurtz. But, and here we begin to appreciate the depth
and complexity of Conrad's story, 'going up that river was like
travelling back to the earliest beginnings of the world'. Kurtz
had gone into the Congo with the highest civilising ideals, yet had
succumbed completely to the power of the wilderness, which, we
are told, had whispered to him things about himself that he did
not know and which 'echoed loudly within him because he was
hollow at the core'. Marlow, who by determined application to his
job as captain had been able to resist both the sinister call of the
wilderness and the debased fellowship of the European exploiters
(sardonically known as 'pilgrims'), found himself irresistibly
drawn to Kurtz, the man who had plumbed the final depths of
savagery and civilisation. With Kurtz Marlow 'accepted this unforeseen partnership, this choice of nightmares forced upon me
in the tenebrous land invaded by these mean and greedy phantoms'. The voyage back to the earliest beginnings of the world was
also a journey into our own deepest darkness, and against the dis-

coveries made in this psychic descent the simpler ideals of work and duty proved no defence: the really hollow civilised man like Kurtz ('All Europe had contributed to the making of Kurtz') had proved capable of descent into absolute evil. In terms of the wider intellectual history of our period we might well remember Freud's claim that man could only be civilised at the cost of suppressing— *not* eradicating—his most primitive drives and impulses. In works of literature like *Heart of Darkness* we are plunged into the imperial experience in its ultimate depths, at a point beyond both primitive savagery and civilised man's assumption of godhead. And at the heart of the darkness of our lives is utter meaninglessness. The contrast with a work like *King Lear* is polar. Lear discovered his own essential humanity in the very depths of madness and despair, but reading this novel of Conrad's we are impelled to wonder if Kurtz's state is the image of the final horror, the end-product of man's loss of faith since Shakespeare's time.

.   .   .   .   .   .

Conrad's earlier story called 'An Outpost of Progress' (first printed in *Tales of Unrest*, 1898) is also set in Africa, but his field is wider than this. In the short story called 'An Anarchist' (which appeared in *A Set of Six* (1908), he tells of a young Parisian caught up in an Anarchist movement and sent to a penal settlement in South America. He manages to escape during a barbarous and savage mutiny, but only to the 'civilisation' of the cattle estate belonging to a famous meat-extracting company, regarded by its American manager as 'the acme of the nineteenth century's achievement'. The Anarchist finds himself in another penal settlement, for the blackmailing manager has no scruples in treating him as a kind of slave to work for the company, which must be economical in its operations because it spends such enormous sums in advertising round the world! We might also, as Sandison does in *The Wheel of Empire*, refer to the Malayan stories Conrad wrote, but a more important novel needs consideration.

Conrad again used a South American location in the long and complicated *Nostromo* (1904), set in the imaginary state of Costaguana. In this great panoramic novel, with its revolutionaries, politicians, journalists, workers, business men, engineers, intellectuals, sailors and priests, all playing their parts in a highly organised pattern of interlinking relationships, Conrad essentially focusses on the connection between moral and material interests. What causes advanced nations to go into underdeveloped countries? One answer might be the pursuit of profit; but if there is one thing *Nostromo* may be said to do it is to deny answers that ignore the complex realities of life. Not all causes are simply commercial. See, for example, the words of the Englishman Charles Gould, inheritor of the mining concession so hated by workers and political idealists in this disturbed South American state:

> What is wanted here is law, good faith, order, security. Anyone can declaim about these things, but I pin my faith to material interests. Only let the material interests once get a firm footing, and they are bound to impose the conditions on which alone they can continue to exist. That's how your money-making is justified here in the face of lawlessness and disorder.
>
> (Part 1, Chapter 6.)

This is not the voice of exploitation pure and simple. It is none the less true that the mine has become a fetish; for the sake of its peaceful working Charles Gould, by no means a Kurtz, had involved himself in the internal politics of Costaguana and had been led to inevitable disillusionment, a state of mind and soul in which words like liberty, democracy, patriotism and government take on 'a nightmarish meaning'. We have already, in chapter 4, seen the way in which people viewing industrial England had recourse to absolutes like nightmare. When lives are seen to stand in the level of dreams, we deduce that the course of history is felt by those living through it to have reached a moment of crisis: the School Board Inspector in Stepney talking of casual dock labourers and the novelist penetrating imaginatively into the possible careers of South American economic imperialists both reached the same kind of value-judgement. And so, by a dreadful irony, Conrad ensures that the Gould Concession, meant to bring salvation to a troubled republic, turns out to be an incubus that in the words of one of the characters will 'weigh as heavily upon the people as the barbarism, cruelty and misrule of a few years ago'.

There are many other aspects to this extraordinary *tour de force* of literature. From a historical point of view there is the fine contrast between the old republican, Georgio Viola, and other revolutionaries in Costaguana. Viola was an austere man with 'a shaggy white leonine head'; his divinities were Liberty and Garibaldi and he was utterly contemptuous of the rabble of revolutionaries around him; 'scoundrels and leperos', he maintained, 'who did not know the meaning of the word "liberty".' He looked back at the deeds of the immortal thousand in their glorious attempt to bring liberty to Italy as if they had been fighting in an age of giants, and was sternly devoted to a 'vast humanitarian idea' in a way that brought forgetfulness of self and personal advantage. (Part 1, Chapters 3 and 4.) But the old man was completely out-of-date in South America. The revolutionary Pedrito Montero, bent on having a share in material prosperity but faced with the intransigent refusal of Charles Gould to hand over the mine in working order, suddenly concluded that 'Republicanism had done its work. Imperial democracy was the power of the future':

> In that attitude, he declared suddenly that the highest expression of democracy was Caesarism: the imperial rule based upon the direct popular vote. Caesarism was conservative. It was strong. It recognized the legitimate needs of democracy which requires orders, titles and distinctions. They would be showered on deserving men. Caesarism was peace. It was progressive. It secured the prosperity of a country.

> (Part 3, chapter 7.)

It can be imagined how the popular vote will be won and just who will share in the wealth of the country.

This is not the place to go into the artistic subtleties of *Nostromo*, such as Conrad's virtuoso manipulation of the sequence of events in his narrative to bring out his themes and sense of values, giving up the easy effects of suspense and surprise by narrating effects before causes and so on. (It is not, many find, an easy novel to read.) But it is important to realise that little more than a bare outline of the structure of ideas has been given above; the whole novel is a very complete embodiment of them and stands in its own right as a substantial creation. Perhaps a single quotation will serve to prove how effortlessly Conrad can move from immediate circumstance to the largest of issues:

> The Capitaz [Nostromo] never checked his speed. At the head of the wharf vague figures with rifles leapt to the head of his horse; others closed upon him—cargadores of the company posted by Captain Mitchell on the watch. At a word from him they fell back with subservient murmurs, recognizing his voice. At the other end of the jetty, near a cargo crane, in a dark group with glowing cigars, his name was pronounced in a tone of relief. Most of the Europeans in Sulaco were there, rallied round Charles Gould, as if the silver of the mine had been the emblem of a common cause, the symbol of the supreme importance of material interests. They had loaded it into the lighter with their own hands. Nostromo recognized Don Carlos Gould, a thin, tall shape, standing a little apart and silent, to whom another tall shape, the engineer-in-chief, said aloud, 'If it must be lost, it is a million times better that it should go to the bottom of the sea.' (Part 2, Chapter 7.)

The silver, in fact, is to prove Nostromo's undoing—he is tempted by it and falls—but this is no more than a single strand in the novel. The passage quoted above emphasises that silver stands for a pressure exerted upon the entire imagined state of Conrad's creation, producing a warp throughout its grain. 'Silver', he wrote in a letter of 7 March 1923,

> is the pivot of the moral *and* material events, affecting the lives of everybody in the tale. That this was my deliberate purpose there can be no doubt. I struck the first note of my intention in the unusual form which I gave to the title of the First Part, by calling it 'The Silver of the Mine', and by telling the story of the enchanted treasure on Azuera, which, *strictly speaking, has nothing to do with the rest of the novel.* [My italics]

One could hardly ask for a better demonstration of the truth that works of literature of this kind are more than mere reflections of the externals of their time: Conrad's letter indicates very clearly that he intended his work to embody his own sense of values, his own estimate of the connection between moral and material values. For the sake of making all this clear he is quite prepared to introduce writing 'which, strictly speaking, has nothing to do with the rest of the novel', in the ordinary narrative sense, that is. His work is historical in a double fashion: it shows how a man of that age estimated characteristic events and people of his time.

At the end of the book one fussy and stupid character, Captain Mitchell, is quite unable to see beyond the apparent facts. For Mitchell material interests have brought triumphant progress to Costuagana. He thinks he has been present at the acting of great history and his ludicrous pomposity on the subject underlines the last irony of the book: the most idealistic service of material interests has admittedly led to order and material prosperity—but it has also meant the ruin of almost everybody's individual life and the loss of genuine freedom of the spirit. In creating this interplay of personal, political, economic and social forces, not only in *Nostromo* but in other works about the interaction between developed and undeveloped parts of the world, Conrad has been 'disturbingly prophetic' of later history. (See Douglas Hewitt's short but very useful *Conrad: A Reassessment*, 1969.) In this connection it is worth recalling that Kipling's famous poem called 'The White Man's Burden' (1899) was addressed not to Britain but to the United States of America, urging that country to take on its proper responsibilities in the Philippines. The very familiarity of the phrase 'Yankee imperialism' in our day is a sign that more rigid successors have almost imposed a new orthodoxy of their own; rightly or wrongly, the critique of colonialism or neo-colonialism is now as obsessive and as comprehensive as ever the imperialist myth itself was in the 1890s. Conrad's work marks the beginning of its decline and the rise of the counter-myth.

.   .   .   .   .   .

Few specialists in literature would deny Conrad major status and attention. He is the subject of dozens of books and hundreds of articles. A *selective* checklist of fiction published in the Spring 1964 number of *Modern Fiction Studies* noted around 90 items on *Heart of Darkness*, by far the most studied of his works though *Nostromo* runs it fairly close. There was a slump in his reputation about the time of his death in 1924, but since that time the writings of critics like F. R. Leavis and Morton Zabel in the 1940s have ensured his classic status. Many critics, too, would maintain that his anti-imperialist works are the solid basis of his reputation. But Conrad was not left-wing in other matters, which is presumably one reason why he does no more than emerge briefly in a footnote of Bernard Porter's recent study, *Critics of Empire: British Radical Attitudes to Colonialism in Africa 1895–1914* (1968), sharing even this humble position with Conan Doyle, who wrote a book called *The Crime of the Congo* in 1910, and Mark Twain, whose *King Leopold's Soliloquy* came out in 1907. There is also a short quotation from a letter of Conrad's to Roger Casement, dated 17 December 1903, to the effect that E. D. Morel's attack on King Leopold's policy and methods was justified, and Porter then comments that *Heart of Darkness* gives 'a terrifying picture of the Congo situation'. In the eyes of a professional historian, whose survey of the relevant evidence is systematic, thorough and properly evaluative, Conrad is a peripheral writer. A short survey of some of those writers Porter does treat at some length will, I think, direct us to important conclusions about the place of different kinds of literature in a society and the nature of their effect on it.

We may first take the case of Mary Kingsley, niece of the Victorian social-reform novelist Charles Kingsley and a remarkable woman in her own right. Porter reproduces a photograph of her in his book; the strong, keen, precise lines of her features seem to underline the actual honesty and forthrightness of her character. He tells us that although she was an imperialist, she became disgusted with the mindless jingoism she met on her return to England after two trips she had made to Africa between 1893 and 1895. She wanted a colonial policy firmly based on anthropological science, one that did not regard the African as a defective European but would rather recognise the true nature and value of African institutions. For the first time, says Porter, we have an 'applied anthropology'; a properly empirical study had provided the possibility of new solutions to colonial problems, which broadly amounted to Indirect Rule—Africans should be helped, but only so that they could develop on their own lines.

Porter also considers the thought of J. A. Hobson in detail. Hobson was the author of a number of books of a progressive nature, especially *Imperialism: A Study* (1902). His thinking about imperial affairs must be related to his thinking on social matters generally, since he was determined to bring ethical considerations to bear on the whole range of human problems. His Ruskinian attack on the inadequacy of narrowly economic criteria will strike a responsive note today when the run-down of a great railway system, the building of motorways and the siting of major airports have all called for an enormously delicate balance between human and economic considerations. For Hobson, purely rational and commercial factors were just a part of social good in the widest definition, though Porter goes on to give major stress to his historically important economic theory. Hobson contended that Europe's surplus capital (and production that the poor could not afford to buy) had brought about the opening of foreign markets and, in effect, the establishment of an empire. His particular views on the causes of the South African War transformed this economic theory into something conspiratorial and deliberate: international financiers, he came to believe, influenced imperial policy for their own profit, private gain overcoming social good. Put simply, as it so often was later, Imperialism is a capitalist phenomenon.

A third important figure in *Critics of Empire* is the tireless campaigner, E. D. Morel. The fundamental cause of the evil found in the Congo State, Morel decided, was that the natives did not own their own land any longer; therefore unable to engage in free commercial activities they were *de facto* slaves. As a writer, then, Morel possessed a particularly horrifying case, a diagnosis and a solution (peasant proprietorship and free trade). It is valuable to look directly at one of his propaganda volumes, *Red Rubber: the Story of the Rubber Slave Trade Flourishing on the Congo in the Year of Grace 1906* (2nd impression, 1907). After an introduction by the colonial administrator Sir Harry H. Johnston, Morel piles up the evidence of colonial atrocities: this part of his book is filled with letters from Congo travellers and missionaries, diaries, statements and reports, all relating the deplorable facts of the situation as seen by a variety of observers. Then, in the section entitled 'Public Works and the Price Thereof', we find Morel rising to heights of rhetoric:

> Gold to pour into the lap of some favoured friend. Gold to be invested in undertakings 'from China to Peru.' Gold to rear palaces, pagodas, and monuments to the Emperor of the Congo in Belgian cities. Gold to purchase properties under brilliant Mediterranean skies. Gold to be hoarded in private treasure-chests of which none but the Royal owner holds the key. Gold to corrupt consciences and manufacture public opinion: to disseminate lying literature through the world, even on the seats of continental railway carriages.

This incantatory repetition of the world 'gold' is very like Conrad's treatment of the word 'silver' (see page 200 above): the stress on an object both valuable in itself and the symbol of an immorality that places wealth above human considerations has an ancestry that stretches back through Ben Jonson's *Volpone* (1606). But this local tactic of style does not really make Morel comparable to Conrad or Jonson. How can the accumulation of many discrete pieces of evidence from a variety of sources have the same total impact as a consistent imaginative world? We may learn from one; we live in the other. It is true that critics have noticed signs of strain in Conrad's prose as he strove to express the full breadth and depth of Marlow's experiences in *Heart of Darkness* but this is a judgement on quite another level. Relatively speaking, Morel's rhetorical engine sounds as loudly as a car in the wrong gear in comparison with the efficient purr of Conrad's.

But, it must here be added, Conrad was not at all widely read until the success of his later novel *Chance* in 1914. Furthermore, writers like Morel, Hobson and Mary Kingsley are non-fictional and very explicit in their analyses and recommendations. Such writings were much more likely to affect the men who actually made or influenced policy than Conrad's were. Porter, we notice, states that Mary Kingsley's books became essential reading for colonial administrators. Many of her ideas have been adopted in practice. Hobson has been very influential, if only indirectly, since a deterministic version of his 'economic taproot of imperialism' was adopted by Lenin. He also influenced Ramsay Macdonald's *Labour and Empire* (1907) and hence Labour's colonial policy. As for Morel, both he and Roger Casement were the founders of the Congo Reform Association in 1904, which in a nonsectarian way brought together a very influential body of people in many walks of life and by constant propaganda had demonstrable effect on the actual course of events in the Congo. Clearly the work of such writers was felt directly in its day and had an even greater influence in the years that followed. Must we then assume that Conrad is historically unimportant, to be read for his own sake as a remarkable literary craftsman but not as anything more than this?

Only if we neglect the changes wrought by time, perhaps. Porter always in his book discriminates carefully between direct and indirect influence and, recognising the fact that imperialists were certainly more predominant about 1900, lays some stress on the way in which Radical anti-imperialists provoked future ideological movement on the left of enormous significance:

> Yet what gives the Radical imperial thinking of these years its greatest import is the 'myth' of economic imperialism it helped to create. . . . Hobson's analysis of colonial expansion was interpreted more rigidly and his term 'capitalist imperialism' was read as a tautology. . . . If myths are a force in world affairs, then the ramifications of this one are indisputable; and Hobson, unwittingly, helped to shape it.

Something very similar, only more delayed in effect, can be claimed for Conrad. Year after year his books continue to be published and read (and not only because they appear on the syllabuses of schools and universities, as cynics might claim), while others sink out-of-print and into near-oblivion. His novels are kept alive by their qualities as literature, and thus his outlook on his age is the myth that can become a force in world affairs when men turn to the past to help them make sense of the history of their own times. A neat

example of this is given in an interesting essay called 'Imperialism:
Conrad's *Heart of Darkness*' (*Journal of Contemporary History* 2,
1967); here Jonah Raskin notices how Conor Cruise O'Brien made
direct reference to Conrad and Leopold's Congo in his book *To
Katanga and Back* (1962). *Heart of Darkness* has become the man
of today's *Inferno*, his illuminating analogy.

.   .   .   .   .   .

Not many writers achieved Conrad's complexity in their approach
to material exploitation and idealistic rule of the less developed
parts of the globe. Conrad's friend, R. B. Cunninghame Graham,
gives us an example of the sarcastic simplicities of some anti-
imperialist writers:

> Thus, through the mist of time, the Celto-Saxon race emerged
> from heathendom and woad, and, in the fulness of the
> Creator's pleasure, became the tweed-clad Englishman. Much
> of the earth was his, and in the skies he had his mansion
> ready, well aired, with every appliance known to modern sani-
> tary science waiting for him, and a large Bible on the chest of
> drawers in every room. Australia, New Zealand, Canada,
> India, and countless islands, useful as coaling stations and
> depots where to stack his Bibles for diffusion amongst the
> heathen, all owned his sway. Races, as different from his own
> as is a rabbit from an elephant, were ruled by tweed-clad
> satraps expedited from the public schools, the universities, or
> were administered by the dried fruits culled from the Imperial
> Bar.

Historically, we see that the reliance on world markets and the
need to protect overseas trading had involved Britain in the control
of sea-routes. Sail had only recently given way to steam—Conrad's
The Mirror of the Sea contains some elegiac prose-poetry on the
subject—therefore, a chain of coaling stations was required,
especially on the route to India. 'The flag has followed the Bible
and trade has followed the flag' (*Saturday Review*, 1897), and so on.
The historical interest of the above passage is considerable. But as
literature, this kind of writing is as limited as some of the imperialist

manifestos we have looked at in the last chapter. It was good rousing stuff for liberal troops, doubtless. 'Niggers', from which the passage was taken, was first published in 1897 (and reprinted, greatly revised, in his *Thirty Tales & Sketches*, selected by Edward Garnett, 1929). It is in form a great tirade, obtaining its main effects by huge accumulations of language: 'rowan, holly, jacaranda, greenheart and pines, larch, willow and all kinds of trees that flourish, rot and die unknown in tropic forests' lead on to 'giraffes and tigers, with jerboas, grey soft chinchillas, elephants, armadillos and sloths, ant-eaters, marmots, antelopes, and the fast-disappearing bison of America.' Eventually we arrive at Cunninghame Graham's central ironic contention that almost all other peoples of the world are niggers—because they differ from us. Indians are; Arabs, too:

> So are Maylays, the Malagasy, Japanese, Chinese, Red Indians, as Sioux, Comanches, Navajos, Apaches with Zapatecas, the Esquimaux, and in the south Ranqueles, Lenguas, Pampas, Pehuelches, Tobas, and Araucanos, all these are 'niggers' though their hair is straight. Turks, Persians, Levantines, Egyptians, Moors, and generally all those of almost any race whose skins are darker than our own, and whose ideas of faith, of matrimony, banking, and therapeutics differ from those held by the dwellers of the meridian of Primrose Hill, cannot escape. Men of the Latin races, though not born free, can purchase freedom with a price, that is, if they conform to our ideas, are rich and wash, ride bicycles, and gamble on the Stock Exchange.

His tone here is distinctly reminiscent of Bernard Shaw rallying stolid English audiences.

Cunninghame Graham had as exotic a career as Conrad. The son of a Scottish laird and a part-Spanish mother, he was a world-wide traveller (Texas, South America, Morocco, etc.) and story-teller, as *Thirty Tales & Sketches* amply demonstrates. See, for example, his comparison of the Argentine Tango newly arrived in a flashily sophisticated Paris hotel with the original dance he had seen years before in a genuine South American rancho. But he was completely opposite in politics from Conrad, who was a deep conservative in most matters. 'England, the land of his adoption he loved fervently', Cunninghame Graham writes in another sketch, 'and could not tolerate that anything with which he had been once familiar should be tampered with, as often happens when a man adopts a second fatherland, for to change that which first attracted him seems a flat blasphemy' ('Inveni Portum: Joseph Conrad'). Cunninghame Graham had actually been one of those arrested in Trafalgar Square on 'Bloody Sunday', 1887 (see page 110 above), and to read Conrad's correspondence with him is to discover the extent of their ideological differences.[1] Both were outsiders, anti-imperialists, strange birds—but on opposite sides in most major questions of social change in their time. The great sweep of Cunninghame Graham's prose in 'Niggers' has a certain excellence: it points to a real attitude in some; its rhetoric, for its particular purpose, achieves the desired effects, and it is highly enjoyable to read, especially aloud. The point is there made: it is oratory. It works by simplification, and if people did exist who thought in the manner that Cunninghame Graham is sarcastically attacking they were not worth very much. Nor is, ultimately, an attack that adopts their own simplifications. With Conrad, on the other hand, it is indisputable that he has created something of great scope and depth, given to us a panoramic view of international relations and a penetrating insight into the human spirit.

Wilfred Scawen Blunt was another great traveller and writer who campaigned against British imperialism, championing the Egyptian nationalist cause in a long poem called 'The Wind and the Whirlwind' (1883):

> Oh insolence of strength! Oh boast of wisdom!
> Oh poverty in all things truly wise!
> Thinkest thou, England, God can be outwitted
> For ever thus by him who sells and buys?

'His voice was a voice as of a Cassandra prophesying in the wilderness, in the days when he warned England that Egypt would be free, that Ireland would become a nation, and that our Indian Empire was seething with revolt' (1927, Cunninghame Graham in *Thirty Tales & Sketches*). Blunt is, in fact, the anti-imperialist counterpart of the imperialist Henley, for both men wrote well when turned inwards upon their own personal experience but shallowly when the full warmth of their passions was engaged with outward events. In public verses they are poetical mastodons, very spectacular but both destined to become extinct. Their art is really a caricature of reality, a point which becomes very evident when we look at a novel like Hilaire Belloc's *Emmanuel Burden* (1904).

In this Belloc gives an ironic historical account of the imaginary M'Korio Delta, ripe for exploitation in 1886:

A Government which comprehended the meaning of the word Imperial proceeded to the partition of Africa. So far as the M'Korio was concerned, that partition was marked by a majestic simplicity. The whole of the right bank was recognised as falling within the sphere of influence of the French, with whose acknowledged possessions in Africa these districts ultimately merged. The whole of the left bank, right up country as far as the Cameroons, was similarly adjudged to Germany. We retained for our portion no useless shadowy sovereignty over the immense spaces of the interior, but the solid and tangible possession of the Delta. . . . By no means the whole of this province is permanently under water. There are several considerable islands of firm earth, sufficient to afford sustenance for a sparse but combative population which is split up into some five or six distinct tribes, but is known to the surrounding natives under the collective name of the Yaba. The reduction of these our fellow-citizens, 'half devil and half child', would probably have proved too heavy a task for any troops save those who had been trained in our own magnificent and permanent school of colonial warfare. As it was, a short campaign sufficed to establish that *Pax* which the commander in his despatches cleverly termed *Brittanica*.   (Chapter 3.)

Such writing contains an element of truth, but it is not the whole truth; careful and rigorous selection of fact has been made before the work is shaped, a feature that is further brought home to us in this book by the illustrations provided for it by G. K. Chesterton.

o

Like Lytton Strachey's *Eminent Victorians*, which came out in 1918, *Emmanuel Burden* can be enjoyed for its wit; it can also be enjoyed for its felicities of invention, but only as long as one is content to remain within the bounds of Belloc's fable. Yet this is to ignore a fundamental purpose of the whole: it is a fable designed to bear an application to real life and as such is only lastingly effective when the reader is convinced, as so often with Swift, that the author has hit upon some strong prevailing tendency in human nature or society. This Belloc can achieve: the description of Emmanuel Burden's last moments seems to me to be one occasion, but more often the book is both more particular and more partial. Discriminations are lost; the fullness of truth is reduced to an unacceptable degree. Or is this to mistake the *genre* and take matters too seriously altogether? Perhaps; it is a subject for debate, certainly. One might begin by asking why so many readers in practice tend to dislike fables and even prefer books of a much more documentary nature, something like Leonard Woolf's *Diaries in Ceylon 1908–1911: Records of a Colonial Administrator. Being the Official Diaries maintained by Leonard Woolf while Assistant Government Agent of the Hambantota District, Ceylon* (1963).

Finally, to prove that complexity and many-sidedness is not necessarily the only good, though a sufficient exposure to propaganda and caricature often tempts us to believe that it is, Hardy's 'Drummer Hodge' comes to mind:

> They throw in Drummer Hodge, to rest
>   Uncoffined—just as found:
> His landmark is a kopje-crest
>   That breaks the veldt around;
> And foreign constellations west
>   Each night above his mound.
>
> Young Hodge the Drummer never knew—
>   Fresh from his Wessex home—
> The meaning of the broad Karoo,
>   The Bush, the dusty loam
> And why uprose to nightly view
>   Strange stars amid the gloam.

> Yet portion of that unknown plain
>> Will Hodge for ever be;
> His homely Northern breast and brain
>> Grow up a Southern tree,
> And strange-eyed constellations reign
>> His stars eternally.

In some ways this is a very definite selection from life. It is impossible to tell what Drummer Hodge was like as an individual.[2] The use of the name Hodge immediately makes him a type figure, as we saw earlier with Richard Jefferies, but in this instance the draining away of personality is deliberate and effective. It establishes firmly one of the few contentions that grow out of the poem. This drummer boy is no different from other victims of war, sent to fight in South Africa, transported like an object from Wessex to the broad Karoo, discarded like an object when his usefulness ceased. The comparison with Rupert Brooke's famous sonnet of 1914, 'The Soldier', is unavoidable, for 'Drummer Hodge' contains no sort of comforting suggestion that there is 'in that rich earth a richer dust concealed': young Hodge is, chillingly, 'portion of that unknown plain'. In human terms, we might feel in response to Hardy's poem, it is not right that young men should be sent to fight for causes they do not understand, and there can be no consolation for their death in a foreign field. Another comparison with a contemporary poem on the other side, by Newbolt, 'The Volunteer', first printed in his *The Sailing of the Long Ships and Other Poems* (1902), underlines the universality of Hardy's three short stanzas. Newbolt's poem seems confined to its time and place:

> 'He leapt to arms unbidden,
>> Unneeded, over-bold;
> His face by earth is hidden,
>> His heart in earth is cold.

> 'Curse on the reckless daring
>> That could not wait the call,
> That proud fantastic bearing
>> That would be first to fall!'

> O tears of human passion,
> Blur not the image true;
> This was not folly's fashion,
> This was the man we knew.

But as we read through 'Drummer Hodge' we feel that here is something greater, a type of unavoidable tragedy. Constellations will continue to west; new, if alien, growth will spring again; strange stars will shine still as drummer boys, wars and all human life pass away beneath. It is not a complex poem, but nor does it fix and define like simple caricatures of reality. It has imaginative potency.

.   .   .   .   .   .

In wider political terms, however, the South African War was dwarfed by subsequent imperial history. A. J. P. Taylor tells us in his *English History 1914–1945* (1965) that when war was declared in 1914 the governments and parliaments of the Dominions were not consulted; in India the viceroy issued the royal proclamation on his own authority. 'Some 50 million Africans and 250 million Indians were involved, without consultation, in a war of which they understood nothing against an enemy who was also unknown to them.' Drummer Hodge, in this view, belonged to more than Wessex and South Africa. By 1917, when half a million Indians were fighting on the British side, India had to be given a certain amount of representation in the Imperial War Cabinet, from which it had previously been excluded as a dependency of the crown. Taylor sees in this action the beginning of the long road that ended in the granting of Indian independence thirty years later. In April 1919 General Dyer opened fire on a crowd of unarmed people at Amritsar and killed 379 of them. Gandhi, the leader of the Indian National Congress, now began his campaign of civil disobedience, so that force became the only method of keeping British rule over the sub-continent. 'Gandhi held the moral lead. The British had only power' is Taylor's comment.

The total situation, of course, was not really clear-cut and in E. M. Forster England produced a novelist who, although committed very strongly to certain principles, managed to write a book reflecting many of the complications that in practice prevent simplified judgements. Forster knew 'the coin that will buy the exact truth has not yet been minted'. It is strange to look back from *A Passage to India* (1924) to some of the early short stories, which seem very escapist in nature. 'The Celestial Omnibus' and 'The Other Side of the Hedge', for example, appear to be rather fanciful ways of avoiding life, making easy fun of those who believed in work and progress: 'We are always learning, expanding, developing. Why, even in my short life I have seen a great deal of advance—the Transvaal War, the Fiscal Question, Christian Science, Radium.' In a preface to the collected edition of his short stories (1954) Forster writes that 'The Machine Stops' was 'a reaction to one of the earlier heavens of H. G. Wells' (*The Time Machine*). It is anti-Utopian, then, though very much in ways that William Morris could have accepted. Most important, however, is the fact that we can find in this fantasy of the future a number of Forster's basic values expressed very clearly, which makes it worth some attention before we look at *A Passage to India*.

In this story the human race is imagined living in a Machine underground. Buttons and switches everywhere bring all that is needed and, despite the Machine's lack of distinctiveness and character, this is preferred to earth and sea and sky above. When Vashti is travelling in an old-fashioned airship to see her son the stars are intolerable, sunrise is horrifying and the blind is pulled to hide the Himalayas, the Caucasus, and 'a golden sea, in which lay many small islands and one peninsula', Greece. Her son Kuno is different: atavistic desires take him through one of the old ventilation hatches of the Machine and he finds himself in Wessex. A link with Hardy is made in this name; there are also points of contact with writers like Kipling and Lawrence. The little hills of Wessex are 'living',

'and the turf that covered them was a skin, under which their muscles rippled, and I felt that those hills had called with incalculable force to men in the past, and that men had loved them. . . .'

His voice rose passionately.

'Cannot you see, cannot all you lecturers see, that it is we that are dying, and that down here the only thing that really lives is the Machine? We created the Machine to do our will, but we cannot make it do our will now. It has robbed us of the sense of space and of the sense of touch, it has blurred every human relation and narrowed down love to a carnal act, it has paralysed our bodies and our wills, and now it compels us to worship it.'

We can hear an echo of the first paragraph in T. S. Eliot's 1941 preface to Kipling's verse: Kipling, according to Eliot, was in some of his works 'discovering and reclaiming a lost inheritance', deliberately reversing 'the values of industrial society' and attempting to convey 'a point of view unintelligible to the industrialised mind'. The second paragraph contains an attitude given powerful expression from Carlyle onwards (see especially the analysis of *Signs of the Times*, 1829, in Raymond Williams's *Culture and Society 1750–1950*, 1963, I.4). It is also, in a very particular way, 'proved' in the course of the action of Forster's story, the key phrase being 'human relation'. When eventually the Machine stops, and human beings conditioned by it are unable to survive its cessation, Vashti and her son touch each other and talk face to face—not through the medium of the Machine. In the darkness and chaos of the end human relations are momentarily re-established.

Forster, to put it very simply, believed that human beings should come together, but he knew the difficulties. In the imperial India of Forster's novel the very term 'Bridge Party', meaning a party in which British and Indians met on an equal footing, is a joke. Adela Quested, new from England and wanting to meet Indians, is regarded as 'cranky'. Her fiancé's mother, Mrs Moore, who brought her out to India, discovers that her son is going to pass on a private conversation she had with an Indian to his official superior. 'Nothing's private in India', he tells her, and this is picked up by Forster's own authorial comment later—'every human act in the East is tainted with officialism'. In some aspects the book seems designed as a satire on the lack of humanity the

British are forced to display on account of their imperial position. One minor character always lives in my memory for the moment when his voice broke into a roar: 'It's not the time for sitting down. It's the time for action. Call in the troops and clear the bazaars.' But his fatuity is at once qualified, since Forster goes on, 'The Major's outbursts were always discounted . . .'. And even this statement is modified: '. . . but he made everyone uneasy on this occasion'. Can one sidle up to truth?

Chapter 5 contains a significant debate between Ronnie Moore and his mother, which exposes the dilemma of the English in India:

'. . . I am out here to work, mind, to hold this wretched country by force. I'm not a missionary or a Labour Member or a vague sentimental sympathetic literary man. I'm just a servant of the Government; it's the profession you wanted me to choose myself, and that's that. We're not pleasant in India, and we don't intend to be pleasant. We've something more important to do.'

He spoke sincerely. Every day he worked hard in the court trying to decide which of two untrue accounts was the less untrue, trying to dispense justice fearlessly, to protect the weak against the less weak, the incoherent against the plausible, surrounded by lies and flattery. That morning he had convicted a railway clerk of overcharging pilgrims for their tickets, and a Pathan of attempted rape. He expected no gratitude, no recognition for this, and both clerk and Pathan might appeal, bribe their witnesses more effectually in the interval, and get their sentences reversed. It was his duty. But he did expect sympathy from his own people, and except from new-comers he obtained it. He did think he ought not to be worried about 'Bridge Parties' when the day's work was over and he wanted to play tennis with his equals or rest his legs upon a long chair.

He spoke sincerely, but she could have wished with less gusto. How Ronny revelled in the drawbacks of his situation! How he did rub it in that he was not in India to behave pleasantly, and derived positive satisfaction therefrom! He reminded her of his public schooldays. The traces of youngman humanitarianism had sloughed off, and he talked like an intelligent and embittered boy. His words without his voice might have impressed her, but when she heard the self-satisfied lilt of them, when she saw the mouth moving so complacently and competently beneath the little red nose, she felt, quite illogically, that this was not the last word on India. One touch of regret—not the canny substitute but the true regret from the heart—would have made him a different man, and the British Empire a different institution.

The last sentence makes a remarkable claim, perhaps too remarkable to be true, though Yeats would have understood. Still, there is no doubt where Forster's sympathies lie: his criticism of the 'undeveloped heart' of imperial administrators comes over strongly. Yet Ronnie's speech is in content a strong reminder of 'the problems of social order': they are not entirely ignored. We may notice as well that Indians are not portrayed as mere victim figures, for even amongst themselves personal relationships do not come easily and indeed, on some occasions are only maintained by 'official' means: see the 'worrying committee of notables, nationalist in tendency, where Hindus, Moslems, two Sikhs, two Parsis, a Jain, and a Native Christian tried to like one another more than came natural to them. As long as someone abused the English, all went well, but nothing constructive had been achieved, and if the English were to leave India, the committee would vanish also' (chapter 9). It is after reading a passage as explicit as this that one sees the full significance of a symbolic moment of relationship in *Kim*, when he spoke to his Tibetan lama,

> forgetting his white blood; forgetting even the Great Game as he stooped, Mohammedan-fashion, to touch his master's feet in the dust of the Jain temple.

It is not only Forster's practical man of action who recalls Kipling's writings to us; so does the more inward theme of connection across the barriers of caste, race and religion.

The central narrative of *A Passage to India* concerns the mysterious assault on Adela Quested in one of the Marabar Caves and the consequent trial of Aziz, her Indian friend. The trial is the time when the gulf between East and West is at its widest and when the baser human emotions are in their worst phase. At the critical moment Adela Quested suddenly withdraws her accusation and the trial shudders to a stop: 'Victory on this side, defeat on that— complete for one moment was the antithesis. Then life returned to its complexities . . .' If at this point we ask where is the centre of interest the answer must, I think, refer to the psychology of Adela Quested. Why on earth did she recant? Had she really been assaulted in the first place? But Forster leaves all this obscure on the personal level: personal as well as social life has its complexities and obscurities. In fact, much of the inner action of *A Passage to India* takes place on a more comprehensive, symbolic plane, some- thing easily shown by quoting the last paragraph of the novel. Two men, one English and one Indian, ride together; they wish to be friends:

> But the horses didn't want it—they swerved apart; the earth didn't want it, sending up rocks through which riders must pass single file; the temples, the tank, the jail, the palace, the birds, the carrion, the Guest House that came into view as they issued from the gap and saw Mau beneath: they didn't want it, they said in their hundred voices, 'No, not yet,' and the sky said, 'No, not there.'

It is impossible to outline the whole symbolic pattern here, but the Marabar Caves demand special attention—for what they represent in the novel and for the stimulus they obviously gave to Forster's geographical imagination:

> They are dark caves. Even when they open towards the sun, very little light penetrates down the entrance tunnel into the circular chamber. There is little to see and no eye to see it, until the visitor arrives for his five minutes and strikes a match. Immediately another flame rises in the depths of the rock and moves towards the surface like an imprisoned spirit: the walls of the circular chamber have been most marvellously polished. The two flames approach and strive to unite, but cannot, because one of them breathes air, the other stone. A mirror

inlaid with lovely colours divides the lovers, delicate stars of pink and grey interpose, exquisite nebulae, shadings fainter than the tail of a comet or the midday moon, all the evanescent life of the granite, only here visible. Fists and fingers thrust above the advancing soil—here at last is their skin, finer than any covering acquired by the animals, smoother than windless water, more voluptuous than love. The radiance increases, the flames touch one another, kiss, expire. The cave is dark again, like all the caves.   (Chapter 13.)

There can be few more beautiful passages in twentieth-century prose. The use of the word 'skin' takes us back to the Wessex of 'The Machine Stops', anti-mechanical, calling with 'incalculable force'—the adjective is fully meant—to men who had loved it. The 'conceit' of the two flames, one of which breathes air and the other stone, is perhaps the finest touch of all, yet it is here exactly that we are made to know unity prevented by ineluctable circumstance—the theme we have already looked at in the sphere of human relations.

From this point we may see the lines of symbolic structure radiating out through the book. The caves are 'extraordinary', but for no known reason. Deeper caves may exist which contain nothing whatsoever, for 'they were sealed up before the creation of pestilence or treasure'. In a cave Mrs Moore has a spiritual experience of horror and absolute negation; the echo converted every word of living speech to 'boum':

But suddenly, at the edge of her mind, Religion appeared, poor little talkative Christianity, and she knew that all its divine words from 'Let there be Light' to 'It is finished' only amounted to 'boum'. Then she was terrified over an area larger than usual; the universe, never comprehensible to her intellect, offered no repose to her soul, the mood of the last two months took definite form at last, and she realized that she didn't want to write to her children, didn't want to communicate with anyone, not even with God.   (Chapter 14.)

On the other hand, at the moment of Adela's *volte-face* at the trial she has a vision of the caves, when 'a match was reflected in the

polished walls—all beautiful and significant, though she had been
blind to it at the time.' When Mrs Moore leaves India the palms tell
her that an echo was not India and the Marabar Caves were not
final (chapter 23). India is also the temple ceremony of the last
part of the book, which is affirmative. It is not rigid or mechanically
perfect; it is human and disorderly and inelegant.[3] One of the
inscriptions actually reads, 'God si Love.' Like Kim's lama, the
unworldly Brahman, Professor Godbole, attempts completeness in
his inner spirit; then, later in the proceedings, in the midst of what
logical Westerners would call 'muddle',

> All sorrow was annihilated, not only for Indians, but for
> foreigners, birds, caves, railways, and the stars; all became joy,
> all laughter; there had never been disease nor doubt, misunder-
> standing, cruelty, fear.

Forster goes on to say that such ecstatic moments are only real
to believers, and when they begin to think about them the moments
become history and fall under the rules of time. Similarly, he only
allows personal relations to survive for a limited period, but his
'not yet' and his 'not there' at the very end of the novel imply that
somewhere and at some time they will be possible. When Empire
ends, perhaps. Just as the human spirit tries 'to ravish the unknown',
finding sometimes ecstatic completeness and sometimes the horror
of negation, so human beings will always attempt to make contact,
finding sometimes enmity and sometimes love. In *A Passage to
India* the realistic and the symbolic patterns coincide, though
never hardening into a petrified mass. This is why as a novel it
remains relevant to more than its own subject-matter and why, I
think, one sentence from chapter 36 demands to be generalised and
applied to imperialism both in life and in literature for the truth it
contains: 'Looking back at the great blur of the last twenty-four
hours, no man could say where was the emotional centre of it, any
more than he could locate the heart of a cloud.'

NOTES

[1] C. T. Watts has recently published an edition, *Joseph Conrad's Letters to R. B.
Cunninghame Graham* (Cambridge, 1969). It has extensive notes and a full introduction.

[2] This is not quite the case with, say, A. E. Housman's very similar poem on the death of his younger brother in the Boer War, no. 17 in *Last Poems* (1922):

Astronomy

The Wain upon the northern steep
  Descends and lifts away.
Oh I will sit me down and weep
  For bones in Africa.

For pay and medals, name and rank,
  Things that he has not found,
He hove the Cross to heaven and sank
  The pole-star underground.

And now he does not even see
  Signs of the nadir roll
At night over the ground where he
  Is buried with the pole.

See also N. Marlow, *A. E. Housman: Scholar and Poet* (1958), pages 88 et seq., for Kipling's influence upon Housman's poems of soldiering and enlistment.

[3] See Forster's letters on the Gokul Ashtami Festival of 1921 in his *The Hill of Devi: being Letters from Dewas State Senior* (1953), pages 100–113.

8: More Strange than True?

M ANY of the writers we have looked at so far had every intention of being relevant in their time. Shaw, Wells, Galsworthy and a host of lesser authors set out to be practical, often chose to embroil themselves in contemporary controversies and certainly saw themselves as very much a part of the society in which they lived and wrote. The rise of modern industrial society offered a challenge both to their humanity and to their sense of the quality of life; they reacted by using what they considered to be the resources of language in an attempt to alter the course of history for the better. It is noticeable how infrequently they celebrated aspects of contemporary existence. (In this respect a poet like Henry Newbolt comes out remarkably well, whatever his faults.) Nevertheless, they did not recoil from it in disgust; they freely criticised but did not reject society. Literary men, in fact, became men of action, albeit in a special sense of the term. On the other hand, we have also come across writings that were not always so practical. These differ widely from each other, but to some extent their authors had all turned aside from a direct and simple involvement with the ordinary business of life. Morris, we have seen, wrote a Utopia, turning his back upon both present and likely future as he gazed longingly into medieval history. Edward Thomas evoked the continuities latent in the ordinary life of his time as he recreated it in his poetry, distilling a long tradition of feeling about rural England especially. Gissing created a fiction of contemporary urban life that had something of the lurid phosphorescence of an older myth, while Forster, writing so painstakingly, obviously even, about human relationships in imperial India was still impelled to find beauty and mystery in some featureless caves and to include characters who led a mystically contemplative inner life. Even Kipling did this. He was not always taking 'a bloomin' day aht, on the blasted 'eath, along with Britannia, 'is gurl', as he is shown doing in the Beerbohm cartoon.

It would not be wise to stress overmuch these slight reorientations and intermittent disengagements, for none of the authors we have mentioned so far leave life far behind: the images, metaphors, symbols or figures they used to transmit less tangible vibrations take their place in a perfectly ordinary scheme. If in some ways or at some moments these authors are pure creators, they keep more than a toe-hold upon solid earth. Indeed, there is often reason to suppose that even the most mysterious examples have been incorporated either for the sake of completeness of record—'There are more things in heaven and earth, Horatio...'—or with the imprecise feeling that if all mundane answers to the problems of life are deficient then perhaps mystical solutions can be found. No-nonsense rationalists will unhesitatingly diagnose a state of temporary derangement and solemnly warn the writer that the average man will not understand. And one of England's greatest critics, Samuel Johnson, can be summoned to testify on the strength of his comments about Gray's *Elegy* that it is the common man who, 'uncorrupted with literary prejudices', will finally decide all claim to literary honours. All of which makes a group of writers towards the end of the century, heirs to the disillusionment with Victorian culture that had been growing since Ruskin's time and carrying to an extreme an increasing separation of artistic values from everyday social and moral ones, look very much of a side-show.

. . . . . .

'The Ancient historians gave us delightful fiction in the form of fact; the modern novelist presents us with dull facts under the guise of fiction. The Blue-Book is rapidly become his ideal both for method and manner.' In this fashion Oscar Wilde unrepentantly rejects one of the most socially involved types of literature in his time. 'As for that great and daily increasing school of novelists for whom the sun always rises in the East-End, the only thing that can be said about them is that they find life crude and leave it raw.'

Much of this essay, 'The Decay of Lying', which appeared in *Intentions* (1891), is light-hearted playing with ideas, as its title reveals. But it is wonderfully clear. He takes the old naive criticism of the writer, that he did not tell the truth because he invented, and accepts it joyfully: 'Lying and poetry are arts—arts, as Plato saw, not unconnected with each other—and they require the most careful study, the most disinterested devotion.' Plato, of course, ultimately decided that poets must be banished from his ideal Republic; Wilde banished the Republic from the world of art. He delights in inverting the expected, as when he writes of young men with a natural gift for exaggeration who 'fall into careless habits of accuracy'. After some neat flicks of the lash for Stevenson, James, Mrs Oliphant and Haggard (who once had the makings of a magnificent liar but is now afraid of being suspected of genius), Wilde passes on to a series of statements which, while few could ever accept them fully, contain more than a grain of truth. Also, some of these contentions rest upon premises we may not accept but which are important in their implications:

> The only beautiful things, as somebody once said, are the things that do not concern us. As long as a thing is useful or necessary to us, or affects us in any way, either for pain or pleasure, or appeals strongly to our sympathies, or is a vital part of the environment in which we live, it is outside the proper sphere of art.

Allowing for the fact that Wilde has not here attempted to stifle *his* personal gift for exaggeration, it is very evident that he is denying the validity of art that is propaganda or that has in some other way 'a palpable design upon us', as Keats put it, or that is dully naturalistic. 'One touch of Nature may make the whole world kin, but two touches of Nature will destroy any work of art'. This is picked up and developed later in a highly interesting section on the decorative arts:

> The whole history of these arts in Europe is the record of the struggle between Orientalism, with its frank rejection of imitation, its love of artistic convention, its dislike to the actual representation of any object in Nature, and our own imitative

spirit. Wherever the former has been paramount, as in Byzantium, Sicily and Spain, by actual contact or in the rest of Europe by the influence of the Crusades, we have had beautiful and imaginative work in which the visible things of life are transmuted into artistic conventions, and the things that Life has not are invented and fashioned for her delight. But wherever we have returned to Life and Nature, our work has always become vulgar, common and uninteresting.

Lewis Carroll's *Alice in Wonderland* (1865) and *The Hunting of the Snark* (1876) are by analogy examples of 'the things that Life has not'; in our period, too, G. K. Chesterton was writing fantasies like *The Napoleon of Notting Hill* (1904) and *The Man Who Was Thursday* (1907). Chesterton often reminds us of Wilde by his fondness for paradox, and even more for his ability to illuminate and irritate almost simultaneously. We think also of Gilbert's Savoy Operas (1875–1889), which Chesterton praised as effective satire *because* they were so detached. In *The Eighteen-Eighties* (edited by De la Mare) he wrote:

If we want to point out what can really be stupid and irrational and dangerous about a vulgar and conceited patriotism, we need a sort of ritual of satire that the irony may have a chance. Thus we find it is against the almost monotonous background of blue waves and bulwarks, in the unreal rigidity of H.M.S. Pinafore [1878] that the sailor is permitted to burst forth into that sublimely logical burlesque:

> He is an Englishman!
> And it's greatly to his credit.

And reaching the ironic heights of:

> But in spite of all temptations
> To belong to other nations,
> He remains an Englishman.

That knocks at one blow all the stuffing out of the stuffy and selfish sort of patriotism; the sort of patriotism which is taking credit instead of giving praise. It lays down for ever the essential and fundamental law; that a man should be proud of England but not proud of being an Englishman.

Chesterton's claim is that points of view of this kind would not be listened to 'in a general atmosphere of the rowdy, the fashionable or the obvious.' Certainly some of the greatest satires in the past have been distanced from reality by one means or another—Dryden's *Absalom and Achitophel*, Swift's *Gulliver's Travels* and Byron's *The Vision of Judgement*—and, at this time, Wilde's *The Importance of Being Earnest* (1895) or Barrie's *The Admirable Crichton* (1902) each have their own 'ritual of satire'. In the latter play the invention of a butler who proves to be a natural leader once he and his employers are wrecked on a desert island is in a comic way useful social criticism of class divisions. In the former Lady Bracknell's reluctance to allow her daughter 'to marry into a cloakroom, and form an alliance with a parcel' is superficially incredible and unreal; underneath, I suspect, such writing has something to do with educating attitudes. To me, it is a very moot point whether great tracts of Wells's *Tono-Bungay* fundamentally communicate any more than a single speech in Act IV from Lady Bracknell:

A moment, Mr. Worthing. A hundred and thirty thousand pounds! And in the Funds! Miss Cardew seems to me a most attractive young lady, now that I look at her. Few girls of the present day have any really solid qualities, any of the qualities that last, and improve with time. We live, I regret to say, in an age of surfaces.

For once, a context is hardly necessary.

When we look at the continuation of this speech ('Pretty child! your dress is sadly simple, and your hair seems almost as Nature might have left it. But we can soon alter all that'), we realise that Wilde does not really exempt himself from criticism: he knows perfectly well that he too lives in 'an age of surfaces'. Nature, we saw in 'The Decay of Lying', cannot be left unchanged, it must be 'transmuted into artistic conventions'. (The old alchemists, remember, transmuted base metal into gold.) This, despite the social criticism (a little touch of English Ibsen in the action), is really much more important. Here we have maintained the absolute primacy of the world of art. The aesthetic experience becomes in

P

practice a kind of religious experience. We must take up these two points in some detail.

.   .   .   .   .   .

The term 'artistic conventions' reminds us that art of any kind has a history. It is not only produced in some relation to life; it takes its place with other works of art for which various modes of presentation have been discovered. Any new work may well seek to place itself in relation to these as well as to ordinary experience. Look, for instance, at the examples of Aubrey Beardsley's work reproduced in this book. Though Beardsley and Wilde did not get on with each other in real life, his drawings undoubtedly conform to Wilde's theories of art. The visual images are not realistic in any simple sense. To begin with, they usually lack a dimension. Proportions are often distorted. Subjects are captured with strong precision of line and purely decorative rhythms are imposed on them. Beardsley is a sophisticated artist, in the sense that his drawings proclaim that they are nothing but art and have their being in a realm only distantly related to the everyday world. The *Volpone* drawing actually illustrates a play of a highly stylised kind in itself. Jonson's hero is first seen on the stage opening a 'shrine' where he can worship his 'saint'—gold; this was the boldly non-naturalistic beginning of a poetic drama. The 'Et in Arcadia Ego' drawing is even more complex in its ancestry: it takes its place in a literary and inconographical tradition traced for us by Erwin Panofsky in his *Meaning in the Visual Arts* (New York, 1955), though unfortunately he does not mention the Beardsley drawing. Arcadia in Virgil and many subsequent pastoral writers is an idealised land of the spirit, a place of eternal spring and inexhaustible pleasures. Later, to rudely summarise Panofsky's scholarly account, there was the tradition begun by Giovanni Francesco Guercino's painting 'Et in Arcadia Ego', in which two shepherds gaze sadly on a piece of masonry surmounted by a very prominent skull, the death's-head or *memento mori*, and also the tradition begun by Nicholas Poussin's second painting on the same theme, in which calmly and gracefully a group of Arcadians trace a sepulchral inscription upon a plain tomb. Thus the translation of the Latin phrase can range from the sombre

'Death even in Arcady' (grammatically correct) to the pleasantly elegiac 'I, too, was in Arcady' (less correct but sanctioned by much usage). After the seventeenth century it was the English who preserved the present happiness menaced by death interpretation; George III, Panofsky tells us, immediately saw this in a Reynold's picture he was shown. Beardsley, too, would seem to belong to the Guercino tradition, but in his own particular manner. Much of his 'Et in Arcadia Ego' is taken up with the tomb, the funeral urn and the dark yew. But there is nothing like a reaction of shock or sadness as far as the figure is concerned. Is the aging dandy even aware that death is in his Arcady? He positively dances over the grass and flowers; elegant, stylish, hardly touching the common earth and, if aware of death, defiantly bent on self-fulfilment. He seems to represent certain aspects of a whole generation of writers and artists in the last decade of the nineteenth century, men like Lionel Johnson, Ernest Dowson, Arthur Symons and Beardsley himself.

Known as the Decadents or Aesthetes, they are revived for us most fascinatingly (though mythically, to be sure) in Yeats's *Autobiographies: Reveries over Childhood and Youth and The Trembling of the Veil* (1926). Yeats called volume 4 of *The Trembling of the Veil* (first published in 1922) 'The Tragic Generation' and writes of Oscar Wilde, for instance, that he was a comedian 'in the hands of those dramatists who understood nothing but tragedy'. Wilde's career undoubtedly ended in a spectacular fall: arrested at the height of his brilliant reputation, tried and sentenced to hard labour for homosexual behaviour, his Arcady turned into Reading Gaol. There have been subsequently those who see in the Wilde trial of 1895 great historical significance—society persecuting its unwanted minorities—but for Yeats, Lionel Johnson was more interesting. He saw in Johnson the type of the true artist who withdraws from the world to cultivate himself and his art ('As for living —our servants will do that for us', Yeats quotes from Villiers de L'Isle Adam's Rosicrucian play *Axël*); yet this artist, half-conscious that some part of him still desires what has been renounced, can find no peace in isolation. In his lifetime Johnson turned night into day, breakfasting when others dined, studying and talking in his considerable library and, Yeats eventually discovered, drinking to excess. There was also the more extraordinary fact that Johnson would invent conversations with famous men of his time like Newman and Gladstone, on which Yeats comments:

> Perhaps this dreaming was made a necessity by his artificial life, yet before that life began he wrote from Oxford to his Tory but flattered family, that as he stood mounted upon a library ladder in his rooms taking a book from a shelf Gladstone, about to pass the open door on his way upstairs to some college authority, had stopped, hesitated, come into the room and there spent an hour of talk. Presently it was discovered that Gladstone had not been near Oxford on the date given; yet he quoted that conversation without variation of a word until the end of his life, and I think believed in it as firmly as did his friends. These conversations were always admirable in their drama, but never too dramatic or even too polished to lose their casual accidental character; they were the phantasmagoria through which his philosophy of life found its expression.
>
> (Section 6.)

We might feel that this is just too silly: contemporary history, in the shape of Gladstone's conversation, purely invented, quite untrue. It was, however, admirably turned, possessing both style and ease; a creation through which a philosophy of life could find expression according to Yeats. And if Yeats was perhaps too close to Johnson to be an unbiased witness, we ourselves may look at some stanzas from one of Johnson's finest poems, 'By the Statue of King Charles at Charing Cross':

> Sombre and rich, the skies;
> Great glooms, and starry plains.
> Gently the night wind sighs;
> Else a vast silence reigns.
>
> The splendid silence clings
> Around me; and around
> The saddest of all kings
> Crowned, and again discrowned.

Comely and calm, he rides
Hard by his own Whitehall:
Only the night wind glides:
No crowds, nor rebels, brawl. . . .

Which are more full of fate:
The stars; or those sad eyes?
Which are more still and great:
Those brows; or the dark skies?

Although his whole heart yearns
In passionate tragedy:
Never was face so stern
With sweet austerity.

Vanquished in life, his death
By beauty made amends:
The passing of his breath
Won his defeated ends.

Brief life, and hapless? Nay:
Through death, life grew sublime.
Speak after sentence? Yea:
And to the end of time. . . .

History again: not even contemporary history: and a lost cause
at that! Johnson might seem to be compounding the felony, but
this poem cannot be so easily dismissed. We are only too well
aware that great figures live after their death as a legendary
inspiration to others, 'speak after sentence', that is. (Yeats's
occultist friend, MacGregor Mathers, 'imagined a Napoleonic role
for himself'—as did Uncle Ponderevo, for that matter. Wells
evidently thought this particular folly common enough to satirize.)[1]
Besides, the poem obviously converts Charles's behaviour into the
perfect myth to express Johnson's 'philosophy of life'. In verses that
move sparely yet weightily, in a style controlled yet forceful,
Johnson chisels verbal significance for us with ritualistic precision:
Charles is seen as one who was no slave to circumstance, therefore
able to meet ignominious death with grace and dignity of spirit.

The meditation of the poem moves on to the inadequacy of the present:

> Our wearier spirit faints,
> Vexed in the world's employ:
> His soul was of the saints:
> And art to him was joy.
>
> King, tried in fires of woe!
> Men hunger for thy grace:
> And through the night I go,
> Loving thy mournful face.
>
> Yet when the city sleeps;
> When all the cries are still:
> The stars and heavenly deeps
> Work out a perfect will.

Charles in this poem is a model for those who strive to make works of art of their lives, attempting to bring the maximum of order to the most intensely known experience. One might wonder if the historical Charles I was worthy of this hagiography. (The author of *Eikonoklastes* ['Image-breaker'], John Milton, would not have thought so, and Marvell's *An Horatian Ode* gave both sides of the question with great beauty and strength of thought.) But who goes to *King Lear* or *Cymbeline* for ancient history's sake? Need we choose between Falstaff, Fastolfe and Oldcastle? There is room for discussion, certainly, but the main point here for us is that Johnson and similar 'wearier spirits' of the nineties could not live up to a high ideal. They actually did lead disordered lives and come to tragic ends; and they became in their turn legends in the imaginative growth of one of the greatest writers of the twentieth century. Through knowing them Yeats came to see the artist as a tragically divided figure, alienated from society but wanting the life of action, unable to maintain the burden of his isolation. And then,

> What portion in the world can the artist have,
> Who has awakened from the common dream,
> But dissipation and despair?
>
> ('Ego Dominus Tuus', 1917.)

To call this group of writers 'escapist' is commonplace, but Frank Kermode makes the shrewd comment in his most stimulating and relevant book, *Romantic Image* (1957), that Yeats was so certain art was not 'escape' that 'he thought of the situation the other way round: art was what you tried to escape from' (page 26).

. . . . . .

At this stage it might seem reasonable for us to drop the Aesthetes. In the last decades of the nineteenth century there was a kind of art and literature based upon a rejection of life. Its creators had deliberately cut themselves off from major movements of history, and the best that can be said for them is that they provided material of a peculiar kind for the imagination of a major poet. What more need be said beyond a remark or two to the effect that just as there came the 'yellow press' catering to an industrial proletariat avid for sensationalism, so there appeared *The Yellow Book* or *The Savoy* providing a more sophisticated version of the same thing? (A point made by Holbrook Jackson as early as 1913, in his *The Eighteen Nineties*.) Is not Wilde's novel *The Picture of Dorian Gray* (1891) a clear proof of how art for art's sake could so easily degenerate into 'sensation for sensation's sake'? Dorian Gray, in fact, took the quest to unintentionally comic lengths:

> At another time he devoted himself entirely to music, and in a long latticed room, with a vermilion-and-gold ceiling and walls of olive-green lacquer, he used to give curious concerts, in which mad gipsies tore wild music from little zithers, or grave yellow-shawled Tunisians plucked at the strained strings of monstrous lutes, while grinning negroes beat monotonously upon copper drums, and, crouching upon scarlet mats, slim turbaned Indians blew through long pipes of reed or brass, and charmed, or feigned to charm, great hooded snakes and horrible horned adders. (Section 11.)

But a little before this point Wilde had given a philosophical basis for the life led by this English disciple of Des Esseintes (hero of a famous French novel, *A Rebours*, published in 1884 by Joris-Karl Huysmans),[2] the new hedonism that

was to have its service of the intellect, certainly; yet, it was
never to accept any theory or system that would involve the
sacrifice of any mode of passionate experience. Its aim, indeed,
was to be experience itself, and not the fruits of experience,
sweet or bitter as they might be. Of the asceticism that deadens
the senses, as of the vulgar profligacy that dulls them, it was to
know nothing. But it was to teach man to concentrate himself
upon the moments of a life that is itself but a moment.

'Self-culture is the true ideal of man', cries Gilbert, one of the
speakers in Wilde's dialogue 'The Critic as Artist' (1891); true
individualism expressing itself through joy will be ensured by
Socialism and Science, Wilde claims in 'The Soul of Man Under
Socialism' (1895), so that man can live 'intensely, fully, perfectly'.
In all these quotations we perceive the influence of the Oxford don
Walter Pater, whose *Studies in the History of the Renaissance* came
out in 1873. This book had a famous summary Conclusion, from
which we may trace much of the theory of the Aesthetic movement
and in which we can discover the source of what is positive in
Aestheticism rather than merely exclusive or scandalous:

The service of philosophy, of speculative culture, towards the
human spirit, is to rouse, to startle it to a life of constant and
eager observation. Every moment some form grows perfect in
hand or face; some tone on the hills or the sea is choicer than
the rest; some mood of passion or insight or intellectual excitement is irresistibly real and attractive to us,—for that moment
only. Not the fruit of experience, but experience itself, is the
end. A counted number of pulses only is given to us of a varie-
gated, dramatic life. How may we see in them all that is to be
seen in them by the finest senses? How shall we pass most
swiftly from point to point, and be present always at the focus
where the greatest number of vital forces unite in their purest
energy?
To burn always with this hard, gem-like flame, to maintain
this ecstasy, is success in life. . . . Well! we are all *condamnés*
as Victor Hugo says: we are all under sentence of death but
with a sort of indefinite reprieve—*les hommes sont tous*

condamnés à mort avec des surcis indéfinis: we have an interval and then our place knows us no more. Some spend this interval in listlessness, some in high passions, the wisest, at least among 'the children of this world', in art and song. For our one chance lies in expanding that interval, in getting as many pulsations as possible into the given time. Great passions may give us this quickened sense of life, ecstasy and sorrow of love, the various forms of enthusiastic activity, disinterested or otherwise, which come naturally to many of us. Only be sure it is passion—that it does yield you this fruit of a quickened, multiplied consciousness. Of such wisdom, the poetic passion, the desire of beauty, the love of art for its own sake, has most. For art comes to you proposing frankly to give nothing but the highest quality to your moments as they pass, and simply for those moments' sake.

'Such manner of life might come even to seem a kind of religion', Pater wrote in *Marius the Epicurean* (1885), 'an inward, visionary, mystic piety . . .' One could live one's life like a piece of divine music, perfect in its order and harmony. Pater also saw that such a life might come into conflict with accepted morality, breaking convention in favour of 'that eager, concentrated, impassioned realization of experience'. He went so far as to remove the Conclusion from the second edition of *The Renaissance* because of the bad effect it might have upon the young, though restoring it later, slightly (and significantly) altered; in *Marius* he writes about the cost of this vision of life in its fullness, 'the sacrifice of a thousand possible sympathies'. Pater really wanted his aestheticism to be a profoundly moral matter, to include ethics, which was a position very similar if not identical to that of Henry James, as we have already seen (page 138 above). But how one should actually behave is not clear at all. It seems impossible to get beyond the pure belief that what is keenly experienced is *ipso facto* moral, and Graham Hough's conclusion in *The Last Romantics* (1949) seems very just: 'There is hardly any kind of conduct which could not be sanctioned by this doctrine', from that of the ascetic to that of the heroine of *Lady Chatterley's Lover*. In historical perspective,

Pater is one version of the Victorian agnostic making a deliberate attempt to convey a 'sort of religious phase possible for the modern mind'. No believer, he yet thought that 'the Church of the Middle Ages, by its aesthetic worship, its sacramentalism, its real faith in the resurrection of the flesh, had set itself against that Manichean opposition of spirit and matter and its results in men's way of taking life'. (See *Marius*, especially ch. 22). In Pater's own time we might note the rise of a 'Ritualist' Movement in the Anglican Church. In 1885 Gladstone appointed Dr Edward King to the bishopric of Lincoln and a few years later he was actually on trial for highly ritualistic practices in divine worship. Then again, many poets of the time were, or became, Catholics: Coventry Patmore, Francis Thompson, Lionel Johnson, Ernest Dowson, and even Wilde himself. Thompson especially stands out as one who revived for the nineteenth century the rich sensuousness combined with spiritual exaltation of the seventeenth-century author Richard Crashaw, Counter-Reformation Catholic and Metaphysical poet:

> *Poet* and *Saint*! to thee alone are given
> The two most sacred names of *Earth* and *Heaven* . . .

is the beginning of Cowley's elegy on Crashaw's death.

· · · · · ·

Thompson's poetry is no more in general favour than Crashaw's today. In his most famous poem, 'The Hound of Heaven', the basic idea of Christ as a lover pursuing the human soul is often thought to be tasteless, though there are precedents, and when this idea is worked out with extravagantly baroque imagery and large rhapsodic surges the damage is done for many readers:

> I pleaded outlaw-wise
> By many a hearted casement, curtained red,
> Trellised with intertwining charities;
> (For, though I knew His love Who followed,
>   Yet was I sore adread
> Lest, having Him, I must have nought beside);

But, if one little casement parted wide,
The gust of His approach would clash it to.
Fear wist not to evade, as Love wist to pursue.
Across the margent of the world I fled,
        And troubled the gold gateways of the stars,
   Smiting for shelter on their clanged bars;
     Fretted to dulcet jars
And silvern chatter the pale ports of the moon.
I said to dawn, Be sudden; to eve, Be soon;
   With thy young skiey blossoms heap me over
     From this tremendous Lover!
Float thy vague veil about me, lest He see!

But whatever the reservations about the particular style and form
Thompson exemplifies one of the main tendencies of religious
development in the nineteenth century: the avoiding of problems
raised by Evolution or the scientific 'higher criticism' of the Bible
by resort to subjective experience—often ecstatic recognition
of a divine world:

   O World invisible, we view thee,
     O World intangible, we touch thee,
   O world unknowable, we know thee,
     Inapprehensible, we clutch thee!

   Does the fish soar to find the ocean,
     The eagle plunge to find the air—
   That we ask of the stars in motion
     If they have rumour of thee there?

   Not where the wheeling systems darken,
     And our benumbed conceiving soars!—
   The drift of pinions, would we hearken,
     Beats at our own clay-shuttered doors.

   The angels keep their ancient places;—
     Turn but a stone, and start a wing!
   'Tis ye, 'tis your estranged faces.
     That miss the many-splendoured thing.
                ('In No Strange Land')

The epigraph to this poem, 'The Kingdom of God is within you', puts it in a completely orthodox context. We may look at a lesser known poem of Thompson's, 'The Mistress of Vision', for writing a little less obviously Christian and more akin to other manifestations of a religion of art. This poem was first printed in a section entitled 'Sight and Insight' in Thompson's *New Poems* (1897). It tells of an enchanted garden in 'visionary May,' at the very core of which is a 'Lady of fair weeping', inaureoled with a light 'most heavenly-human'—

> Like the unseen form of sound,
> Sensed invisibly in tune,

whose singing contains ancient secrets. Her mystic knowledge can only be won through pain ('from spear and thorn alone') and in an imaginative realm beyond death or its psychic equivalent:

> 'When earth and heaven lay down their veil,
> And that apocalypse turns thee pale;
> When thy seeing blindeth thee
> To what thy fellow-mortals see;
> When their sight to thee is sightless;
> Their living, death; their light, most lightless;
> Search no more—
> Pass the gates of Luthany, tread the region Elenore.'

Professor Kermode's comments on the goddess Moneta, in Keats's *The Fall of Hyperion*, seem to apply to Thompson's mysterious Lady. Both represent an older, imaginative source of knowledge, the intuitively discovered secrets that a world bent on rational and scientific explanations of life unhesitatingly rejects. (See *Romantic Image*, pages 8–10). But Thompson's subsidiary references to spear and thorn hook his later Romanticism to Christianity; his way of negation connects 'saint' and 'singer'. (Lionel Johnson's conversation with Cardinal Newman—his own invention, of course—began rather splendidly with Newman's greeting: 'I have always considered the profession of a man of letters to be a third order of the priesthood'!) A Beardsley drawing, 'Of a Neophyte, and how the Black Art was revealed unto him', which is reproduced amongst the illustrations of this book, guides our attention to more heterodox versions of poetry as religion. The revelation made to the neophyte may be of a black art, but it is still a revelation of secrets undiscoverable by mere logic and the discursive powers of the mind. The desire to combat materialistic, reductive accounts of life and the universe, besides making Edward Burne Jones decide to paint more angels, brought into being a multitude of occultist movements, which proved irresistibly attractive to writers and artists. Magic and art joined hands and, some would say, closed their eyes.

．　．　．　．　．　．

In 1875 the notorious Madame Blavatsky founded Theosophy as a new and higher synthesis of knowledge, claiming that she had access to arcane doctrine preserved from ancient times by 'Masters' living in Tibet. She survived denunciation by the newly founded Society for Psychical Research and in 1888 established an Esoteric Section which Yeats joined, 'deprived' as he was 'by Huxley and Tyndall of the simple-minded religion of [his] childhood' (*The Trembling of the Veil*, Book 1). He also joined a body with a much greater interest in magic, the so-called 'Hermetic Students' (Order of the Golden Dawn), founded by MacGregor Mathers, translator of *The Kabbalah Unveiled* (1887). Yeats says in his notes to *The Trembling of the Veil* that Mathers's instructor in magic had lived in France, and it is well worth referring to chapter 7 of Richard Ellmann's *Yeats: the Man and the Masks* (1961) for a useful summary of the cults swarming in Paris at the end of the century and the interest in magic of French artists and writers: 'Magic offered to the symbolists, many of whom studied it, a reinforcement of their belief in the power of word or symbol to evoke a reality otherwise inaccessible.' Through Theosophy Yeats was encouraged to continue finding correspondence between fairy tale and folklore, dream and vision. (It was in 1890 that Sir James Frazer the anthropologist brought out his stylish comparative study of myth and ritual, *The Golden Bough*, in which he attempted to show the essential likenesses beneath the diversity of custom and belief in many lands.) The cabbalistic magic of

MacGregor Mathers put more stress on symbols as a source of power and so his influence ran very naturally with that of another friend of Yeats, Arthur Symons, It was Symons who introduced contemporary French literature to English readers in his book *The Symbolist Movement in Literature* (1899), dedicated to Yeats, 'the chief representative of that movement in our country.' Through symbolism the poet could pierce through to the common inner experience of humanity and make it perceptible in symbols that are not mere translations but concrete embodiments of that reality itself, healing Pater's spirit and matter division; he could also place himself in the tradition of William Blake—'the first great *Symboliste* of modern times and the first of any time to preach the indissoluble marriage of all great art with symbol', Yeats wrote in *The Savoy* for 1896. Sensibility, isolation, joy and suffering strangely mingled, religious or magical insight into the secrets of life, the power of the symbol to *be* ultimate reality—we could hardly be farther from the main preoccupations of Shaw, the Webbs, Wells and the Fabian Society, or Booth, Stead, Gissing and the East End. The sun rose, not in the East End but in Paris, or in quite another realm, Luthany perhaps,

> Like a silver thurible
> Solemnly swung, slowly,
> Fuming clouds of golden fire, for a cloud of incense-smoke.

But we cannot linger in its mystic glow, for it is time to consider perhaps the greatest poet of the coming age, William Butler Yeats.

·   ·   ·   ·   ·   ·

If people were to accept the theory that poetry moves us because of its symbolism, what change should one look for in the manner of our poetry? A return to the way of our fathers, a casting out of descriptions of nature for the sake of nature, of the moral law for the sake of the moral law, a casting out of all anecdotes and of that brooding over scientific opinion that so often extinguished the central flame in Tennyson, and of that vehemence that would make us do or not do certain things; or, in other words, we should come to understand that the beryl stone was enchanted by our fathers that it might unfold the pictures in its heart, and not to mirror our own excited faces, or the boughs waving outside the window.

I quote these words from an essay Yeats wrote at the turn of the century, 'The Symbolism of Poetry' (now printed in *Essays and Introductions*, 1961), because Tennyson is so representative a Victorian author, a man who wrote for a middle-class public about the things they knew in a way that they could understand. This simple author-public relationship Yeats repudiated.[3] Referring to the works of Sir Charles Gavan Duffy in the second book of *The Trembling of the Veil*, Yeats maintained that 'in all his writings, in which there is so much honesty, so little rancour, there is not one sentence that has any meaning when separated from its place in argument or narrative, not one distinguished because of its thought or music.' Compare the last sentence of the passage quoted above, with its enchanted beryl stone, symbol of imaginative creation, but both concrete and indefinable in analytic terms, lucent with its own mysterious vitality, unlimited, self-subsistent. With the coalescence of native Romantic and French *symboliste* traditions in the last decades of Victoria's reign the courses of ordinary history and of much fine literature go their separate ways; from this period many devoted authors feel that they are living in an alien society with alien values, and that they cannot, or will not distort their difficult art for the sake of communicating easily with the average reader. 'Is it not certain that the Creator yawns in earthquake and popular displays, but toils in rounding the delicate spiral of a shell?' (*The Trembling of the Veil*, Book 2). No longer can a major author like Tennyson speak out in his own society and be met on equal terms by one of its political leaders, both sharing a common idiom of rational, easily comprehensible discourse. (A poet like Browning is, I think, a special case in this context.) Nor can it all be thought of as a late, eccentric and unfortunate development of Romanticism, as unhappy in its consequences for artists driven into isolation (or dissipation) as it was for readers forced into philistinism. It was this without a doubt—perhaps more in theory than in practice sometimes. But we have also seen how Henry James knew the conflict between the demands of art and those of society; the same point is maintained in an impressive letter of 1902 by another great author of the time, Joseph Conrad. (This is the one in which he defended himself and his artistic ideals to William Blackwood, publisher of *Blackwood's Magazine*, which would have been the perfect vehicle for Conrad had he been no more than a writer of exotic adventure stories.) To Tennyson and the Cambridge 'Apostles' the Palace of Art proved morally uninhabitable. He wrote a poem with that title to say so in 1832. But the wind changed and not all who ran before it were out-and-out Aesthetes.

Yeats himself, however, though he had learnt much from the Aesthetes, did not remain content with what he had discovered and, he wrote to George Russell in 1904, he became exasperated with 'the sweet insinuating feminine voice of the dwellers in that country of the shadows and hollow images'. His poetry in the new century grew to be more energetic, topical and critical of real life, but the criticism came from a man who in art and in matters of belief had journeyed in 'far other worlds, and other seas' (Innisfree, for example). In a poem like 'September 1913'—the very fact that it is a date means that Yeats is writing of time and history—he shows what he thinks of the Ireland of his day:

> What need you, being come to sense,
> But fumble in a greasy till
> And add the halfpence to the pence
> And prayer to shivering prayer, until
> You have dried the marrow from the bone?
> For men were born to pray and save:
> Romantic Ireland's dead and gone,
> It's with O'Leary in the grave.

His distaste for materialism and pietism is obvious; they are to him the ruination of Ireland, they dry 'the marrow from the bone'. The deeds of the political martyrs who tried to make Ireland into a true nation have been wasted. But we also see that these deeds of Irish patriotic history turn into a myth in Yeats's verse and, as the poem goes on, are removed from time to become limitless symbols of freedom, equivalents in the poetic universe of the wild geese that fly out over the water (though as George Moore brings out in 'The Wild Goose', there is also a historical reference to the Irishmen who used to fight in foreign armies):

> Was it for this the wild geese spread
> The grey wing upon every tide;
> For this that all that blood was shed,
> For this Edward Fitzgerald died,
> And Robert Emmet and Wolfe Tone,
> All that delirium of the brave?
> Romantic Ireland's dead and gone,
> It's with O'Leary in the grave.

Yeats had met O'Leary, leader of the Fenian movement and a very remarkable man (he even thought that perhaps the English character was better than the Irish but that the Irish could not turn English), when in 1884 he returned to Dublin after long years of imprisonment and exile. He was a magnetic figure, whose memory was still green many years later when Yeats in his old age wrote the poem 'Beautiful Lofty Things'. Patriot rather than politician, he was in his day a great moral force whose influence is made manifest in *The Trembling of the Veil*, Book 2, and for very clear reasons: 'he no more wished to strengthen Irish Nationalism by second-rate literature than by second-rate morality', for instance. Yet even this man could not draw the whole of Yeats's allegiance. 'How could he like verses that were all picture, all emotion, all association, all mythology? He could not have approved of my criticism either, for I exalted Mask and Image above the eighteenth-century logic which he loved, and set experience before observation, emotion before fact.' When Yeats left Aestheticism behind him, he did not remake himself entirely in another school. One might say, perhaps, that he changed its initial letter to a lower case—aestheticism.

An even better known figure who came to play a part in Yeats's myth of Irish nationalism was Charles Stuart Parnell, leader of the Irish Home Rule party:

Q

> If you have revisited the town, thin Shade,
> Whether to look upon your monument
> (I wonder if the builder has been paid)
> Or happier-thoughted when the day is spent
> To drink of that salt breath out of the sea
> When grey gulls flit about instead of men,
> And the gaunt houses put on majesty:
> Let these content you and be gone again;
> For they are at their old tricks yet.
>
> ('To a Shade'.)

Yeats associated the treatment of Parnell after the O'Shea divorce revelations in 1890 (the echoes were still reverberating in James Joyce's 'Ivy Day in the Committee Room', one of the stories in *Dubliners*, 1914)[4] with that meted out to Hugh Lane some twenty or so years later when he wished to give his collection of modern French paintings to Dublin. When difficulties arose over the provision of a suitable gallery, Yeats became convinced that his contemporaries lacked wisdom and generosity: other cities, he wrote in a note of 1914 we can read in his *Collected Poems*, had been stupid over works of genius, 'but Dublin is the capital of a nation, and an ancient race has nowhere else to look for an education. . . . Against all this we have but a few educated men and the remnants of an old traditional culture among the poor.' (How reminiscent that is of George Sturt!) He goes on, 'Both were stronger forty years ago, before the rise of our new middle class which made its first public display during the nine years of the Parnellite split, showing how base at moments of excitement are minds without culture.' The last phrase, of course, underlines what a dilemma faced Yeats: nothing if not human, one is glad to report, here he was himself in a spasm of excitement and public controversy; if not quite in the market place at least at the door of the palace of art. A great issue was at stake for him, the place of culture in the national community he hoped to help shape, but it is a relief to see how in a poem of 1914 he was able to subdue his rage and turn from what Norman Jeffares has called his 'Swiftian savagery' (see *W. B. Yeats: Man and Poet*, 1962) on the subject of contemporary realities to the serene but vital contemplation of an ideal character:

> Maybe a twelvemonth since
> Suddenly I began,
> In scorn of this audience,
> Imagining a man,
> And his sun-freckled face,
> And grey Connemara cloth,
> Climbing up to a place
> Where stone is dark under froth,
> And the down-turn of his wrist
> When the flies drop in the stream;
> A man who does not exist,
> A man who is but a dream;
> And cried, 'Before I am old
> I shall have written him one
> Poem maybe as cold
> And passionate as the dawn.'
>
>   ('The Fisherman')

Such a brief sketch! But this figure was an escape from despondency for Yeats, as the Leech Gatherer had been for Wordsworth and the rural craftsman for Sturt. Yeats's fisherman has the loneliness of the one and the skill of the other; and he is 'but a dream', of art.

One other great public controversy engaged Yeats during these years: the furore over John Synge's *The Playboy of the Western World* when it was put on at the Abbey theatre in 1907.[5] The riots at its first performance have become a legend. Yeats was roused to heated defence of Synge and his work. He had met Synge in 1896 and advised him 'to go to the Aran Islands and find a life that had never been expressed in literature.' Synge found amongst Irish peasants his subjects and, as Yeats saw it, though shy and timid himself, 'an invalid and full of moral scruple', he created 'now some ranting braggadocio, now some tipsy hag full of poetical speech, and now some young man or girl full of the most abounding health': dramatic personae or masks, in other words, who seemed to be his anti-types but in which he 'paraded all the desires of his heart' (*The Trembling of the Veil*, Book 4). In this way he escaped from mere private dreaming. It is well worth taking note of two significant comments from Anne Saddlemayer's introduction to the fourth volume of Synge's *Collected Works* (1968; general editor, Robin Skelton). First, though the central fact of *The Playboy of the Western World* (that peasants would welcome a young man who had killed his father and even admire his courage) was based on real-life happenings, Synge claimed that this was relatively unimportant: 'The story—in its *essence*—is probable, given the psychic state of the locality.' Second, in one of his notebooks we find Synge concerning himself with the place of such literature in a society as it lives through time. A passage dealing with 'mature drama'—'the deeper truth of general life in a perfect form and with mature philosophy'—ends with a truly seminal comment: 'Journalism may be literary, literature is always scriptural.' This must be one of the most incisive summaries of the aesthetic creed ever written.

.   .   .   .   .   .

The year 1914 was of some importance in Ireland. Irishmen joined the colours, including Erskine Childers, the author of *The Riddle of the Sands* (1903), a fine adventure story in which young English yachtsmen discovered a plan for a German invasion of England. Even Synge's peasants in the far South-West of Ireland, on the isles of Blasket, felt the effects of the ensuing war as they found the sea covered in wreckage: 'There was no spending. Nothing was bought. There was no need. It was to be had on the top of the water . . .' (Maurice O'Sullivan, in his vivid *Twenty Years A-Growing*, rendered from the original Irish by Moya Llewelyn Davies and George Thomson, 1933). But the key date in Irish history is Easter Monday 1916, when the Republic was proclaimed in Dublin. Although Roger Casement landed in a German submarine with a warning to call off the rising, a few hundred young men came out 'in the name of God and of the dead generations', seized the General Post Office and fought valiantly for a few days. The executions that followed turned a sluggish public sympathy

in their favour. Yeats's poem 'Sixteen Dead Men' makes this very
plain:

> O but we talked at large before
> The sixteen men were shot,
> But who can talk of give and take,
> What should be and what not
> While those dead men are loitering there
> To stir the boiling pot?

This simple, ballad-like poem shows by contrast the deeper and
more moving quality of his 'Easter 1916', a poem that opens with
a recollection of 'September 1913'. The people Yeats had then
despised,

> Being certain that they and I
> But lived where motley is worn,

had resigned their parts in the 'casual comedy' and had been
transformed into figures in a great and universal tragedy:

> All changed, changed utterly:
> A terrible beauty is born.

The last sentence is, of course, sharply ambiguous. Irish patriots
could be seen as terrible *and* as heroically beautiful. He had known
the 'rebels' before, he shows us in the second section of the poem:

> That woman's days were spent
> In ignorant good-will,
> Her nights in argument
> Until her voice grew shrill.
> What voice more sweet than hers
> When, young and beautiful,
> She rode to harriers?
> This man had kept a school
> And rode our wingèd horse;
> The other his helper and friend
> Was coming into his force;
> He might have won fame in the end,
> So sensitive his nature seemed,

> So daring and sweet his thought.
> The other man I had dreamed
> A drunken, vainglorious lout.
> He had done most bitter wrong
> To some who are near my heart,
> Yet I number him in the song . . .

Constance Marcievicz, Pearse, MacDonagh, MacBride (who had married the woman Yeats loved, Maud Gonne)—all had lost their diverse individualities in attaining heroic stature. They became part of a myth for their people:

> I write it out in a verse—
> MacDonagh and MacBride
> And Connolly and Pearse
> Now and in time to be,
> Wherever green is worn,
> Are changed, changed utterly:
> A terrible beauty is born.

Yet, as we have seen with O'Leary, Yeats could not commit himself entirely, and the third section of the poem contains the inner reasons why the beauty of their heroism was also appalling:

> Hearts with one purpose alone
> Through summer and winter seem
> Enchanted to a stone
> To trouble the living stream.
> The horse that comes from the road,
> The rider, the birds that range
> From cloud to tumbling cloud,
> Minute by minute they change;
> A shadow of cloud on the stream
> Changes minute by minute;
> A horse-hoof slides on the brim,
> And a horse plashes within it;
> The long-legged moor-hens dive,
> And hens to moor-cocks call;
> Minute by minute they live:
> The stone's in the midst of all.

From the grey eighteenth-century houses of the beginning of 'Easter 1916'—it was, we remember, eighteenth-century logic that O'Leary loved—to the living stream with its horse and rider and birds is a step into another world; but Yeats has not really deserted historical circumstance. The stone troubles the living stream and seems to deny it: we realise that Yeats cannot accept the petrifying inhumanity of absolute patriotism, even though he has appreciated the magnitude of the sacrifice involved and known what it will mean for Ireland. This is, inevitably, an inadequate paraphrase, since in this section of the poem he has invoked the right of the artist to speak through symbolic images and thereby detach himself to some extent from the lives and actions he is engaged with. At the same time, in the poem as a whole there has been no attempt to gloss over what might be called the journalistic aspects of the subject, 'ignorant good-will', daring and sweet thought, and so on. This poem can become 'scriptural' for those who respond to it.

'Easter 1916' manages to encompass the tension in Yeats between his public and private concerns. In two other poems, 'On a Political Prisoner' (Constance Marcievicz) and 'The Leaders of the Crowd', the balance tips heavily on the private side. Though they are technically accomplished works, the former especially, other poems we must look at seem to show that at this stage in his development Yeats required room in which to convey the full complexities of his attitude and bring out the total interplay between public and private concerns.

·   ·   ·   ·   ·   ·

> Now that we're almost settled in our house
> I'll name the friends that cannot sup with us
> Beside a fire of turf in th'ancient tower,
> And having talked to some late hour
> Climb up the narrow winding stair to bed:
> Discoverers of forgotten truth
> Or mere companions of my youth,
> All, all are in my thoughts tonight being dead.

With this beautiful grave opening we are introduced to the old square castle at Ballylee in Galway which Yeats had bought in

1917. It is, of course, fanciful to say that the old friends are introduced to his new home and its hospitality, because Lionel Johnson,
John Synge and George Pollexfen (Yeats's uncle) were all dead at
the time of composition:

> They were my close companions many a year,
> A portion of my mind and life, as it were,
> And now their breathless faces seem to look
> Out of some old picture-book;
> I am accustomed to their lack of breath . . .

It is in this sense that they live, first in Yeats's imagination and
then in the poem he has created. But they are not recalled for
their own sakes alone; they are summoned to play their part in a
more complex myth, since this poem is an elegy, entitled 'In
Memory of Major Robert Gregory'. Gregory was the son of Yeats's
aristocratic friend and sympathiser, Lady Gregory; she and her
home, the nearby Coole Park, stood for what Wells had wanted
Bladesover to symbolise, a noble, cultured and beautiful order
that was dying in the thin air of the modern age. She was Yeats's
co-director in the company that ran the Abbey theatre and wrote
a number of short plays that are often comic ('Spreading the News',
1904) and sometimes touching ('The Gaol Gate', 1906). They can
also, we might note, get down to the human bedrock of the Irish
situation ('The Rising of the Moon', 1907). Her son, a flier killed
on the Italian front early in 1918, had been soldier, scholar and
painter. He was, for Yeats, a latter-day Renaissance man, another
Sir Philip Sidney:

> I am accustomed to their lack of breath
> But not that my dear friend's dear son
> Our Sidney and our perfect man,
> Could share in that discourtesy of death.

In another short poem Yeats wrote on Robert Gregory, 'An Irish
Airman Foresees His Death', we learn that it was neither law nor
duty that sent him out to fight against the Germans; he went for
much more inward reasons, personal and mystical:

I know that I shall meet my fate
Somewhere among the clouds above;
Those that I fight I do not hate,
Those that I guard I do not love;
My country is Kiltartan Cross,
My countrymen Kiltartan's poor,
No likely end could bring them loss
Or leave them happier than before.
Nor law, nor duty bade me fight,
Nor public men, nor cheering crowds,
A lonely impulse of delight
Drove to this tumult in the clouds;
I balanced all, brought all to mind,
The years to come seemed waste of breath,
A waste of breath the years behind
In balance with this life, this death.

To return to the 'Elegy', we can see that he was for Yeats more than
an ordinary painter. In the following stanza we might discount
Yeats's assessment of his potential, but it would be a pity to miss
the significance of the *kind* of artist Gregory was and the tradition
that lay behind his work:

We dreamed that a great painter had been born
To cold Clare rock and Galway rock and thorn,
To that stern colour and that delicate line
That are our secret discipline
Wherein the gazing heart doubles her might.
Soldier, scholar, horseman, he,
And yet he had the intensity
To have published all to be a world's delight.

One of his paintings is reproduced amongst the illustrations of this
book. Even in black and white something of its lonely visionary
quality, the figures and natural objects bound together in a
mysterious sympathy, comes across to us. The painting has that
slightly hallucinatory character of images seen in a dream, at once
picturesque and inspired. Yeats saw Gregory as a painter in the

tradition of Blake, Samuel Palmer and Edward Calvert, and Professor Kermode in his subtle and scholarly analysis in chapter 2 of *Romantic Image* has underlined the importance of this fact in the major design of the elegy. Gregory was 'a maker of symbols, of images perceptible to the Blakean eye' and therefore absorbed in an intensely private activity, but he managed to escape into the life of action; it was 'a delighted escape from a typical cruel dilemma imposed by the nature of the artist and exacerbated by modern decadence.' Yeats, in creating this fine elegy for a man who, he believed, had succeeded in reconciling action and contemplation within himself (this only happened in a relationship, we recall, in *Kim*), has given us a complex symbol of the deepest-lying difficulties of the artist in the twentieth century. Solving them drove Gregory to a 'tumult in the clouds' and ended in his death.

Yeats himself, another creator, was left alive, in a land that found no peace in 1918 with the rest of the world. War came to Ireland when Britain took measures thought necessary to pacify a rebellious part of itself and when most of Ireland did precisely the same for the right of a small nation to determine its own future. Fifty years later we are unhappily familiar with the consequences of such a situation: violence, 'authorised' reprisals, casual slaughters and destruction:

> Now days are dragon-ridden, the nightmare
> Rides upon sleep; a drunken soldiery
> Can leave the mother, murdered at her door,
> To crawl in her own blood, and go scot-free;
> The night can sweat with terror as before
> We pieced our thoughts into a philosophy,
> And planned to bring the world under a rule,
> Who are but weasels fighting in a hole.
>
> ('Nineteen Hundred and Nineteen')

The actual incident of women being shot by Black and Tans from a passing lorry was referred to by Yeats in a speech made at Oxford on 17 February 1921. Professor Jeffares quotes from a contemporary press-cutting of the debate in the Union:

The rural policeman who attended to take the dying deposi-
tions of the women shot from a passing lorry in Galway, was
not allowed to do so, and the man who went for the doctor was
shot. The verdict of the military enquiry was that the woman
was struck by a descending bullet fired from the lorry 'as a pre-
cautionary measure'. . . . 'I do not know', declared Mr. Yeats,
'which lies heaviest on my heart—the tragedy of Ireland or the
tragedy of England.'

Both poetry and prose display the same quality of passionate
engagement with particular case and general situation, but the
poem is an infinitely richer statement. 'Nineteen Hundred and
Nineteen' begins by evoking the many 'ingenious lovely things'
made in ancient Athens, now lost for ever. This, however sad, is
a fact of life.

> But is there any comfort to be found?
> Man is in love and loves what vanishes,
> What more is there to say? That country round
> None dared admit, if such a thought were his,
> Incendiary or bigot could be found
> To burn that stump on the Acropolis,
> Or break in bits the famous ivories,
> Or traffic in the grasshoppers or bees.

Ireland, too, during the time of 'The Troubles' illustrates the same
general truth for Yeats. He goes on to pour scorn upon the hopes
there had been of a cultural renascence in Ireland, not excluding
his own former idealism:

> O but we dreamed to mend
> Whatever mischief seemed
> To afflict mankind, but now
> The winds of winter blow
> Learn we were crack-pated when we dreamed.

IV

> We, who seven years ago
> Talked of honour and of truth,

> Shriek with pleasure if we show
> The weasel's twist, the weasel's tooth.

Despairingly, he now sees this nightmare as the beginning of a new and terrible age when

> All men are dancers and their tread
> Goes to the barbarous clangour of a gong.

In the strange prose work Yeats was writing about this time, *A Vision* (1925; revised 1937), he included amongst other things a theory of history. History is said to move in cycles, the period from the time of Christ being almost one cycle or 'great year'. There are resemblances to Oswald Spengler's 'logic of history' in his book *The Decline of the West* (1918), where he maintained that Western culture was in its last phase of decline, a late time manifested by traditionless city-dwellers uprooted from the land and despising it—money-serving, unspiritual, devoid of art, not a folk but a mass. The terrors that Yeats associated with the last phase of the cycle since Christ might seem to have already been powerfully expressed in the quotations above, but it is in the final poem of 'Nineteen Hundred and Nineteen' that the spring tide of Yeats's rhetoric really floods in:

VI

> Violence upon the roads: violence of horses;
> Some few have handsome riders, are garlanded
> On delicate sensitive ear or tossing mane,
> But wearied running round and round in their courses
> All break and vanish, and evil gathers head:
> Herodias' daughters have returned again,
> A sudden blast of dusty wind and after
> Thunder of feet, tumult of images,
> Their purpose in the labyrinth of the wind;
> And should some crazy hand dare touch a daughter
> All turn with amorous cries, or angry cries,
> According to the wind, for all are blind.
> But now wind drops, dust settles; thereupon

There lurches past, his great eyes without thought
Under the shadow of stupid straw-pale locks,
That insolent fiend Robert Artisson
To whom the love-lorn lady Kyteler brought
Bronzed peacock feathers, red combs of her cocks.

There is a famous dictum of T. S. Eliot to the effect that great poetry can communicate before it is understood. It is not hard to appreciate in this extraordinary passage the wearing down of what is fine and noble, the sterile blast of dusty wind, noise, tumult, confusion and insanity, irrational swinging from love to rage and, finally, the dragging syllables that bring evil to life in sub-human shape and the sudden tautening of the verse as the love-lorn victim sacrifices things of earthly beauty and colour to that bleached-out form. We could deepen our appreciation by looking into Arthur Symons's poem, 'The Dance of the Daughters of Herodias', or into Oscar Wilde's play *Salome* (1894). We might look also at one of Yeats's own early poems. 'The Hosting of the Sidhe', and at the note he wrote upon it about the gods of ancient Ireland, the Sidhe, who 'journey in whirling wind, the winds that were called the dance of the daughters of Herodias in the Middle Ages, Herodias doubtless taking the place of some old goddess.' These figures destroy human hopes and happiness; they bring ruin upon wisdom and beauty; they make us, like Herod in Wilde's play, feel a wind blowing and hear 'in the air something that is like the beating of wings, like the beating of vast wings' (though how banal these images are in comparison!). Then there are the names Yeats has taken from a British Museum manuscript: Lady Kyteler and Robert Artisson, her incubus. (She had been brought before the Kilkenny Inquisition in 1324 for dealings in magic.) The curious unity of Yeats's mind is apparent: from the painfully present realities of his time in history it reaches out into fairytale and history, into literature, folklore and myth, fusing related complexities into perfectly controlled surges and eddies of visionary expression. He is not just a representative writer who mirrors his age in its own undistinguished terms; he is an individual who embodies his consciousness of that age in a uniquely personal myth. Dispassionately, later, we *might* wish to say that poems like 'Nineteen Hundred and Nineteen' are too crisis-dominated. (On a simple level the holding of a highly successful Swift Tercentenary Conference in 1967 showed that the people of Dublin are not always 'at their old tricks yet'.) Where values are involved it is difficult to judge, but one fact seems very clear indeed: many of the writers of our period would be in the dock with Yeats. Much of its significant literature turned out to be a vision of despair, decadence, nightmare, thunder of feet, tumult of images . . . But those last phrases are borrowed, of course.

.   .   .   .   .   .

Yeats's formulations, symbolic though they may be, come very aptly to mind. To attempt to translate them into ordinary terms can only be a temporary expedient, as I think we can see from that well-known poem, 'The Second Coming'. This already contains, in lines 7 and 8 for instance, powerful direct statement; it also contains metaphors ('anarchy is loosed upon the world'), metaphors with symbolic force ('the falcon cannot hear the falconer') and pure symbols (the 'vast image' from the Great Memory of which all our lesser memories are part). These, surely, *add* immensely to any conceivable paraphrase, however long.

> Turning and turning in the widening gyre
> The falcon cannot hear the falconer;
> Things fall apart; the centre cannot hold;
> Mere anarchy is loosed upon the world.
> The blood-dimmed tide is loosed, and everywhere
> The ceremony of innocence is drowned;
> The best lack all conviction, while the worst
> Are full of passionate intensity.
>
> Surely some revelation is at hand;
> Surely the Second Coming is at hand.
> The Second Coming! Hardly are those words out
> When a vast image out of *Spiritus Mundi*
> Troubles my sight: somewhere in sands of the desert
> A shape with lion body and the head of a man,

A gaze blank and pitiless as the sun,
Is moving its slow thighs, while all about it
Reel shadows of the indignant desert birds.
The darkness drops again; but now I know
That twenty centuries of stony sleep
Were vexed to nightmare by a rocking cradle,
And what rough beast, its hour come round at last,
Slouches towards Bethlehem to be born?

In Yeats's system the cycle of history since the birth of Christ is coming to its end, and the countermovement will before long begin with some catastrophic happening. This poem of 1920 has many memorable lines and haunting images. Its 'fearful symmetry' could not have been framed by any other poet of the time, but has it perhaps reached a level of both statement and symbolism too remote from the Irish experience that is its invisible foundation? Has too much reality been strained out of the myth contained in this poem? Yeats, too, we remember, had been in Arcady—has he merely created its perfect antitype, just as distanced from reality though antithetic in values? To my mind, once one gets over the exhilaration of riding the tiger, 'The Second Coming' suffers in comparison with Yeats's 'Meditations in Time of Civil War' (1921–23), a poem with which we must conclude this survey of Yeats's verse.

When De Valera and others refused to accept the treaty signed in 1921 by the Chairman of the Irish delegation with Lloyd George, Irishmen took up arms against each other and civil war broke out. Erskine Childers was shot at dawn. Yeats's 'symbolical tower seemed likely to be attacked by unsymbolical men and weapons at any moment, and husband and wife frequently ran to the window to look out when signs of gunfire were especially close', Ellmann tells us.

V

The Road at My Door

An affable Irregular,
A heavily-built Falstaffian man,

> Comes cracking jokes of civil war
> As though to die by gunshot were
> The finest play under the sun.
>
> A brown Lieutenant and his men,
> Half dressed in national uniform,
> Stand at my door, and I complain
> Of the foul weather, hail and rain,
> A pear-tree broken by the storm.
>
> I count those feathered balls of soot
> The moor-hen guides upon the stream,
> To silence the envy in my thought;
> And turn towards my chamber, caught
> In the cold snows of a dream.

There is no loss of reality; history of the simplest personal kind, in fact, is provided for us. But the last line is a reminder of Yeats's ranging imagination, which moves to bring images from past and future into symbolic relationship with present experience. Poem I, for instance, entitled 'Ancestral Houses', evokes the beauty and abundance of life associated with great houses (the literary tradition stretching back to such splendid poems as Ben Jonson's 'To Penshurst', Thomas Carew's 'To Saxham' and Andrew Marvell's 'Upon Appleton House'). Yeats must have had in mind those of Ireland, like his friend Lady Gregory's, but also Lady Ottoline Morell's house and gardens at Garsington. (Compare page 139, above). They stood for so much that was civilised in life, 'though now it seems', Yeats continues,

> As if some marvellous empty sea-shell flung
> Out of the obscure dark of the rich streams,
> And not a fountain, were the symbol which
> Shadows the inherited glory of the rich.

The whole tradition of living (for Yeats, incidentally, the offspring of 'violence' and 'bitterness' seeking its antitype in 'sweetness' and 'gentleness') had lost its vital creative force; no longer a flowing fountain of rich experience but a finished, discarded object, however beautiful.

Yeats literally at this time in his life retired into his ancient tower and relative isolation, accepting change because of his awareness (or belief) that 'only an aching heart/Conceives a changeless work of art.' The middle poems of 'Meditations' describe the private 'monument and fitting symbol' he made, but Poems VI and VII recreate the furious realities of civil war, which prove to be far more disturbing than the ending of a traditional great-house culture. These realities of war threaten more than physical existence: they subvert inner equilibrium:

> A barricade of stone or wood;
> Some fourteen days of civil war;
> Last night they trundled down the road
> That dead young soldier in his blood:
> Come build in the empty house of the stare. [starling]
>
> We had fed the heart on fantasies,
> The heart's grown brutal from the fare;
> More substance in our enmities
> Than in our love; O honey-bees,
> Come build in the empty house of the stare.

Yeats gives his testimony of the profoundly uncreating forces at large in Ireland—his last stanza above becomes absolutely general in its application—and, lest we should imagine that rebuilding will be as easy as it is for bees, he looks pessimistically to the future in the final poem, 'I See Phantoms of Hatred and of the Heart's Fullness and of the Coming Emptiness'. Once again there are weird but unforgettable amalgamations:

> Their legs long, delicate and slender, aquamarine their eyes,
> Magical unicorns bear ladies on their backs.
> The ladies close their musing eyes. No prophecies,
> Remembered out of Babylonian almanacks,
> Have closed the ladies' eyes, their minds are but a pool
> Where even longing drowns under its own excess;
> Nothing but stillness can remain when hearts are full
> Of their own sweetness, bodies of their loveliness.

R

The cloud-pale unicorns, the eyes of aquamarine,
The quivering half-closed eyelids, the rags of cloud or of lace,
Or eyes that rage has brightened, arms it has made lean,
Give place to an indifferent multitude, give place
To brazen hawks. Nor self-delighting reverie,
Nor hate of what's to come, nor pity for what's gone,
Nothing but grip of claw, and the eye's complacency,
The innumerable clanging wings that have put out the moon.

I turn away and shut the door, and on the stair
Wonder how many times I could have proved my worth
In something that all others understand or share;
But O! ambitious heart, had such a proof drawn forth
A company of friends, a conscience set at ease,
It had but made us pine the more. The abstract joy
The half-read wisdom of daemonic images,
Suffice the ageing man as once the growing boy.

One critic has justly remarked of the 'Meditations' and 'Nineteen Hundred and Nineteen' that there is in them 'an interplay of individual attitude and public event which it is not easy to parallel' (Graham Martin, 'The Later Poetry of W. B. Yeats', in *The Modern Age*, ed. Boris Ford, 1961). This comment points directly to their unique value. One might also say that there is in them an interplay of individual and public language, and it is amazing how wide a range Yeats manages: for instance, 'indifferent multitude' and 'brazen hawks' are within a line of each other above, syntactically equated. It is not possible to pretend that Yeats is an easy poet. More often than not it is only wise to seek scholarly and critical guidance. Fortunately, Yeats has been very well served by his commentators, and though what Ellmann calls 'esoteric Yeatsism' can be overstressed, we should not look to him for anything like the continuous lucidity of his fellow Irishman, Bernard Shaw. Shaw was intelligent enough, actually, to give the Aesthetics a lot of their due (witness the dialectical successes he allows the poet Marchbanks in *Candida*, 1897), but like H. G. Wells with Henry James, he was undoubtedly on the other side of the fence. When Yeats asked Shaw for an Irish play to stage in the Abbey Theatre, Shaw wrote *John Bull's Other Island* (1904). It is, as we might have expected, jestingly serious about Irishmen:

> *Doyle* It's all dreaming, all imagination. He can't be religious. The inspired Churchman that teaches him the sanctity of life and the importance of conduct is sent away empty; while the poor village priest that gives him a miracle or sentimental story of a saint, has cathedrals built for him out of the pennies of the poor. He can't be intelligently political: he dreams of what the Shan Van Vocht [Poor Old Woman] said in ninetyeight. If you want to interest him in Ireland you've got to call the unfortunate island Kathleen ni Hoolihan and pretend she's a little old woman. It saves thinking. It saves working. It saves everything except imagination, imagination, imagination . . .

Cathleen ni Houlihan (1902) was a patriotic play by Yeats, about which in later years he was to ask:

> Did that play of mine send out
> Certain men the English shot?

But whatever its effect upon its audience, and it seems to have been considerable, it was definitely not realistic in Shaw's sense. Against this we can set Yeats's reaction to Shaw's *Arms and the Man* (1894):

> I listened to *Arms and the Man* with admiration and hatred. It seemed to me inorganic, logical straightness and not the crooked road of life, yet I stood aghast before its energy as today before that of the Stone Drill by Mr. Epstein or of some design by Mr. Wyndham Lewis. He was right to claim Samuel Butler for his master, for Butler was the first Englishman to make the discovery that it is possible to write with great effect without music, without style, either good or bad, to eliminate from the mind all emotional implication and to prefer plain water to every vintage, so much metropolitan lead and

solder to any tendril of the vine. Presently I had a nightmare that I was haunted by a sewing-machine, that clicked and shone, but the incredible thing was that the machine smiled, smiled perpetually. Yet I delighted in Shaw as a formidable man. He could hit my enemies and the enemies of all I loved, as I could never hit, as no living author that was dear to me could ever hit.

Here, it seems to me, is the great divide opening between writers about the turn of the century. If Shaw is, in Yeats's near-lethal phrase, like a sewing machine that clicks, shines and smiles perpetually, then Yeats, in the eyes of men like Shaw, is even at his most realistic like one of those Greek sculptures of Centaurs, which join to a body that is a miracle of equine and human naturalism—a *stylized* head. Ordinary Centaurs are extraordinary enough, but Yeats is the Centaur with a difference.

We leave both men with their writing careers unfinished. Shaw's *Saint Joan*, his best-known play, is yet to come and Yeats has still to publish his greatest poems, 'Byzantium', 'Coole Park and Ballylee', 'The Municipal Gallery Revisited' and so on. Other poems on Casement and Parnell will revert to a kind of savage and jingoistic simplicity, but nothing of this kind is able to cancel the authentic mastery of the poems we have been studying. 'Try to get the most out of your material, but always in such a way as to honour it most', Morris wrote in his 'Art and Industry'. This, it seems to me, is just what Yeats has done: he took the history of his time, public and personal, and honoured it by using all the resources of language to encompass its complexities. His poetry is an admittedly intuitive response to experience, always suspect to plain and sensible men; he thrived on the tensions between artist and man of action, refusing to turn his writing into either a pleasant adjunct to serious living or a tool to be used in the world's business. At his best Yeats can weld internal and external events into imaginative symbols without losing either immediacy or subtlety of human reaction, 'for wisdom is a butterfly and not a gloomy bird of prey' he used to claim. In the hard times of the twentieth century the most remarkable of modern authors proved able to resist the inheritors of nineteenth-century Gradgrindery[6] and, indeed, to carry the campaign right out of the Aesthetic side-show into which other writers had fled because of it.

NOTES

[1] H. G. Wells in his *Daily Express* controversy with Churchill in 1920 wrote that he was 'obsessed by dreams of exploits and a career. . . . He is a great student and collector of the literature of Napoleon, that master-adventurer. Before all things he desires a dramatic world with villains—and one hero.' See Vincent Brome, *Six Studies in Quarrelling* (1958), page 61. See also Wells's *Outline of History* (1923).

[2] It is, for the scholar Mario Praz, 'the pivot upon which the whole psychology of the Decadent Movement turns . . . all the prose works of the Decadence, from Lorrain to Gourmont, Wilde and D'Annunzio, are contained in embryo in *A rebours*.' See the section 'Byzantium', in *The Romantic Agony* (1933), Chapter 5.8.

[3] This is not to say by any means that Tennyson played to the gallery. The drafts of his unpublished poem, 'Wherefore, in these dark ages of the press . . .', are most illuminating in this connexion and show that his 'sense of Art' was like that of James, a kind of conscience that would prevent him seeking public acclaim at any cost. The drafts have been printed from the Trinity College, Cambridge, manuscripts by Christopher Ricks in the *Times Literary Supplement* for 21 August 1969.

[4] R. B. Cunninghame Graham had attempted to convey Parnell's magnetism in 'A Memory of Parnell' (1906). See *Thirty Tales & Sketches*, ed. R. Garnett.

[5] It offended both religious and national feelings. Performances had to be continued under police protection.

[6] See Dickens's *Hard Times* (1854), chapter 2: 'Thomas Gradgrind, sir. A man of realities. A man of facts and calculations. A man who proceeds upon the principle that two and two are four, and nothing over . . .'

9 : Drift into War

In his *England in the Nineteenth Century 1815–1914* (1950), David Thomson writes that nearly every year from 1895 onwards brought either a war or a war-scare. After the Boer War in particular, a new level of hysteria in international affairs led to the competitive building-up of national armaments and to the establishment of a new system of protective alliances between states. In Britain matters reached such a pitch that mythical airships of an invading force were seen over the coast by many 'eyewitnesses' in 1913—the counterpart of today's flying saucers, Thomson suggests. In other spheres of national life there were a great wave of strikes in industry, which involved violence and shooting, and, constantly seething, the intractable problem of Ulster, still with us today. Many of the people living in Northern Ireland wanted no part of the Home Rule being fought for by the rest of the country ('Orange bitters will not mix with Irish whiskey'), and in this they were supported by the Conservative Unionist Party. Bonar Law actually suggested that the Army should disobey orders if asked to coerce Ulster and Lord Willoughby de Broke—we have already come across this intransigent peer—urged that the Army Annual Act should not be passed. This was in 1914, with war-preparations of an unprecedented kind being made in Europe. To these signs of unrest and anarchy on all sides, seen by George Dangerfield in his *The Strange Death of Liberal England 1910–1914* as part and parcel of the same general release of pent-up energies and passions, must be added the resort to violence by some sections of the Suffragette Movement. Since it is often said that the position of women in a society is an index of its civilisation, it is worth looking a little more closely at the movement and one or two of its literary aspects.

In 1903, at 82 Nelson Street in Manchester, Mrs Emmeline Pankhurst founded the Women's Social and Political Union, a militant society. Their motto was clear and succinct: Deeds, not Words. They derived their policy from Charles Parnell and the Irish party in the preceding century: they had no wish to be loved, they wished to shock and outrage. Mrs Pankhurst admitted in her autobiography, *My Own Story* (1914), that she had put into practice the political lesson taught her when her husband stood as a Liberal candidate in 1885. Home Rulers successfully opposed him, and so Suffragettes made a practice of attacking government candidates in by-elections. One example might be the defeat of Winston Churchill in North-West Manchester in 1908, though Constance Rover notes in her centenary study, *Woman's Suffrage and Party Politics 1866–1914* (1967), that a spectacular intervention in this by-election was made by the Manchester Barmaids' Association. He must have been a dead duck from the start! (Other reasons for his defeat are suggested by Randolph S. Churchill in his *Winston S. Churchill: Young Statesman 1901–1914*, 1967, pages 258–60; the complications of Churchill's attitude to Woman's Suffrage, his 'ambivalent attitude', are also dealt with in this volume.) But Dr Rover goes on to refer to far more serious incicents. Hunger strikes by suffragettes in prison were met by forcible feeding, which changed the temper of the movement considerably: from about 1909 came the stone-throwing, window smashing, firing the contents of pillar boxes and other forms of arson, the damaging of pictures (including the Sargent portrait of Henry James at the Royal Academy) and, most unfortunate of all, the death of Miss Davison, who threw herself in front of the King's horse at the 1913 Derby. This kind of activism is reflected in H. G. Wells's *Ann Veronica* of 1909, which is, even so, much closer to a conventional novel than most of the Wells books we have looked at so far. Ultimately, of course, it is intended as a 'guide to conduct' in real life.

Chapter 10 of *Ann Veronica* is full of realistic details of the suffragette movement and its activities (though not particularly convincing *in toto*). The heroine joins 'The Women's Bond of Freedom' and meets one of its leaders, a striking young woman, forceful and animated, but 'about as capable of intelligent argument as a runaway steam-roller'. 'She was a trained being', Wells continues, 'trained by an implacable mother to one end', and we remember that two of Mrs Pankhurst's daughters, Christabel and Sylvia, worked in the movement. Ann Veronica was then enlisted for a raid on the House of Commons. There follows a description of this raid told in burlesque style ('minute figures of determined women at war with the universe'), the struggles with police, the cries of spectators ('Who'll mind the baby nar?'), the night in the cells and, next morning, the appearance in court before a disgusted magistrate. The following chapter deals with Ann Veronica's prison experiences, and here Wells's critical attitude expressed through the treatment of the raid and its aftermath becomes more explicit in Ann Veronica's consequent self-examination. She becomes disillusioned, not with the cause of woman's suffrage but with its militant manifestations. Even in prison these existed in the form of imitating animal noises before the mid-day meal,

> until the whole place was alive with barkings, yappings, roarings, pelican chatterings, and feline yowlings, interspersed with shrieks of hysterical laughter. To many in that crowded solitude it came as an extraordinary relief. It was better even than the hymn-singing. But it annoyed Ann Veronica.
>
> 'Idiots!' she said, when she heard this pandemonium, and with particular reference to the young lady with the throaty contralto next door. 'Intolerable idiots! . . .'
>
> It took some days for this phase to pass, and it left some scars and something like a decision. 'Violence won't do it', said Ann Veronica, 'begin violence, and the woman goes under. . . .
>
> 'But all the rest of our case is right. . . . Yes.'

Wells, in fact, makes the militant suffragette movement just a phase his heroine has to live through, carefully tailoring it to fit into two pretty self-contained chapters. His views are historically interesting in a representative sense, for there is little doubt that violence, for all its initial success in attracting public attention to the suffragette case, brought diminishing returns in public sympathy in the long run and antagonized many who were in a position to help. It is not surprising to learn that Churchill, who in 1909 had been attacked with a dog-whip at Bristol railway station, told a deputation of suffragettes shortly afterwards that he was bound to say he thought their cause had marched backwards. Yet as far as literary criticism of *Ann Veronica* is concerned, Wells's fundamental lack of approval of militancy has given these two chapters a rather hard gloss, more suitable perhaps for some kind of satiric form than a novel. They do not associate easily with the more sensitive chapters about the problems encountered by a young woman who feels she must break away from her overbearing father, a man quite incapable of conceiving that a daughter could want a degree and a career of her own:

> His ideas about girls and women were of a sentimental and modest quality; they were creatures, he thought, either too bad for a modern vocabulary, and then frequently most undesirably desirable, or too pure and good for life. He made this simple classification of a large and various sex to the exclusion of all intermediate kinds; he held that the two classes had to be kept apart even in thought and remote from one another. Women are made like the potter's vessels—either for worship or contumely, and are withal fragile vessels.
>
> (Chapter 1, 3.)

His daughter, however, is a descendant of 'the girls of the eighties' who 'broke bounds and sailed away on bicycles'; she is like Forster's Lucy Honeychurch in *A Room With a View* (*1908*), who seeks 'beauty rather than short skirts and latch keys. But independence was certainly her cue' (chapter 19). The chapters in which Wells describes his heroine's break contain some of the best writing in the book, though it could be argued that towards the end of the novel he avoids hardness only to fall into the opposite trap of sentimental improbability. We might adapt, in fact, one of the father's better mixed metaphors and say that the life of a novelist (rather than a young girl) is set about with prowling pitfalls, from which he must be shielded at all costs.

There were other, more whole-hearted opponents of female suffrage. Matthew Arnold's niece, Mrs Humphry Ward, was one of the moving spirits in the formation of the Women's National Anti-Suffrage League in 1908, which later merged with the Men's League—the Countess of Jersey very properly resigning the Presidency to the Earl of Cromer. (See *Woman's Suffrage*, chapter 9.) Kipling, who was featured in the *Anti-Suffrage Review* as a prominent supporter, sent a poem 'The Female of the Species' to the *Morning Post* in 1911. It is too long to quote in full (the whole poem may be read in *Rudyard Kipling's Verse: Inclusive Edition 1885–1932*, 1933), but the opening quatrains will give an idea of its quality; they include its famous refrain:

When the Himalayan peasant meets the he-bear in his pride,
He shouts to scare the monster, who will often turn aside.
But the she-bear thus accosted rends the peasant tooth and nail,
For the female of the species is more deadly than the male.

When Nag the basking cobra hears the careless foot of man,
He will sometimes wriggle sideways and avoid it if he can.
But his mate makes no such motion where she camps beside
    the trail,
For the female of the species is more deadly than the male.

When the early Jesuit fathers preached to Hurons and
    Choctaws,
They prayed to be delivered from the vengeance of the squaws.
'Twas the women, not the warriors, turned those stark
    enthusiasts pale,
For the female of the species is more deadly than the male.

It is hard to suppose that any opponent would be converted by this poem. It is undoubtedly amusing at this distance in time, but really takes its place with jumble sales, rallies, and other means of maintaining the cohesion (coherence?) of the converted. 'There was the music of the harp/And the clear song of the bard'—the language of *Beowulf* needs translation now, but social roles remain, it would seem, as the millenia roll by. Kipling sang for his clan in his day and even now may touch the heart of some misogynist, but the outbreak of war in August 1914 put an end to campaigning on either side. Before it ended, women, in quite changed circumstances, had gained the vote.

.   .   .   .   .   .

Although it is always wise to bear in mind the historian Maitland's warning that what is now long in the past was once in the future, it is true to say that the Great War had been feared and anticipated for many years beforehand. There are innumerable examples we could take. The essay from Conrad we have already quoted from, 'Autocracy and War', which was prompted by the Russo-Japanese conflict of 1904–5 and appeared in the *Fortnightly Review* for July 1905, is firstly a powerful indictment of Russia; but it also attacks Prussia, 'the evil counsellor of Russia on all the questions of her Polish problem'. Conrad feared 'Pan-Germanism', especially in the new century and under changing conditions:

Industrialism and commercialism—wearing high-sounding names in many languages (*Welt-politik* may serve for one instance) picking up coins behind the severe and disdainful figure of science whose giant strides have widened for us the horizon of the universe by some few inches—stand ready, almost eager, to appeal to the sword as soon as the globe of the earth has shrunk beneath our growing numbers by another ell or so. And democracy, which has elected to pin its faith to the supremacy of material interests, will have to fight their battles to the bitter end, on a mere pittance. . . .

The essay, which Conrad apparently thought highly of, ends with sarcasm about Germany's naval expansion under Admiral Alfred von Tirpitz and a portentous warning borrowed from the French statesman Gambetta:

The German eagle with a Prussian head looks all round the horizon not so much for something to do that would count for good in the records of the earth, as simply for something good to get. He gazes upon the land and upon the sea with the same covetous steadiness, for he has become of late a maritime eagle,

268 · DRIFT INTO WAR

and learned to box the compass. He gazes north and south, and east and west, and is inclined to look intemperately upon the waters of the Mediterranean when they are blue. The disappearance of the Russian phantom has given a foreboding of unwonted freedom to the *Welt-politik*. According to the national tendency this assumption of Imperial impulses would run into the grotesque were it not for the spikes of the pickelhaubes peeping out grimly from behind. Germany's attitude proves that no peace for the earth can be found in the expansion of material interests which she seems to have adopted exclusively as her only aim, ideal, and watchword. For the use of those who gaze half-unbelieving at the passing away of the Russian phantom, part Ghoul, part Djinn, part Old Man of the Sea, and wait half-doubting for the birth of a nation's soul in this age which knows no miracles, the once-famous saying of poor Gambetta, tribune of the people (who was simple and believed in the 'immanent justice of things') may be adapted in the shape of a warning that, so far as a future of liberty, concord, and justice is concerned: '*Le Prussianisme—voilà l'ennemi!*'

Conrad was by no means the only writer of the time to be concerned about the German menace. The Preface to volume 20 of the Atlantic Edition of H. G. Wells's *Works* tells us that its longest story, *The War in the Air*, which had been published first as a magazine serial in 1908, had been held back 'after novels published so late as 1916 in order to group it with various other of the writer's forecasts that anticipated the Great War.' With it in volume 20, in fact, are shorter pieces like 'The Land Ironclads', first published in the *Strand Magazine* in 1903, which describes a tank attack; an article on the significance of 'The Coming of Blériot' (July, 1909), which sees in this French aviator's successful crossing of the Channel a clear proof of the backwardness of English technology, and also a warning that from the military point of view Britain is no longer an inaccessible island:

Here the air is full of the clamour of rich and prosperous people invited to pay taxes, and beyond measure bitter. They are going to live abroad, cut their charities, dismiss old servants, and do all sorts of silly, vindictive things. We seem to be doing feeble next-to-nothings in the endowment of research. Not one in twenty of the boys of the middle and upper classes learns German or gets more than a misleading smattering of physical science. Most of them never learn to speak French. Heaven alone knows what they do with their brains!

Aeronautics, Wells saw, opened the way to an entirely new kind of warfare, and one which he feared would inevitably lead to the breakdown of civilisation and social organisation as he knew it. Along with this, as another major premise, *The War in the Air* depends upon his belief that war could be started by Imperial Germany in the shape of an airship attack on the United States. In the midst of these literally earth-shattering events, Wells placed one of his little men, a figure like Kipps or Polly, who accidentally blunders 'into the hot focus of Welt-Politik'. This was a great airship park, developing on a colossal scale the discoveries of Hunstedt and Stossel, Wells writes, giving Germany 'before all other nations a fleet of airships, the air power and the Empire of the world':

They were altogether fishlike. For the great airships with which Germany attacked New York in her last gigantic effort for world supremacy—before humanity realised that world supremacy was a dream—were the lineal descendants of the Zeppelin airship that flew over Lake Constance in 1906, and of the Lebaudy navigables that made their memorable excursions over Paris in 1907 and 1908. (Chapter 3.5.)

The parenthesis in the above quotation is interesting. Bert Smallways is taken with the invading air-fleet across the Atlantic where it met the American navy in battle and was successful. Wells takes the large historical view: here were the ironclad battleships, which first came into existence during the Crimean War and had since then involved 'enormous expenditure of human energy and resources' to maintain through their various stages from novelty to obsolescence, destroyed by 'cheap things of gas

and basketwork . . . smiting out of the sky!' World supremacy
appears to be attainable. But, after New York has been attacked
and has surrendered, resistance breaks out afresh; an airship is
shot down and then those who are trying to repair it are 'rushed
by an armed mob, and . . . killed after a fierce disorderly struggle':

> The difficulty of the Germans in both these cases came
> from the impossibility of landing any efficient force or, indeed,
> any force at all from the air-fleet. The airships were quite
> unequal to the transport of any adequate landing parties;
> their complement of men was just sufficient to manoeuvre
> and fight them in the air. From above they could inflict
> immense damage; they could reduce any organised govern-
> ment to a capitulation in the briefest space, but they could
> not disarm, much less could they occupy, the surrendered
> areas below. They had to trust to the pressure upon the
> authorities below of a threat to renew the bombardment. It
> was their sole resource. No doubt, with a highly organised
> and undamaged government and a homogenous and well-
> disciplined people that would have sufficed to keep the peace.
> But this was not the American case. Not only was the New
> York government a weak one and insufficiently provided with
> police, but the destruction of the City Hall and Post-Office
> and other central ganglia had hopelessly disorganised the co-
> operation of part with part. The street-cars and railways had
> ceased; the telephone service was out of gear and worked
> only intermittently. The Germans had struck at the head,
> and the head was conquered and stunned—only to release
> the body from its rule. New York had become a headless
> monster, no longer capable of collective submission. Every-
> where it lifted itself rebelliously; everywhere authorities and
> officials, left to their own initiative, were joining in the arming
> and flag-hoisting and excitement of that afternoon.
>
> (Chapter 6.5.)

Imagination is often thought of as a wild, undisciplined faculty, but
the above passage shows, I think, that in Wells there was a strong
logical component: his invention thrust out leaves and tendrils

from a stem of reasoned speculation. He goes on to write passages of horrific power about the fighting that eventually becomes world-wide, but along with this he always strives to draw the necessary consequences of his prophetic conceptions. Chapter 8 is explicit upon 'the special peculiarities of aerial warfare': the fact that large urban populations are placed under stress (he remarks on the experience of Paris in 1871, 'a comparatively light' experience), the ineffectiveness of Zeppelins against each other and the impossibility of air power being able to counter what could be called guerilla operations. Chaos, not world supremacy, is the result of the War in the Air initiated by Germany.

Chapter 11 pushes the argument to its conclusion, seeing Progress in Western Europe and America as no more than an accidental balance on the right side, 'infinitely more complex and delicate in its adjustments' than people of Wells's time suspected, and which they foolishly thought of as a fact of life in relation to which they bore no moral responsibility. They ignored the lessons of history, especially the collapse of every previous civilisation. Speaking from the point of view of a man of the future, Wells asks,

Could mankind have prevented this disaster of the War in the Air? An idle question that, as idle as to ask could mankind have prevented the decay that turned Assyria and Babylon to empty deserts or the slow decline and fall, the gradual social disorganisation, phase by phase, that closed the chapter of the Empire of the West. They could not, because they did not, they had not the will to arrest it. What mankind could achieve with a different will is a speculation as idle as it is magnificent. And this was no slow decadence that came to the Europeanised world; those other civilisations rotted and crumbled down, the Europeanised civilisation was, as it were, blown up. Within the space of five years it was altogether disintegrated and destroyed. Up to the very eve of the War in the Air one sees a spacious spectacle of incessant advance, a world-wide security, enormous areas with highly organised industry and settled populations, gigantic cities spreading gigantically, the seas and oceans dotted with shipping, the land netted with rails and open

ways. Then suddenly the German air-fleets sweep across the
scene, and we are in the beginning of the end.

.　　　.　　　.　　　.　　　.　　　.

There is not much doubt that Wells is the kind of writer who was
fully engaged with the life and activities, in the largest sense, of his
own age; furthermore, he had both the impulse to look back into
history (one of his works is called *The Outline of History*, 1920) and
then to extrapolate into the unknown future (another, a very important one to him, is called *Anticipations*, 1901). Professional
historians may well have reservations about Wells's accomplish-
ment; even the veriest amateur with the advantage of hindsight can
see the failures in his prophecies. At the very time I am drafting
these lines three American astronauts, Neil Armstrong, Edwin
Aldrin and Michael Collins, are on the way to the moon, with the
intention of setting foot on it for the first time. Apollo 11, it is
hardly necessary to say, does *not* depend for its motion upon a
mysterious, gravity-resisting substance called Cavorite, as the
voyaging sphere did in Wells's *The First Men in the Moon* (1901)!
On the other hand, Apollo 11 is not the more 'realistic' projectile
from a gun we read about in Jules Verne, either; and in addition,
Wells's romance is truly extraordinary for the fertility of invention
he displayed in creating it and for the excellence of his descriptions
of the lunar world. Critics have rightly praised chapter seven's
wonderful (the word is not lightly used) descriptions of sunrise on
the moon and the rapid growth of vegetation in the following
chapter. There is, too, the memorable description of the machine
that was the source of the streams of blue light running through the
underground caverns (chapter 14) and the imaginatively resourceful
way one of those streams is used in the pages that follow. His
narrator tells us:

And after all, I *do* remember one other thing besides the
purely personal affair, which is, that a sort of gutter came
presently across the floor of the cavern, and then ran along by
the side of the path of rock we followed. And it was full of that
same bright blue luminous stuff that flowed out of the great

machine. I walked close beside it and I can testify it radiated not a particle of heat. It was brightly shining, and yet it was neither warmer nor colder than anything else in the cavern.

As the two men walk along down their tunnel,

'Trickle, trickle,' went the flowing light very softly, and our footfalls and their echoes made an irregular paddle, paddle.

Further along the tunnel, and after some paragraphs of conversation, they come to a declivity and the little stream dips suddenly out of sight:

In another moment, as it seemed, we had reached the edge. The shining stream gave one meander of hesitation and then rushed over. It fell to a depth at which the sound of its descent was absolutely lost to us. Far below was a bluish glow, a sort of blue mist—at an infinite distance below. And the darkness the stream dropped out of became utterly void and blank, save that a thing like a plank projected from the edge of the cliff and stretched out and faded and vanished altogether. There was a warm air blowing up out of the gulf.

For a moment I and Cavor stood as near the edge as we dared, peering into a blue-tinged profundity. And then our guide was pulling at my arm.

That is a moment one does not easily forget, and as far as it is possible to reduce the workings of the fantastic imagination to mere details of craftsmanship, it seems to derive much of its power from the verbal life given to that cold-blue and brilliant stream.

The last chapters of *The First Men in the Moon* give an account of the Selenites, peculiar insect-like creatures met with in these subterranean passages, and is just as remarkable, for they are incredibly differentiated according to their function in society:

They differed in shape, they differed in size, they rang all the horrible changes on the theme of Selenite form! Some bulged and overhung, some ran about among the feet of their fellows. All of them had a grotesque and disquieting suggestion of an insect that has somehow contrived to mock humanity; but all

s

seemed to present an incredible exaggeration of some particular feature: one had a vast right fore-limb, an enormous
antennal arm, as it were; one seemed all leg, poised, as it were,
on stilts; another protruded the edge of his face mask into a
nose-like organ that made him startlingly human until one saw
his expressionless gaping mouth. The strange and (except for
the want of mandibles and palps) most insect-like head of the
mooncalf-minders underwent, indeed, the most incredible
transformations: here it was broad and low, here high and
narrow; here its leathery brow was drawn out into horns and
strange features; here it was whiskered and divided, and there
with a grotesquely human profile. One distortion was particularly conspicuous. There were several brain cases distended
like bladders to a huge size, with the face mask reduced to
quite small proportions.   (Chapter 24.)

This is still Wells allowing complete freedom to what Dryden in
the preface to *Annus Mirabilis* called the 'nimble Spaniel' of a
writer's imagination, letting it beat over and range 'through the
field of Memory'; in this case, surely, the memory of the young man
who had won a scholarship in 1884 to the Royal College of Science
at South Kensington. But there is a serious theme as well. Bernard
Bergonzi has noted that the possible future condition of humanity
was a topic that occupied Wells throughout his life and that in 1885
he delivered a paper on it to his College Debating Society (*The
Early H.G. Wells: A Study of the Scientific Romances*, Manchester,
1961, page 36).

This paper, called 'The Past and Future of the Human Race',
may be conveniently read in a revised version printed amongst the
essays of *Certain Personal Matters: A Collection of Material, Mainly
Autobiographical* (1898). Its new title there is 'Of A Book Unwritten.'
A statement of Darwin's, made in that most famous book of his,
On the Origin of Species by Means of Natural Selection (1859)—
'Judging from the past, we may safely infer that not one living
species will transmit its unaltered likeness to a distant futurity'—
stands in the background of the young Wells's contention (through
one Professor Holzkopf) that man, no different from other species

subject to evolution, 'will undergo further modification in the future, and at last cease to be man, giving rise to some other type of animated being.' And so Wells imagines our remote descendants, hopping on their hands, with enormous brains and withered legs and abdomens, human tadpoles living in deep galleries below ground. These wierd beings are evidently comparable to the higher orders of Selenites on the moon, especially the extraordinary Grand Lunar, that ne plus ultra of intellectual development, but Bergonzi underlines the ambiguous attitude Wells has to all these speculative end-products of evolutionary processes. Are they admirable or are they detestable? If future societies are going to evolve in such ways, should we be pleased or should we be horrified? Selenite society represents 'an extreme, and even grotesque, type of the totally organized social order that was increasingly to be the ideal of his utopian speculations', Bergonzi writes; and Wells, he goes on to suggest, is like his own hero of *The First Men in the Moon*. When Mr Cavor first comes across young Selenites confined in jars to be turned into specialised machine minders, 'he both admires a society that could do such things, and is dismayed by the results in practice.'

·   ·   ·   ·   ·   ·

Historically speaking, both the ideas and the attitudes of Wells are of exceptional interest. He continues and intensifies the kind of fired imagination displayed by that Victorian hero of Mrs Gaskell's *North and South*, John Thornton, who saw in James Nasmyth's invention of the steam-hammer a glorious move in 'the war which compels, and shall compel, all material power to yield to science.' After all, since the early years of Victoria's reign scientists had gone on to discover or develop ideas of much greater potential. Wells refers in the early pages of *The First Men in the Moon* to 'those Röntgen rays there was so much talk about a year or so ago', for example; these are the x-rays discovered by Wilhelm Röntgen in 1895. And, just about the time Wells was writing this book, which was serialised in the *Strand Magazine* for 1901, Max Planck announced his revolutionary quantum hypothesis. On 14 December 1900, classical physics was questioned in one aspect of its very foundations, and fundamental concepts were successfully challenged. Wells can be seen as providing a literary equivalent to scientific triumphs that could only be properly grasped by experts, and while his ideas and inventions are often incredible even now, he does generate excitement of a similar kind. Less fantastic, and to be expected from a man who joined the Fabian Society, are Wells's socio-political interests, which deserve more attention than I have given them so far.

When the Grand Lunar began to question Cavor about his life on earth (we remember Gulliver's conversations with the king of Brobdingnag and his Houyhnhnm master[1]), it becomes necessary to explain to this all-powerful ruler of the moon the nature of Democracy. I have always liked the Grand Lunar's first reaction to Cavor's outline of the democratic method:

When I had done he ordered cooling sprays upon his brow, and then requested me to repeat my explanation conceiving something had miscarried.

'Do they not do different things, then?' said Phi-oo.

Some, I admitted, were thinkers and some officials; some hunted, some were mechanics, some artists, some toilers. 'But *all* rule,' I said.

'And have they not different shapes to fit them to their different duties?'

'None that you can see,' I said, 'except perhaps, for clothes. Their minds perhaps differ a little,' I reflected.

'Their minds must differ a great deal,' said the Grand Lunar, 'or they would all want to do the same things.'

In order to bring myself into a closer harmony with his preconceptions, I said that his surmise was right. 'It was all hidden in the brain,' I said; 'but the difference was there. Perhaps if one could see the minds and souls of men they would be as varied and unequal as the Selenites. There were great men and small men, men who could reach out far and wide, and men who could go swiftly; noisy, trumpet-minded men, and men who could remember without thinking. . . . [The record is indistinct for three words.]

He interrupted me to recall me to my previous statement. 'But you said all men rule?' he pressed.

'To a certain extent,' I said, and made, I fear, a denser fog with my explanation.

He reached out to a salient fact. 'Do you mean,' he asked, 'that there is no Grand Earthly?'

Again, I think, a very effective line. Yet more important than the details of technique is what Bergonzi has acutely characterised as the product of Wells's early individualism and later, swift acceptance of a collectivist frame of reference: the doctrine of the 'élite', a governing aristocracy of technologists and managers. (See *The Early H. G. Wells*, pages 169–70.) It dates from 1897, when in Book II, Chapter 7, of *The War of the Worlds* the 'Artilleryman' looks forward to the superior human beings who will come together and find a way of defeating the Martian invaders. In this work, probably the finest of Wells's romances, is 'the first suggestion of the need for an intellectual and physical élite which was increasingly to dominate his sociological thinking, and which received its most systematic expression in the Samurai of *A Modern Utopia*' (page 138). It is not surprising that Bergonzi should also note the beginnings of interest in the thought of Friedrich Neitzsche in England during the 1890s, the assimilation of his thought to that of Darwin, and the possibility that Wells's Samurai and later versions of an élite 'may be attempts to give a sociological embodiment to the *Übermensch*' (pages 10–11). The intellectual influence generally of such thinkers is incalculably great. Shaw's *Man and Superman* (1903), especially its preface, Act III (the Don Juan in Hell sequence) and appended *Revolutionists' Handbook*, is another illustration of this.

In Cavor's conversation with the Grand Lunar, the subject of earthly wars is also touched upon:

I told them an ironclad could fire a shot of a ton twelve miles, and go through twenty feet of iron—and how we could steer torpedoes under water. I went on to describe a Maxim gun in action, and what I could imagine of the battle of Colenso. The

Grand Lunar was so incredulous that he interrupted the translation of what I had said in order to have my verification of my account. They particularly doubted my description of the men cheering and rejoicing as they went into (?battle)

'But surely they do not like it!' translated Phi-oo.

I assured them men of my race considered battle the most glorious experience of life, at which the whole assembly was stricken with amazement.

The last sentence is worth bearing in mind, for later in this chapter we will be reading some of its most famous illustrations, writings more widely known than perhaps any works from this period. The whole passage shows, too, that for all the science-fiction quality of *The First Men in the Moon*, it bears a relation to contemporary realities, though not to any great extent, one must admit. We might also note here that *The War of the Worlds* is in its more powerfully mythic way related to *The War in the Air*. The latter is a relatively plain statement about the practical dangers facing the island of Britain with the development of airships and, later in the story, aeroplanes. But the quotation from its eleventh chapter on page 271 above concerning the fate of the 'Europeanised world', complacent, heedless, ripe for destruction and therefore inevitably subjected to apocalyptic terrors, is a proof of Wells's attempt to rise above the minutiae of day-to-day technological reality and arrive at some grander pattern of events. The balance between fantastic myth and reality is different in all these works, yet they all express feelings of apprehension, malaise and lost vitality. That this mood was not confined to Wells we have already seen in works like Gissing's *The Nether World* and Hardy's *Tess of the D'Urbervilles*; or compare Gosse's comments on Ibsen quoted on pages 128–9 above. We know too, that these feelings were not confined to literature. Historians have claimed that a phenomenon like jingoism, for all its bluster, is an expression of anxiety and tension, and we have already considered the early twentieth-century panics and war-scares, strikes and suffragette violence. Most disturbing, perhaps, of all, was the feeling that all these external events had their origin deep within man himself: one remembers the famous and *Strange Case of Dr*

Jekyll and Mr Hyde (1886), and A. E. Housman's poem 'The Welsh
Marches', which appeared in *A Shropshire Lad* (1896):

> The sound of fight is silent long
> That began the ancient wrong;
> Long the voice of tears is still
> That wept of old the endless ill.
>
> In my heart it has not died,
> The war that sleeps on Severn side;
> They cease not fighting, east and west,
> On the marches of my breast.
>
> Here the truceless armies yet
> Trample, rolled in blood and sweat;
> They kill and kill and never die;
> And I think that each is I.
>
> None will part us, none undo
> The knot that makes one flesh of two,
> Sick with hatred, sick with pain,
> Strangling—When shall we be slain?

Alongside this we must put the introductory poem of Housman's
More Poems (1936):

> They say my verse is sad: no wonder;
>   Its narrow measure spans
> Tears of eternity, and sorrow,
>   Not mine, but man's.
>
> This is for all ill-treated fellows
>   Unborn and unbegot,
> For them to read when they're in trouble
>   And I am not.

·   ·   ·   ·   ·   ·

In the new century, as F. T. Marinetti's 1909 Futurist Manifesto
shows, *avant-garde* theorists were rejecting the past and its values,
welcoming war and danger and aggression, seeing beauty only in
struggle and the violent, amoral speed and power of machines,
more wonderful to them than the Winged Victory of Samothrace.

One is tempted to say when reading the Manifesto that the English representative of Futurism is Toad of Toad Hall, who began his wildly comic career in Kenneth Grahame's *The Wind in the Willows* (1908), but there is nothing funny about the machines and the new implements of war provided by applied science in 1914:

> So now must I,
>   Bird of the night,
> Towards the sky
>   Make wheeling flight,
> And bear my poison o'er the gloomy land,
> And let it loose with hard unsparing hand.
>
> The chafers boom
>   With whirring wings,
> And haunt the gloom
>   Which twilight brings—
> So in nocturnal travel do I wail
> As through the night the wingèd engines sail.
>
> Death, Grief, and Pain
>   Are what I give.
> O that the slain
>   Might live—might live!
> I know them not, for I have blindly killed,
> And nameless hearts with nameless sorrow filled.

These stanzas are from a poem called 'Nox Mortis', by Paul Bewsher; it is quoted in Maurice Hussey's recent anthology, *Poetry of the First World War* (1967), along with a poem by Jeffery Day, an air ace who was killed in action. As Hussey says, such poetry had novel forms of experience for its subject, though we must not forget H. G. Wells's prose. Day was very successful in rendering the sensation of flight in a poem with the unpromisingly 'poetic' title of 'On the Wings of the Morning'. It is a fairly long poem, so it is not given in full here:

> My turning wing inclines towards the ground;
>   The ground itself glides up with graceful swing
> and at the plane's far tip twirls slowly round,

then drops from sight again beneath the wing
   to slip away serenely as before,
   a cubist-patterned carpet on the floor.

Hills gently sink and valleys gently fill.
   The flattened fields grow ludicrously small;
slowly they pass beneath and slower still
   until they hardly seem to move at all.
      Then suddenly they disappear from sight,
      hidden by fleeting wisps of faded white.

The wing-tips, faint and dripping, dimly show,
   blurred by the wreaths of mist that intervene.
Weird, half-seen shadows flicker to and fro
   across the pallid fog-bank's blinding screen.
      At last the choking mists release their hold,
      and all the world is silver, blue, and gold.

The last line shows that Day is not always able to resist the temptation to over-compose his picture, to make an appropriate setting in which to dream 'a happy dream of golden days', but he has evolved a most effective verse-movement and syntax to recreate his experience. I think his last stanza will show this also:

The scattered hues and shades of green and brown
   fashion themselves into the land I know,
turning and twisting, as I spiral down
   towards the landing ground; till, skimming low,
      I glide with slackening speed across the ground,
      and come to rest with lightly grating sound.

Not that these poems provided a revolutionary new style to match the novelty of their material. This is true of much of the poetry written early in the Great War, which can often be related to the Georgian anthologies edited by Edward Marsh from 1912 onwards. Rupert Brooke's 'The Old Vicarage, Grantchester', dated Café des Westens, Berlin, May 1912, centrally demonstrates the way in which the Georgian poets Marsh gathered together had reduced the scale of the kind of poetry we have seen in chapter 6 above (the

voices of various imperial nightingales) as they turned to simpler
and more homely themes:

> Just now the lilac is in bloom,
> All before my little room;
> And in my flower-beds, I think,
> Smile the carnation and the pink;
> And down the borders, well I know,
> The poppy and the pansy blow . . .
> Oh! there the chestnuts, summer through,
> Beside the river make for you
> A tunnel of green gloom, and sleep
> Deeply above; and green and deep
> The stream mysterious glides beneath,
> Green as a dream and deep as death.
> —Oh, damn! I know it! . . .

But here we must break off to admit that this is not just a sentimental idyll nor the 'charming' poem it has been called. The
colloquial 'damn' introduces a much more realistic Brooke a few
lines later:

> Here am I, sweating, sick, and hot,
> And there the shadowed waters fresh
> Lean up to embrace the naked flesh.
> *Temperamentvoll* German Jews
> Drink beer around;—and *there* the dews
> Are soft beneath a morn of gold.
> Here tulips bloom as they are told;
> Unkempt about those hedges blows
> An English unofficial rose . . .

We might, at this point, feel that a Masefield-like earthiness on the
subject of sweat still leaves the patriotism about rural England
quite intact, but as the poem continues we discover that this realism
is extended to the complexity of the poet's attitude, whilst at the
same time the subject-matter becomes a sort of Trollopian fantasy:

> And in that garden, black and white,
> Creep whispers through the grass all night;
> And spectral dance, before the dawn,

A hundred Vicars down the lawn;
Curates, long dust, will come and go
On lissom, clerical, printless toe;
And oft between the boughs is seen
The sly shade of a Rural Dean . . .
Till, at a shiver in the skies,
Vanishing with Satanic cries,
The prim ecclesiastic rout
Leaves but a startled sleeper-out,
Grey heavens, the first bird's drowsy calls,
The falling house that never falls.

God! I will pack, and take a train,
And get me to England once again!
For England's the one land, I know,
Where men with Splendid Hearts may go . . .

We might well wonder how seriously we should take this poem at
any particular point, and there are other bewilderments to come
before we arrive at the emotional lines leading up to the famous
conclusion:

Say, is there Beauty yet to find?
And Certainty? and Quiet kind?
Deep meadows yet, for to forget
The lies, and truths, and pain? . . . oh! yet
Stands the Church clock at ten to three?
And is there honey still for tea?

My own belief is that Brooke is trying to have it more ways than
both (if such an expression can be allowed), thus demonstrating his
native superiority to presumed Germanic regularity and inflexibility.
A somewhat unpleasant superiority, one might say; or more subtly,
the inevitable result of a relatively sophisticated mind, at *that*
period in history, failing to subdue itself to pastoral quietism and
patriotic simplicity.

.   .   .   .   .   .

When war came, however, Brooke broke these 'furies of complexity' and spoke out with greater directness:

If I should die, think only this of me:
  That there's some corner of a foreign field
That is for ever England. There shall be
  In that rich earth a richer dust concealed;
A dust whom England bore, shaped, made aware,
  Gave, once, her flowers to love, her ways to roam,
A body of England's, breathing English air,
  Washed by the rivers, blest by suns of home.

And think, this heart, all evil shed away,
  A pulse in the eternal mind, no less
    Gives somewhere back the thoughts by England given;
Her sights and sounds; dreams happy as her day;
  And laughter, learnt of friends; and gentleness,
    In hearts at peace, under an English heaven.

This sonnet, 'The Soldier', has been subjected to much hard criticism since Easter 1915, when it was praised by Dean Inge in St Paul's. D. J. Enright, in his essay 'The Literature of the First World War' (*The Modern Age*, ed. B. Ford) has suggested that for all the reiteration of 'England' and 'English', 'an odd uncertainty as to whether the poet is praising England or himself—"a richer dust"—remains despite that reiteration.' I do not really think this is so if the poem is read by itself, but it is actually the fifth in a sequence published first in *New Numbers* in December 1914, and then reprinted in *1914 & Other Poems* (1915), which ran through impression after impression. The first poem in the sequence, 'Peace', undoubtedly seems to contain elements too personal to be those of a representative young Englishman:

Now God be thanked Who has matched us with His hour,
  And caught our youth, and wakened us from sleeping,
With hand made sure, clear eye, and sharpened power,
  To turn, as swimmers into cleanness leaping,
Glad from a world grown old and cold and weary,
  Leave the sick hearts that honour could not move,
And half-men, and their dirty songs and dreary,
  And all the little emptiness of love!

Brooke speaks for many of his contemporaries at the beginning of this octave, but the last two lines at least seem to invite precise and personal questions. If the poem is compared from this point of view with Hardy's 'Drummer Hodge' or Newbolt's 'The Volunteer' (see pages 210–12 above), the difference is clear. It is possible to argue, I think, that 'The Soldier' should on these grounds be allowed to stand by itself as a set-piece, when possibly only the sharpest ears will catch unwanted overtones of subjective obsession.

That Brooke should identify himself with England is given considerable ratification by the reaction to his death in the Aegean and his burial on 23 April, 1915, 'the day of Shakespeare and St. George.' He became for many the very essence of the best England could sacrifice in her cause. Bernard Bergonzi's *Heroes' Twilight: A Study of the Literature of the Great War* (1965) is very pertinent indeed on the subject of the Rupert Brooke legend and its amazing efflorescence. He stresses a point of considerable relevance for us: the reception of the sonnets was such that even now it is difficult to discuss them as literature. 'They are,' he writes, 'works of very great mythic power, since they formed a unique focus for what the English felt, or wanted to feel, in 1914–15: they crystallize the powerful archetype of Brooke, the young Apollo, in his sacrificial role of the hero-as-victim. Considered, too, as historical documents, they are of interest as an index to the popular state of mind in the early months of the war.' Maurice Hussey, too, states that they both won a public for war-poetry and encouraged others to write it; without them poetry might not have become the dominant art-form it did at the time.

This was not an unmixed blessing, however, when the poetry of Robert Nichols is considered. His very brief experience at the Front in the Royal Field Artillery was distilled into two volumes of verse: *Invocation: War Poems and Others* (1915) and *Ardours and Endurances* (1917). The latter became a best-seller, and Nichols himself took to public readings of his own poetry and that of famous contemporaries, some of whom were not exactly pleased. Robert Graves wrote rather waspishly that he 'started a legend of Siegfried [Sassoon], himself and me as the new Three Musketeers, though the three of us had never once been together in the same room.' One sees in his poetry the heroic, sacrificial attitude so common in the earlier part of the war, as in 'Boy':

> In a far field, away from England, lies
> A Boy I friended with a care like love;
> All day the wide earth aches, the cold wind cries,
> The melancholy clouds drive on above.
>
> There, separate from him by a little span,
> Two eagle cousins, generous, reckless, free,
> Two Grenfells, lie, and my Boy is made man,
> One with these elder knights of chivalry.

No one should be contemptuous of the actual deeds of such young men, but we may sharply question the mode of Nichols's celebration, which is a task performed for us in some detail by J. H. Johnston's *English Poetry of the First World War: A Study in the Evolution of Lyric and Narrative Form* (1964).

The problem with such verses is that they undoubtedly spring from genuine emotions in the writers and they do meet very real needs in their readers. The outbreak of war, at least, is a time when there are few firm pacifists—Bertrand Russell, who in 1918 spent six months in prison for anti-war activities, was one and D. H. Lawrence, whose autobiographical account of the war years can be read in the bitter chapter 10 of his novel *Kangaroo* (1923), was another. But it was more usual for authors to lend their pens to the war effort, sometimes in a very straightforward way indeed: 'A little while ago, during a short visit to America, I was often questioned about the Dardanelles Campaign. People asked me why that attempt had been made, why it had been made in that particular manner, why other courses had not been taken, why this had been done and that either neglected or forgotten, and whether a little more persistence, here or there, would not have given us the victory.' This could hardly be called incisive! It is the very unpretentious opening to John Masefield's *Gallipoli* (1916), much of which is similarly plain exposition of the Dardanelles campaign ('Let the reader imagine . . .'), with maps and photographs, some of which can only be described as homely. It was meant to appeal to a wide public. There are in addition quotations from the *Song of Roland* at the beginning of each Section and at special moments the prose gathers itself up to the height of the great argument:

> They saw the hump of Achi Baba flicker and burn and roll up to heaven in a swathe of blackness, and multitudinous brightness changing the face of the earth, and the dots of our line still coming, still moving forward, and halting and withering away, but still moving up among the flashes and the darkness, more men, and yet more men, from the fields of sacred France, from the darkness of Senegal, from sheep-runs at the ends of the earth, from blue-gum forests, and sunny islands, places of horses and good fellows, from Irish pastures and glens, and from many a Scotch and English city and village and quiet farm; they went on and they went on, up ridges blazing with explosion into the darkness of death. Sometimes, as the light failed, and peak after peak that had been burning against the sky grew rigid as the colour faded, the darkness of the great blasts hid sections of the line; but when the darkness cleared they were still there, line after line of dots, still more, still moving forward and halting and withering away, and others coming, and halting and withering away, and others following, as though those lines were not flesh and blood and breaking nerve, but some tide of the sea coming in waves that fell yet advanced, that broke a little farther, and gained some yard in breaking, and were then followed, and slowly grew, that halted and seemed to wither, and then gathered and went on, till night covered those moving dots, and the great slope was nothing but a blackness spangled with the flashes of awful fire.
>
> (Pages 82–3.)

It would be snobbish to say that this passage lacks literary qualities. The accumulation of phrases in the first sentence, which expresses both the movement of the force and the breadth of its international composition, is economical, and though the description may lack sensuous immediacy, this is clearly part of Masefield's rather more objective, epic intention. If it is suggested that the

heroic mode is no longer viable in the modern age, the answer
might well be that many find it acceptable even today—and 'old
soldiers' are understandable exceptions. Yet given these conces-
sions, there is some limpness in the language, I think: the sea image
towards the end, for instance, evokes little more than the feeling
that it was a lengthy, halting advance. The words Synge wrote in a
notebook form in one's mind: 'Journalism may be literary, literature is always scriptural.' Once again, the danger of propaganda to
literature becomes an issue. It will perhaps save repetitious commentary here if I note that Alfred Harmsworth, Lord Northcliffe,
who ended the war as Director of Propaganda, had a sonnet written
in his honour by Sir William Watson, entitled 'The Three Alfreds'.
In 1915, Northcliffe and his newspapers had attacked Kitchener
over the shell shortages in France and Watson approved of his
actions, so in his sonnet he claims that Northcliffe, though 'neither
King nor bard', had

> Saved England, saved her not less truly than
> Her hero of heroes saved her long ago.

Some heady new wine was going into some old literary bottles.

Along with Rupert Brooke's famous sonnets perhaps the most
well-known poem of the Great War is Julian Grenfell's 'Into
Battle', published in the *Times* on the very day that his death was
announced, 27 May 1915. Eldest son of a peer, educated at Eton and
Balliol, excelling in both intellectual and physical activity, it must
have seemed utter loss when this brilliant young man was cut down
by a shell-splinter. Or was it loss? His poem opens with these
words:

> The naked earth is warm with spring,
>   And with green grass and bursting trees
> Leans to the sun's gaze glorying,
>   And quivers in the sunny breeze;
> And life is Colour and Warmth and Light,
>   And a striving evermore for these;
> And he is dead who will not fight;
>   And who dies fighting has increase.

The paradox of that last line finds its explanation in the next stanzas, which proclaim a mystical unity with nature and its eternal processes:

> The fighting man shall from the sun
>> Take warmth, and life from the glowing earth;
> Speed with the light-foot winds to run,
>> And with the trees to newer birth;
> And find, when fighting shall be done,
>> Great rest, and fullness after dearth.

> All the bright company of Heaven
>> Hold him in their high comradeship,
> The Dog-Star, and the Sisters Seven,
>> Orion's Belt and sworded hip.

This looks back to Shelley's elegy on the death of Keats, *Adonais* (1821), especially its nineteenth stanza:

> Through wood and stream and field and hill and Ocean
> A quickening life from the Earth's heart has burst
> As it has ever done, with change and motion
> From the great morning of the world when first
> God dawned upon chaos . . . ,

and the last stanza of all:

> Whilst, burning through the inmost veil of Heaven,
> The soul of Adonais, like a star,
> Beacons from the abode where the Eternal are.

The long tradition of pastoral elegy in Europe stretches back through *Lycidas* ('sunk low, but mounted high') to the eclogues of Virgil and Moschus, but more closely relevant to Grenfell's poem is chapter 7 of *The Story of My Heart* (1883), in which Jefferies writes a great paean on 'the intense life of the senses' and physical effort. (Grenfell, it appears, was an exceptional athlete.) Jefferies can sympathise 'with the chase and the hunter eagerly pursuing, whose javelin trembles to be thrown; with the extreme fury of feeling, the whirl of joy in the warriors from Marathon to the last

T

battle of Rome, not with the slaughter, but with the passion—the life in the passion . . .'. He goes even further in the next paragraph:

> So deep is the passion of life that, if it were possible to live again, it must be exquisite to die pushing the eager breast against the sword. In the flush of strength to face the sharp pain joyously, and laugh in the last glance of the sun—if only to live again, now on earth, were possible. So subtle is the chord of life that sometimes to watch troops marching in rhythmic order, undulating along the column as the feet are lifted, brings tears in my eyes.

Take this to its conclusion, omit the if-clauses, and we have something very like the last stanzas of 'Into Battle':

> And when the burning moment breaks,
>   And all things else are out of mind,
> And only joy of battle takes
>   Him by the throat, and makes him blind,
>
> Through joy and blindness he shall know,
>   Not caring much to know, that still
> Nor lead nor steel shall reach him, so
>   That it be not the Destined Will.
>
> The thundering line of battle stands,
>   And in the air death moans and sings;
> But day shall clasp him with strong hands,
>   And Night shall fold him in soft wings.

'The blood is wiser than the intellect' is a phrase that might sum up the philosophy of these lines; the fatalistic acceptance of death is all energy and high spirits and resolution. Grenfell's letters, too, show that he was really inspired by the way in which the Empire rallied to Britain's cause and that in France he discovered love for the profession of arms—and for 'one's fellow-man so much more when bent on killing him.'

·   ·   ·   ·   ·   ·

J. H. Johnstone, who quotes this phrase in *English Poetry of the First World War*, found it a 'cryptic remark that is subject to a number of interpretations.' Perhaps one of Kipling's Boer War poems, 'Piet', will provide the beginning of an explanation:

> An' when there wasn't aught to do
> But camp and cattle-guards,
> I've fought with 'im the 'ole day through
> At fifteen 'undred yards;
> Long afternoons o' lyin' still,
> An' 'earin' as you lay
> The bullets swish from 'ill to 'ill
> Like scythes among the 'ay.
>   Ah there, Piet!—be'ind 'is stony kop,
>   With 'is Boer bread an' biltong, an' 'is
>   flask of awful Dop;
>   'Is Mauser for amusement an' 'is pony
>   for retreat,
>   I've known a lot o' fellers shoot a dam'
>   sight worse than Piet.

'Piet' comes in the section entitled 'Service Songs' in Kipling's *The Five Nations* (1903), where one's eye is also caught by 'Columns':

> 'What are our orders an' where do we lay?'
> (*Time, an' 'igh time to be trekkin' again!*)
> You came after dark—you will leave before day,
> '*You section, you pompom, an' six 'undred men!*'

> Down the tin street, 'alf awake an' unfed,
> 'Ark to 'em blessin' the Gen'ral in bed!...

This is hardly different in tone from Grenfell's amusing 'Prayer for Those on the Staff' and its light satire at the expense of men living sybaritically, in a safer place:

> Fighting in mud, we turn to Thee,
> In these dread times of battle, Lord,
> To keep us safe, if so may be,
> From shrapnel, snipers, shell and sword.

But not on us, for we are men
   Of meaner clay, who fight in clay,
But on the Staff, the Upper Ten,
   Depends the issue of the Day.

The staff is working with its brains,
   While we are sitting in the trench;
The Staff the universe ordains
   (Subject to Thee and General French)

God help the Staff—especially
   The young ones, many of them sprung
From our high aristocracy;
   Their task is hard and they are young.

O Lord, who mad'st all things to be,
   And madest some things very good,
Please keep the extra A.D.C.
   From horrid scenes, and sight of blood.

See that his eggs are newly laid,
   Not tinged as some of them—with green;
And let no nasty draughts invade
   The windows of his Limousine.

Bergonzi's comment on these lines is that its satire is good-humoured, 'but it points forward to Siegfried Sassoon's savage verses which expressed the front-line soldier's resentment of the imbeciles of the Staff.' These, too, Kipling can match:

The General got 'is decorations thick
   (The men that backed 'is lies could not complain),
The Staff 'ad D.S.O.'s till we was sick,
   And the soldier—'ad the work to do again!
                           ('Stellenbosh')

There is even a poem in *The Five Nations* that gives a not-unsympathetic view of deserters:

There is no need to give our reasons, though
   Gawd knows we all 'ad reasons which were fair;

But other people might not judge 'em so,
    And now it does not matter what they were.

What man can size or weigh another's woe?
    There are some things too bitter 'ard to bear.
Suffice it we 'ave finished—Domino!
    As we can testify, for we are there,
In the side-world where 'wilful-missings' go.

This indication of Kipling's range may be fitly concluded with the reminder that throughout his career he wrote about ships and the Navy. This is a Service that literary authorities rarely seem to mention: one gets the impression that almost all the authors were in the trenches, with one or two others, like Cecil Lewis, author of *Sagittarius Rising* (1936), flying above them. Naval authors seem to have been like the German Grand Fleet, mostly in harbour.[2] But Kipling, author of 'The Destroyers' (1898) and the extraordinary dramatic monologue 'M'Andrew's Hymn' (1893), wrote a number of poems about the war at sea, 1914–18. There is one on the battle of Jutland, 'The Verdicts', others called 'Mine Sweepers', 'The Lowestoft Boat', 'The North Sea Patrol' and so on. Kipling once went down in a submarine himself—

We'll duck and we'll dive like little tin turtles,
We'll duck and we'll dive underneath the North Seas,
Until we strike something that doesn't expect us.
From here to Cuxhaven it's go as you please!

The first thing we did was to dock in a minefield,
Which isn't a place where repairs should be done;
And there we lay doggo in twelve-fathom water
With tri-nitro-toluol hogging our run.

The next thing we did, we rose under a Zeppelin,
With his shiny big belly half blocking the sky.
But what in the—Heavens can you do with six-pounders?
So we fired what we had and bade him good-bye.

            (From *The Fringes of the Fleet*, 1915.)

It is *not* great literature, but it seems to have scarcity-value!

The chameleon quality of Kipling as a writer is again brought out when the jog-trot insouciance of these submarine verses is read alongside the tough-minded dialogue of his story 'Sea-Constables: A Tale of '15' (in *Debits and Credits*, 1926). This is a tale in the form of a four-sided conversation about the relentless shadowing of a neutral captain who tried to run a cargo of oil to Germany. He is finally forced to run in to a small Irish port and turn over his oil to an Admiralty agent; and here comes another turn of the screw for the squeamish, because the neutral, ill with bronchial pneumonia in a doctorless town, had expected to be taken to England on his surrender. The response to this is: 'I said there wasn't any question of surrender. If he'd been a wounded belligerent, I might have taken him aboard, though I certainly shouldn't have gone a yard out of my course to land him anywhere; but as it was, he was a neutral—altogether outside of the game.' The argument continues, ultimately to end with a stroke of literary craftsmanship intended to spare the reader nothing:

> 'Then I'm a dead man, Mr. Maddingham,' he said.
> 'That's *your* business,' I said. 'Good afternoon.'
> And I went out.
> 'And?' said Winchmore, after some silence.
> 'He died. I saw his flag half-masted next morning.'

It is not a pleasant story; nor was it meant to be. It bears a great similarity to Kipling's 'Mary Postgate' (in *A Diversity of Creatures*, 1917), which tells of an English spinster's merciless satisfaction when a wounded German airman dies in her garden, because she has lost in battle the young man she had helped bring up and not long before seen a child killed by a German bomb before her eyes. Such stories can be taken as 'philosophical' propositions: this is what life is really like in time of war, whatever the tender-minded may care to believe. 'Mary Postgate' is the more plausible of the two stories, I think, and goes deeper into human nature, but neither can be ignored in any study of war-time psychology and the literature that reflects it.

Kipling knew perfectly well that there would be dissentients in the 'game' of war. In 1917 he wrote a poem called 'The Holy War', which claimed that John Bunyan had 'mapped for those who follow, / The world in which we are.' Bunyan prophesied the enemy without and within:

> All enemy divisions,
>   Recruits of every class,
> And highly screened positions
>   For flame or poison-gas;
> The craft that we call modern,
>   The crimes that we call new,
> John Bunyan had 'em typed and filed
>   In Sixteen Eighty-two.
>
> Likewise the Lords of Looseness
>   That hamper faith and works,
> The Perseverance-Doubters,
>   And Present-Comfort shirks,
> With brittle intellectuals
>   Who crack beneath a strain—
> John Bunyan met that helpful set
>   In Charles the Second's reign.
>
> Emmanuel's vanguard dying
>   For right and not for rights,
> My Lord Apollyon lying
>   To the State-kept Stockholmites,
> The Pope, the swithering Neutrals,
>   The Kaiser and his Gott—
> Their rôles, their goals, their naked souls—
>   He knew and drew the lot.

It is a comprehensively framed indictment, with all the vituperative energy we have come to expect of Kipling (*swithering* Neutrals!). The International Socialist Congress at Stockholm, which had produced a peace programme in August, and a peace initiative from the Pope are expected targets. Complications arise when it is realised that some of the 'brittle intellectuals / Who crack beneath a strain' were also members of Emmanuel's vanguard. But then, life is like that, we might say, if we were feeling philosophical.

NOTES

[1] See another volume in this Series: R. W. Harris, *Reason and Nature in the Eighteenth Century*, 1968, pages 137–8. The two conversations could be very usefully compared and contrasted as a critical exercise.

[2] Miss Catherine Reilly, of the Central Library, Manchester, who is preparing a bibliography of First World War poetry, knows of very few examples, and these the equivalent of 'soldier songs'. Sir Henry Newbolt was involved in the Official History of the War at Sea, but it seems that Harold Owen's reticence may be typical: 'I do not like talking about my war experiences [which] differed little from those of thousands of others in wartime.' A little of his naval experience may be incidentally gleaned from his *Journey from Obscurity: Wilfred Owen 1893–1918* (1963–65).

10: Pro Patria Mori

A Soldier's Declaration

I am making this statement as an act of wilful defiance of military authority, because I believe that the war is being deliberately prolonged by those who have the power to end it. ... I have seen and endured the suffering of the troops, and can no longer be a party to prolong these sufferings for ends which I believe to be evil and unjust. ...

On behalf of those who are suffering now I make this protest against the deception which is being practised on them; also I believe that I may help to destroy the callous complacence with which the majority of those at home regard the continuance of agonies which they do not share, and which they have not sufficient imagination to realize.

July 1917   S. Sassoon

July was the month in which the third battle of Ypres, popularly known as Passchendaele, began: one of the great battles of the war, with casualties running into hundreds of thousands. It is a fittingly dreadful background to the refusal sent by Lieutenant Sassoon, then just coming to the end of a convalescent leave in England, to his commanding officer.

There are two important points to bear in mind when reading this protest. First, Sassoon, had been a poet in the Brooke mould, idealistic and committed to battle:

> The anguish of the earth absolves our eyes
> Till beauty shines in all that we can see.

> War is our scourge; yet war has made us wise,
> And fighting for our freedom, we are free.
>
> ('Absolution'.)

This poem, written in 1915, identifies Sassoon as one of 'the happy legion' of fighting soldiers, able to be inspired by the death of his own brother at Gallipoli and ready to proclaim that they had 'made an end of all things base' ('To My Brother'). This is exactly what Brooke had claimed in his first sonnet, when he turned away from 'a world grown old and cold and weary'. An even more extraordinary poem by Sassoon, 'The Kiss', was inspired by a V.C.'s 'Spirit of the Bayonet' address:

> To these I turn, in these I trust—
> Brother Lead and Sister Steel.
> To this blind power I make appeal,
> I guard her beauty clean from rust.

Quite seriously intended at first, Robert Graves tells us, it was later put forward as a satire (*Goodbye to All That*, 1929, chapter 25). Remembering Henley's 'The Song of the Sword' (see page 168 above) this can be accepted at its face value, though it seems almost unbelievable in the light of stanzas like the following:

> Sweet Sister, grant your soldier this:
> That in good fury he may feel
> The body where he sets his heel
> Quail from your downward darting kiss.

This is a romanticising of the enthusiasm which used to be thought proper when bayonet fighting was taught, both then (see *Goodbye to All That*, chapter 21) and much later. Second, we must also realise that the 'act of wilful defiance of military authority' was made by a man who had been a positive daredevil in action at the front. In the semi-fictional *Memoirs of An Infantry Officer* (1930), part of a trilogy that includes *Memoirs of a Fox-hunting Man* (1928) and *Sherston's Progress* (1936), Sassoon certainly makes it appear so:

Then I rushed at the bank, vaguely expecting some sort of scuffle with my imagined enemy. I had lost my temper with the man who had shot Kendle; quite unexpectedly, I found myself looking down into a well-conducted trench with a great many Germans in it. Fortunately for me, they were already retreating. It had not occurred to them that they were being attacked by a single fool; and Fernby, with presence of mind which probably saved me, had covered my advance by traversing the top of the trench with his Lewis gun. I slung a few more bombs, but they fell short of the clumsy field-grey figures, some of whom half turned to fire their rifles over the left shoulder as they ran across the open towards the wood, while a crowd of jostling helmets vanished along the trench. Idiotically elated, I stood there with my finger in my right ear and emitted a series of 'view-holloas' (a gesture which ought to win the approval of people who still regard war as a form of outdoor sport). Having thus failed to commit suicide, I proceeded to occupy the trench—that is to say, I sat down on the fire-step, very much out of breath and hoped to God the Germans wouldn't come back again. (Part IV.3.)

The evident irony in this passage is meant to be that of a maturer Sherston (the name of its hero) looking back upon his younger self. We discover, too, from a straight autobiographical work Sassoon wrote, *Siegfried's Journey* (1945), that the young Sherston is a much simpler character than his creator was at the time, a figure with whom readers could feel some sympathetic bond of identity. But the bravery was true enough: Sassoon, a poet and more complex being than Sherston, was actually awarded the Military Cross for heroism in the field. Michael Thorpe has called attention to the approval shown by ordinary soldiers like Frank Richards, whose *Old Soldiers Never Die* (1933) refers enthusiastically to Mr Sassoon on several occasions. (See *Siegfried Sassoon: A Critical Study*, 1966.) The protest, then, acquires great force from the man who made it: one who had joined up at the beginning of the war—neither Brooke nor Owen had done this—and had fought bravely through the terrible Somme offensive of July 1916. This is the struggle generally thought of as the turning point in the 1914–18 war, when idealism died. In early 1917, after some months sick leave in England, he was back in France, only to be wounded during the battle of Arras. In May he published the collection of his poems called *The Old Huntsman*, which forms a perfect record of reversal, from the idealism of the poems we have been considering to bitter and savage satire, 'deliberately devised to disturb complacency':

> The House is crammed: tier beyond tier they grin
> And cackle at the Show, while prancing ranks
> Of harlots shrill the chorus, drunk with din;
> 'We're sure the Kaiser loves our dear old Tanks!'
>
> I'd like to see a Tank come down the stalls,
> Lurching to rag-time tunes, or 'Home, sweet Home',
> And there'd be no more jokes in Music-halls
> To mock the riddled corpses round Bapaume.

In the first stanza he has captured the atmosphere of a certain Liverpool music hall and the crude patriotism of its show; he has also, in the next stanza, caught the sudden flash of anger that a soldier might feel at its inane optimism. But it is a response on the same level, so that it is very easy to see the application of the comment Graves made about him in *Goodbye to All That*: 'the direction of Siegfried's unconquerable idealism changed with his environment; he varied between happy warrior and bitter pacifist.' In general, however, Sassoon's loss of faith in the cause for which he was fighting was representative of this generation of younger writers in France—Graves himself, Wilfred Owen, Osbert Sitwell, Herbert Read and others, we are told, could no longer believe in the war, even if they fought on.

·   ·   ·   ·   ·   ·

There is an even wider historical context. Both Sassoon and Owen were affected greatly by reading Henri Barbusse's *Le Feu* (1916; English translation, *Under Fire*, 1917), which was a work of intense protest against the war and its effects upon humanity. In 1917, widespread mutinies occurred in the French army and were put down with severity. There is no doubt that the horrors of trench warfare, one of the novelties of the 1914–18 battles, broke men's spirits. A recent book by George Coppard, who joined up as a boy of sixteen, says bluntly, 'Some men who met their end before a firing squad would have willingly fought the enemy in hand-to-hand combat, but they simply could not endure prolonged shell and mortar fire' (*With A Machine Gun to Cambrai*, 1969). It is, of course, always necessary to remember the individual nature of some experiences. Wyndham Lewis, for instance, in the war-time sections of his autobiographical *Blasting and Bombardiering* (1937) certainly gives the impression of merciless shelling and constant diving for safety into shell-holes, but he also talks of having slept through 'scores of full-dress bombardments'. Very frequently he writes with humour and cool self-mockery: 'As time went on, I found that there was one situation in which I did not at all enjoy finding myself. I did not like to be subjected to indiscriminate shell-fire when undressed. Lay me to rest in a flea-bag and I jib at shelling.' Lewis has an eye for the arresting detail ('a high naval dignitary on horseback'—who regarded a dangerous spot near Nieuport as 'a standing challenge to the Nelson Touch') and the ability to recount a marvellous story, such as the one in the chapter entitled 'Hunted with Howitzers'. But the very fact that *Blasting and Bombardiering* is so effectively written, that these stories are so distanced and controlled in the telling, underlines the length of time after the First World War it was published; it bears in some ways more relation to the prospects of the Second, which is a useful reminder of the care needed in treating works of literature, even non-fictional ones, as historical documents.

Sassoon's *Memoirs of An Infantry Officer* is a very different book, focussed upon a more naive and suffering hero, but also written with a degree of detachment. His own war poetry, more of which was published in the volume called *Counter-Attack* (1918), points up the difference:

> If I were fierce, and bald, and short of breath,
>   I'd live with scarlet Majors at the Base,
> And speed glum heroes up the line to death.
> ('Base Details'.)

An officer came blundering down the trench:
'Stand-to and man the fire-step!' On he went . . .
Gasping and bawling, 'Fire-step . . . counter-attack!'
  Then the haze lifted. Bombing on the right
  Down the old sap: machine-guns on the left;
  And stumbling figures looming out in front.
  'O Christ, they're coming at us!' Bullets spat,
And he remembered his rifle . . . rapid fire . . .
And started blazing wildly . . .

                                    ('Counter-Attack')

And, all because his brother had gone west,
Raved at the bleeding war; his rampant grief
Moaned, shouted, sobbed, and choked, while he was kneeling
Half-naked on the floor. In my belief
Such men have lost all patriotic feeling.

                                    ('Lamentations')

There is not much artistic transmutation of experience in such
poetry, only enough to thrust stark realities upon the reader or
turn them into contemptuous sarcasm:

'He's a cheery old card,' grunted Harry to Jack
As they slogged up to Arras with rifle and pack.
But he did for them both with his plan of attack.

                                    ('The General')

The word 'Arras' places it firmly in its historical context, as does
the colloquial accuracy of the language, yet on the whole such
poems, and they are typical, seem to stay rooted in their time. We
may contrast them with a poem called 'The Dug-Out', which is one
of Sassoon's poems that manages, I think, to retain the emotions
aroused on its first reading:

Why do you lie with your legs ungainly huddled,
And one arm bent across your sullen cold
Exhausted face? It hurts my heart to watch you,
Deep-shadow'd from the candle's guttering gold;
And you wonder why I shake you by the shoulder;

Drowsy, you mumble and sigh and turn your head . . .
You are too young to fall asleep for ever;
And when you sleep you remind me of the dead.

There is more than one source of information about Sassoon's protest and its context in the history of the time. The semi-fictional account in Part 10 of *Memoirs of An Infantry Officer* is not altogether easy to accept in some of its details. Is it possible, for instance, that Sherston would have had to look up the word 'integrate' in a dictionary? (The purpose of this, presumably, is to underline how very unsophisticated he was in comparison with Thornton Tyrrell, the civilian sage who was advising him.) For some portions of the story, however, there is a control provided by *Goodbye to All That*, because Graves was the friend who appeared at the critical moment, managed to obtain a medical board for Sassoon and, eventually, the care of the psychologist W. H. R. Rivers at Craiglockhart. There is, too, the much later *Siegfried's Journey* (1945) to bridge the gaps in Sassoon's personal history. As far as the wider history of the time is concerned, the second volume of Bertrand Russell's autobiography does a great deal to fill in the picture of the pacifist circles with which Sassoon became associated (Russell was Sherston's Thornton Tyrrell). There were the people who used to visit Garsington, the home of Philip and Lady Ottoline Morell—writers like Aldous Huxley and Lytton Strachey—but Russell makes it very evident that they were not at all numerous and met with a lot of opposition. He himself was deprived of his Trinity College Lectureship in 1916, when he was convicted and fined for writing a pamphlet objecting to the sentence of two years' hard labour passed on a Conscientious Objector; in 1918 he actually went to prison for six months for writing in an article that American troops would be used as strike-breakers, a task to which he claimed they had become accustomed in their own country. The letters he prints from this period are equally revealing. There is one from H. G. Wells stating his belief that not many Conscientious Objectors were genuine, and letters full of admiration for Russell from Arthur Graeme West, whose literary relics were published as *The Diary of a Dead Officer* in 1919.[1] This juxtaposition might serve as an illustration of the gap that opened between those at the front and most of the people at home: 'Every one talked a foreign language; it was newspaper language,' wrote Robert Graves when he got back to England in 1916 after being wounded. 'I found serious conversation with my parents all but impossible' (chapter 21).

.　　.　　.　　.　　.　　.

Whatever the rights and wrongs of this conflict may be—Graves was not alone in calling attention to it, as Wilfred Owen's 'The Parable of the Old Man and the Young' savagely confirms—the men at the front had one indisputable advantage. It is to them we must look for the record of the human realities of war in the twentieth century. Famous literary men were given access to military records and taken on tours in France to be shown a judicious selection of the sights, but clearly this could be no substitute. Out of first-hand experience sprang an intense if limited literature, based first of all upon a rejection of the conventional attitudes that had been the early response at the outbreak of war:

> God! how I hate you, you young cheerful men,
> Whose pious poetry blossoms on your graves
> As soon as you are in them . . .
> 　　　　　　　　　Hark how one chants—
> 'Oh happy to have lived these epic days'—
> 'These epic days'! And *he'd* been to France,
> And seen the trenches, glimpsed the huddled dead
> In the periscope, hung on the rusty wire:
> Choked by their sickly foetor, day and night
> Blown down his throat: stumbled through ruined hearths,
> Proved all that muddy brown monotony . . .

The limitations of West's attitude are patent. Hate for the mis-guided is an extravagant emotion for its cause, and if 'God! how I hate you, you young cheerful men' should be diluted because it is typically slangy, it is still true to say that nothing else in his poem modifies its impact. West's *Diary* records his disillusionment not only with exalted attitudes to war but with all values, and thus shows how at least one young man was breaking under the strain. It is an acceptable revelation in that sense at least. More important is one of the poems at the end of the book, *Night Patrol*, which sets out to do little more than be a faithful record of experience, gaining immeasurably from this near-disconnection with the fragile and strained personality of its author. While 'God! how I hate you' is wide open to the charge of being the production of a shell-shocked mind, 'Night Patrol' can only be admired for its controlled poise.

It begins with orders, bare and practical:

> 'Over the top! The wire's thin here, unbarbed
> Plain rusty coils, not staked, and low enough:
> Full of old tins, though . . .'

The progression of the phrases is that of ordinary speech, as lacking in refinement and cultivation as the ruined landscape the patrol reached through the wire:

> The sodden ground was splashed with shallow pools,
> And tufts of crackling corn-stalks, two years old,
> No man had reaped, and patches of spring grass,
> Half-seen, as rose and sank the flares, were strewn
> With the wreck of our attack: the bandoliers,
> Packs, rifles, bayonets, belts, and haversacks,
> Shell fragments, and the huge whole forms of shells
> Shot fruitlessly—and everywhere the dead.

The passage is, of course, very like Burgundy's speech about wartorn France in the last act of *Henry V*, a picture of fertility and beauty spoiled and waste:

> Her fallow leas
> The darnel, hemlock, and rank fumitory,
> Doth root upon, while that the coulter rusts
> That should deracinate such savagery . . .

But Burgundy's speech continually harps upon the husbandry, order and civilisation that must be restored, in a way that has no parallel in West's flinty record. No hope budded where 'the dead men stank through all':

v

> They lay, all clothed,
> Each in some new and piteous attitude
> That we well marked to guide us back; as he,
> Outside our wire, that lay on his back and crossed
> His legs Crusader-wise; I smiled at that . . .

'There's honour for you! Here's no vanity!' exclaimed Falstaff when he came across the body of Sir Walter Blunt on Shrewsbury field (*1 Henry IV*, V.iii.32). It is life alone that Falstaff and this patrol were intent on saving.

> From him, a quarter left, lay a small corpse,
> Down in a hollow, huddled as in a bed,
> That one of us put his hand on unawares.
> Next was a bunch of half-a-dozen men
> All blown to bits, an archipelago
> Of corrupt fragments, vexing to us three,
> Who had no light to see by, save the flares.
> On such a trail, so lit, for ninety yards
> We crawled on belly and elbows, till we saw,
> Instead of lumpish dead before our eyes,
> The stakes and crosslines of the German wire.
> We lay in shelter of the last dead man,
> Ourselves as dead, and heard their shovels ring
> Turning the earth, their talk and cough at times.
> A sentry fired and a machine-gun spat;
> They shot a flare above us, when it fell
> And spluttered out in the pools of No Man's Land,
> We turned and crawled past the remembered dead;
> Past him, and them, and him, until,
> For he lay some way apart, we caught the scent
> Of the Crusader and slid past his legs,
> And through the wire and home, and got our rum.

Realistic though it may be, West's unemphatic language is now and again lit by a brief flare of rhetoric ('an archipelago / Of corrupt fragments'), or by an adjective that for all its accuracy is poignant in its associations ('the lumpish dead'), or by the inversion of some splendid ideal ('we caught the scent / Of the Crusader'). For us, today, the plain pragmatism of the phrase 'the remembered dead'—to find one's way back by—is in strangely sad contrast with one of the best known stanzas of Laurence Binyon's 'For the Fallen' (1915):

> They shall not grow old, as we that are left grow old:
> Age shall not weary them, nor the years condemn.
> At the going down of the sun and in the morning
> We will remember them.

But the contrast with the full heroic mode of celebration is absolute:

> All furnish'd, all in arms;
> All plum'd like estridges, that with the wind
> Bated like eagles having lately bath'd;
> Glittering in golden coats, like images;
> As full of spirit as the month of May
> And gorgeous as the sun at midsummer;
> Wanton as youthful goats, wild as young bulls.
> (*1 Henry IV*, IV.i.97.)

Shakespeare felt able to include a speech like this in a play that also contained the antics of Bardolph and Falstaff; a twentieth-century battlefield did not permit either grandeur or jollity for men like West. 'The dethronement of the soft cap clearly symbolised the change that was coming over the war, the induration from a personal crusade into a vast machine of violence . . .' wrote Edmund Blunden in his *Undertones of War* (1928). And this machine would not stop, or so it seemed at the time.

·   ·   ·   ·   ·   ·

Where West has concentrated on record in 'Night Patrol' Wilfred Owen regarded himself as the spokesman of humanity, the man who was to express, to use his famous phrase, 'the pity of War'. He was in France from January until June 1917, when he was sent to Craiglockhart, and had undergone experiences of a kind that caused him to feel that official religion and patriotism could not be more incompatible. Sassoon, who met him at the hospital, says in *Siegfried's Journey* that he stimulated Owen 'towards writing with compassionate and challenging realism', but that he was only reinforcing an impulse 'already strong within him'. Later in that year he rejoined his battalion in France, drafting a famous Preface to his verses: 'Above all I am not concerned with Poetry. My Subject is War, and the pity of War. The Poetry is in the pity. . . . All a poet can do today is warn.' The last phrase brings us up short; because it looks as though we are again to be faced with propaganda. We are. But it is not the kind of propaganda that converts its subject-matter into some type of ideal, as we may see from looking at 'Exposure', one of Owen's earlier war poems dating from February 1917. It begins:

> Our brains ache, in the merciless iced east winds that
> knive us . . .
> Wearied we keep awake because the night is silent . . .
> Low, drooping flares confuse our memory of the salient . . .
> Worried by silence, sentries whisper, curious, nervous,
> But nothing happens.

This looks something like West's realism, rather more personal and emotional, and displaying more obvious craft of expression—one might instance the use of half-rhymes: 'knive-us' and 'nervous'; 'silent' and 'salient'. As the poem goes on the technique becomes more evident:

> Pale flakes with fingering stealth come feeling for our faces—
> We cringe in holes, back on forgotten dreams, and stare, snow-
> dazed,
> Deep into grassier ditches. So we drowse, sun-dozed,
> Littered with blossoms trickling where the blackbird fusses.
> Is it that we are dying?

> Slowly our ghosts drag home: glimpsing the sunk fires, glozed
> With crusted dark-red jewels: crickets jingle there;
> For hours the innocent mice rejoice: the house is theirs,
> Shutters and doors, all closed: on us the doors are closed,—
> We turn back to our dying.

But this is technique that any critic would wish to defend, as when Edmund Blunden made the fine comment about Owen's use of half-rhyme or 'pararhyme': 'What he made of it is felt at its fullest, perhaps, in the solemn music of 'Strange Meeting', but again and again by means of it he creates remoteness, darkness, emptiness, shock, echo, the last word' (Memoir, *The Poems of Wilfred Owen*, 1931). Again, the waking dream of home in 'Exposure' is deliberately beautiful and harmonious, to sharpen the contrast with the misery of the dreamers. It provides a peculiar contrast, too, with Yeats's situation during the Civil War:

> We are closed in, and the key is turned
> On our uncertainty; somewhere
> A man is killed, or a house burned,
> Yet no clear fact to be discerned:
> Come build in the empty house of the stare.

> ('Meditations in Time of Civil War', VI.)

To Owen, the clear facts could hardly be avoided, and his poetry shows a constant preoccupation with the horrors of twentieth-century warfare, with gassing and blinding, the 'Batter of guns and shatter of flying muscles / Carnage incomparable, and human squander', men dying like cattle, jabbing and parrying with the bayonet. But he is able to go beyond the immediate realities and express the depths of human despair and isolation. It is propaganda, but it is not facile or superficial.

It can hardly be claimed that Owen is as great a poet as Yeats, though considering the age at which he died that is not to be expected. The name of John Keats is frequently and naturally invoked by critics: both were poets of astonishing achievement in their brief lives and both wrote poems with flaws as great as their felicities. It has been pointed out how 'Exposure' is a kind of terrible parody of the Ode to the Nightingale and how one of Owen's major poems, 'Strange Meeting', is reminiscent of both *Endymion* and *Hyperion*. 'Strange Meeting' begins with a scene that brings to mind the huge drama of Keats's fallen Titans in their agony and despair:

It seemed that out of battle I escaped
Down some profound dull tunnel, long since scooped
Through granites which titanic wars had groined.
Yet also there encumbered sleepers groaned,
Too fast in thought or death to be bestirred.
Then, as I probed them, one sprang up, and stared
With piteous recognition in fixed eyes,
Lifting distressful hands as if to bless.
And by his smile, I knew that sullen hall,
By his dead smile I knew we stood in hell.

The real and the nether world come together in visionary relationship: the trenches and tunnels, the saps and counter-saps, are given
their true name. In this timeless and mythical world Owen can,
somewhat awkwardly, bring out the spiritual loss that war entails,
the death of those who might have been able to give the world
what it would always be in need of:

     I mean the truth untold,
The pity of war, the pity war distilled.
Now men will go content with what we spoiled,
Or, discontent, boil bloody, and be spilled.
They will be swift with swiftness of the tigress,
None will break ranks, though nations trek from progress.
Courage was mine, and I had mystery;
Wisdom was mine, and I had mastery;
To miss the march of this retreating world
Into vain citadels that are not walled.
Then, when much blood had clogged their chariot-wheels
I would go up and wash them from sweet wells,
Even with truths that lie too deep for taint.
I would have poured my spirit without stint
But not through wounds; not on the cess of war.
Foreheads of men have bled where no wounds were.

Owen voices here the high Romantic conception of the poet, one
who was a seer in spite of all the adverse pressures, and one who
could retain for the benefit of humanity those deeper truths that are

inevitably lost when, to remember Yeats's meditations in time of civil war, 'innumerable clanging wings . . . have put out the moon.' That is, as long as he is allowed to survive. Owen was killed in 1918.

In this recovery of the poet's full role in society, Owen's poetry has, as Bergonzi states, 'done more than any other work in English to form a sensibility that can grasp the nature of technological war. If Brooke and Binyon seem irrecoverably anachronistic, then that is largely because of what we have learnt from Owen' (*Heroes' Twilight*, page 134). The poem 'Dulce et Decorum Est', a description of the horrors of a gas attack, proves this to the hilt:

> Gas! GAS! Quick, boys!—an ecstasy of fumbling,
> Fitting the clumsy helmets just in time,
> But someone still was yelling out and stumbling
> And floundering like a man in fire or lime.—
> Dim through the misty panes and thick green light,
> As under a green sea, I saw him drowning.
>
> In all my dreams before my helpless sight
> He plunges at me, guttering, choking, drowning.
>
> If in some smothering dreams, you too could pace
> Behind the wagon that we flung him in,
> And watch the white eyes writhing in his face,
> His hanging face, like a devil's sick of sin;
> If you could hear, at every jolt, the blood
> Come gargling from the froth-corrupted lungs,
> Obscene as cancer, bitter as the cud
> Of vile, incurable sores on innocent tongues,—
> My friend, you would not tell with such high zest
> To children ardent for some desperate glory,
> The old Lie: Dulce et decorum est
> Pro patria mori.

There had never been anything like gas before, as Robert Graves tells us in his sardonic way:

Here we were issued with gas-respirators and field dressings. This was the first respirator issued in France. It was a gauze-pad filled with chemically-treated cotton waste, to be tied across the mouth and nose. It seems it was useless against German gas. I never put it to the test. A week or two later came the 'smoke-helmet', a greasy grey-felt bag with a talc window to look through, but no mouthpiece. This also was probably ineffective against gas. The talc was always cracking and there were leaks where it was stitched into the helmet.

These were early days of trench-warfare, the days of the jam-tin bomb and the gas-pipe trench-mortar. It was before Lewis or Stokes guns, steel helmets, telescopic rifle-sights, gas-shells, pill-boxes, tanks, trench-raids, or any of the later improvements of trench warfare.

(*Goodbye to All That*, chapter 12.)

Looking back now to the poem, after this passage of professional and ironic prose, we can see how Owen was straining every nerve to ensure that the experience of gas in action is lived in all its dire intensity. 'I have seen inner indecision racing in his mind', wrote his brother in the third volume of *Journey from Obscurity* (1965), 'but it did not appear in his face.' It does not appear in this poem; some kinds of truth are indisputable. But if we refer again to Hardy's 'Drummer Hodge' (a work that has made itself a kind of poetic touchstone in this book), 'Dulce et Decorum Est' is made to seem a poem stretched upon a bed of Procrustean dialectic—a sweet and fitting way to die for one's country against the newest way of death. It is the tension between two things only, and, uneasily, after the first impact, we ask ourselves if this is enough. That an ideal shrivels in contact with reality does not make this particular poem slickly cynical, but how large is that reality? Is 'Drummer Hodge' exclusive in this way? Or, we might well ask, does not Owen's own poem 'Futility', though weaker technically, reach out to more universal history?

> Move him into the sun—
> Gently its touch awoke him once . . .
>
> Think how it wakes the seeds—
> Woke, once, the clays of a cold star.

Are limbs, so dear-achieved, are sides,
Full-nerved—still warm—too hard to stir?
Was it for this the clay grew tall?
—O what made fatuous sunbeams toil
To break earth's sleep at all?

. . . . . .

One of the finest works to come out of the great war, David
Jones's *In Parenthesis* (1937), also registers the change in the nature
of battle during 1916, providing a compressed equivalent of the
substance of the rural/industrial myth we examined in the early
chapters of this book. Jones, in fact, draws this analogy in his
Preface, when he writes that 'in the earlier months there was a
certain attractive amateurishness, and elbow-room for idiosyn-
crasy that connected one with a less exacting past.' George Sturt's
writings come to mind as Jones notes the ending of the period of
the individual rifleman of the Boer War or the 'Bairnsfather' war
(referring to Bruce Bairnsfather's popular cartoon of 'Ol' Bill')
and then goes on, 'Just as now there are glimpses in our ways of
another England—yet we know the truth. Even while we watch
the boatman mending his sail, the petroleum is hurting the sea.
So did we in 1916 sense a change. How impersonal did each new
draft seem arriving each month, and all these new-fangled gadgets
to master.' This is the germ of the book in some ways: like Edward
Thomas, whose poems we have seen sending roots back into
English history, or Rudyard Kipling, whose stories in *Puck of
Pook's Hill* (1906) and *Rewards and Fairies* (1910) reach back even
further into Romano-British history, or like all the medievalising
writes from Rossetti and Morris to Belloc and Chesterton, David
Jones searches for tradition and continuity. He writes a prose-
poetry richly embroidered with allusions to history told in song
and story. For us he must be of exceptional interest. His work is
the product of the historical imagination; he continually sought
to bring the past to bear upon present realities and found in his
created amalgam a myth that for him at least, and for us if we are
able to respond to it, made sense of the fragmented, dehumanised
world in which he found himself in 1916. Modern civilisation, we

have seen already, was for many writers a failure. Jones was another who rejected the optimistic view that progress in a material sense was true cultural advance. Rather, he wished to assimilate his present appalling experience in battle to the experience of others before him, to realise how men, in the deepest and most important ways of all, imitate what has gone before. History is a sacred ritual for Jones, and hence comes the interlocking pattern of references to Malory's *Morte d'Arthur*, Shakespeare's *Henry V*, Welsh epics like Aneirin's *Y Goddoddin*, the Bible, the Catholic liturgy, and so on, not to mention popular songs and ballads and common sayings. There are limitations, perhaps. It is clearly a national rather than an international myth: the kind of civilised consciousness and sensibility created does not go much beyond Britain, for the Biblical and liturgical elements Jones incorporates have long been filtered through British souls. But, unlike many of the writers we have been looking at, Jones evolved an order out of the most chaotic experience; he survived in more than the physical sense. With such large considerations in mind, we may now be surprised to encounter the fullness of present reality achieved by *In Parenthesis*. Imagine a sergeant lecturing a private,

On addressing commissioned officers—it was his favourite theme. John Ball stood patiently, waiting for the eloquence to spend itself. The tedious flow continued, then broke off very suddenly. He looked straight at Sergeant Snell enquiringly —whose eyes changed queerly, who ducked in under the low entry. John Ball would have followed, but stood fixed and alone in the little yard—his senses highly alert, his body incapable of movement or response. The exact disposition of small things—the precise shape of trees, the tilt of a bucket, the movement of a straw, the disappearing right boot of Sergeant Snell—all minute noises, separate and distinct, in a stillness charged through with some approaching violence— registered not by the ear nor any single faculty—an on-rushing pervasion, saturating all existence; with exactitude, logarithmic, dial-timed, millesimal—of calculated velocity, some mean chemist's contrivance, a stinking physicist's destroying toy.

He stood alone on the stones, his mess-tin spilled at his feet. Out of the vortex, rifling the air it came—bright, brass-shod, Pandoran; with all-filling screaming the howling crescendo's up-piling snapt. The universal world, breath held, one half second, a bludgeoned stillness. Then the pent violence released a consummation of all burstings out; all sudden up-rendings and rivings-through—all taking-out of vents—all barrier-breaking—all unmaking. Pernitric begetting—the dissolving and splitting of solid things. In which unearthing aftermath, John Ball picked up his mess-tin and hurried within; ashen, huddled, waited in the dismal straw. Behind 'E' battery, fifty yards down the road, a great many mangolds, uprooted, pulped, congealed with chemical earth, spattered and made slippery the rigid boards leading to the emplacement. The sap of vegetables slobbered the spotless breech-block of No. 3 gun.

(Part 2.)

One thesis, the perversion of the course of nature through man's scientific interference, stands out very clearly. 'Was it for this the clay grew tall?' But like Owen, Jones in the passage above has no intention of glossing over the physical impact of the event, an act of war; language is forced into expressive shapes regardless of pale convention: 'with all-filling screaming the howling crescendo's up-piling snapt. The universal world, breath held, one half second, a bludgeoned stillness.' It is obviously not commonplace literature, but Jones, we find, lets us in on his secrets in a most remarkable way. In this work, which can be fitted into no standard category of literature and which demands—there is no avoiding it—application, are internal clues and threads to lead us through the labyrinth. In the quotation above, for instance, the first paragraph mentions the 'exact disposition of small things . . .' The grand and mythic, in other words, does not forbid a concern (such as that displayed by Imagist poets like Herbert Read or Richard Aldington) with direct treatment of the thing in itself. Another passage from part 3 of *In Parenthesis* has always seemed to me to be valuable as an exposé of Jones's method, unwinding its intricacies and inviting us to live into the work's three-dimensional meaning. In this section the men are moving up to the front by night, in the rain, through a broken, ravaged landscape, each following the other, till an obstacle causes them all to halt:

> So they stood waiting; thick-textured night cloaked.
>
> So he dreamed where he slept where he leaned, on piled material in the road's right ditch.
>
> Stepping over things in the way, can't lift knee high enough —it makes the thigh ache so—more of them in front as far as you can see—can't go to left or right—this restricting corridor —higher ones, hurdles on 'jerks-ground':
>
> Up, up—o-ver
> Up pup—o-verr.
>
> Gorilla-sergeant, in striped singlet, spring-toed, claps his hands like blackman-master: Get over—you Ball—you cowson.
>
> Obstacles on jerks-course made of wooden planking—his night phantasm mazes a pre-war, more idiosyncratic skein, weaves with stored-up very other tangled threads; a wooden donkey for a wooden hurdle is easy for a deep-sleep trans-formation-fay to wand
> carry you on dream stuff
> up the hill and down again
> show you sights your mother knew,
> show you Jesus Christ lapped in hay with Uncle Eb and his diamond dress-stud next the ox and Sergeant Milford taking his number, juxtapose, dovetail, web up, any number of con-cepts, and bovine lunar tricks.

This is not the conventional articulation of smiling public men, but it is not chaotic. The physical effort of moving, we can appreciate, lives on in the mind; and the mind can of course recall memories of physical training back in England—those incredibly bounding sergeants *did* seem like another species—and then move even further back into childhood and its wonders, because the human mind can, as Jones writes, 'juxtapose, dovetail, web up, any number of concepts, and bovine lunar tricks.'

The passage forms an 'idiosyncratic skein'. It is John Ball's dream. Yet who is John Ball? Though he is a central character in

Jones's book, we do not learn much about him in civilian life;
also, he bears the name of a Kentish priest in the 1381 Peasants'
Revolt, in whose Blackheath sermon everyone was called John
(for policy's sake). At the end of *In Parenthesis*, he suddenly
becomes one with its author. All in all, then, we deduce John
Ball's representative humanity. The book as a whole rests upon
the power of man to hold past and present together in suspension,
to knit together twentieth-century soldiers with others who have
fought and died before them, to live into the experience of others
when faced with the same basic stresses and strains, and to repeat
their reactions when like circumstances recur. 'Lance Corporal
Lewis sings where he walks, yet in a low voice, because of the
Disciplines of the Wars.' So, too, did Shakespeare's Fluellen complain that the mines were 'not according to the disciplines of the
war' and rage at the 'tiddle-taddle' and 'pibble-pabble' coming
from the camp at night (*Henry V*, III, ii and IV. i). In this there
is similarity, and even where contrasts are found, they are not simply
and harshly satiric in the manner of much war-poetry. This we
may see from a longer, brilliant passage on trench-life in Part 3:

> You can hear the silence of it:
> you can hear the rat of no-man's-land
> rut-out intricacies,
> weasel-out his patient workings,
> scrut, scrut, sscrut,
> harrow out-earthly, trowel his cunning paw;
> redeem the time of our uncharity, to sap his
> own amphibious paradise.
> You can hear his carrying-parties
> rustle our corruptions through the night-
> weeds—contest the choicest morsels in his
> tiny conduits, bead-eyed feast on us; by a
> rule of his nature, at night-feast on the
> broken of us.
> Those broad-pinioned;
> blue-burnished, or brinded-back;
> whose proud eyes watched the
>   broken emblems

> droop and drag dust,
> suffer with us this metamorphosis.
>   These too have shed their fine feathers;
> these too have slimed their dark-bright coats;
> these too have condescended to dig in.
>   The white-tailed eagle at the battle ebb,
>   where the sea wars against the river
> the speckled kite of Maldon
> and the crow
> have naturally selected to be un-winged;
> to go on the belly, to
> sap sap sap
> with festered spines, arched under the moon; furrit
> with whiskered snouts the secret parts of us.
>   When it's all quiet you can hear them:
> scrut scrut scrut
> when it's as quiet as this is.
>   It's so very still.
>   Your body fits the crevice of the bay in the
> most comfortable fashion imaginable.
>   It's cushy enough.

The passage about the birds refers back to the tenth-century Anglo-Saxon poem, *The Battle of Brunanburh*, which we may look at in Tennyson's fairly close translation:

> Many a carcase they left to be carrion,
> Many a livid one, many a sallow-skin—
> Left for the white-tailed eagle to tear it, and
> Left for the horny-nibbed raven to rend it, and
> Gave to the garbaging war-hawk to gorge it, and
> The gray beast, the wolf of the weald.

Anglo-Saxon poems like *Beowulf* and *The Battle of Maldon* contain comparable passages, showing how typical a theme it used to be. David Jones, writing of 1916, just before the battle of the Somme and the assault on Mametz wood, moulds the modern variant; those dire birds of ancient epic dwindle into rats. Like the

men who had to fight in a twentieth-century battle, they have
'condescended to dig in'. There is irony in the phrase, for the
metamorphosis brings out the lack of nobility in modern trench-
warfare; nevertheless, the complexity of the truth is not insulted,
for Jones also shows that in intervals of relative peace and
security men could settle down as comfortably as the rats,
making themselves a cushy paradise. A soldier's life was not
always composed of unremitting horror and unrelieved degrada-
tion. The Tommie could often make a joke about such things as
waterlogged trenches and the 'silent navy' of the journalists, as
Jones well knew: 'Why not parade the Jolly Tars and Jack's the
boy—we could do with a silent diver's mate, we could do with a
tin fish to shift him up in the Islands [isolated posts on the Festubert
front], and that Rooshun roller wants more juice . . .' (Part 5, and
notes). A. J. P. Taylor, who mentions Jones and Frank Richards
in his *English History 1914–1945* (1965), has stated that the
Tommies speak mainly in the songs which survive in the oral
tradition, 'self-depreciatory and often obscene'. It is also true to
say that *In Parenthesis* catches the very idiom of the Tommies'
minds and tongues.

·   ·   ·   ·   ·   ·

David Jones's book makes many other literary memorials of the
Great War seem unimaginably minor, but two poems stand out
from the ruck and incidentally illustrate the great range of possible
response good writers can bring to the same events. Isaac
Rosenberg's 'Dead Man's Dump' (1917) and Herbert Read's
The End of a War (1933) both belong to the kind of literature that
transcends its immediate occasion, but in very different ways. In
Rosenberg's poem, despite what has been said, the immediate
occasion is brutally present:

> The plunging limbers over the shattered track
> Racketed with their rusty freight,
> Stuck out like many crowns of thorns,
> And the rusty stakes like sceptres old
> To stay the flood of brutish men
> Upon our brothers dear.

> The wheels lurched over sprawled dead
> But pained them not, though their bones crunched,
> Their shut mouths made no moan.
> They lie there huddled, friend and foeman,
> Man born of man, and born of woman,
> And shells go crying over them
> From night till night and now.

One has merely to look at the adjectives and verbs to appreciate how Rosenberg has stuck to raw experience, yet by the time one has read to the third line it becomes evident that Rosenberg is unfolding a larger relevance. David Jones at bottom sought a way of symbolically *elevating* novel ways of making war:

> We who are of the same world of sense with hairy ass and furry wolf and who presume to other and more radiant affinities, are finding it difficult, as yet, to recognise these creatures of chemicals as true extensions of ourselves, that we may feel for them a native affection, which alone can make them magical for us. It would be interesting to know how we shall ennoble our new media as we have already ennobled and made significant our old—candle-light, fire-light, Cups, Wands and Swords, to choose at random. (Preface).

Presumably the fact that both classical 'Pandoran' and chemical 'pernitric' occur as adjectives in the passage quoted above reflects one aspect of his effort. But for Rosenberg, a freight of barbed wire brought associations of utter pain and sacrifice; Jones's 'We search how we may see formal goodness in a life singularly inimical, hateful, to us' belongs, it would seem, to a less tragic personality.

'Dead Man's Dump' drives on, passionate and questioning, discovering death as the moment when Earth fastens upon her human prey. Then,

> None saw their spirits' shadow shake the grass,
> Or stood aside for the half used life to pass
> Out of those doomed nostrils and the doomed mouth,
> When the swift iron burning bee
> Drained the wild honey of their youth.

Where in the first stanza there were similes, now there is complete fusion of tenor and vehicle; the iron bullet or shrapnel is a bee and youth is honey sweet and clear. The intensity of metaphoric identification excludes the kind of emblematic significance lent to Cups, Wands and Swords; it also makes nature's processes appear irremediably inimical to man. Earth is not a mother, but a Black Widow spider.

> Maniac Earth! howling and flying, your bowel
> Seared by the jagged fire, the iron love,
> The impetuous storm of savage love.
> Dark Earth! dark Heavens! swinging in chemic smoke,
> What dead are born when you kiss each soundless soul
> With lighting and thunder from your mined heart,
> Which man's self dug, and his blind fingers loosed?

It is man who makes dreadful love to Earth with his exploding mines and saps—the third battle of Ypres was prefaced by a spectacular one—and man who unites himself to great uncreating Nature so that she brings forth only dead bodies. Soulless violation of Earth's integrity ends in still-birth.

This stanza has been criticised. It has been thought the weakest part of the poem, hectic and over-elaborate, twopence-coloured not penny-plain. But it is perhaps best seen as a great spiritual explosion in the middle of the poem, the complete realisation of the answer to an earlier question about the blown-up men: 'Who hurled them out? Who hurled?' Man himself is the Great Anarch. Again, this stanza has been thought an unwanted digression from the narrative reality that began with the plunging limber. It may not, however, be too indulgent to a poem that is possibly not in its final form if we see the sudden return to narrative reality in the next stanza as the dramatically concrete embodiment of a realised basic meaning. Man makes earth a monstrous place, and he it is who suffers the utterly harrowing physical consequences:

> A man's brains splattered on
> A stretcher-bearer's face;
> His shook shoulders slipped their load,

W

> But when they bent to look again
> The drowning soul was sunk too deep
> For human tenderness.

From this point on, it seems to me, the poem is incontrovertibly great. Remembering Wordsworth's Lucy poem, or Lear's last speech, one might say that some lines are derivative in a very general way:

> The grass and coloured clay
> More motion have than they,

but would any other poet have written the next line?

> Joined to the great sunk silences.

At such lines, when abstract and concrete come together, we recall Rosenberg's admiration for John Donne's poetry; and this closeness to the earlier poet is reinforced when we discover that Rosenberg is prepared to push beyond 'great sunk silences'. A lesser poet might have stopped, well satisfied with a line like this, but Rosenberg goes on with the imaginative boldness of Donne in his 'Nocturnal on St Lucy's Day'. Absolutes must be explored:

> Here is one not long dead;
> His dark hearing caught our far wheels,
> And the choked soul stretched weak hands
> To reach the living word the far wheels said,
> The blood-dazed intelligence beating for light,
> Crying through the suspense of the far torturing wheels
> Swift for the end to break
> Or the wheels to break,
> Cried as the tide of the world broke over his sight.

> Will they come? Will they ever come?
> Even as the mixed hoofs of the mules,
> The quivering-bellied mules,
> And the rushing wheels all mixed
> With his tortured upturned sight.
> So we crashed round the bend,

> We heard his weak scream,
> We heard his very last sound,
> As our wheels grazed his dead face.

The first of these two stanzas attempts to penetrate the mystery of the last moments of a dying man, the time when, borrowing another of Rosenberg's images from the poem 'In War', the dark soul is flickering; but the intolerably hopeless attempt to hang on is shattered in the next stanza. When the plunging limber comes, life just gutters out.

There is a solidity about Rosenberg's poem that is sometimes present in Read's *The End of A War*. Its first section, 'Meditation of the Dying German Officer', begins in a very similar way, though obviously about an easier death:

> Ich sterbe . . . Life ebbs with an easy flow
> and I've no anguish now. This failing light
> is the world's light: it dies like a lamp
> flickering for want of oil. When the last jump comes
> and the axe-head blackness slips through flesh
> that welcomes it with open but unquivering lips
> then I shall be one with the Unknown
> this Nothing which Heinrich made his argument
> for God's existence: a concept beyond the mind's reach.
> But why embody the Unknown: why give to God
> anything but essence, intangible, invisible, inert?

These are images as finely specific as Rosenberg's, but by the end of the quotation his poem has become a technically metaphysical argument about God's existence. And so it continues, shuttling between the fact,

> But still I hear a distant gunfire, stirring in my ear
> like a weary humming nerve,

and the philosophy:

> Faith in self comes first, from self we build
> the web of friendship, from friends to confederates
> and so to the State. This web has a weft

>in the land we live in, a town, a hill
>all that the living eyes traverse. There are lights
>given by the tongue we speak, the songs we sing,
>the music and the magic of our Fatherland.
>This is a tangible trust.

The imagery is well manipulated, but in a functional way; here
meaning—Read's recreation of the reasoning underlying German
racial solidarity—is primary, although he was perfectly capable of a
higher intensity of fusion of form and content:

>My brow falls like a shutter of lead, clashes
>on the clenched jaw. The curtain of flesh
>is wreathed about these rigid lines
>in folds that have the easy notion of a smile.
>So let them kiss earth and acid corruption:
>extinction of the clod.

A note at the end of the entire poem explains that Read had
picked a particular incident to 'serve as a focus for feelings and
sentiments otherwise diffuse', which shows that the incident was
not of overwhelming importance in itself. Nor are the feelings and
sentiments those of pity or scorn or despair, or any of the more
usual emotions found in war poetry: 'It is not my business as a poet
to condemn war (or, to be more exact, modern warfare).' Here we
might well react like Dr Johnson when reading *Lycidas*—to say
that where there is leisure for exactness there is little grief. But
Read gives an answer that would have done for Milton too: 'I
only wish to present the universal aspects of a particular event.
Judgement may follow, but should never precede or become
embroiled with the act of poetry. It is for this reason that Milton's
attitude to his Satan has so often been misunderstood.' The attitude
is highly aesthetic in the way it excludes ethics, and the resulting
poem often transcends reality in a much more generalised way than
Rosenberg's 'Dead Man's Dump'. The incident itself, as if to
emphasise the degree of impersonality Read achieves, is particularly
horrific. (There is as much of a surprising gulf between 'strong'
subject and intellectual treatment as there is with a play like

Pirandello's *Six Characters*.) An English battalion was induced by a badly wounded German officer to enter a machine-gun ambush in a village; in revenge at being so deceived the German officer is killed and later, as things are settling down in the cleared village, the dreadfully mutilated body of a young girl is discovered. It is a story almost begging for sensational treatment, and indeed, 'atrocity stories' were a stock-in-trade for some writers of the Great War period.

Read avoids all temptations. The second section, 'Dialogue Between the Body and the Soul of the Murdered Girl' begins with an emblem-book description of the wounds of the girl ('Red lips that cannot tell / a credible tale') and continues with a certain amount of narrative; but all is designed to lead up to a philosophical dilemma. The girl, we find, had been a patriotic spy; one part of her could not believe in the value of death without a cause:

SOUL

In this war
many men have perished not blessed
with faith in a cause, a country or a God
not less martyrs than Herod's Victims, Ursula's Virgins
or any massed innocents massacred.

BODY

Such men give themselves not to their God but to their fate
die thinking the face of God not love but hate.

SOUL

Those who die for a cause die comforted and coy;
believing their cause God's cause they die with joy.

The final section, 'Meditation of the Waking English Officer', belongs to the following morning as he wakens to hear the bells ringing for the armistice—'Suspended life / renews its rhythmic beat.' The meditation that follows is very fine, the thoughts of the officer turning and twisting as he strives to find the grounds of his existence so miraculously saved, when there had been

> no fair joy
> no glory in the strife, no blessed wrath.
> Man's mind cannot excel
> mechanic might except in savage sin.
> Our broken bodies oiled the engines: mind was grit.

He had rejected the 'lonely pride' of pacifism and given himself unresisting to the storm, but in its darkness he found only the terrors of negation:

> The individual lost: seventy years
> seventy minutes, have no meaning.

And so the inner debate continues. How easy it is to believe in God in the right circumstances;

> But haggard in the face of death
> deprived of all earthly comfort, all hope of life,
> the soul a distilled essence, held
> in a shaking cup, spilled
> by a spit of lead, saved
> by chance alone
> very real
> in its silky bag of skin, its bond of bone,
> so little and so limited,
> there's no extenuation then.

There is much more in this poem than has been indicated, but enough has been described to show the contemplative level on which it moves. It can hardly be said to be an abstract poem, as the quotations show; it is not a treatise. At the same time, Read keeps strict control over his plunges into the solidly real, and there is the constant sense that the actual subserves a spiritual analysis, a search into concepts and motives lying deep behind war:

> Now I see, either the world is mechanic force
> And this the last tragic act, portending
> endless hate and blind reversion
> back to the tents and healthy lusts
> of animal men: or we act
> God's purpose in an obscure way.

The organisation of *The End of A War* (one can see it in broad outline from the section-titles) is firm and clear, whereas any defender of the structure of Rosenberg's 'Dead Man's Dump' is conscious that he may be resorting to special pleading. Rosenberg was killed in action and therefore unable to revise the poems appearing in *The Collected Works* of 1937 (edited by G. Bottomley and D. Harding). But the originality and power he displayed is undeniable. It stands as one of the most impressive records of the Great War, a record that for all its specificity burns through to a vision of man-begotten chaos. These two individual visions of war's meaning are complementary; together they say more than almost any other works of the time. If we consider, as we perhaps should, their limitations, we must use exceptional yardsticks. Both poems, we might say, do not make up a *Troilus and Cressida*, but their quality is indicated by the fact that this fine Shakespearian play should seem relevant. Such poems explore psychological, moral, ideological and spiritual complexities of human experience in history, at those special times when man meets ultimates of life and death. Literature in them serves what might be thought its most important cultural purpose, even though it guards jealously its own necessary aesthetic independence.

· · · · · ·

There are many other literary reflections of the Great War it has not been possible to examine in any detail. Other works by Read, such as his classic prose piece *In Retreat* (1925), or by Rosenberg, such as his poem called 'Daughters of War'—huge cloudy symbols he himself believed made up his finest creation—could be looked at. There are excellent poems by writers like Edmund Blunden, Charles Sorley and others; there are the prose works of Henry Williamson, H. G. Wells, T. E. Lawrence, Arnold Bennett and others. The Great War was such an enormous experience that it inevitably impinged upon every sphere of life, so that even amongst the innocent memories of a Cambridge childhood and youth it surfaces in a surprising way:

At night she often lay awake, struggling with the problem of why God allowed suffering. Like Man Friday, she asked: 'Why

God no kill the Devil?' And like Robinson Crusoe she found the question very difficult to answer. . . . Aunt Etty was far too honest to quibble, and never did satisfy herself with an answer; but when pushed too far, she would turn to a short list of subjects, about which she was annoyed. She kept these ready for use as counter-irritants, so that she could feel pleasantly indignant about them, when she was not able to sleep. During the 1914 War, the thought of Admiral Jellicoe's weak mouth was a very satisfactory standby; and the untrustworthiness of Winston Churchill at this time, or the immorality of H. G. Wells, often sent her comfortably off to sleep.

This short passage is from Gwen Raverat's sharp, affectionate and very human *Period Piece: A Cambridge Childhood* (1952), a book to be highly recommended for its recreation of the decades before the war, when for a lady it was an important duty to go to London to shop and 'Onward Christian Soldiers' was always sung by her daughter's school on the night before a hockey match, *fortissimo*.

One of the most complete and satisfying works available, which extends over both the pre-war period and the war itself, is Ford Madox Ford's *Parade's End*. This consists of four books (*Some Do Not*, 1924; *No More Parades*, 1925; *A Man Could Stand Up*, 1926; and *Last Post*, 1928), although a number of critics have preferred Ford's later opinion that the last volume is not an integral part of the sequence. *Parade's End* is a dazzling display of selective impressionist technique, which at the same time registers the impact of the war upon the whole way of life in English society:

He seemed to see his draft: two thousand nine hundred and ninety-four men he had command of for over a couple of months—a long space of time as that life went—men he and Sergeant-Major Cowley had looked after with a great deal of tenderness, superintending their morale, their morals, their feet, their digestions, their impatiences, their desires for women. . . . He seemed to see them winding away over a great stretch of country, the head slowly settling down, as in the Zoo you will see an enormous serpent slowly sliding into its water-tank. . . . Settling down out there, a long way away, up against

that impassable barrier that stretched from the depths of the
ground to the peak of heaven. . . .
   Intense dejection: endless muddles: endless follies: endless
villainies. All these men given into the hands of the most
cynically care-free intriguers in long corridors who made plots
that harrowed the hearts of the world. All these men toys: all
these agonies mere occasions for picturesque phrases to be put
into politicians' speeches without heart or even intelligence.
Hundreds of thousands of men tossed here and there in that
sordid and gigantic mud-brownness of mid-winter. . . . By God,
exactly as if they were nuts wilfully picked up and thrown over
the shoulder by magpies. . . . But men. Not just populations.
Men you worried over there. Each man a man with a backbone,
knees, breeches, braces, a rifle, a home, passions, fornications,
drunks, pals, some scheme of the universe, corns, inherited
diseases, a greengrocer's business, a milk walk, a paper stall,
brats, a slut of a wife. . . .

(No More Parades, Part I. 1.)

   There is a peculiarly modern tone and movement in this internal
monologue of Christopher Tietjens, Ford's hero, a man of strong
Tory principles who yet became progressively disillusioned with the
defects of the governing classes and more and more convinced of
the breakdown of true social order and discipline. The title of the
whole work, *Parade's End*, has a wide significance. More, then, than
wartime disillusionment is involved: there is the smell of decay
about the total fabric of Victorian civilisation. Ford expresses as
powerful a distaste for corruption in English society as Wells does
in *Tono-Bungay*. Tietjens is a man of integrity exploited and
harried by lesser and dishonest men, a symbolic figure who is yet,
as Bergonzi says, 'always recognizable as a living human being:
fair, red-faced, large, slow-moving' (*Heroes' Twilight*, chapter 9).
His relationship with his wife Sylvia is anguished and complicated,
and when he turns from its bitterness to the young suffragette
Valentine Wannop, the problems increase. His first meeting with
her at a suffragette demonstration shows society at its most brutish
and his chivalrous actions are immediately misinterpreted. The

long, misty night ride they took together in a dog-cart ends in disaster:

> Not ten yards ahead Tietjens saw a tea-tray, the underneath of a black-lacquered tea-tray, gliding towards them: mathematically straight, just rising from the mist. He shouted: mad: the blood in his head. His shout was drowned by the scream of the horse: he had swung it to the left. The cart turned up: the horse emerged from the mist: head and shoulders: pawing. A stone sea-horse from the fountain of Versailles! Exactly like that! Hanging in air for an eternity: the girl looking at it, leaning slightly forward.
>
> The horse didn't come over backwards: he had loosened the reins. It wasn't there any more. The damndest thing that *could* happen! He had known it would happen. He said:
>
> 'We're all right now!' There was a crash and scraping: like twenty tea-trays: a prolonged sound. They must be scraping along the mud-guard of the invisible car . . .
>
> (Some Do Not, Part I.7.)

This personal disaster is recalled through verbal repetition on the first page of the next volume, *No More Parades*. It grows, so to speak, into an act of war against a nation:

> An immense tea-tray, august, its voice filling the black circle of the horizon, thundered to the ground. Numerous pieces of sheet-iron said, 'Pack. Pack. Pack.' In a minute the clay floor of the hut shook, the drums of ears were pressed inwards, solid noise showered about the universe, enormous echoes pushed these men—to the right, to the left or down towards the tables, and crackling like flames among vast underwood became the settled condition of the night.

Parade's End is a work of continuous relevance, with, as Paul L. Wiley writes in his *Novelist of Three Worlds: Ford Madox Ford* (Syracuse, N.Y., 1962), 'interwoven motifs and overlapping episodes—in short . . . a complex total impression of a distinct but vanished stage in the life of a people.' It is true we find a perceptible and constant bias throughout the work, a certain romanticising of old English virtues. We have often met this before and its constancy means that it can be allowed for. But *Parade's End* is the kind of fiction that belongs in the great tradition of the novel—for its psychological and social analysis, its fully realised characters and the perpetual brilliance of its impressionist prose, which fixes typical moments of history with all the sense of actuality that we expect of the novel as a form. Read, we recall, found that at the armistice, 'Suspended life / renews its rhythmic beat.' Ford, as a novelist, would not move on such a transcendental plane; real life at his armistice is much more untidy:

> At least they weren't over there! They were prancing. The whole world round them was yelling and prancing round. They were the centre of unending roaring circles. The man with the eyeglass had stuck a half-crown in his other eye. He was well-meaning. A brother. She had a brother with the V.C. All in the family.
>
> Tietjens was stretching out his two hands from the waist. It was incomprehensible. His right hand was behind her back, his left in her right hand. She was frightened. She was amazed. Did you ever! He was swaying slowly. The elephant! They were dancing! Aranjuez was hanging on to the tall woman like a kid on a telegraph pole. The officer who had said he had picked up a little bit of fluff... well, he had! He had run out and fetched it. It wore white cotton gloves and a flowered hat. It said: 'Ow! Now!'... There was a fellow with a most beautiful voice. He led: better than a gramophone. Better....
>
> *Les petites marionettes, font! font! font!* ...
>
> On an elephant. A dear, meal-sack elephant. She was setting out on ...
>
> (*A Man Could Stand Up*, Part III.2.)

Literature can serve its cultural purpose in very diverse ways, we find, and history survives in an amazing variety of literary documents.

NOTES

[1] See especially Dennis Welland, 'Arthur Graeme West: A Messenger to Job', in *Renaissance and Modern Essays: Presented to V. de Sola Pinto*, ed. G. R. Hibbard, 1966.

11 : The Modern and the New

THE experience of world war for writers who were actually engaged in fighting and dying was, as we have seen, a great spiritual crisis, one which thoroughly upset traditional assumptions and undermined standard attitudes. Nevertheless, when we think of the case of Yeats, the poems of whose middle period we looked at and evaluated in chapter 8, we cannot say that the conventions of literary *expression* were transformed by English war-poets to anything like the same extent. Rosenberg might have developed a comparable body of work. A poem like Wilfred Owen's 'The Show', a nightmare vision, had interesting potential. But neither Owen nor Rosenberg survived the war, and it is not to them that we must look for the most seminal writing of the last decade of our period or for the writing that clearly demonstrates the greatest possibilities of literary form. In some ways, too, the very magnitude of the historical event enforced a narrowing of focus, a concentration upon what seemed to be the immediate needs of the situation between 1914 and 1918, as in the case of authors like Kipling, Wells (*Mr Britling Sees It Through*, 1916) and Masefield, not to mention the many others who lent their pens to the war effort. And amongst those who came to do the very reverse, like Sassoon, one can see from later poems and letters that the anti-war imperative had equally led to a distortion of natural vision. Such factors also tend to disguise the truth that a fundamental revolution in attitudes had already begun well before the war and, in some writers at least, had led to work to which the word 'modern' might most appropriately be applied. We may begin by looking at some of the early novels of E. M. Forster.

In his first novel, *Where Angels Fear to Tread* (1905), we find a

feature we have already noted in his short story 'The Machine
Stops'—a conflict of values. The opening chapter of the novel sets
in opposition to each other the romantic glamour of Italy and the
dull respectability of the London suburb of Sawston. Sawston is all
convention and Book Club, mediocrity and Progressive Whist,
bazaars and boredom. The place reappears in his next novel, *The
Longest Journey* (1907), and its school in particular is shown to
exert a deadening influence. We are to some extent reminded of
Lawrence's Ursula Brangwen when we find that Forster's hero,
Rickie Elliot, is becoming severe in class, since he finds it to be the
most expedient way of teaching, and is deliberately curbing his own
enthusiasms to avoid problems. Its headmaster has one criterion—
'success: success for the body in this life or for the soul in the life to
come.' Conflict of values is again the ground-plan of *Howards End*
(1910), in which Forster achieves a much more substantial embodiment of his themes. Like Conrad, Forster shows himself engaged
with 'material interests', a fact we can see very clearly from the
description of Christmas Shopping in chapter 10. 'We always give
the servants money,' says Mrs Wilcox to Forster's heroine Margaret
Schlegel. What follows brings out the materialism in a way that
Louis Macneice was to develop in later years (see his *Autumn
Journal*, 1939), but also with a degree of realistic acceptance of its
actuality which is significant:

'Yes, do you, yes, much easier,' replied Margaret, but felt the
grotesque impact of the unseen upon the seen, and saw issuing
from a forgotten manger at Bethlehem this torrent of coins and
toys. Vulgarity reigned. Public houses, besides their usual
exhortation against temperance reform, invited men to 'Join
our Christmas goose club'—one bottle of gin, etc., or two,
according to subscription. A poster of a woman in tights
heralded the Christmas pantomime, and little red devils, who
had come in again that year, were prevalent upon the
Christmas cards. Margaret was no morbid idealist. She did not
wish this spate of business and self-advertisement checked. It
was only the occasion of it that struck her with amazement
annually.

We have in fact already heard Margaret acknowledging that her own fine way of life depends upon her private income; she stands on it as if it were an island, whilst the poor are sunk deep below the surface of the sea. At times, she says, it seems that the 'lowest abyss is not the absence of love, but the absence of coin', and when accused of Socialism, she continues,

> Call it what you like. I call it going through life with one's hand spread open on the table. I'm tired of these rich people who pretend to be poor, and think it shows a nice mind to ignore the piles of money that keep their feet above the waves. I stand each year upon six hundred pounds, and Helen upon the same, and Tibby will stand upon eight, and as fast as our pounds crumble away into the sea they are renewed—from the sea, yes, from the sea. (Chapter 7.)

Over against such liberal, progressive values are set those of people like the Wilcoxes. Their actions over the house that gives the book its title are very revealing. When Mrs Wilcox dies, they discover that she has left a scribbled pencil note to the effect that she wants Howards End to go to Margaret Schlegel; to Mrs Wilcox it was more than a mere piece of property and she had come to regard Margaret as her spiritual heir. But the reactions of her family—they suppress all knowledge of the note and cast it on the fire—are broadly symbolic of their inner nature. Forster's narrative at this point, we cannot but help notice, repeats the terms used in the Christmas shopping passage quoted above, 'unseen' and 'seen':

> The practical moralist may acquit them absolutely. He who strives to look deeper may acquit them—almost. For one hard fact remains. They did neglect a personal appeal. The woman who had died did say to them, 'Do this,' and they answered, 'We will not.'
>
> The incident made a most painful impression on them. Grief mounted into the brain and worked there disquietingly. Yesterday they had lamented: 'She was a dear mother, a true wife: in our absence she neglected her health and died.' Today they thought: 'She was not as true, as dear, as we supposed.' The

desire for a more inward light had found impression at last, the unseen had impacted upon the seen, and all that they could say was 'Treachery.' Mrs Wilcox had been treacherous to the family, to the laws of property, to her own written word. How did she expect Howards End to be conveyed to Miss Schlegel? Was her husband, to whom it legally belonged, to make it over as a free gift? . . . (Chapter 11.)

And so on. They are being thoroughly worldly and practical in this affair—and yet they are not to be utterly despised. Margaret Schlegel, we are told in chapter 12, sees that they have certain virtues, even if not the first-rate ones: they are neat and decisive and obedient. Such people, she thinks, form civilisation and form character; they keep the soul from becoming sloppy. Margaret actually decides to marry Henry Wilcox, in order 'to escape from the island of moneyed privilege, to connect the ideals of the Schlegels to the business world that supplies them with their independence' (C. B. Cox, *The Free Spirit: A Study of Liberal Humanism*, 1963, page 78).

Married to Henry Wilcox in this attempt to make contact with a very real side of life, Margaret at one point goes down to the empty Howards End, getting away from London, rush, bustle and motor cars. At the farm where she calls for the key, she meets with a disappointment, for in place of the expected simple friendliness she encounters a most finished and would-be genteel young lady:

Stunned, Margaret did not move from the best parlour, over which the touch of art nouveau had fallen. But the other rooms looked in keeping, though they conveyed the peculiar sadness of a rural interior. Here had lived an elder race, to which we look back with disquietude. The country which we visit at weekends was really a home to it, and the graver side of life, the deaths, the partings, the yearnings for love, have their deepest expression in the heart of the fields. All was not sadness. The sun was shining without. The thrush sang his two syllables on the budding guelder-rose. Some children were playing uproariously in heaps of golden straw. It was the presence of sadness at all that surprised Margaret, and ended

by giving her a feeling of completeness. In these English farms,
if anywhere, one might see life steadily and see it whole, group
in one vision its transitoriness and its eternal youth, connect—
connect without bitterness until all men are brothers.

(Chapter 33.)

There is no need to repeat what has been said in earlier chapters
about the rural myth, but it is worth noticing the phrase to 'see life
steadily and see it whole', which derives from Matthew Arnold's
words about Sophocles. Forster, in fact, follows Arnold as a critic
of all that makes for lack of harmony in life, anything which
prevents cultural development in human beings and society, in
which the perfected individual should be able to carry others along
with him. (See *Culture and Anarchy*, 1869.) The weight of feeling is
very strong and very traditional. But Forster's associated effort to
come to terms with the realities of his own age in history and join
the seen to the unseen, harmonise outer and inner values, is not
very plausibly worked out in his novel. He could not really connect
with the new world, although he could recognise it clearly:
'London was but a foretaste of this nomadic civilisation which is
altering human nature so profoundly, and throws upon personal
relations a stress greater than they have ever borne before. Under
cosmopolitanism, if it comes, we shall receive no help from the
earth' (chapter 31). Other, more revolutionary ideas than these
were abroad, and the place we must look for some of them is
Cambridge about the turn of the century.

Cambridge at that time contained the men who began the great
reaction against the dominating idealistic school of philosophers in
this country, though it may be thought a truly peculiar dispensation
of Providence that the new currents of thought should come to be
known as 'Oxford philosophy'. In 1892 G. E. Moore went up to
Cambridge to study classics, but changed to philosophy and in 1903
published his famous *Principia Ethica*. The nature of his influence
is put very simply by Bertrand Russell, who in the first volume of
his autobiography writes that 'it was an intense excitement, after

having supposed the sensible world unreal, to be able to believe
again that there really were such things as tables and chairs'
(*Autobiography: 1872–1914*, 1967). The epigraph of *Principia Ethica*,
we might notice here, is equally plain: 'Everything is what it is, and
not another thing' (Bishop Butler). Nor is it surprising to find that
the title of one of Moore's later articles is 'In Defence of Common
Sense'. In his ethical thought Moore claimed that good is the
simplest of notions, like yellow, and therefore 'incapable of any
definition, in the most important sense of that word (*Principia*,
Cambridge 1954, page 9). It just is so. Later in the *Principia* (page
188) Moore argued that 'the most valuable things, which we
know or can imagine, are certain states of consciousness, which
may be roughly described as the pleasures of human intercourse
and the enjoyment of beautiful objects', which was to be another
of his highly influential statements. Amongst philosophers Moore is
regarded as a great questioner, a man who raised problems, which
he then attempted to make precise and to solve. 'But when he was
faced with criticism,' F. Copleston tells us in *A History of Philosophy*, volume 8, part 2 (1966), 'he never brushed it aside. . . . it was
his habit to give serious consideration to the critic's remarks and to
give due weight to his point of view.' This alone is a great intellectual
virtue, but Moore went even further: if he was perplexed, he said
so, and if convinced he had been wrong, admitted it without
further ado. Russell records that only by a trick was he able to make
Moore tell a lie. He asked Moore if he always spoke the truth—and
received the answer 'No'! In one of Forster's novels, *A Room With a
View* (1908), there is an amusing account of the difficulties involved
in being completely honest in life. The novel begins with two ladies,
abroad in Italy but living in a pension which might as well have
been in England, with portraits of the late Queen and the late poet
laureate hanging heavily framed on the wall, together with a notice
of the English Church (Rev. Cuthbert Eager, M.A. Oxon.). There
is no mistaking the stifling Victorian atmosphere. When the ladies
are heard complaining that their rooms lack the view they had been
promised, a stranger offers them his own and his son's room, only
to be coldly snubbed by the older of the two ladies. The younger
feels that it is more than a mere matter of rooms and views: it

X

involves a whole mental outlook upon life. Eventually, an English clergyman of their acquaintance persuades them to take the offer and provides, in all innocence, a perfect comment upon the state of English genteel society:

> 'He is rather a peculiar man.' Again he hesitated, and then said gently: 'I think he would not take advantage of your acceptance, nor expect you to show gratitude. He has the merit—if it is one—of saying exactly what he means. He has rooms he does not value, and he thinks you would value them. He has no more thought of putting you under an obligation than he thought of being polite. It is so difficult—at least I find it difficult—to understand people who speak the truth.'

Jane Austen, one knows, would have appreciated the confession in the last sentence.

As so often is the case with English novelists, the fictional account can be matched in real life. Leonard Woolf, who went up to Cambridge a few years later than Forster in 1899, has spoken in one of the volumes of his autobiography of Moore's profundity and passion for truth: 'When Moore said, "I *simply* don't understand *what* he means," the emphasis on the "simply" and the "what" and the shake of his head over each word gave one a glimpse of the passionate distress which muddled thinking aroused in him' (*Sowing: An Autobiography of the Years 1880–1904*, 1960). Woolf learnt from Moore that he should not accept any given system of belief without using his common sense to assay it. He goes on to testify that at Cambridge he reacted against 'bourgeois Victorianism', encouraged to revolt by Moore's 'ingenuous passion for truth' and also 'the climate of scepticism and revolt into which we were born.' (The other leaders he names in this connection are Swinburne; Shaw, in *Man and Superman*; Samuel Butler, in *The Way of All Flesh*; and, 'to some extent', Hardy and Wells.) There is a powerful feeling communicated by Leonard Woolf that Cambridge meant to him the relaxation of a fusty and stultifying grip, a social and intellectual emancipation from the rules and conventions of 'the last days of Victorian civilisation.' As Lytton Strachey exultantly cried on the publication of *Principia Ethica*, 'The age of reason has come!' Both Strachey and Woolf were, of course, members of the Bloomsbury Group, artists and writers who met frequently in the new century and who had roughly the same taste and *Weltanschauung*. Other members were Maynard Keynes, Clive Bell, Roger Fry and the four children of Sir Leslie Stephen, one of whom, Virginia, married Leonard Woolf. The experimental novels for which she became justly famous appeared outside our period, but we can see in her early critical essays, especially 'Mr Bennett and Mrs Brown' and 'Modern Fiction' (reprinted in *The Captain's Deathbed*, 1950, and *The Common Reader, First Series*, 1925), how emancipated she was as far as traditional forms and modes of writing were concerned, thus paralleling in art what her husband and those like him had discovered in life. When human relations change, she maintains in 'Mr Bennett and Mrs Brown', then there is inevitably 'a change in religion, conduct, politics and literature.' She repudiated the novel as it was written by Arnold Bennett and John Galsworthy, saying that it failed to capture life; in her own concentration upon the full rendering of experience and in her attempt to capture its essence, she developed a style which has been likened to that of Cézanne in painting. (His art had been introduced to London by one of the Bloomsbury Group, Roger Fry, in the Post-Impressionist exhibitions of 1910 and 1912.)

With G. E. Moore as a philosopher is coupled the name of Bertrand Russell, again a revolutionary influence. Father Copleston writes that he is for many the best known of British philosophers, 'a prophet of liberal humanism, a hero of those who regard themselves as rationalists, free from the shackles of religious and metaphysical dogma and yet at the same time devoted to the cause of human freedom, as against totalitarianism, and of social and political progress according to rational principles' (*History*, volume 8, part 2, chapter 19). Some of his writings are difficult and technical in nature, and, to the layman, not easy to see the value of, though professionals seem to agree that they are very impressive, particularly in the field of mathematical logic. He himself, writing for laymen in the first volume of his autobiography about one of his early intellectual setbacks, remarks, 'It seemed unworthy of a grown man to spend his time on such trivialities, but what was I to do?' We might, however, look again at Leonard Woolf's account of his Cambridge years to gain an impression of the impact made by a radical thinker upon his time, for in matters of influence and change in values what a man seems to represent is in some ways as important as what he actually is:

> Russell used to come to Moore's rooms sometimes in order to discuss some difficult problem that was holding him up. The contrast between the two men and the two minds was astonishing and fascinating. Russell has the quickest mind of anyone I have ever known; like the greatest of chess players he sees in a flash six moves ahead of the ordinary player and one move ahead of all the other Grand Masters. However serious he may be, his conversation scintillates with wit and a kind of puckish humour flickers through his thought. Like most people who possess this kind of mental brilliance, in an argument a slower and duller opponent may ruefully find that Russell is not always entirely scrupulous in taking advantage of his superior skill in the use of weapons. Moore was the exact opposite, and to listen to an argument between the two was like watching a race between the hare and the tortoise. Quite often the tortoise won—and that, of course, was why Russell's thought had been so deeply influenced by Moore and why he still came to Moore's rooms to discuss difficult problems.

Woolf shows obvious admiration for Russell's intellect, only slightly qualified by his comment on dialectical methods. In 1914 Russell went to Harvard to act as a temporary professor of philosophy, where he met a very silent postgraduate student who only once made a memorable remark—to the effect that Heraclitus reminded him of Villon. The student, however, was regarding his tutor with a much sharper gaze than Woolf's:

> When Mr. Apollinax visited the United States
> His laughter tinkled among the teacups.
> I thought of Fragilion, that shy figure among the birch-trees,
> And of Priapus in the shrubbery
> Gaping at the lady in the swing.

In the palace of Mrs. Phlaccus, at Professor Channing-
Cheetah's
He laughed like an irresponsible foetus.

The impact Russell made upon the society of Harvard was evidently profoundly disturbing. What could be more grotesque than 'an irresponsible foetus', the kind of phenomenon Aubrey Beardsley drew in his more bizarre moments. There is in Eliot a degree of psychological resistance to Russell that is quite missing in Leonard Woolf, but as the poem continues, we discover that Eliot was very well aware of how slow and dull were the people Russell met in America. At Harvard, too, was a 'bourgeois Victorianism' unable to cope with Russell's almost incredible intellectual and emotional energy of spirit:

I looked for the head of Mr Apollinax rolling under a chair
Or grinning over a screen
With seaweed in its hair.
I heard the beat of centaur's hoofs over the hard turf
As his dry and passionate talk devoured the afternoon.
'He is a charming man'—'But after all what did he mean?'
'His pointed ears. . . . He must be unbalanced.'—
'There was something he said that I might have challenged.'
Of dowager Mrs Phlaccus, and Professor and Mrs Cheetah
I remember a slice of lemon, and a bitten macaroon.

If the near-contemporary testimony of Woolf and Eliot, so different in tone but so similar in certain essential respects, is to be credited, it was high time that the slice of lemon and the bitten macaroon should be thrown away. The cold current of the new century was just beginning to strike chill. As Dryden sang two hundred years before,

'Tis well an Old Age is out
And time to begin a New.
                    (*The Secular Masque, 1700*)

    .   .   .   .   .   .

But Eliot's resolute mythologizing of Russell has surely given us the clue that there ought to be some qualifications, even of the

non-fictional prose account by Leonard Woolf. Many of the
Bloomsbury Group, we find, belonged to a Cambridge society
founded about 1820 called the Apostles, which had subsequently
contained many of the most intellectually eminent men at the
university. To young men who were fortunate enough to be invited
to join this society about the turn of the century there came an
intensified sense of intellectual liberation. Wilfred Stone has described Forster's 'thankfulness at being received in this company'
and connected it with 'the euphoric relief in escaping to Cambridge
(or Oxford) from the stupefying boredom of late-Victorian households and public schools' (*The Cave and the Mountain: A Study of
E. M. Forster*, 1966, chapter 3). We may compare what we have
seen Forster writing of the undeveloped heart of Reggie Moore
(see page 216 above); the public school was for Forster the anti-
type of Cambridge. None of this would appear to qualify earlier
statements, but if we now look at Russell's autobiography again
to see what he himself thought of the twentieth-century history of
quintessential Cambridge, we discover major reservations:

> The tone of the generation some ten years junior to my own
> was set mainly by Lytton Strachey and Keynes. It is surprising
> how great a change in mental climate those ten years had
> brought. We were still Victorian; they were Edwardian. We
> believed in ordered progress by means of politics and free
> discussion. The more self-confident amongst us may have
> hoped to be leaders of the multitude, but none of us wished to
> be divorced from it. The generation of Keynes and Lytton
> did not seek to preserve any kinship with the Philistine. They
> aimed rather at a life of retirement among fine shades and
> nice feelings, and conceived of the good as consisting in the
> passionate mutual admirations of a clique of the élite. This
> doctrine, quite unfairly, they fathered upon G. E. Moore,
> whose disciples they professed to be.   (Chapter 3.)

His point seems well worth bearing in mind, for while the revolt
against Victorian civilisation is an undoubted fact of cultural
history, here we have the warning of one of its leaders that in his
view it was carried to an extreme. Nevertheless, while it may be

true to say that these young men of Cambridge wanted to be good rather than do good, there is still the fact that continuities had been shattered and that a genuinely 'modern' morality had been developed. Strachey's *Eminent Victorians* of 1918 may stand as the most obvious work of iconoclasm performed, with its attempted demolition of four great representative Victorians: Dr Thomas Arnold of Rugby, Florence Nightingale, General Gordon and Cardinal Manning.

.   .   .   .   .   .

Even in Strachey's extreme form, however, we have not yet dis-covered the full extent of the new age's revolt. Stephen Spender's *The Struggle of the Modern* (1963) elaborates a very helpful dis-tinction between classes of writers. On the one side he places men like Shaw and Wells, confident that they are capable of evaluating the tendencies of the age to which they belong and that by their writings they can affect those tendencies, using the most up-to-date and progressive criteria. These he calls 'contemporaries'. On the other side he groups the writers he calls 'moderns', men like Rimbaud, Joyce, Proust and Eliot, who feel that they have been affected by their age and that 'they had somehow to reflect and respond to the effects of such conditioning in their art: perhaps by allowing unconscious forces to erupt through its surfaces; or perhaps by the cultivation of an extreme critical awareness, as it were an uninterrupted stream of communication with the values of the past, in what they wrote.' (Part 2. 1.) The 'moderns', in this special sense of the word, believe that they will thus produce a genuinely new art, which will be a synthesis of both past and present. They are progressive in that they are as firmly committed to the present as 'contemporaries', but, paradoxically, they are strongly traditional because of their constant awareness of past history. We have, in fact, already considered this point when looking at David Jones's *In Parenthesis* (1936), a work in the true line of descent from the great modern writings of the first decades of the twentieth century. The modern movement is cosmopolitan: both Europe and America contributed. It is by no means confined to literature, as we may see by a brief consideration of Picasso, an artist so revolutionary that some sixty years later there are many people still adamantly refusing to respond to his work. The critic John Golding has called the Cubist movement of the early years of this century the most complete and radical artistic revolution since the Renaissance; in aesthetic terms, he states, 'a portrait by Renoir will seem closer to a portrait by Raphael than it does to a Cubist portrait by Picasso' (*Cubism: A History and An Analysis 1907–1914*, 2nd edition, 1968). Yet Golding also notes that Cubist artists owe a debt to their predecessors, painters like Seurat, Douanier Rousseau, Cézanne and Gaugin, and through Gaugin back to primitive art. Even so, a study of the portrait of a young girl with a mandolin reproduced amongst the illustrations will show how truly revolutionary Picasso's art was in 1910 when it was painted.

We see that solid forms have been broken down and analysed into a number of smaller areas, which are, so to speak, presented individually for our inspection. Traditional perspective is ignored; all forms are faceted into one plane. Not only this: the figure of the young girl is in a sense sinking into its surroundings, which are treated in a very similar way. The process is not quite driven to its logical extreme, however, as it was in some paintings. There is, in this portrait, a more realistic and sculptural effect about the curves of the breast and the mandolin, especially in comparison with the treatment of the head. The Gris portrait of Picasso, which we have also reproduced, brings out more boldly the implications of the artistic discoveries of Picasso (and Braque): it is more un-compromising in its analysis, intellectual rather than instinctive, methodical—almost mechanical. When it was first exhibited at the 1912 *Salon des Indépendants*, it was regarded, says Golding, as having 'the character of a tribute to the *chef d'école*.' It is indeed a striking work, though it is undeniable that many will see it as an act of appropriate revenge rather than tribute. As for the 'Con-struction for Noble Ladies' by Schwitters, which dates from 1919, this is included so that we may compare it with the examples of Victorian art amongst the other illustrations—and meditate on the flow of history and the movements of the human spirit in the course of a generation or so. We could also compare the musical activities of Schoenberg with those of his contemporary, Cecil Sharp. From 1900 onwards the performance of Schoenberg's advanced music was accompanied by hostile demonstrations; in 1908, *Grove's Dictionary* tells us, he produced the first works 'in which the tonal system is definitely suspended.' Yet from 1907 onwards Cecil Sharp was bringing out his *Morris Book, Country Dance Book* and the like, basing them on older sources like John Playford's *English Dancing Master* (1651), though for purely practical reasons translating them 'into modern and intelligible language.' This is a revival, not a *synthesis* of old and new. It is history as re-creation, very pleasurable indeed but not in the least modern in Spender's sense.

. . . . . .

We cannot at this point ignore the existence of one of the most influential of all modern critical works, the essay by T. S. Eliot called 'Tradition and the Individual Talent', which was published in the *Egoist* in 1919 and has been reprinted in his *Selected Essays* (1932). Eliot begins with the statement that people tend to praise a writer for those features of his work that are most distinctive and in which he differs from his predecessors. Per contra, Eliot believes that the best parts of a writer's work are those in which his artistic ancestors are most fully alive. The essay, clearly of vital relevance in a book on history and literature, continues by carefully side-stepping the criticism that traditionalism of this kind could possibly involve slavish imitation and then reaches one of its most famous passages (for a short essay it is surprising how many of these there are):

Tradition is a matter of much wider significance. It cannot be inherited, and if you want it you must obtain it by great labour. It involves, in the first place, the historical sense, which we may call nearly indispensable to anyone who would continue to be a poet beyond his twenty-fifth year; and the historical sense involves a perception, not only of the pastness of the past, but of its presence; the historical sense compels a man to write not merely with his own generation in his bones, but with a feeling that the whole of the literature of Europe from Homer and within it the whole of the literature of his own country has a simultaneous existence and composes a simultaneous order. This historical sense, which is a sense of the timeless as well as of the temporal and of the timeless and of the temporal together, is what makes a writer traditional. And it is at the same time what makes a writer most acutely conscious of his place in time, of his own contemporaneity.

Eliot goes on to say that once the new work of art has been created something happens to all preceding works of art, because 'the existing monuments form an ideal order among themselves, which is modified by the introduction of the new (the really new) work of art among them.' For this reason all poets should be as fully aware as possible of the main current of past culture and write in conscious relation to it. The poet, in fact, Eliot writes in one of the less plausible passages of this essay, must sacrifice himself to something more valuable, extinguish his own personality. This too, is the note on which Eliot ends, stating that the poet will not be able to achieve this impersonality unless he surrenders his egoistic self to the work to be done. 'And he is not likely to know what is to be done unless he lives in what is not merely the present, but the present moment of the past, unless he is conscious, not of what is dead, but of what is already living.'

This kind of timeless and static order achieved by an individual mind is not what we normally think of as historical, since we tend rather to imagine a sequence of events, the experience of mankind in the process of unrolling through time. A conception like Eliot's is very different from that expressed in the classic introduction to Hippolyte Taine's *History of English Literature* (1864). Far from believing that the artist could extinguish himself, Taine wrote that the work of art was the equivalent of a fossil, which one goes behind in order to form some idea of the animal that produced it. And when the critic reaches the inner being of the man who created the work of art, he must then consider the artist as shaped by his race, his milieu and his historical moment. All kinds of factors determine the way in which an artist writes—the hereditary character of his people, climate, political events, existing cultural developments and so on. This is literature as the product of history. Nevertheless, Eliot's formulations, which we must never forget were those of a practising creative artist, show history and literature in a fruitful relationship. A simple example might be an early poem, 'Cousin Nancy', which appeared in his *Prufrock and Other Observations* (1917):

> Miss Nancy Ellicott
> Strode across the hills and broke them,
> Rode across the hills and broke them—
> The barren New England hills—
> Riding to hounds
> Over the cow-pasture.
>
> Miss Nancy Ellicot smoked
> And danced all the modern dances;
> And her aunts were not quite sure how they felt about it,
> But they knew that it was modern.
>
> Upon the glazen shelves kept watch
> Matthew and Waldo, guardians of the faith,
> The army of unalterable law.

In some ways this is a fairly simple poem, a portrait of an up-to-date and rather carefree young lady, a contemporary descendant of those 'girls of the eighties' and Beardsley's superb lady golfer. But what is Eliot's attitude towards this novelty? The answer seems to depend on the last line, which is a reference to a sonnet by Meredith called 'Lucifer in Starlight'. This sonnet tells of Lucifer rising again from his dark dominion and almost managing to revive his old revolt, but then he looked at the stars and realised he could never succeed:

> Around the ancient track marched, rank on rank,
> The army of unalterable law.

Nancy Ellicott has not escaped from her egotistic self and its desires; her rebellion is as futile as Lucifer's was. She is not truly 'modern'.

A much more interesting poem is 'The Love Song of J. Alfred Prufrock', which seems to have been finished as early as 1911 and was first published in *Poetry* (*Chicago*) in June 1915. It begins by placing itself in a great (and by now very familiar) literary tradition with an epigraph from Dante's *Inferno*. The quotation is from the words of Count Guido de Montefeltrano when he spoke confidently to Dante in Hell, because he was sure that Dante, too, was one of the dead. (We are fortunate in being able to refer for this kind of information to B. C. Southam's most useful booklet, *A Student's Guide to the Selected Poems of T. S. Eliot*, 1968.) Eliot's vision in 'The Love Song', then, is associated with a kind of death in life. This we see again, later in the poem, when the sadly limp Mr Prufrock wonders if it would have been worth it

> To say: 'I am Lazarus, come from the dead,
> Come back to tell you all, I shall tell you all'—
> If one, settling a pillow by her head,
>> Should say: 'That is not what I meant at all.
>> That is not it, at all.'

Prufrock is ever frustrated; he lacks the courage to meet any sort of challenge:

> For I have known them all already, known them all,
> Have known the evenings, mornings, afternoons,
> I have measured out my life with coffee spoons;
> I know the voices dying with a dying fall
> Beneath the music from a farther room.
>> So how should I presume?

The lines about the coffee spoons and music take us past the poor, indecisive Prufrock to the society in which he has his being. We seem to be back in the world of the Channing-Cheetahs and their kind, back with toast and tea and talk with neither salt nor savour:

> In the room the women come and go
> Talking of Michelangelo.

The great Italian artist is manipulated by Eliot rather in the way John Davidson used him in his poem 'The Crystal Palace', though with less sharpness—'This music hath a dying fall'. In both poems, however, the deficiencies of the present moment are indicated at such points. Poor Prufrock's love song ends in unacted desires and wistful dreams:

> I grow old . . . I grow old . . .
> I shall wear the bottoms of my trousers rolled.
>
> Shall I part my hair behind? Do I dare to eat a peach?
> I shall wear white flannel trousers, and walk upon the
>   beach.
> I have heard the mermaids singing, each to each.
>
> I do not think that they will sing to me.
>
> I have seen them riding seaward on the waves
> Combing the white hair of the waves blown back
> When the wind blows the water white and black.
>
> We have lingered in the chambers of the sea
> By sea-girls wreathed with seaweed red and brown
> Till human voices wake us, and we drown.

The verse is rhythmic but hardly rigidly patterned; the transitions and sequences of meaning are sometimes clear but often obscure. There is a deliberate denial of simple expectation on the part of the reader, a degree of difficulty which exceeds that of a Browning monologue (which undoubtedly used to succeed in capturing the ellipticalities of real-life conversation). Overall, there are the strange connections between past and present, where the prosaic if novel fashion of trouser turn-ups, for instance, is placed next to the echo of Donne's wit and bold extravagance. How could a Prufrock ever attain to the energy of this?

> Go and catch a falling star,
>   Get with child a mandrake's root,
> Tell me where all past years are,
>   Or who cleft the devil's foot,
> Teach me to hear mermaids singing . . .

A poet writing with the past in his mind can achieve such constant, illuminating juxtapositions and echoes.

One of the most important features of these early poems is that

Eliot is speaking through characters or masks like Prufrock. In the next poem, 'Portrait of a Lady' (1910), we find an equally un-heroic protagonist: 'I smile, of course,/And go on drinking tea.' 'Gerontion' of 1919 is another exceptional poem of this kind, the soliloquy, dryly despairing, of an old man near death, who realises that his life has never amounted to anything. He had been a failure. He sits, empty and unredeemed, like all those others who had disregarded salvation and lived in spiritual sloth:

> After such knowledge, what forgiveness? Think now
> History has many cunning passages, contrived corridors
> And issues, deceives with whispering ambitions,
> Guides us by vanities. Think now
> She gives when our attention is distracted
> And what she gives, gives with such supple confusions
> That the giving famishes the craving. Gives too late
> What's not believed in, or if still believed,
> In memory only, reconsidered passion. Gives too soon
> Into weak hands, what's thought can be dispensed with
> Till the refusal propagates a fear. Think
> Neither fear nor courage saves us. Unnatural vices
> Are fathered by our heroism. Virtues
> Are forced upon us by our impudent crimes.
> These tears are shaken from the wrath-bearing tree.

The verse itself is a pastiche of various Elizabethan dramatists, fitting the meditation of Elliot's character into literary tradition; and so too is the content of the verse, these thoughts of 'a dry brain in a dry season', generalised to the experience of people in history. The past in this poem is as deficient as the present, since Gerontion's private agony is that of mankind, always deceived and ever bewildered. History is a labyrinth. If, as Southam suggests, the 'contrived corridors' glances at the so-called Polish Corridor, the strip of land taken from Germany by the Versailles treaty which became the most resented of its settlements, we have an example of those precise references to contemporary life so fascinating to men like Shaw and Wells—but usually neglected by Eliot.[1] It fades here into the background of the poem; it is, so to speak, a facet that is already facing the reader and which does not have to be turned on some axis from the vanishing perspective of history. The past and the present co-exist in Gerontion's mind; the images thrown up are kaleidoscopic and horribly chaotic:

> What will the spider do,
> Suspend its operations, will the weevil
> Delay? De Bailhache, Fresca, Mrs Cammel, whirled
> Beyond the circuit of the shuddering Bear
> In fractured atoms. Gull against the wind, in the windy
>   straits
> Of Belle Isle, or running on the Horn,
> White feathers in the snow, the Gulf claims,
> And an old man driven by the Trades
> To a sleepy corner.

A concentrated allusion in the early part of the poem points to *The Education of Henry Adams* (1918), in which Adams describes the Maryland spring, an 'intermixture of delicate grace and passionate depravity.' The theory of history Adams formulated in this work seems relevant to 'Gerontion', since Adams saw the new century as no longer a unity but a multiple thing, where order is but a dream man attempted to impose upon the law of nature, chaos:

Nevertheless, he could not pretend that his mind felt flattered by this scientific outlook. Every fabulist has told how the human mind has always struggled like a frightened bird to escape the chaos which caged it; how—appearing suddenly and inexplicably out of some unknown and unimaginable void; passing half its known life in the mental chaos of sleep; victim even when awake to its own ill-adjustment, to disease, to age, to external suggestion, to nature's compulsion; doubting its sensations, and, in the last resort, trusting only to instruments and averages—after sixty or seventy years of growing astonishment, the mind wakes to find itself looking blankly into the void of death.

Always, Adams writes, the human mind has tried to adjust itself to conditions,

until at last, in 1900, a new avalanche of unknown forces had
fallen on it, which required new mental powers to control.
If this view was correct, the mind could gain nothing by flight
or by fight, it must merge in its super-sensual multiverse, or
succumb to it.   (Chapter 31.)

Both Adams and Eliot, in a more compressed and allusive way,
are giving us theories of human development and the pressures
upon man as the universe he lives in explodes in complexity. There
are other aspects of Eliot's argument in the poem, particularly
those which evoke a centre of permanence and stability, 'the still
point of the turning world', which are brief hints of what is to come
in his future writings. At this stage of his career, however, he saw
'the immense panorama of futility and anarchy which is contemporary history'. Prufrock and Gerontion are its sterile representatives. The phrase I have quoted, we might note, comes from a piece
of Eliot's critical prose in *The Dial* for 1923, in which he defends
the method James Joyce used in *Ulysses* of continuous comparison
with Homer's *Odyssey*. The criticism can also be taken as a guide
to Eliot's own method, even more properly than it can be applied
to Joyce's:

> In using the myth, in manipulating a continuous parallel
> between contemporaneity and antiquity, Mr Joyce is pursuing
> a method which others must pursue after him. They will not
> be imitators, any more than the scientist who uses the dis-
> coveries of an Einstein in pursuing his own, independent,
> further investigations. It is simply a way of controlling, of
> ordering, of giving a shape and a significance to the immense
> panorama of futility and anarchy which is contemporary
> history. It is a method already adumbrated by Mr Yeats, and
> of the need for which I believe Mr Yeats to have been the first
> contemporary to be conscious. It is a method for which the
> horoscope is auspicious. Psychology (such as it is, and whether
> our reaction to it be comic or serious), ethnology, and *The
> Golden Bough* have concurred to make possible what was
> impossible even a few years ago. Instead of narrative method,
> we may now use the mythical method. It is, I seriously believe,

a step toward making the modern world possible for art, toward . . . order and form.

Eliot here speaks of the modern movement, in Stephen Spender's definition of the adjective.

.   .   .   .   .   .

The intention of such writers is to place contemporary history in the same plane as the past and in so doing to create a modern myth that brings shape to the flux of events. Often, these new works can embody value-systems, though the avoidance of direct statement and reliance upon implication make it difficult to tease them out. In broad terms, myths, we might say, have always been ways in which human beings have expressed their deepest and most intuitive sense of themselves and of the universe. Human history, Nicholas Berdyaev writes in his book *The Meaning of History* (1923; translated by G. Reavey, 1936), 'is not an objective, empirical datum; it is a myth . . . the story preserved in popular memory of a past event . . . revealing an ideal world'. Moreover,

Each man represents by virtue of his inner nature a sort of microcosm in which the whole world of reality and all the great historical epochs combine and coexist. He is not merely a minute fragment of the universe, but rather a world in his own right, a world revealed or hidden according as consciousness is more or less penetrating and extensive. In this development of self-consciousness the whole history of the world is apprehended, together with all the great epochs which historical science investigates, by submitting them to the critical test of historical monuments, scriptures and archaeological data.

(Chapter 2.)

Certainly in a poem like 'Gerontion' Eliot seems to be attempting to make the past history of human beings present in the consciousness of his characters—a history, Eliot evidently feels, of confusion and loss.

Ulysses was not published in full until 1922, but there is a great deal to be gained from looking at some of Joyce's earlier writings.

Y

The first story in *Dubliners* (1914) is called 'The Sisters', and is mediated through the mind of a man remembering his childhood, a time that seemed heavy with mysterious significance. The adults he heard speaking about an old priest he had known were prone to hints and unexplained allusions. The priest had just died, paralysed and demented, and with plausible realism Joyce makes the child notice details both large and small, beautiful and sordid, when taken to visit the corpse:

> I went in on tiptoe. The room through the lace end of the blind was suffused with dusky golden light amid which the candles looked like pale thin flames. He had been coffined. Nannie gave the lead and we three knelt down at the foot of the bed. I pretended to pray but I could not gather my thoughts because the old woman's mutterings distracted me. I noticed how clumsily her skirt was hooked at the back and how the heels of her cloth boots were trodden down all to one side. The fancy came to me that the old priest was smiling as he lay there in his coffin.

In Richard Ellmann's monumental biography of Joyce (New York, 1959), there are various comments quoted in which Joyce explains what he intended when he wrote the story in 1904. He was, to begin with, trying to convert 'the bread of everyday life into something that has a permanent artistic life of its own'. Next, if it should seem that this ideal truth or lasting myth relates to no more than an individual, we have Joyce's word that the group of stories he was writing were to be called *Dubliners*, 'to betray the soul of that hemiplegia or paralysis which many consider a city.' This is not by any means made explicit in 'The Sisters'. The story reads like bald reality, the succession of trivial remarks and incidents we all know to be the bread of everyday life—'Mind you, I noticed there was something queer coming over him latterly'. At the same time, there is a wealth of unstated meaning that we, like the child, feel we must grasp. The very way in which the story is told, its form, pushes the plain fact into the realm of significant myth. This is true of other stories in the collection, like 'After the Race', which counterpoints the cosmopolitan sophistication of racing-car people with a young Dubliner's naivety. He is led, in his pride and excitement at being with them, to losses at cards he cannot afford. Again, there is a contemptuous realism in the narration, but the very opening of the story brings out its real content:

> The cars came scudding in towards Dublin, running evenly like pellets in the groove of the Naas Road. At the crest of the hill at Inchicore sightseers had gathered in clumps to watch the cars careering homeward, and through this channel of poverty and inaction the Continent sped its wealth and industry. Now and again the clumps of people raised the cheer of the gratefully oppressed.

In the last and finest story of *Dubliners*. 'The Dead', there is in the compass of a single story the full demonstration of one of Dangerfield's *aperçus* in *The Strange Death of Liberal England*, when he claims that the highest form of social history is fiction. Read in cold blood, this seems brilliantly incredible, but read after Joyce's story it appears to be the sober truth. Once more we notice that it is a matter of turning the fading perspectives of history into the plane of the present, or, to put in another way, to make the past come alive in a present reality. All through this story both past and present exercise their pressure upon our attention. Richard Ellmann's chapter called 'The Backgrounds of "The Dead"' makes it obvious how Joyce's imagination as he lived in voluntary exile abroad was sending down innumerable rootlets into his own memories of Ireland. The festive occasions, the Irish oratory, a pathetic lover who dies, book reviews for the *Daily Express* and so on are all known to belong to Joyce's own experience or that of his wife, and there is a pervasive sense of absolute authenticity—the servant girl, for instance, who when chaffed about her prospects of marriage, replies bitterly, 'The men that is now is only all palaver and what they can get out of you.' The hero of 'The Dead', Gabriel Conroy, ran up against Joyce's own difficulties in a country alive with nationalist feeling he could not share. We find, in fact, another reference to the preoccupation of writers like Yeats and Synge with the West of Ireland and its presumed value to modern men. Conroy is cornered at the party in his aunt's house by a Miss Ivors, who has 'a crow to pluck' with him, the fact that he writes for an English paper. She gives him the derisive name of 'West Briton'. Later in the party she suggests that he should join a group going to the Aran Islands (which Yeats had advised Synge to visit), not far from the birthplace of Conroy's wife, a country girl. Something like the following conversation must have been heard more than once in those days:

'But you will come, won't you?' said Miss Ivors, laying her warm hand eagerly on his arm.

'The fact is,' said Gabriel, 'I have just arranged to go—'

'Go where?' asked Miss Ivors.

'Well, you know, every year I go for a cycling tour with some fellows and so—'

'But where?' asked Miss Ivors.

'Well, we usually go to France or Belgium or perhaps Germany,' said Gabriel awkwardly.

'And why do you go to France and Belgium,' said Miss Ivors, 'instead of visiting your own land?'

'Well,' said Gabriel, 'it's partly to keep in touch with the languages and partly for a change.'

'And haven't you your own language to keep in touch with— Irish?' asked Miss Ivors.

'Well,' said Gabriel, 'if it comes to that, you know, Irish is not my language.'

Their neighbours had turned to listen to the cross-examination. Gabriel glanced right and left nervously and tried to keep his good humour under the ordeal, which was making a blush invade his forehead.

'And haven't you your own land to visit,' continued Miss Ivors, 'that you know nothing of, your own people, and your own country?'

'O, to tell you the truth,' retorted Gabriel suddenly, 'I'm sick of my own country, sick of it!'

Everything rings true about this dialogue: the humourless insistence of the young lady and the way in which she talks through

Gabriel's answers, emphasised by the parallelism of the syntax in the two questions about language and the land; also, the sudden turning of the worm at the end of the passage, unbearably embarrassed and goaded into repetition of an extravagant phrase: 'sick of my own country, sick of it'. Conroy's unease and easily shaken poise on this topic have been foreshadowed earlier in this beautifully constructed story by touches like the reference to his wife's goloshes. The wife thinks they are funny—and one of his aunts does not even know what they are. They have to be explained, with the rider that Gabriel says everyone wears them on the Continent. 'O, on the Continent', is the enigmatic murmur of his aunt. Gabriel, like the young man in 'After the Race', obviously has visions of a finer, freer existence out of Ireland and its narrow ways. Throughout the story, Gabriel Conroy is not quite accepted in the society to which he so evidently belongs. He is a forerunner of Leopold Bloom in *Ulysses*.

If this were all, 'The Dead' would be one of those pieces of literature distinguished for the credibility of their documentation. Irish society, its types, its language and its manners are deftly recorded. The description of the feast and Gabriel's carving of the goose, for instance, is a minor masterpiece, worth comparing with its comic English counterpart in H. G. Wells's *The History of Mr Polly*. But the story begins to gain an extraordinary resonance when it harks back into history.

At the table, we notice, the conversation turns to the topic of the great singers of the past who used to visit Dublin from abroad; their names are repeated reverently—'Those were the days . . . when there was something like singing to be heard in Dublin', when the carriage-horses of a great *prima donna* were unyoked and the gallery boys pulled her through the streets to her hotel. Later in the feast, Gabriel makes a sentimental and oratorical speech, partly aimed at Miss Ivors, who has, however, left the party— another frustration for him. 'This new generation,' he proclaims, 'educated or hyper-educated as it is, will lack those qualities of humanity, of hospitality, of kindly humour which belonged to an older day.' So far, perhaps, this is no more than generalised nostalgia for the past, but Joyce goes on to bring the past to life in the imagination of Gabriel and his wife. A tenor sings an old song plaintively and uncertainly in the distance, and Gabriel

> stood still in the gloom of the hall, trying to catch the air that the voice was singing and gazing up at his wife. There was grace and mystery in her attitude as if she were a symbol of something.

It is a moment of revelation to Gabriel; later, he sees his wife, still under the spell of the song, 'standing right under the dusty fanlight and the flame of the gas lit up the rich bronze of her hair.' It is as if in the dusty failure of Gabriel's existence there is at least the illumined beauty of his wife and what he believes to be the fundamental fire of their marriage relationship. Joyce portrays Gabriel then as dizzy with renewed love: he can hardly wait to be alone with her and feel her come to him. But, when they are at last together in their hotel room, Gabriel discovers that she is withdrawn from him in spirit, back into her own history, remembering through the pathos of the song they have heard her own first lover, who, though dying of consumption, had stood in her garden in the rain to say that he did not wish to live, and had died a week later. This is all based upon a real incident in the life of Joyce's wife, but the footnote hardly matters. Joyce has shown the past pressing upon the present in the most nakedly human way: the dead have come out of history to live again, to such an extent that even Gabriel gradually forgets his own frustration and, as his wife sleeps beside him, finds pity for his dead rival:

> The tears gathered more thickly in his eyes and in the partial darkness he imagined he saw the form of a young man standing under a dripping tree. Other forms were near. His soul had approached that region where dwell the vast hosts of the dead. He was conscious of, but could not apprehend, their wayward and flickering existence. His own identity was fading out into a grey impalpable world: the solid world itself, which these dead had one time reared and lived in, was dissolving and dwindling.

We are now nearing the end of this story. Gabriel is sinking in sleep, losing himself in a vision of the unity that can join both then and now in the human mind. The life and festivities of the party, so keenly observed and authentically recorded, give way to the melancholy rhythms of his internal being; the thoughts of his conscious mind are shown sinking down into the sensations of the unconscious, the prose movements losing their day-time tension for the flaccidity of will-less slumber, images taking over the burden of the meaning; there is an unavoidable connection between living and dead, present and past history:

A few light taps upon the pane made him turn to the window. It had begun to snow again. He watched sleepily the flakes, silver and dark, falling obliquely against the lamp-light. The time had come for him to set out on his journey westward. Yes, the newspapers were right: snow was general all over Ireland. It was falling on every part of the dark central plain, on the treeless hills, falling softly upon the Bog of Allen and, farther westward, softly falling into the dark mutinous Shannon waves. It was falling, too, upon every part of the lonely churchyard on the hill where Michael Furey lay buried. It lay thickly drifted on the crooked crosses and headstones, on the spears of the little gate, on the barren thorns. His soul swooned slowly as he heard the snow falling faintly through the universe and faintly falling, like the descent of their last end, upon all the living and the dead.

Ellmann has naturally drawn attention to that strange sentence, 'The time had come for him to set out on his journey westward', for this was the very thing Gabriel had refused to do and evidently scorned. But half-asleep, Ellmann suggests, he accepts the west, the place of primitive feelings and impulses, the country that was fundamentally his own whatever his conscious mind preferred. A letter we have already referred to in chapter 2 contains a sentence that now needs more careful consideration: 'My intention was to write a chapter of the moral history of my country and I chose Dublin for the scene because that city seemed to me the centre of paralysis.' This is a very positive statement, its criticism supported by Joyce's own abandonment of Ireland, 'the old sow who eats her farrow.' But unless we assume that the ending of 'The Dead' is satirical, we must realise that the writing of the moral history of Ireland was subject to deep psychic undertows. These, we may feel, Joyce found in his imaginative penetration of his character's being, fictional and yet so close to Joyce himself. Perhaps there are lessons to be learnt by historians in general.

. . . . . .

Joyce's other major work falling within our period, *A Portrait of the Artist as a Young Man*, was published in the *Egoist* between 1914 and 1915 with the encouragement and support of Ezra Pound, who had heard about Joyce from Yeats. *A Portrait* is a *bildungsroman* (novel of development) in form and as such it could hardly begin at a much earlier stage than it does:

> Once upon a time and a very good time it was there was a moocow coming down along the road and this moocow that was coming down along the road met a nicens little boy named baby tuckoo. . . .
>
> His father told him that story: his father looked at him through a glass: he had a hairy face.
>
> He was baby tuckoo. The moocow came down the road where Betty Byrne lived: she sold lemon platt.
>
> > *O, the wild rose blossoms*
> > *On the little green place.*
>
> He sang that song. That was his song.
>
> > *O, the green wothe botheth.*
>
> When you wet the bed first it is warm then it gets cold. His mother put on the oilsheet. That had the queer smell.
>
> His mother had a nicer smell than his father. She played on the piano the sailor's hornpipe for him to dance. He danced:
>
> > *Tralala lala,*
> > *Tralala tralaladdy,*
> > *Tralala lala,*
> > *Tralala lala.*

Uncle Charles and Dante clapped. They were older than his father and mother but uncle Charles was older than Dante.

Pound, then in London and militantly engaged in reforming English literature—Wyndham Lewis calls him the 'impresario' of the moderns, 'the men of 1914', in *Blasting and Bombardiering*— was delighted with his discovery. It is perhaps odd to find so sophisticated and revolutionary a novel beginning in this childish way, through readers opening their *Cornhill Magazine* for the August of 1864 would have found another starting with 'the old rigmarole of childhood.' But this earlier *jeu d'esprit* did not last for more than a sentence. Joyce, unlike Elizabeth Gaskell in *Wives and Daughters*, meant to keep out of his novel and did not intervene in order to guide and control the responses of his readers. He had some incentive to play such a part, since *A Portrait of the Artist as a Young Man* is in many ways autobiographical, yet Joyce allowed his work to speak for itself to an extent that critics still quarrel about his attitude to its central character. We can see from the passage quoted above how directly he is rendering the sense-impressions of childhood and a similar, if more complex, rendering of experience continues throughout the novel. It would be wrong, however, to ignore the more subtle ways in which this book is organised: it is an elaborately wrought and formed work of art, a portrait, in fact.

The warmth followed by cold of bed-wetting is more than just a vivid sensation remembered from childhood; it is also the first example of a recurrent motif. Within a few pages, Joyce's hero, Stephen Dedalus, is shown recalling how he had been shouldered into a ditch by another boy . . . 'And how cold and slimy the water had been!' In the next section of the novel, Dedalus wanders about the docks and quays of Dublin, 'wondering at the multitude of corks that lay bobbing on the surface of the water in a thick yellow scum . . .' All these repetitive fragments begin to glint in the substance of the narrative and, we discover, undergo their own development which matches the emotional and spiritual changes of the central figure. Those we have just brought together are associated with discomfort on the whole, just as Stephen Dedalus is ill-at-ease in Irish society, but by the end of section 4 water has become as regenerative as the rain that Eliot's Gerontion was hopelessly waiting for:

He was alone. He was unheeded, happy and near to the wild heart of life. He was alone and young and wilful and wild-hearted, alone amid a waste of wild air and brackish waters and the sea-harvest of shells and tangle and veiled grey sunlight and gayclad lightclad figures of children and girls and voices childish and girlish in the air.

A girl stood before him in midstream, alone and still, gazing out to sea. She seemed like one whom magic had changed into the likeness of a strange and beautiful sea-bird. Her long slender bare legs were delicate as a crane's and pure save where an emerald trail of seaweed had fashioned itself as a sign upon the flesh. Her thighs, fuller and soft-hued as ivory, were bared almost to the hips, where the white fringes of her drawers were like feathering of soft white down. Her slate-blue skirts were kilted boldly about her waist and dove-tailed behind her. Her bosom was as a bird's, soft and slight, slight and soft as the breast of some dark-plumaged dove. But her long fair hair was girlish: and girlish, and touched with the wonder of mortal beauty, her face.

She was alone and still, gazing out to sea; and when she felt his presence and the worship of his eyes her eyes turned to him in quiet sufferance of his gaze, without shame or wantonness. Long, long she suffered his gaze and then quietly withdrew her eyes from his and bent them towards the stream, gently stirring the water with her foot hither and thither. The first faint noise of gently moving water broke the silence, low and faint and whispering, faint as the bells of sleep; hither and thither, hither and thither; and a faint flame trembled upon her cheek.

—Heavenly God! cried Stephen's soul, in an outburst of profane joy.

He turned away from her suddenly and set off across the strand. His cheeks were aflame; his body was aglow; his limbs were trembling. On and on and on and on he strode, far out over the sands, singing wildly to the sea, crying to greet the advent of the life that had cried to him.

Compared with the youth who had wandered dissatisfied and embittered by the thick yellow scum of Dublin docks, this Stephen has caught a sight of a brave new world. A few pages before his vision of the wading girl the taunting cries of bathing boys had forced him to meditate upon the significance of his unIrish name. Why was he called Dedalus? What did it mean that he bore a name echoing that of the fabulous Daedalus, the great artificer and creator of the wings that bore human beings above the earth?

Was it a quaint device opening a page of some medieval book of prophecies and symbols, a hawk-like man flying sunward above the sea, a prophecy of the end he had been born to serve and had been following through the mists of childhood and boyhood, a symbol of the artist forging anew in his work-shop out of the sluggish matter of the earth a new soaring impalpable imperishable being?

There is much that is ninetyish here—the dedicated artist soaring above the ordinary world, utterly separated from it in spirit though pursued by its coarse cries. There is also the Joycean intention to take 'the sluggish matter of the earth' and make it new. As Joyce manipulates his 'parallel between contemporaneity and antiquity' (see page 352 above), we are made to realise the moment of decision to be an artist has come to Stephen. 'He would create proudly out of the freedom and power of his soul, as the great artificer whose name he bore . . .' This resolution is sealed by the strange moment of revelation when he sees the wading girl in the moving water. The novel ends with a full confirmation. Stephen leaves 'home, fatherland and church' behind him, escaping from the old man in the west of Ireland with his red-rimmed horny eyes who thinks 'there must be terrible queer creatures at the latter end of the world,' and goes 'to encounter for the millionth time the reality of experience and to forge in the smithy of my soul the uncreated conscience of my race.' The very last words of all are a prayer to his spiritual father: 'Old father, old artificer, stand me now and ever in good stead.' Old father, lost in antiquity almost, but still living in this new synthesis of past and present. Joyce, like John Synge in Yeats's elegy on Major Robert Gregory, 'chose the living world for text', but at least in the physical sense journeyed away from the west of Ireland and its 'race / Passionate and simple' as John Synge's heart.

It must be very clear by now that this novel about a young man's personal development is also what its title accurately confirms, another variant of the situation of the artist. Stephen is portrayed as a young man who was offered the highest vocation his society could offer, ordination to the priesthood as a member of the Jesuit order. But the very completeness of resignation demanded by this particular vocation threatened his freedom: 'His destiny was to be elusive of social or religious orders. . . . He was destined to learn his own wisdom apart from others or to learn the wisdom of others himself wandering among the snares of the world' (Part 4). Stephen is always an isolated figure; and one parallel Joyce produced, we might notice, belonged to recent history. Once again the figure of Parnell stepped upon a literary stage and underwent the processes of transformation into myth—this time into a myth with positively Manichean characteristics. His career and fate caused the gigantic and lengthy quarrel at Stephen's first Christmas dinner with adults and ended the season of goodwill with a bang:

> Dante shoved her chair violently aside and left the table, upsetting her napkin-ring which rolled slowly along the carpet and came to rest against the foot of an easy-chair. Mr Dedalus rose quickly and followed her towards the door. At the door Dante turned round violently and shouted down the room, her cheeks flushed and quivering with rage:
>
> —Devil out of hell! We won! We crushed him to death! Fiend!
> The door slammed behind her.
>
> Mr Casey, freeing his arms from his holders, suddenly bowed his head on his hands with a sob of pain.
>
> —Poor Parnell! he cried loudly. My dead king!
> He sobbed loudly and bitterly.
>
> Stephen, raising his terror-stricken face, saw that his father's eyes were full of tears.   (Part 1.)

James Joyce as well as his creations associated himself with the figure of a proud and betrayed Parnell. Like Yeats, Joyce believed Parnell's shade would continue to haunt Ireland,

This lovely land that always sent
Her writers and artists to banishment
And in a spirit of Irish fun
Betrayed her own leaders, one by one.
'Twas Irish humour, wet and dry,
Flung quicklime into Parnell's eye . . .
                    ('Gas from a Burner')

Both men fastened on this political and moral tragedy as a focus
for their disappointment with their own nation and the way it
failed to reach their ideal standards.

     .   .   .   .   .   .

England, too, roused one modern writer to paroxysms of
contempt:

> It was in 1915 the old world ended. In the winter 1915–16 the
> spirit of the old London collapsed; the city, in some way,
> perished, perished from being a heart of the world, and
> became a vortex of broken passions, lusts, hopes, fears, and
> horrors. The integrity of London collapsed and the genuine
> debasement began, the unspeakable baseness of the press and
> the public voice, the reign of that bloated ignominy, *John Bull*.

This quotation comes from chapter 12, 'The Nightmare', of D. H.
Lawrence's *Kangaroo* (1923), the novel he wrote after a visit to
Australia. His memory of the war-time years ends with a sight of
England seen from a departing boat, looking like 'a grey, dreary-
grey coffin sinking in the sea behind, with her dead grey cliffs and
the white, worn-out cloth of snow above.' The American Ezra
Pound seems to confirm this diagnosis of the spiritual state of
England in the sequence of short poems called *Hugh Selwyn
Mauberley* (1920). Pound lived in London between 1908 and 1920,
regarding it as the centre of civilisation and being correspondingly
largely exasperated with it, as we see when he says of his *Homage to
Sextus Propertius* (1919): 'it presents certain emotions as vital to
me in 1917, faced with the infinite and ineffable imbecility of the
British Empire, as they were to Sextus Propertius some centuries
earlier, when faced with the infinite and ineffable imbecility of the

Roman Empire' (*Letters*, ed. D. D. Paige, 1951, page 310). Many
of the poems of *Hugh Selwyn Mauberley* remind us of Henry
James's assessment of English philistinism and the way it affected
creative artists:

> The age demanded an image
> Of its accelerated grimace,
> Something for the modern stage,
> Not, at any rate, an Attic grace;
>
> Not, not certainly, the obscure reveries
> Of the inward gaze;
> Better mendacities
> Than the classics in paraphrase!
>
> The 'age demanded' chiefly a mould in plaster,
> Made with no loss of time,
> A prose kinema, not, not assuredly, alabaster
> Or the 'sculpture' of rhyme.

Pound himself called *Mauberley* 'a study in form, an attempt to
condense the James novel' in a letter to Felix Schelling. The
connection with stories like James's 'The Figure in the Carpet' and
'The Next Time' has been analysed in J. J. Espey's *Ezra Pound's
Mauberley: A Study in Composition* (1955). Both James and Pound
felt strongly the vulgarity of the age and the way in which literary
and financial values were intertwined. In the poem entitled 'Mr
Nixon', who may well be based on Arnold Bennett, Pound satirises
the way some writers achieved their enormous public success:

> In the cream gilded cabin of his steam yacht
> Mr Nixon advised me kindly, to advance with fewer
> Dangers of delay. 'Consider
>   'Carefully the reviewer.
>
> 'I was as poor as you are;
> 'When I began I got, of course,
> 'Advance on royalties, fifty at first,' said Mr Nixon,
> 'Follow me, and take a column,
> 'Even if you have to work free. . . .

'I never mentioned a man but with the view
'Of selling my own works.
'The tip's a good one, as for literature
'It gives no man a sinecure.
'And no one knows, at sight, a masterpiece.
'And give up verse, my boy,
'There's nothing in it.'

Mr Nixon is the true descendant of George Gissing's Jasper Milvain in *New Grub Street* (1891), a tradesman of literature. Gissing's sociological document of the literary life in late-Victorian London, quite as solid as *The Nether World* in its accumulation of detail, is an early example of a general concern with the state of culture at a time when newspapers and periodicals were being tailored to fit the public taste and 'serious' writers were beginning to feel the pressures of the commercial system.

Even in the places where art was fostered, Pound shows in *Mauberley*, the true artist was not at home. In poem 12 of the first sequence Mauberley meets his patroness:

'Daphne with her thighs in bark
'Stretches toward me her leafy hands,'—
Subjectively. In the stuffed-satin drawing-room
I await The Lady Valentine's commands . . .

Daphne was changed into a laurel when being chased by Apollo, and a laurel wreath, the traditional acknowledgement of the poet, is what Mauberley wants from his patroness; but he cannot really believe in the value of the approbation of a fashionable society hostess,

Knowing my coat has never been
Of precisely the fashion
To stimulate, in her,
A durable passion;

Doubtful, somewhat, of the value
Of well-gowned approbation
Of literary effort,
But never of The Lady Valentine's vocation:

> Poetry, her border of ideas,
> The edge, uncertain, but a means of blending
> With other strata
> Where the lower and higher have ending . . .

Donald Davie has recently suggested that it was in emulating Gautier—the quotation about Daphne comes from 'Le Château du Souvenir', and the tight-packed quatrains are another indication of the debt owed to *Emaux et Camées* (1830)—that Pound discovered the secret of purifying and raising 'to a new power attitudes that in life were callow and unresolved' (*Ezra Pound: Poet as Sculptor*, 1965, page 98). This comment seems to me to be particularly valuable. Apart from the new angle it gives on the past-present synthesis that has been one of the topics of this chapter, it provides a clue to the conviction that some of these *Mauberley* poems inspire in the reader. An author complaining about the ingratitude, intolerance, incomprehension, and so on of society is always a suspect witness, obviously with a *parti pris*. How can his testimony about the predicament of the artists carry conviction even if true? But if the poet's beliefs and feelings have survived their transformation into taut, compressed and highly disciplined artistic form, then, perhaps, we are more ready to take seriously the work of a man admittedly 'out of key with his time.' Somehow, thinking of Tennyson's 'Locksley Hall Sixty Years After', the laconic seems more convincing than the wholesale.

The phrase 'out of key with his time' comes from the opening poem of *Mauberley*, 'E.P. Ode pour l'Election de Son Sepulchre'. Its last two stanzas display almost all the characteristics we have come to expect from the 'tradition of the modern': they are difficult, allusive, cosmopolitan, uncompromising, and they hold the values of the past in suspension with those of the present:

> His true Penelope was Flaubert
> He fished by obstinate isles;
> Observed the elegance of Circe's hair
> Rather than the mottoes on sun-dials.

> Unaffected by 'the march of events',
> He passed from men's memory in *l'an trentiesme*

De son eage; the case presents
No adjunct to the Muse's diadem.

Meaning and feeling could not be much more distilled. Like Flaubert, this poet devotes himself to his difficult craft; like the 'tragic generation' Yeats knew, he is in the service of a dangerous but beautiful enchantress. Inevitably, he is unconcerned with facile mottoes or events 'that shake mankind' (see 'Locksley Hall', lines 165–6); as far as all that is concerned, Pound writes in ironical echo of the medieval French poet Francois Villon, he passed out of public notice in his thirtieth year. Much more could be said in exegesis of this poem, as the Pound commentators have amply demonstrated, but it must be very clear by now that this generation of 'modern' writers was more radical than any others in their age. The period after 1900, as we have seen, saw many sharp reactions against the Victorian era, but none in literature as definitive as the one we associated with the names of Pound, Joyce and Eliot. That revolutionaries should be vitally concerned with their own epoch is only to be expected, but that these particular revolutionaries should also be concerned to relate themselves to past epochs is much more surprising. Whether the re-imagining of the relationship between past and present demanded the discontinuous forms they devised is a large proposition that the practice of poets like Hardy and Edward Thomas goes some way to question. Ultimately, I think, their new forms were worth the finding for the enjoyment that they give, but I would not myself care to defend the necessity of them in the first place.

NOTES

[1] C. K. Stead, in chapter 6 of *The New Poetic*, adds the suggestion that 'the phrase "fractured atoms" would not have occurred to Eliot a year earlier—since it was in June 1919, at the time of the Versailles conference, that the first splitting of the atom (by Ernest Rutherford) was announced.'

Z

12 : Epilogue : The End of the Beginning

IT might have been wise to have ended this book with the great modern writers poised, theoretically and practically, to continue with the most important works—Pound's *Cantos*; Eliot's *The Waste Land, Four Quartets* and several plays; Joyce's *Ulysses* and *Finnegans Wake*. But Clio, Muse of history, lifts a warning finger. In 1918, after years of careful preservation, Robert Bridges at last judged the time ripe to publish a small edition of the poems of a friend who had died years before, in 1889. It consisted of 750 copies, which took ten years to exhaust. His friend, Gerard Manley Hopkins, had been a pupil of Pater's at Oxford and academically very successful, but in 1868, after being received into the Roman Catholic Church by Dr (later Cardinal) Newman, he accepted the very discipline that was to be spurned by Joyce's Stephen Dedalus. And when Hopkins became a Jesuit, he set about burning all the poetry he had written, determined to write no more unless ordered to do so—which from a purely literary point of view might be held to justify Stephen in his refusal to serve. The ironies multiply when we learn that Hopkins was sent by his superiors to be Professor of Greek literature at University College, Dublin, which Joyce was to attend some years later. There Hopkins was often acutely unhappy in the deepest sense of the word, but, fortunately, he was by now composing verse again. In 1888, he wrote a poem that does not look in the least out of place in the era of Pound and Picasso and Schoenberg, some two decades afterwards. The poem, 'That Nature is a Heraclitean Fire and of the comfort of the Resurrection', is one of his greatest:

> Cloud-puffball, torn tufts, tossed pillows|flaunt forth, then chevy on an air-

built thoroughfare: heaven-roysterers, in gay-gangs|they
    throng; they glitter in marches.
Down roughcast, down dazzling whitewash,|wherever an elm
    arches,
Shivelights and shadowtackle in long|lashes lace, lance, and
    pair. . . .

Difficult, experimental and innovatory verse, without a doubt; the
product of an intense effort to capture what he used to call the
'inscapes' of things, their distinctive selves; combined with a
powerful drive to make patterns of words, their sounds and shapes.
Language itself in this poem seems to take on the actuality of the
nature that is its subject, but it still retains what all nature's pelting
energies together do not possess—meaning; and this, too, Hopkins
works into patterns of thought and emotion:

      Million-fuelèd,|nature's bonfire burns on.
But quench her bonniest, dearest|to her, her clearest-selvèd
    spark
Man, how fast his firedint,|his mark on mind, is gone!
Both are in an unfathomable, all is in an enormous dark
Drowned. O pity and indig|nation! Manshape, that shone
Sheer off, disseveral, a star,|death blots black out; nor mark
      Is any of him at all so stark
But vastness blurs and time|beats level. . . .

It becomes clear at this point in the poem that Hopkins has
joined the innumerable poets who have lamented the transience of
this life of ours; as we read the last lines above, so original and so
newly forged, memories of other lines nag at the edges of the
mind:

    O, how shall summer's honey breath hold out
    Against the wrackful siege of batt'ring days,
    When rocks impregnable are not so stout,
    Nor gates of steel so strong, but Time decays?

But even if Shakespeare's sixty-fifth sonnet, or even those variously
shaped poems classified by George Puttenham in 1589, lie behind
Hopkins's lines, they are still part of a poem that is genuinely new

in Eliot's special usage of the word. Hopkins is an individual talent in a tradition, which must alter, belatedly, to accommodate his work. It is a great pleasure to discover in the notes of the standard fourth edition (*The Poems of Gerard Manley Hopkins*, edited by W. H. Gardner and N. H. Mackenzie, 1967) a quotation from a letter Hopkins wrote on 25 September 1888, in which he says of this very poem, 'The effect of studying masterpieces is to make me admire and do otherwise.' He is in fact referring to his distillation of 'a great deal of early Greek philosophical thought', but the way the letter goes on very much underpins the general contention we have borrowed from Eliot: 'So it must be on every original artist to some degree, on me to a marked degree. Perhaps then more reading would only *refine my singularity*, which is not what you want.' It is the modernist paradox over again.

Of course, there are many senses in which it is positively misleading to think of Hopkins as anything other than a Victorian poet. The poem we are looking at ends with a major reversal of Stephen Dedalus's *Non serviam*, when in language which might appear to have come from *Ulysses* but which was actually written by a Victorian poet ordered into exile in Ireland, Hopkins assuages his pity and indignation at man's snowflake existence with the comfort of the Resurrection:

> Across my foundering deck shone
> A beacon, an eternal beam.|Flesh fade, and mortal trash
> Fall to the residuary worm;|world's wildfire, leave but ash:
> In a flash, at a trumpet crash,
> I am all at once what Christ is,|since he was what I am, and
> This Jack, joke, poor potsherd,|patch, matchwood, immortal
> diamond,
> Is immortal diamond.

We might also refer to a very different poem, but one which still shows Hopkins to be a true Victorian. This is the phenomenally obscure 'Tom's Garland upon the Unemployed' of 1887, which turns upon the image of the state as a human body—as in Menenius's speech (*Coriolanus*, I.i.94). Fortunately for us Hopkins has provided a lengthy prose explanation ('O, once explained, how

clear it all is!' he cries happily), from which we gather that in socio-
political affairs he was at the stage before Gissing when he wrote
The Nether World. Hopkins can still be angry with radicals who
want to upset the state. One should know and appreciate one's
place, even if, like the navvy's, it is a lowly one:

> What! Country is honour enough in all us—lordly head,
> With heaven's lights high hung round, or, mother-ground
> That mammocks, mighty foot.

Yet Hopkins is also very aware of what he calls 'the curse of our
times', the fact that some unfortunates 'share care with the high
and obscurity with the low, but wealth or comfort with neither':

> But nó way sped,
> Nor mind nor mainstrength; gold go garlanded
> With, perilous, O nó; nor yet plod safe shod sound;
> Undenizened, beyond bound
> Of earth's glory, earth's ease, all; no one, nowhere,
> In wide the world's weal; rare gold, bold steel, bare
> In both; care, but share care—
> This, by Despair, bred Hangdog dull; by Rage,
> Manwolf, worse; and their packs infest the age.

The poem is full of mid-Victorian earnestness in its thought and a
somewhat conservative balance in its attitudes. But then, nobody
could possibly imagine it was by Tennyson and, if the editor of
The Month (the Jesuit magazine) is any guide when turning down
one of the very greatest of Hopkins's poems, 'The Wreck of the
Deutschland', such poetry would never have suited the great
Victorian public.

It begins to look as though Hopkins is modern in form because
he was such an ardent experimentalist, but that his ideas, feelings
and attitudes very frequently belong to the nineteenth century or
even earlier. Now and again, a particular poem will make us doubt
this simple conclusion. There is one he wrote in the last year of his
life, 'The shepherd's brow . . .', which has only recently been given
its place amongst the finished poems. Eliot's Prufrock comes to
mind as its last lines expound futility and shift abruptly into self-
denigration:

Man Jack the man is, just; his mate a hussy.
And I that die these deaths, that feed this flame,
That . . . in smooth spoons spy life's masque mirrored: tame
My tempests there, my fire and fever fussy.

But there is character in its moods here rather than states of mind; decision rather than drift in the movement of thought. Another poem, the beautifully turned sonnet 'To R.B.' (the last finished poem of all), might almost have been written to prove the Yeatsian formula, 'Only an aching heart / Conceives a changeless work of art.' Its sestet is perfect:

Sweet fire the sire of muse, my soul needs this;
I want the one rapture of an inspiration.
O then if in my lagging lines you miss

The roll, the rise, the carol, the creation,
My winter world, that scarcely breathes that bliss
Now, yields you, with some sighs, our explanation.

·   ·   ·   ·   ·   ·

In all probability it is a futile exercise to attempt to anchor such an individual poet in his own or in any other age; nor is it fair, concentrating as we have upon the poems written during the last few years in Dublin, to ignore the occasions when thoughts ceased to grind against thoughts and all Hopkins's great powers combined to remarkable effect. He was not always tormented by ill health or by scruples about the award of half-marks in examining or by Catholic support for the Irish cause or by spiritual dryness. His poem 'Harry Ploughman', for instance, finely brings us back to the concerns of the rural literature we began with as it re-creates for us a man and a 'vanishing life':

Hard as hurdle arms, with a broth of goldish flue
Breathed round; the rack of ribs; the scooped flank; lank
Rope-over thigh; knee-nave; and barrelled shank—
          Head and foot, shoulder and shank—
By a grey eye's heed steered well, one crew, fall to;
Stand at stress. . . .

He leans to it, Harry bends, look. Back, elbow, and liquid
    waist
In him, all quail to the wallowing o' the plough. 'S cheek
    crimsons, curls
Wag or crossbridle, in a wind lifted, windlaced—
       See his wind- lilylocks -laced . . .

A poem of this quality makes me wonder if literature can serve
any better end than to preserve a human being and his way of life
for future generations. This is more than a matter of placing a bee
in translucent amber for us all to gape at whenever we feel the
need for some release from the complications of today's urban
existence; that limber dance of language does not spring out of
anything as lax as the cultivated man's temporary nostalgia for the
simple life. What we encounter, most enduringly, in such poetry is a
relationship between men, which is even more evident in another
poem Hopkins wrote in the first year of our period, 'Felix Randal'.
It is undoubtedly based on his experience as a priest ministering to
the sick:

This seeing the sick endears them to us, us too it endears.
My tongue had taught thee comfort, touch had quenched thy
    tears,
The tears that touched my heart, child, Felix, poor Felix
    Randal;

How far from then forethought of, all thy more boisterous
    years,
When thou at the random grim forge, powerful amidst peers,
Didst fettle for the great grey drayhorse his bright and
    battering sandal!

With 1880 nearly a century behind us now, there are not many
adults who know an actual farrier and there must be many children
who have never seen one at his work. But this is to consider the
poem on a relatively superficial level; in these lines it is Felix
Randal *and* Gerard Manley Hopkins who exist again in our moved
imaginations. We meet a poet using language with an almost
agonised awareness of its intrinsic possibilities, but also with a true

sense of its manifold connections with the actuality of a country's history. Such poetry is not just made out of words related to ideas and emotions, words to be manipulated for ultimately fiercely selfish purposes of the writer, however objective the mode chosen. Hopkins undoubtedly did write at unpropitious times, alienated and turned in upon himself. The so-called 'terrible sonnets' are their record; the evidence, presumably, that made Michael Roberts in his introduction to *The Faber Book of Modern Verse* speak of crisis and tension, fractured personalities and decaying societies— 'Sometimes, as in the case of Hopkins, the problem which is his today is the world's tomorrow.' At other times, however, Hopkins lifted his eyes and turned them fully on the world about him, becoming, like Conrad's novelist, 'the preserver, the keeper, the expounder, of human experience' in a far more complete sense. Then literature embodied history, of a kind that won't be found by digging, anywhere.

Select Bibliography

ARNOLD, MATTHEW
  Mixed Essays (1879)
  Discourses in America (1885)
  Essays in Criticism, Second Series (1888)

ASHBY, M. K.
  Joseph Ashby of Tysoe 1859–1919: A Study of English Village
    Life (1961)

BARRIE, SIR JAMES M.
  Auld Licht Idylls (1888)
  A Window in Thrums (1889)
  The Admirable Crichton (1902)
  Peter Pan (1904)

BELLOC, JOSEPH HILAIRE
  The Path to Rome (1902)
  Emmanuel Burden (1904)
  Mr. Clutterbuck's Election (1908)
  The Servile State (1912)

BENNETT, ARNOLD
  A Man from the North (1898)
  Anna of the Five Towns (1902)
  The Old Wives' Tale (1908)
  Clayhanger (1910)
  The Card (1911)
  Lord Raingo (1926)

BOOTH, WILLIAM
  In Darkest England and the Way Out (1890)

BOURNE, GEORGE
  See STURT

BROOKE, RUPERT
  Poems (1911)
  1914 and Other Poems (1915)

CHESTERTON, GILBERT K.
  The Napoleon of Notting Hill (1904)
  The Man Who Was Thursday (1908)
  The Victorian Age in Literature (1913)
  The Flying Inn (1914)

CONRAD, JOSEPH
  The Nigger of the 'Narcissus' (1897)
  Tales of Unrest (1898)
  Lord Jim (1900)
  Heart of Darkness (1902)
  Nostromo (1904)
  A Personal Record (1906)
  The Mirror of the Sea: Memories and Impressions (1906)
  The Secret Agent (1907)
  A Set of Six (1908)
  Under Western Eyes (1911)
  Chance (1914)

CUNNINGHAME GRAHAM, R. B.
  Thirty Tales & Sketches, Selected by Edward Garnett [from The
    Ipané (1899), etc.] (1929)

DAVIDSON, JOHN
  In a Music-Hall and Other Poems (1891)
  Fleet Street Eclogues (1893–6)
  Ballads and Songs (1894)
  New Ballads (1897)
  The Last Ballad and Other Poems (1899)
  Testaments (1901–8)
  Selected Poems (1905)
  Fleet Street and Other Poems (1909)

ELIOT, T. S.
  Prufrock and Other Observations (1917)
  Poems (1919)
  Ara Vos Prec (1920)
  The Sacred Wood (1920)
  The Waste Land (1922)

FABIAN ESSAYS
  See SHAW

FORD, FORD MADOX
  The Good Soldier (1915)
  Some Do Not (1924)
  No More Parades (1925)

A Man Could Stand Up (1926)
Last Post (1928)

FORSTER, E. M.
Where Angels Fear to Tread (1905)
The Longest Journey (1907)
A Room With a View (1908)
Howards End (1910)
The Celestial Omnibus and Other Stories (1911)
A Passage to India (1924)
The Eternal Moment and Other Stories (1928)

GALSWORTHY, JOHN
The Silver Box (1906)
The Man of Property (1906)
The Country House (1907)
Strife (1909)
Fraternity (1909)
Justice (1910)
The Patrician (1911)
A Bit of Love (1915)
The Foundations (1917)
In Chancery (1920)
The Skin Game (1920)
To Let (1921)

GEORGE, HENRY
Progress and Poverty (1879)

GISSING, GEORGE
Workers in the Dawn (1880)
The Unclassed (1884)
Demos: A Story of English Socialism (1886)
Thyrza (1887)
The Nether World (1889)
New Grub Street (1891)
Charles Dickens: A Critical Study (1898; rev. 1902)
The Private Papers of Henry Ryecroft (1903)

GRAVES, ROBERT
Over the Brazier (1916)
Fairies and Fusiliers (1917)
Country Sentiment (1920)
Goodbye to All That (1929; rev. 1957)

HAGGARD, SIR HENRY RIDER
King Solomon's Mines (1885)
She (1886–7)

Nada the Lily (1892)
Marie (1911–12)
Child of Storm (1913)

HARDY, THOMAS
Tess of the D'Urbervilles (1891)
Jude the Obscure (1896)
Wessex Poems and Other Verses (1898)
Poems of the Past and the Present (1902)
The Dynasts (1903–8)
Time's Laughing-Stocks (1909)
Satires of Circumstance (1914)
Moments of Vision (1917)

HENLEY, WILLIAM ERNEST
In Hospital (1875)
The Song of the Sword and Other Verses (1892)
London Voluntaries (1893)
For England's Sake: Verses and Songs in Time of War (1900)
Works (1921)

HOPKINS, GERARD MANLEY
The Poems of Gerard Manley Hopkins, ed. Robert Bridges (1918)

HOUSMAN, ALFRED EDWARD
A Shropshire Lad (1896)
Last Poems (1922)
More Poems (1936)

JAMES, HENRY
The Portrait of a Lady (1881)
The Princess Casamassima (1886)
The Spoils of Poynton (1897)
The Awkward Age (1899)
The Ambassadors (1903)
The Golden Bowl (1904)

JEFFERIES, RICHARD
Hodge and His Masters (1880)
The Story of My Heart (1883)
The Life of the Fields (1884)
The Open Air (1885)
Amaryllis At the Fair (1887)
The Toilers of the Field (1892)
The Hills and the Vale (1909)

JOHNSON, LIONEL PIGOT
The Art of Thomas Hardy (1894)
Poems (1895)

Ireland, and Other Poems (1897)
Poetical Works, intro. Ezra Pound (1915)

JONES, DAVID
In Parenthesis (1937)

JONES, HENRY ARTHUR
Saints and Sinners (1891)

JOYCE, JAMES
Chamber Music (1907)
Dubliners (1914)
A Portrait of the Artist As a Young Man (1916)
Exiles (1918)
Ulysses (1922)

KIPLING, RUDYARD
Life's Handicap (1891)
Recessional and Other Poems (1899)
Stalky and Co. (1899)
Kim (1901)
The Five Nations (1903)
Puck of Pook's Hill (1906)
Rewards and Fairies (1910)
Sea Warfare (1916)
A Diversity of Creatures (1917)
Twenty Poems (1918)
Verse: Inclusive Edition (1919, 1921, etc.)
Debits and Credits (1926)

LAWRENCE, DAVID HERBERT
The White Peacock (1911)
Sons and Lovers (1913)
The Rainbow (1915)
Women in Love (1920)
England My England and Other Stories (1922)
Kangaroo (1923)
Collected Poems (1928)

LEWIS, PERCY WYNDHAM
Tarr (1918)
Blasting and Bombardiering (1937)

MASEFIELD, JOHN
The Tragedy of Nan and Other Plays (1909)
The Everlasting Mercy (1911)
Dauber (1913)
Gallipoli (1916)

MASTERMAN, C. F. G.
  The Condition of England (1909)

MAUGHAM, WILLIAM SOMERSET
  Liza of Lambeth (1897)
  Of Human Bondage (1915)

MOORE, GEORGE
  A Mummer's Wife (1885)
  Confessions of a Young Man (1888)
  Esther Waters (1894)
  The Untilled Field (1903)
  The Lake (1905)
  Hail and Farewell (1911–14)

MORRIS, WILLIAM
  A Dream of John Ball (1888)
  News From Nowhere (1890)

NEWBOLT, SIR HENRY
  Admirals All and Other Verses (1897)
  The Island Race (1898)
  The Sailing of the Long Ships and Other Poems (1902)
  Clifton Chapel, and Other School Poems (1908)

OWEN, WILFRED
  Poems, ed. S. Sassoon (1920); ed. C. Day Lewis (1963)

PATER, WALTER HORATIO
  Studies in the History of the Renaissance (1873; rev. 1888)
  Marius the Epicurean (1885)

POUND, EZRA LOOMIS
  Personae (1909)
  Ripostes (1912)
  Homage to Sextus Propertius (1917)
  Hugh Selwyn Mauberley (1920)

READ, HERBERT EDWARD
  Naked Warriors (1919)
  The End of a War (1933)

ROSENBERG, ISAAC
  Collected Works, ed. G. Bottomley and D. Harding (1937)

RUSSELL, BERTRAND A. W.
  The Principles of Mathematics (1903)
  Principia Mathematica [with A. Whitehead] (1910–13)
  Mysticism and Logic, and Other Essays (1918)

SASSOON, SIEGFRIED
  The Old Huntsman (1917)

Counter-Attack (1918)
Memoirs of a Fox-Hunting Man (1928)
Memoirs of an Infantry Officer (1930)
Sherston's Progress (1936)
Siegfried's Journey (1945)

SHAW, GEORGE BERNARD
Ed. Fabian Essays (1889)
The Quintessence of Ibsenism (1891; enl. 1913)
Widowers' Houses (1893)
Mrs Warren's Profession (1894)
Arms and the Man (1894)
The Philanderer (1895)
Candida (1898)
Man and Superman (1903)
Major Barbara (1907)
John Bull's Other Island (1907)
Heartbreak House (1917)

STURT, GEORGE
The Bettesworth Book (1901)
Memoirs of a Surrey Labourer (1907)
Change in the Village (1912)
The Wheelwright's Shop (1923)
A Small Boy in the Sixties (1927)
Journal 1890–1927, ed. E. D. Mackerness (1967)

SYNGE, JOHN MILLINGTON
Riders to the Sea (1904)
The Playboy of the Western World (1907)

TENNYSON, ALFRED
Tiresias and Other Poems (1885)
Locksley Hall Sixty Years After (1886)
Demeter and Other Poems (1889)

THOMAS, PHILIP EDWARD
Richard Jefferies (1909)
Poems, 1917
Collected Poems, ed. De la Mare (1928)

THOMPSON, FRANCIS
Poems (1893)
Sister Songs (1895)
New Poems (1897)

THOMSON, JAMES
The City of Dreadful Night and Other Poems (1880)

WATSON, WILLIAM
  The Purple East: A Series of Sonnets on England's Desertion
    of Armenia (1896)
  New Poems (1909)

WELLS, HERBERT GEORGE
  The Time Machine (1895)
  The War of the Worlds (1898)
  Love and Mr Lewisham (1900)
  The First Men in the Moon (1901)
  Kipps (1905)
  The War in the Air (1908)
  Tono-Bungay (1909)
  Ann Veronica: A Modern Love Story (1909)
  The History of Mr Polly (1910)
  The New Machiavelli (1911)
  Boon: Being a First Selection from the Literary Remains of
    George Boon (1915)
  Mr Britling Sees It Through (1916)
  Experiment in Autobiography (1934)

WEST, ARTHUR GRAEME
  The Diary of a Dead Officer (1919)

WILDE, OSCAR FINGAL
  Intentions (1891)
  The Picture of Dorian Gray (1891)
  Salomé (1894)
  The Importance of Being Earnest (1895)
  The Soul of Man Under Socialism (1895)
  The Ballad of Reading Gaol (1898)
  De Profundis (1905, 1913)

WOOLF, VIRGINIA
  The Voyage Out (1915)
  Night and Day (1919)
  The Common Reader (1925–32)
  The Captain's Death-Bed (1950)

YEATS, WILLIAM BUTLER
  The Wandering of Oisin and Other Poems (1889)
  Cathleen Ni Houlihan (1902)
  The Green Helmet and Other Poems (1910; enl. 1912)
  Responsibilities (1914; enl. 1916)
  Reveries over Childhood and Youth (1915)
  The Wild Swans at Coole (1917; enl. 1919)
  Michael Robartes and the Dancer (1920)

The Trembling of the Veil (1922)
A Vision (1925; rev. and enl. 1937)
Autobiographies (1926, 1955)

For more extensive bibliographies and help with critical works, see
  The Concise Cambridge Bibliography of English Literature, ed.
  George Watson, 2nd edition (1965).
J. I. M. Stewart, Eight Modern Writers [Hardy, James, Shaw,
  Conrad, Kipling, Yeats, Joyce, Lawrence] (1963).
S. C. Chew and R. D. Altick, The Nineteenth Century and After,
  in A Literary History of England, ed. A. C. Baugh, 2nd edition
  (1967).

Index